Urban and Rural Transport

LAUNA
FALMER
jeanius at
JEAN JEANIE
MODEL
VILLAGE
TORQUAY
CENTRAL AVE.
B
KENTS
CAVERN
TORQUAY
TOP OF THE TOWN
918 GTA

Urban and Rural Transport

R.W. Faulks

LONDON

IAN ALLAN LTD

First published 1981

ISBN 0 7110 1056 0

Published by Ian Allan Ltd, Shepperton, Surrey; and printed by Ian Allan Printing Ltd at their works at Coombelands in Runnymede, England

Contents

Preface

Foreword
by
Mr Robert Brook FCIS FCIT FBIM
Deputy Chairman and Chief Executive
National Bus Company

At last we have an up-to-date textbook that deals with the operational side of the bus industry.

The publication of Rex Faulks' 'Urban and Rural Transport' fills a very large gap. It provides essential reading for all students of passenger transport, particularly those who will become specialists in bus operations.

Not only is it a manual of instruction, it sets out to stimulate ideas and advance thinking on present-day operational problems.

Not only is today's student tomorrow's operations manager — he is tomorrow's teacher — and he will owe and acknowledge a great deal to the insight and inspiration provided by Mr Faulks' book.

Urban and Rural Transport has been written to meet the needs of students who have entered the transport industry with a view to specialising in bus operation — a subject which has never been over-endowed with basic text books which give overall coverage and provide introductory reading. Whilst much interesting literature on buses and trams is readily available, it is written for the enthusiast rather than the serious student and for academic purposes is little more than a pleasant background material. The works of R. S. Pilcher and L. D. Kitchin, both experts in their day, have long since been dated, W. T. Lambden's *Bus and Coach Operation* no longer reflects current developments and sadly he did not live to prepare a revision. Mr Lambden's untimely passing has meant a loss to the industry of a wise counsellor; to the student a source of knowledge and the written word and to the present author a personal friend. His departure from this world has left a gap in transport literature.

Although few text books on the subject have been written, some names have just been mentioned, high standards have been set and it is never easy to follow in the footsteps of the masters; far less to emulate them. Nevertheless, life must go on and there is a need by those who are seeking a career 'on the buses' for the gap to be filled. At the risk of being presumptuous, therefore, it can be said that this book has been written for that very purpose and it is hoped that the pages which follow will give some help and guidance to transport students. It is further hoped that those not engaged directly in operations but are 'out on the wings', being staff of county councils who whilst not themselves in the business of running buses do have responsibility for broad policy control over the services provided, will also derive benefit and their particular requirements have not been overlooked.

In the course of preparation, as far as passenger transport is concerned the following syllabuses in particular have been borne in mind:

(a) Qualifying examination of the Chartered Institute of Transport:
  Transport Management Practice:
  G Road Passenger Transport
  J Urban Transport

(b) Graduateship examination of the Institute of Traffic Administration:
  Transport Operation (Road Passenger)
(c) Certificate in road passenger transport of the Royal Society of Arts:
  Road Passenger Transport Operation
  Road Passenger Transport Planning
(d) Examinations organised by universities, polytechnics and technical colleges following advanced studies in transport or approved courses containing a transport input, to the extent appropriate.

Limited coverage has also been made of parts of the syllabuses of Rail Transport and Transport Policy and Planning of the Chartered Institute of Transport and Development of Modern Transport and Transport Operation (Rail) of the Institute of Traffic Administration. The movement of freight and physical distribution has not been dealt with.

Having thus set out the stall with its emphasis on bus operating techniques, mention of railways might at first sight suggest an irrelevancy. But this is not so for the reasons which are to be explained in Chapter 2. A treatise on road passenger transport would be incomplete without reference to trams, particularly in view of the forthcoming energy situation, which leads into light rapid transit, heavy rapid transit and — railways. Certainly, a line has to be drawn but the demarcation must lie beyond the point where a diesel bus becomes an electric trolleybus. The very fact that the Chartered Institute of Transport has introduced the subject 'Urban Transport' into its revised examination structure is in itself indicative of the need for a multi modal approach to movement within urban areas. Nevertheless, what follows is insufficient for the requirements of budding railwaymen and no pretence is made that this is also a text book on railway operation. Even within its declared ambit the scope is relatively basic and assumes little previous knowledge or experience. The book is, therefore, essentially for the trainee and not for the manager who in any case has available to him a prolific supply of reports, papers and other material, being the products of research, seminars and the like, all of an advanced and technical nature and on specific topics, only some of which he is likely to find time to read.

It will quickly become apparent that a transport service is the product of the combined efforts of a multiplicity of separate disciplines, the majority of which are independent sciences in their own right. The contents of the pages which follow are, however, confined to pure transport matters. In other words, they cover operating and commercial practices. References to mechanical engineering, accountancy, legal, staff and planning aspects are made only to the extent to which it is necessary for those in the operating and commercial departments to be familiar with these ancillary subjects. Although entire chapters are devoted to finance, planning and statutory controls, in no way must they be construed as adequate coverage for readers in these particular studies. In any case useful material is already available for aspirants in these fields. Particularly as far as the legal profession is concerned the information given here is descriptive only and does not represent adequate coverage of law as such.

The fundamentals of general transport topics are covered in the sister book *Principles of Transport* by the same author. The information contained in that particular work is not duplicated here but the relevant parts are developed to cover in greater detail the operational and commercial techniques within this one facet of transport. The reader should note particularly that statutory control, trade organisations, the structure of the bus industry, administration, staff matters and finance have all been considered in some depth in *Principles of Transport*. The coverage is adequate for bus operating purposes and the information has not been repeated. *Urban and Rural Transport* is complementary to but not an alternative to *Principles of Transport*. By the nature of its purpose, *Principles of Transport* presents facts and the author has made no attempt to superimpose opinions on the resultant issues. In proceeding now beyond the principles and into the application of different techniques actual working methods are examined in some detail and it becomes more appropriate for personal views and preferences to be expressed. To this extent, therefore, *Urban and Rural Transport* could become a little more controversial than *Principles of Transport*. Nevertheless, this is a text book intended as a basis for study. Far from wishing to impose upon the reader a set of opinions, it is hoped that a presentation in this way will stimulate thought and mental argument. Facts and theory must be known and understood but application reflects the attitude of the individual who will develop his own thoughts and inclinations, all with the benefit of knowledge and experience. Where opinions have been expressed, care has been taken to identify them as such. The purpose of a text book is to teach; it is a manual of instruction. It must, therefore, contain accurate information but a discussion on resultant practices is also a helpful teaching aid. At this stage subjective thought is appropriate and a subsequent dialogue stimulating (with plenty of scope for the critics as well!). Fact is one thing and opinion is another and there must be no confusion between the two.

Another slight variation in presentation is that *Principles of Transport*, which introduces the subject of transport before it is split into its modal parts relates principles to practice by the inclusion of a large number of living examples. Although limited reference is made in *Urban and Rural Transport* to current practices amongst operators, in this more specialised work, theory must be examined in greater depth and for this purpose, real life examples are liable to contain extraneous features which cloud the fundamental issues and for this reason have not always been used for explanatory purposes. For similar reasons, the presentation of statistical data has been avoided as far as possible. Furthermore, statistics quickly become dated and are likely to relate to one country only (in this case the UK). Except, therefore, where a simplified presentation is helpful, readers are referred elsewhere for any information of this kind which they might require.

Finally, even with a single author, a work such as this can seldom be accomplished without some help from other people. *Urban and Rural Transport* has been no exception and acknowledgement of the provision of information by individuals within certain bodies or undertakings is duly recorded adjacent to the appropriate figure or plate. Assistance in checking specific facts by the Secretary of the Confederation of British Road Passenger Transport and the Chief Inspecting Officer of Railways is also gratefully acknowledged. Where illustrations have been provided from outside sources, due acknowledgement appears on the page concerned.

It was said earlier that a text book must contain accurate information and it is sincerely hoped that no misrepresentation has arisen. Although every effort has been made to verify certain of the detail with those who are directly concerned, if an error has crept in responsibility must remain that of the author. It is unfortunate that the necessary lead time between preparation and publication tends to be such that what is written, whilst correct at the time, is liable to be overtaken by subsequent events. Given an industry which is always in the public eye and hence sensitive to popular opinion together with a dynamic government, all within a changing world, such circumstances cannot always be avoided but again it is hoped that the effects will be minimal.

The author also wishes to record his appreciation and thanks to Mr R. Brook, Deputy Chairman and Chief Executive of the National Bus Company and Mr A. F. Beckenham, Director of Education and Training of the Chartered Institute of Transport for their help and encouragement; to his secretary, Mrs June Haywood, for the preparation of the script for processing, and to his wife for her forbearance and proof checking. Without such assistance the burden of preparation might have made the task impossible.

In presenting this work it is hoped that the managers of tomorrow will derive some benefit from its pages. Perhaps also it will be of some interest to that strong body of loyal enthusiasts and to anyone else who, although not directly connected with the industry, see a fascination in riding on buses.

RWF
January, 1980

Introduction

Transport is an all-embracing subject. Its science covers the movement of passengers, be they travelling a short distance on a local bus or across the face of the earth by a jet airliner; the movement of merchandise — and there are many different ways of doing that — and physical distribution which, as well as actual transport, involves also materials handling, packaging, warehouse location and management and inventory control. Transport management consists of a collection of people drawn from many different disciplines. Engineers, accountants, lawyers, administrators, sociologists and town and country planners all have an important input but their learning is not confined to transport. The people concerned are specialists within their own particular calling but they are not necessarily also experts in the art of moving people or goods and most could work equally well within an industry other than public transport. The transport specialist as such and the one who must learn the art of movement and who could not easily exercise his skills in any other field is the operator and he generally confines his expertise to one particular mode.

Urban and rural transport is here interpreted as local public passenger transport, which is predominantly bus. But in Great Britain the Local Government Act, 1972 and the Transport Act, 1978 place responsibility on county councils to develop, in consultation with operators, policies which promote the provision of coordinated and efficient systems covering all forms of public passenger transport. The theory is that the natural advantages of each should be properly exploited in order that the most suitable systems local to county areas might be developed. With broad policy control (and financial support) of town and country planning, highways, traffic and parking and local public passenger transport in the hands of a single authority (ie, a county council), a move away from the one-time traditional commercial policies of bus operators is inevitable. Unremunerative bus services for example might become justified if their presence avoids more costly expenditure on other things. This is a time of change. New criteria for service provision is likely to emerge and the bus can no longer be considered in isolation. The chapters which follow give proper recognition to these changing circumstances.

It follows that if this concept of urban passenger transport is to be pursued, modes other than the bus cannot be ignored, at least at the planning stage. Alternatives to buses will become of even greater importance as the energy situation deteriorates, which it is predicted to do. Whilst it is feasible that between now and the turn of the century the battery vehicle will have been developed to the extent that it will be able to undertake all of the functions at present being performed by the diesel engine, it has not, as yet, been proved. Even today there are situations where line dependent systems are more appropriate than the conventional bus and a dearth of oil could easily accelerate a swing in this direction in order to maximise the use of electricity for propulsion purposes. Whilst, therefore the bus is the predominant feature of this subject, trams, trolleybuses and local railways are also a part of the overall urban transport scene.

Although public transport facilities are more profuse in some areas than in others, there are relatively few parts of the inhabited world which have no bus service at all. It follows that many different operating organisations are managed by many different types of people with as many different methods of conducting their businesses and subject to varying statutory rights and obligations but all with the common purpose of carrying passengers to the places where they want to go as expeditiously and as economically as possible. Passenger requirements and accepted standards vary not only between countries but in different areas within the same country. Local customs and practices have grown up within managements and amongst the staff and passengers. What might be regarded as an impossible inhibition in one town could be seen as an indispensable aid to operation in another perhaps less than 100 miles away. This parochial outlook is gradually being broken down within the senior and middle management grades by training schemes and wider promotion opportunities which have eliminated much of the in-breeding which at one time existed. Similar circumstances do not apply within the trade unions whose platform staff members are less likely to move around. Hence local habits die hard and in the treatment of a subject of this kind it is neither practicable nor particularly necessary to discuss the infinite variety of local practices. Readers with some local experience may, therefore, see statements within these pages which are strange to them and with which they might not readily agree. This does not, however, make anybody wrong.

Even at managerial level there are differences of opinion regarding such fundamental issues as the practicalities of one-man operation, methods of fare collection and vehicle design, not to mention different staff agreements and working practices. What this really shows is the inadvisability of being too dogmatic on a particular topic as it is unlikely that any one line of thinking will be completely in error or even completely right. One-man operation is a particular case in point. Whilst this method of working has for many years found general acceptance throughout Europe and North America, the bus conductor still remains a part of the British scene. Collectively within the major publicly owned British bus undertakings there are still 33 conductors for every 100 drivers employed.* As single manning is still a little controversial in the UK (again more in some areas than in others) this way of working cannot be taken for granted as an operator overseas might do. It therefore becomes an important part of the study of bus operation. In this context it may be noted in passing that in the British bus industry, working without a conductor has by popular acceptance become known as 'one-man operation' or 'OMO' for short. Some will say that in the UK this violates the terms of the Sex Discrimination Act, 1975. However, the Interpretation Act, 1889 stipulates that in statutory documents, the term 'he' will be deemed to embrace 'he' or 'she' where appropriate. It is, therefore, regarded as unnecessarily pedantic to elucidate further on nouns or pronouns of an agreed common gender. As parliament is prepared to accept this, the writer also proposes to use the masculine which, by inference, includes the feminine as well and no violation of the Sex Discrimination Act is intended.

Reference to the legislature introduces the feature that transport is governed by complex legislation. Even the trivial point just mentioned involved parliament and in all facets of the subject there are many statutory requirements which are much more fundamental than that. This, of course, applies to all nations but overseas, even if the laws are similar in principle, they are likely to be different in detail. Remembering what was said earlier, the law is a profession in its own right. Lawyers do not have to be busmen and busmen do not have to be lawyers. Nevertheless, because the operation of public transport is so closely bound with the statutes busmen cannot be ignorant of these legal requirements and the subject must form an important part of any work on transport operation. But this notwithstanding, it is clearly impracticable to give comprehensive coverage of the statutory background as it applies to each individual country. Whilst, therefore, the text which follows deals with the science of running buses and trams as is applicable to the world at large, references to legal matters relate only to British law. Even though circumstances may be similar overseas, the foreign student cannot assume that what is the case in the United Kingdom necessarily applies elsewhere.

Transport is movement and where there is movement there is a potential hazard. It is right, therefore, that there should be strict controls backed by the force of law in the interests of public safety. But the provision of transport facilities is also very much a political animal. Certainly as far as local public passenger transport is concerned it is something which is always in the public eye and in this more than in any other science the average layman seems to consider his knowledge and wisdom to be infinitely superior to that of the professional manager. Whilst, therefore, some regulation is essential, there is also political whim and in a country where the pendulum swings periodically between left and right it is not surprising that successive governments have seen fit to introduce new arrangements. Thus over the past three decades or so there have been Transport Acts in the years 1947, 1953, 1962, 1968, 1978 and now 1980 quite apart from those other enactments which, although not specifically mentioning transport in their title, have had no less an impact on all who are involved in the carriage of goods and people. Whilst some of this legislation makes little contribution to the science of actually running buses and trams, the facts must be known and it was the promise of the 1980 Act which has delayed publication of this first edition of *Urban and Rural Transport.*

The preparation and subsequent emergence of the Transport Act, 1980 has made the production of this work particularly difficult. Its period of gestation embraced a change of government in the United Kingdom followed by a policy document, a Transport Bill and finally the introduction of the act itself. This means that when work commenced, such fundamental changes to the licensing system as were destined to come could not have been foreseen let alone written about. Whilst at the end of 1979 it was apparent that changes were imminent, it was not until 1980 that details of the new legislation could be confirmed and even then the implementation of some of the provisions of the new act were not automatic but subject to introduction by the minister. This left very little time to complete a book if it was to be ready for the following academic year and even though every effort has been made to ensure accuracy, at the time of writing, although the new law can be explained, it is done without the benefit of experience of the working of the revised licensing arrangements. The policy document claimed that the hitherto existing licensing system for public service vehicle operation was difficult to understand, daunting to new entrants, hampered initiative and restricted competition. The author certainly accepts that it was difficult for the practitioner to understand but he shares the apprehension of the industry as to whether

*Source: *Transport Statistics — Great Britain 1967-1977;* HMSO

simplification needed to be accompanied by such fundamental changes of principle. The PSV licensing system as it originated in the Road Traffic Act, 1930 stood for 50 years without any substantial change except that in recent years, in deference to public pressure, parliament nibbled at the controls and superimposed on existing legislation a succession of amendments whereby under certain circumstances the licensing laws were relaxed — and thus came the complications. But in 1980, what the industry sees as a black cloud is bursting over the express services, annihilating quantity controls and thereby exposing the established services to unfettered competition which could harm everybody and benefit nobody. That is one viewpoint and it certainly is a reminder of conditions as they were in the 1920s which was the very reason why quantity licensing was introduced in the first place. However, a socialist government swept away quantity licensing from road haulage in its 1968 Transport Act without, it seems, any particularly disastrous effects and on this hypothesis it could be argued that a conservative administration is justified in thinking similarly about the longer distance road passenger services.

However, with urban and rural transport being provided mainly by local bus services, express services do not figure largely in this subject. But there is at least a grey cloud over the local stage carriage services which might not blow away. Whilst quantity control has so far been retained within this category, albeit in a different form, a somewhat ominous remark in the policy document that this would be for the time being is supported by the new act which makes provision for trial areas where no quantity control will be exercised for any road passenger service. Even the relatively near future is, therefore, a little obscure and should local bus networks also become subject to uncontrolled competition the results could be serious. Not many stage services are profitable and under the protection of the licensing system operators have for years endeavoured to give a comprehensive service by cross-subsidisation between routes and as and when that has become insufficient, losses have been made good from public funds. If under these circumstances local pirates are permitted to come in and take the few crumbs which are still to be had it is difficult to see where the benefits will lie.

That, however, is by the way. The point being made here is that in introducing the subject, it is important to realise that the law appertaining to bus and coach operation is, at the time of writing, undergoing a fundamental change which is being implemented as the minister so orders by statutory instrument. Chapter 8 which deals with statutory controls covers the relevant provisions of the 1980 Transport Act but on the assumption that the minister has, in fact, so ordered.

1
Historical Background

Introduction

This is not a historical treatise. The evolution of buses and trams and trains has been well documented and a host of excellent literature on the subject is readily available for both the serious student and the enthusiast of this most fascinating aspect of passenger transport. But if there is to be an appreciation of the present and an understanding of why certain things are happening now and are likely to happen in the future, there must also be a knowledge of how things have developed in the past. Nevertheless, references to what has gone before will be no more than is necessary to acquaint the reader with the events which have led to the situation as it is now in the 1980s. Whilst, therefore, a little bit of history is essential, this chapter will not be one of the longest.

The Growth of a Network

It was in 1829 that George Shillibeer introduced the first horse bus in London from the 'Yorkshire Stingo' on the Marylebone Road to the Bank. It was in 1830 that George Stephenson inaugurated the first steam hauled railway passenger train between Liverpool and Manchester in the north of England. The year 1830 or thereabout can therefore be regarded as the 'beginning of time' as far as the subject matter of this book is concerned and the subsequent 150 years has seen a process of evolution and development leading to the network of services which is now provided. From that time onwards, enterprising bands of people set themselves up to provide transport services as a means of earning their livelihood and in so doing, destined the shape of the things which were to come. Certainly it was done for private gain (with financial risk) and some perished in the process but the services which they provided fulfilled a community need. Small privately owned undertakings mushroomed and with a view to maximising revenue, concentrated on what were regarded as the more lucrative routes. But bus proprieters (and railway managements as well) knew, perhaps better than the passengers, which areas were likely to have the greatest potential. They decided what the people would most probably use and provided the services accordingly. The technique of what is now known in popular parlance as 'marketing' is not, therefore, really so very new. More is to be said about marketing in Chapter 7. It was this early development of lines of communication which helped to determine subsequent geographical patterns of town and country.

So far, 'network' has been used as a collective term, referring to both bus and train but in reality, the two developed quite independently. Historically, it is of no small significance as will be seen in due course that although both appeared on the scene at a similar time period, the railway train produced its own power whilst the bus had to be hauled by a horse. It was soon realised that a horse could pull a greater load if the vehicle had smooth steel wheels which ran on smooth steel rails than it could if running on the uneven surface of a road on account of the lower resistance. It was the same principle as applied to water transport and which had already justified the construction of canals. Steel lines were therefore laid in the roadway on the more important traffic routes and so the street tramway was born. The first horse trams came to Great Britain in the early 1860s and electric traction followed with Magnus Volk opening his short electric railway along the seafront at Brighton in 1883 and the first successful electric street tramway in Great Britain becoming operational at Blackpool in 1885.

However, it was not only private enterprise which helped to lay the foundations of the transport system as it is known today. Over the past decade or more there has been a deal of legislation which has brought politics and public ownership into transport and the present day student will tend to accept this situation as part of the natural course of events. Whilst this was not generally the case before the 1940s when most of Britain's transport was in private hands there was even then one important exception and one which has its roots way back in the past. It is also one which is particularly topical for the subject matter of this book. Municipalities own and operate the local buses in many towns at home and overseas. As far as Great Britain is concerned, the reason for this can be traced to parliamentary action back in the 19th century when, as already noted, trams were becoming very much a part of the urban scene. To encroach a little on Chapter 8 and referring now to British law, parliamentary authority is necessary for the construction of a railway, light railway or tramway (which includes trolleybuses). This was a complication at a time when tramways were developing and the Tramways Act, 1870 was passed with a view to simplifying the procedure. This it did, which is a matter for Chapter 8. What, however, is important in this context and what will lead into Chapter 3 is that this Act of 1870 was also instrumental in bringing local government into the urban transport arena. With tramways being developed by private enterprise, the Tramways Act, 1870, among other things, gave to local authorities the power to acquire compulsorily if they so decided (but not necessarily to operate) local tramway systems. These powers could be exercised at 21 years from their inception and thereafter at seven yearly intervals and the purchase price for such acquisitions needed to contain no recognition of goodwill. In other words, the price was based virtually on scrap value of the assets to be acquired. This, of course, gave very little incentive to tramway promoters even though, in the event, some systems were never acquired in this way. What it did do was to introduce local authorities to local passenger transport. Many such authorities did exercise their powers if only to resuscitate tramways which had become run-down for the very reason that owners would not risk sinking capital into an enterprise which could be taken from them on unfavourable terms. Other tramway systems came into being under local authority control at the outset and in due course their tramway interests led to bus interests as well and hence the patterns of ownership as will be considered in Chapter 3 were evolved.

So much for the political background. To return to the development of the 'system' regardless of the form of ownership and control, the electric tramway came into being in the 1880s and from that time onwards local networks spread out from urban centres into what, in some cases, could almost be termed the nearby countryside. This process was often followed by the construction of rows of terraced houses adjacent to the routes and so the neighbourhoods began to develop. It was in this way that local transport (in the form of tramways) moulded the pattern and the layout of many of our older established towns, particularly within the first few miles of the centre and the development process can be traced in this way. The important point to note here is that in this example transport came first and development followed. The ability to travel made the area attractive for living, it increased land values and readers will doubtless be able to identify districts within their own home towns which owe their origins to the tram.

On the same principle but on a national scale so also did the railway help to shape geographical patterns. Main line railways linked the major centres. Often, competing lines served the same pairs of centres via different routes on a competitive basis. But in so doing, they also opened up the intermediate territory. Longer distance railway services are not the subject of consideration here but it is nevertheless of interest to note how the railways played their part in this development process. Just as tramways influenced the growth of towns, so also did the presence of a railway increase land values and encourage expansion. In some cases there was a negative reaction. Public pressure at the time on occasions prevented this new found method of communication from disturbing the alleged peace of fashionable and established residential areas with the result that powers could not be obtained to construct and the lines had to be a mile or two distant. The folly of such policies are now apparent with some railway stations sited at inconvenient distances from the places which they purport to serve. There are other instances where townships away from the more historical centres have grown up around the railway. In Surrey, Surbiton near to Kingston and Redhill near to Reigate are examples. What, however, is more to the point as far as local transport is concerned is that with main line railways came not only the fast inter-city trains (to use a more recent term) but also the stopping services and the branch lines.

At this juncture it is opportune to recall the point made with some emphasis in a previous paragraph that whilst both buses and trains first appeared on the scene around the 1830s, the latter was steam propelled whilst the former had to rely on animal power. For local journeys the electric tram came around the 1880s but it was not until the 1900s that the internal combustion engine became a reality. By that time steam trains were travelling at fast speeds and had established themselves as the most suitable means of conveyance for destinations beyond the reach of urban tramways. It was this incidence of development of first the steam engine and then the petrol engine some 70 years later which was responsible for the proliferation of railway branch lines and the rise of the intricate railway network which was destined to be severely pruned in the 1960s. Had the petrol engine come first it is quite possible that many of the lesser used and now defunct railway lines would never have been built in the first place. The closing of branch lines and the institution of railway replacement bus services, long lamented by some, is really doing nothing more than correcting an unnatural development caused by this historical accident, unless of course a future energy situation dictates a return to fixed track systems!

Transport and Land Use

Great play is made today of the affinity between local passenger transport and land use. Further references will be made both in this chapter and in subsequent chapters as to how local government, at least in Great Britain, has now been organised to plan, among other things, for good or for ill, the parallel development of land use, transport and related factors with a view to the achievement of optimum benefits from what are, in effect, separate disciplines. It is, of course, true that the design and location of residential areas, for example, in relation to industrial estates and commercial and shopping centres does have a strong effect on the pattern and hence the cost of the provision of local passenger transport. Much unnecessary expense has arisen in the past to bus operators because of the unsatisfactory layout of built-up areas and on this reasoning it is good sense to allow transport to be at least one of the dictates of land use. The corporate planning concept takes into account the requirements not only of all vehicular traffic but also of pedestrians and the environment. This could however militate against the proper penetration by buses of, say, shopping centres. Those responsible for the provision of transport facilities are very conscious of the fact that this is a service industry and that their passengers should always be carried to the places where they want to go and not to where it happens to be convenient to take them. The more sophisticated approach to town planning is therefore welcome providing the basic philosophy continues to make this possible and an anti-bus lobby is not allowed to predominate. Nevertheless, the old order does seem to be changing and it is pertinent, therefore, to see to what extent this is either necessary or desirable.

Conclusions on the Land Use Connection

To conclude this brief historical review designed to illustrate the relationship between transport and land use, there are three different stages of affinity between the two, being:

(a) Speculative transport managements open up new lines of communication into otherwise barren areas. With these new facilities, people follow and land becomes valuable. New dormitory areas come into being, sometimes accompanied by commerce and industry.
(b) New development areas are created to accommodate population growth and overspill and transport managements have at least a moral duty to cater for the resultant new demands as best they can.
(c) Land use and transport is considered collectively with a view to optimum benefits and to facilitate the provision of a transport system with maximum economy and efficiency.

Stage (c) does, of course, present itself, at least in theory, as the ideal and it is the now fashionable approach to issues of this kind. Ideals, however, are one thing and personal opinions and preferences are sometimes another and the gap between theory and reality must never be underestimated. Even if responsibility for land use and transport policies is placed under a single administration, that organisation must have separate functional departments for each. History and the experience of human nature does not produce evidence of any easier relationships between internal departments within a single organisation than might exist between separate entities and the success of the theory at stage (c) must stand the test of practical application. Furthermore, organisational integration cannot be regarded as the automatic cure for all planning ills as local councils must represent the electors and some people are prone to resist control, preferring a more liberal approach than is possible under what they see to be 'big brother' in the shape of overall planning authorities. The principle is not, therefore, necessarily easily accepted by either management or the public. But this is now the present, not the past and the subject has got beyond the limits of this chapter. The thoughts (and they are presented only as thoughts) will be further considered in Chapters 3 and 5.

Vehicles

Just as an elementary knowledge of how service patterns have evolved helps one to understand why things are now provided in the way that they are, so will a cursory look at vehicle designs over the years throw some light on present day problems and practices in this particular field.

An examination of the historical photographs of buses and trams at different periods depicted on pages 88-94 shows how present day designs as will be considered in Chapter 10 have evolved.

The point has already been made that a load can be moved more easily with the lower resistance which results from smooth steel wheels running on smooth steel rails. A comparison of the bus and the tram in use at the turn of the century clearly illustrates the greater capacity of trams and the reason for their introduction in the first instance. As far as the bus is concerned, there has been a gradual process of 'bigger and better' with each new generation of vehicle whilst the tram reached its zenith in terms of capacity and, at least in the United Kingdom, comfort, early on in its career. This is a clue to the subsequent fortunes of these two modes to which further consideration must now be given.

The Development and Demise of the Tram

No study of urban passenger transport would be complete without reference to the tram, even though, in the United Kingdom, there is now only one undertaking, being Blackpool Corporation, which continues to operate this form of transport. In many other parts of the world, including Europe and North America, some excellent tramway systems are still functional and they make a valuable contribution to the transport requirements of the communities which they serve. There could, if circumstances happen to be appropriate, even be a repetition of history with a universal tramway revival in the future but that is a matter for Chapter 12. The present situation is that trams had their heyday in the 1920s and the mode has since suffered a decline and has now become extinct in some places and severely truncated in others. Only by a historical review can it be seen why this has come to pass.

Remember two important factors to which attention has already been drawn. The first is that a horse can pull a greater weight on rails than on a road. The second is that electricity as a form of motive power came before the general acceptance of the petrol engine. Reference again to the selection of illustrations of buses and trams over the developing period indicates that for urban transport trams generally had the advantage in terms of capacity right up to the time of the introduction of the large front entrance, rear engined buses such as the Leyland Atlantean which first appeared in 1958, by which time trams were disappearing anyway. Whilst, however, capacity was a major reason for the introduction of the tram in the first place, it was not also a reason for the final supremacy of the bus as the tram still has a capacity potential. Popularity focuses on comfort and in this respect the tram has been at a disadvantage in the United Kingdom, not because of any inherent characterisic but because no attempt was made to modernise antiquated hardware. Whilst a rail-borne vehicle is able to give a very comfortable ride it is hardly surprising that a bus new in the 1950s compared favourably with trams built up to some 40 years earlier but which were, nevertheless, still running. As far as comfort is concerned, a high standard can be expected from the modern tramway. The explanation why tramway systems were allowed to run-down in favour of the bus would therefore seem to lie elsewhere. This is in fact the case and the reasons are economic as a result of the high cost of the way, the vehicles and the power together with the inflexibility of a fixed track system. However, as far as the cost of fuel is concerned, although the price of electricity is now no longer favourable in comparison with petrol and diesel oil, there are indications that such a situation may well not remain.

To summarise, therefore, it can be said that originally the tram progressed in advance of the bus. But new technology (which, as far as the buses are concerned was in the shape of pneumatic tyres, improved suspension, better performance, greater comfort and more economical operation) in due course put the bus ahead of the tram in terms of public appeal. Add to this the growing diseconomies of the tram and the operating disadvantages of being tied to a track, particularly when the road is heavily congested with other vehicles, and there were reasons for not applying the benefits of similarly advanced technology to the trams, with the results as have been shown. Not all trams, however, were directly replaced by buses. Some undertakings, although not prepared to spend money on updating their tramways were also not ready to dispense with electric traction.

Trolleybuses

The trolleybus, or trackless tram as it was known in some places, was a vehicle designed to combine the electric propulsion of the tram with the manoeuvrability of the bus. Whilst it certainly achieved the former it did not go more than part way towards the achievement of the latter as although it could to some extent weave amongst other traffic, this was possible only to the limits of its trolley booms and the vehicles could not be diverted at short notice along other thoroughfares. Nevertheless, as far as flexibility was concerned, this represented something better than the tram and for all intents and purposes the trolleybus took over where the tram left off. The point has already been made in the previous sub-section that whereas each generation of new buses became more impressive than the last, the trams, after a flying start, were not similarly progressive and by the 1930s they had lost most of their attractiveness as far as the general public was concerned. This is not to say that they could not have been made equally if not more acceptable than buses had managements and national policy been so motivated. In the event, however, the electric vehicles' answer to the bus, at least in Great Britain, was not better trams but trolleybuses, the comfort of which and hence passenger acceptance was equal to that of the bus. Although isolated examples of trolleybus systems had been around since 1911 the heyday was not until the 1930s when local networks were developed on a large scale throughout the UK and elsewhere. When, however, the vehicles and equipment became time expired, decisions were taken not to renew but instead to close the systems and run buses in their place. By that time, as has been stated in the case of the tram, electricity as a form of motive power together with the need for capital equipment had made it uneconomic relative to the diesel bus. By so converting to form one common system, complete integration could be achieved and the disadvantages of running two separate systems were eliminated.

As was the case with trams, as the number of different systems diminished, so also did the demand for vehicles and equipment. Manufacturers gradually dropped out of the business and the systems which were left found it increasingly difficult to survive. The result was that in the UK, the last trolleybus ran (in Bradford) in 1972. Like the tram, examples of the mode remain overseas, including Europe and North America.

But history has a habit of repeating itself. This however is something for the future and for discussion in Chapter 12.

Private Cars

Whilst it could be said that as this is a text book on public transport, private transport has no legitimate place in it, private transport does, nevertheless, have some very important repercussions. The private car shares the use of a common highway, causes congestion and hence delays buses. It also abstracts traffic from buses. On the other hand, if all of the car drivers and their passengers who travel in the peak periods demanded instead a seat on a bus, it would produce at best a heavier peak commitment which would likely be uneconomic and at worst an extra demand at a busy time for which it would be difficult or impossible to cater and hence would be an embarrassment. However, regardless of the effects on buses, people want cars and it cannot be denied that for those who are prepared, able and qualified to drive, nothing can match the private vehicle in terms of convenience and comfort. Public feeling in this respect is amply demonstrated by the table at Fig 1 which shows the number of private cars and private vans licensed in the UK at five yearly intervals from 1930. The trend is clear. In the 1930s, to run a car was a prestige symbol and the exception rather than the rule. True, many people so did but there were plenty who did not and were pleased to utilise the services of public transport, not only for the journey to work but for pleasure purposes as well. Then came World War II which completely distorted everybodys' way of life and traffic patterns along with it. More congenial conditions did not return until the late 1940s. In the aftermath of war, although there was money, there was little to spend it on. Food and, more importantly for this topic, petrol, was rationed and new cars were virtually unobtainable. Only then, however, after years of restriction and gloom could pent up feelings be released and people wanted to get out and about. Private transport was not available and public transport was in great demand. This was now the heyday of the bus but it was not to last. As cars and petrol became more easily available and society became more affluent, so the private vehicle appeared on the roads in ever increasing numbers and bus patronage dwindled, particularly outside the peaks when travel was optional and mostly for pleasure purposes. On many of the rural services double deck vehicles were replaced by single deckers, hourly services were reduced to two-hourly and then to odd journeys prior to being withdrawn altogether. In the towns the trend was less apparent but it was still there. What was very noticeable was the persistently increasing volume of vehicular traffic and the resultant congestion and delay.

This, therefore, is the background which has led to the changing fortunes of buses and which may be summarised as follows:

(a) The combined effects of the erosion of traffics and heavy increases in costs have necessitated hefty fares increases.
(b) With a large part of the traffic already gone, high fares discouraged much of what was left.
(c) Bus loadings, particularly in rural areas, fell to negligible proportions.
(d) Bus services were no longer economic, even after allowing for cross-subsidisation and were reduced and withdrawn.
(e) There remains a hard core of people, mainly the young and the elderly, without access to cars and who, if without buses, suffer hardship.

Year	*000*
1930	1,075
1935	1,505
1940	1,456
1945	1,522
1950	2,307
1955	3,609
1960	5,650
1965	9,131
1970	11,802
1975	14,061

Fig 1 Number of Private Cars and Private Vans licensed in the UK at five yearly intervals from 1930./Source: *Transport Statistics — Great Britain*, HMSO.

Co-ordination and the New Situation

It was the rural areas which first felt the harsh repercussions of this trend. In the towns, high frequency services could be reduced and still give an acceptable albeit more expensive facility for a lesser number of people. These passengers were, within limits, able to afford, perhaps unwillingly, higher fares, at least for travelling to and from work where their salary justified a certain level of expenditure for travel purposes. To what extent they were prepared to go is a matter for consideration in Chapter 7.

In 1959 the British Government set up a Committee under the chairmanship of Professor D. T. Jack to study rural services. This Committee, which reported in 1961, concluded that the decline in rural bus services was causing hardship to a few people and inconvenience to more. Among the possible solutions considered by the Committee were the carriage of fare-paying passengers on school buses, extended use of mini-buses, combination of the carriage of goods and passengers and carriage of passengers in 'postal buses'. The major recommendation, however, was a measure of financial aid to support rural bus services. This report was followed by a series of local enquiries, the findings of which were published in 1965. A white paper of the British government entitled *Transport Policy* published in 1966 drew attention, among other things, to the problems which were arising as a result of the proliferation of the private car and to quote from paragraph 9 of that document.*

'Those who manage or work on London Transport,

**Transport Policy;* Cmnd 3057, HMSO

British Railways and provincial bus services are struggling to reconcile two mutually contradictory objectives: to provide an adequate service for the public and to pay their way. As a result they are finding it increasingly difficult to do either.'

By this time it was not only rural transport which was finding it either difficult or impossible to survive. The finances of all bus undertakings were in a parlous state and on the railway, notwithstanding heavy pruning by Dr (now Lord) Beeching in 1963 of many of the cross-country and branch line local stopping trains serving rural areas, on the passenger side it was really only some of the more important inter-city services which were still viable.

The white paper contained some of the first indications of Government thinking towards subsidies for public transport and also to the overall systems concept. To quote again from paragraph 9 of *Transport Policy*.

'New thinking is required, not only about types and combinations of public transport, but also about how they should be financed.'

And from paragraph 10:

'If the public sector of transport is to play its important role effectively, its different elements can no longer operate in isolation . . .
Passenger services . . . must be adapted to local needs. The urgent need for integration of road and rail services is now emerging . . .
The ways of ensuring this integration, and the forms it should take, must be decided in consultation with the Regional Economic Planning Councils and local authorities . . .'

In 1967, *Transport Policy* was followed by another white paper *Public Transport and Traffic** which was, in effect, a prelude to the Transport Act, 1968. The following extract from paragraph 2 is pertinent to this narrative

'The provision of transport — whether public or private — can no longer be considered in isolation from other developments. It must be built into the whole planning of our community life so that no factory is sited, no housing estate or "overspill" developed, no town re-planned without the implications of the movement of people and goods having been studied and incorporated from the outset. In other words, transport must become the servant of the planners, not their master.'

The 1968 Transport Act duly came and with it a reorganisation of much of Britain's transport and subsidies for local passenger services, be they road or rail. Even then, the situation has not remained static. Subsequent acts have modified certain arrangements, particularly on the financial side. But this is now getting into present day reality and more correctly the subject of subsequent chapters.

The purpose of this brief historical review is to see how and why the present situation has been reached. The background to the changes is, of course, finance. All the time that operators could give an acceptable service without recourse to public funds the managements went their way subject only to licensing and other statutory controls as will be described in Chapter 8. Once taxpayers' and ratepayers' money is used for revenue support or capital grants, however, it is inevitable that politics must become involved. In a country which is somewhat finely balanced between opposing shades of political opinion it is likely that government policy towards transport (and everything else for that matter) will change every now and again. This does not facilitate management's task. Neither does it facilitate writing a book because what is government policy at the time of preparation might have changed by the time the work is published but this is only repeating the remarks which were made in the Introduction.

The trend today, at least in Great Britain, is towards controlled planning whatever might be the dislike by some of this type of approach. What was once a commercial enterprise has become a social service. Competition within urban and rural passenger transport has been replaced by co-ordination subject to any effects of the Transport Act, 1980. Legislation now requires virtually every passenger transport undertaking to co-operate with each other and county councils are transport co-ordinating authorities. Similar trends can be detected overseas, particularly in countries where, like Great Britain, support from public funds is necessary if essential services are to be maintained and where a planning process is necessary if the natural growth of traffic has produced intolerable conditions on the highways. To relieve this particular problem, capital expenditure is often likely to be warranted, which is yet another reason for some sort of government control. Many of the developing countries have not yet reached this situation. Students from these areas can benefit from the experiences of others but it does not necessarily follow that they must emulate British practices precisely as they are today.

**Public Transport and Traffic*; Cmnd 3481 HMSO

2
The Infrastructure

Interpretation

The term 'infrastructure' is relatively new and will not be found in all dictionaries. Having said this, it is certainly not the intention of the author to do anything which might perpetuate the use of words which have now become popular albeit inaccurate common jargon, however widely accepted they might be. Neither is it intended to repeat for the British reader fashionable phrases imported from across the Atlantic unless there are good reasons so to do. There are occasions, however, when it is not easy to find in a single word something which adequately embraces a broad subject which has many parts. There is just such a case with the mass of different items on which capital must be spent to run buses and trains such as highways, track and stations. The term 'infrastructure' has been aptly described by the European Commission as 'a system of communications and services as backing for operation' which is precisely what this chapter is all about. Now to be considered are the highways, the bus stations, the railway to the extent that it is relevant in the urban and rural context and all the physical assets and facilities which are necessary for operation or, in a word, the infrastructure.

Roads

The Highway Network

A general review of the different forms of way applicable to the various modes of transport is contained in the contemporary work *Principles of Transport*. Very briefly, the way may be natural or artificial and it may be available either for the sole use of one particular transport service or it may be shared by many different users. Buses, of course, use the national highway network (which consists of artificially constructed roads) along with all other types of road user, be they for the conveyance of passengers or goods either as part of a public transport service or in the form of private and personalised vehicles, together being collectively referred to as vehicular traffic. The use of the highway is, therefore, very much on a shared basis. Although this inhibits free movement, some amelioration of what is becoming a more and more unsatisfactory situation lies in the fact that the cost of using that way is also shared.

National or local government is responsible for the construction of roads and they are paid for out of public funds derived from taxation and local rates. Road users, however, which includes bus operators, are taxed for the privilege of so doing. As a general principle this can take the form of a vehicle tax and/or a fuel tax. A third method is the application of tolls. Different countries apply different methods to varying degrees. In Great Britain there is a tax on both vehicles and fuel with only a few isolated examples of tolls which are payable for the use of certain bridges and tunnels. There is also a tax on the purchase price of private vehicles when they are bought. Elsewhere there are examples where the entire revenue is derived from the sale of fuel which, unlike the vehicle tax, relates expenditure directly to the extent of use. Although in Great Britain, there is now no direct link between revenue (from fuel and vehicle taxation) and expenditure (on construction and maintenance of roads), the writer does not accept a popular contention that road users have the free use of a permanent way. It is true that a road fund, created by the Development and Road Improvement Funds Act, 1909, was finally abolished by the Miscellaneous Financial Provisions Act, 1955 after having been raided for other purposes since 1926. Nevertheless, the fact must remain that road users are taxed and this should be construed as payment for the use of the way for if they did not use the way they would not pay tax. Whether or not there is a specific fund for this purpose is a technicality. In the event, British road users not only pay for their roads but for a lot of other things as well. In Great Britain in the year 1977/78 only a little more than one third* of the total revenue from motor taxation was actually spent on highway construction and maintenance. Even, however, if it is acknowledged that it is those who use the roads that have to pay for them, they do share the costs. This means that expenditure by bus operators, for example in respect of vehicle taxation is very small indeed compared with the railway which has to construct and maintain its own private tracks on its own private land; a matter which is further discussed in Chapter 4.

In Great Britain roads are classified according to their traffic value and those which provide a national network for through traffic are known as trunk roads or special roads such as motorways. Traffic, transport and highway

*Source: *Transport Statistics — Great Britain;* HMSO

functions are the responsibility of county councils who are, therefore, the highway authorities except that central government deals with trunk roads and motorways. District councils maintain minor and possibly other roads as well for county councils on an agency basis. Both county and district councils may provide car parks. The funding of highway projects is administered through the TPP process as is considered in Chapter 4. Although the trunk road programme is not a part of TPP submissions it does influence local highway strategy and will therefore have a strong bearing on county proposals. But this information is of only partial concern to bus operators. The piece which is of real interest is who is in overall control of the highway, being not only its construction but also its use, which means responsibility for traffic movements. The railway, which has its own private way is an authority only unto itself (subject to any government regulations). The bus operator is one of many users of somebody else's way and he must, therefore, know and have satisfactory working arrangements with that third party. It has been said that it is the appropriate county council which is the highway authority (subject to certain powers which are conferred on district councils) and it is Section 187 of the Local Government Act, 1972 which so decrees.

Traffic Control

It has been said that the road is a public and common way shared by many different types of user of which the bus is but one. It is for this very reason that there must be an independent highway authority. The users may be classified into various broad groups as is shown at Fig 2 which refers to registered vehicles in Great Britain in 1978 and which puts into sharp relief the ratio of buses and coaches to other traffic. Public passenger transport is only a very small part. The figures shown are correct to only one decimal place but put in another way, on average only about one vehicle in every 232 on the British roads in 1978 was a bus or coach. This gives a measure of the situation although in reality traffic is not, of course, as evenly spread as this. On certain thoroughfares buses could on occasions be the only vehicles in sight. Nevertheless it is clear that the bus has a lot of competition when seeking not only passengers but road space as well. This aspect will be further considered in

Basic Classification	**Types of Vehicles Included**	**Percentage of whole in terms of vehicles in use in the year 1978**
Passenger		
Private personalised vehicles	Private transport in the form of private cars	79.2
	Private transport in the form of motor cycles, mopeds, scooters and three wheelers	7.3
Buses and coaches	Public transport, being stage and express carriage services including excursions and tours. Also private hire which is in effect private transport once on the road under contract	0.4
Taxis	A hybrid. A public facility whilst plying for hire but private once the vehicle is engaged	0.2
Goods		
All vehicles adapted for the carriage of merchandise	A very wide variety of vehicles and traffic carried. Vehicles range from small vans to very large tankers, pantechnicons and the like with some exceptional loads. Many are specialised and may be rigid or articulated. Some are providing a public haulage service whilst others are 'own account' being used as part of a trade or business other than transport	9.6
Miscellaneous	Specialised vehicles adapted for duties other than for the carriage of passengers or goods	3.3

Fig 2 Classification of Road Traffic in Great Britain in terms of Vehicles in use in the year 1978./Source: *Basic Road Statistics, 1979;* British Road Federation.

connection with bus priorities. In the absence of any such priorities (and overall there are few) the bus must take its place with every other vehicle and conform to general traffic regulations. Certain rules of the road are laid down by the minister which drivers have a statutory duty to observe. Further advice on road behaviour is contained in the Highway Code,* an official document which is not in itself mandatory although any violation would not help the driver in proceedings resulting from a subsequent accident. Traffic discipline is regulated by signs and light signals and is subject to the overall supervision and control of the police.

A glance again at Fig 1 will remind the reader (if he is not already only too well aware) that the amount of private cars on the road is multiplying rapidly. As the numbers grow, so traffic congestion increases and road construction programmes have failed to keep pace with the ever increasing demands and various palliatives have been and still are being introduced. The British government has tended to veer away from building new urban motorways because of the cost and the impact on the environment. Instead, the general policy is to maximise the use of existing resources aided by less ambitious projects designed to speed traffic flow and traffic management schemes are constantly being introduced by highway authorities to ease pressure. These provide for better use of available roadspace by such measures as uni-directional traffic flows, the reduction or elimination of conflicting traffic movements which means particularly the banning of turns across the path of facing traffic and the prohibition or control of kerbside parking or even loading and unloading merchandise. On occasions these measures require some relatively minor road reconstruction work before they are introduced but even what is thereby becoming traffic engineering is far less costly than the provision of new highways. These traffic management and traffic engineering schemes do, however, often result in somewhat devious routes and important traffic objectives within the central cores of towns are sometimes no longer directly accessible as a result. Vehicles are, therefore, on occasions forced to travel, for example, beyond a commercial centre via a newly created one-way system on the periphery to approach the required destination from the opposite direction. For a through bus route this is at worst impracticable and at best inconvenient and unsatisfactory. Either a setting down/picking up point somewhat distant from the popular traffic point is necessary or else a circuitous time-consuming and hence costly working is necessary. It is the duty of the bus operator to protect the interests of his passengers as far as he is able and to take them where they want to go. To the highway authority, which is responsible for the free flow of all traffic, the bus is just one of many in terms of vehicle numbers and as was shown in Fig 2, a relatively small part. Note however that this is in terms of vehicle numbers and not the number of people involved which would present a very different picture and will be the subject of further discussion. Not only is there an obvious need to avoid the use of additional vehicles and staff which longer routes could easily require, it is the purpose of buses to take passengers where they want to go and as expeditiously as possible. It is understandable, therefore, that operators like to be very closely involved in any traffic management and traffic engineering considerations and to get if possible some preferential treatment. More is to be said about bus priorities and their justification but before so doing, there is one further aspect of traffic management which deserves special attention. It is urban traffic control.

One method of traffic management not so far mentioned is the co-ordinated control of traffic light signals over a wide area. This produces benefits when the density of such signals is relatively high which, according to Department of Transport guidelines, means more than 30 sets in total and not less than 10 per square mile. Traffic management of this kind is known as urban traffic control and its effect is to reduce vehicle journey times by co-ordinating the operation of traffic signals and by giving priority to the heavier traffic flows. There is also a built in system to monitor faults in traffic lights which otherwise can pass without official detection for indeterminate periods and cause much havoc in the process. The system requires a control room in which a computer governs traffic signals in accordance with various time plans which may be selected automatically and which cater for most of the predictable traffic patterns. The controller may, however, override the system manually to cater for any exceptional circumstances either by substituting an alternative fixed plan or by controlling the signals at a particular junction. To enable this to be done, the controller is assisted by closed circuit television. Strategically placed rotatable cameras are able to scan the area and by display on a series of screens in the control room the controller has a visual indication of the actual traffic situation. Also, a wall map of the area is necessary on which is portrayed the main road network with illuminated indications of the operational modes of control of each set of traffic lights in force at the time.

There is, of course, scope for further types of traffic control and traffic restraint by adaptions of this type of arrangement. For example, by computer calculation, access on to particular highways could be controlled to ensure that the volume of traffic at any one time does not exceed road capacity with the resultant congestion which is now becoming almost a way of life. This would, of course, involve queueing at the entry points but even then the subsequent improved traffic flow could compensate for time spent in this way.

**Highway Code*; HMSO

Whilst the highway authority (in Great Britain the county councils) is responsible for traffic control, with the availability of the equipment as described there is clearly a case for a link up with the police (who are responsible for enforcement) and bus managements. The system offers considerable scope in this respect. Alternatively, these bodies could institute their own closed circuit television sytems but if there is to be any control over general traffic arrangements, consultation and agreement with the highway authority is necessary.

Bus Priorities

With traffic congestion becoming ever more acute there can be little dispute on the need for measures designed to relieve some of its worst effects. Even so, it is debatable whether any resultant restraints should be applied as much to the bus as to the private car. It is likely that whilst the bus operator will make a case for preferential treatment for buses, motorists, supported by motoring organisations will take a different view and make representations accordingly. To this background it must be remembered that the resultant arrangements rest with the highway authority branch of the county council, which means that local policy is in the hands of locally elected politicians subject only to the broad framework as laid down by central government. Some councils are more bus minded than are others but there are very few places where an anti-bus lobby is without at least some support. This exemplifies just one need for effective public relations to make sure that the public gets the message but this is something for Chapter 7.

When considering the ratio of buses to other vehicles in Great Britain as depicted at Fig 2 the case for bus priorities might not appear to be very strong. However, in terms of potential capacity a different situation emerges. Buses are able to carry anything up to about 80 passengers and those running on local services within large towns frequently do, particularly in the peaks. This is in stark contrast to the private car whose average occupancy is about 1.6 people. Certainly the bus is a larger vehicle but in about four times the road space compared with the car, it can carry some 50 times as many people. When road space is at a premium, therefore, the case for moving people by public rather than private transport is very strong. Looked at in this light it is surprising that some politicians and some local authority staff as well still remain unenlightened in this respect. It must, nevertheless, be accepted that it is right and proper for the highway authority to do everything in its power to facilitate the free flow of traffic generally. It is also true that people want cars and it is understandable that no politician would be prepared to antagonise public opinion by imposing restraints on private transport without very good reason and that reason will have to be something better than just making life easier for the buses. But it has been shown how traffic management schemes can react unfavourably on buses and a plea for special recognition should in no way be interpreted as a bid to muzzle a competitor.

Bus priority measures may take the following forms:

(a) Facilities for stopping on freeways and other roads where parking, loading or unloading is prohibited.
(b) Authority to make right turns (or left turns where the rule of the road is to keep to the right) barred to other traffic for the purpose of reducing conflicting vehicular movements.
(c) Activation of traffic lights in their favour by buses by means of special equipment placed on the vehicle.
(d) Special bus lanes (usually the near side lane) which allows buses (in single file) to proceed ahead of other road users held in traffic blocks. (The practicability of a bus lane is dependent of course on there being an adequate width of road to allow at least a second lane for general traffic).
(e) Contra-flow operation along what have otherwise become one-way streets. This is, in effect an extension of the bus only lane principle but against the normal traffic flow.
(f) The use of through routes denied to other traffic by the provision of special 'bus gates' being, in effect, no entry signs which buses only are permitted to pass.
(g) The use of roads denied to all other traffic; in other words, bus only roads.
(h) Special provision for buses built into a system of urban traffic control. This could take the form of special computer programming for selected bus routes, separate and unrestricted access for buses on to a highway for which other traffic might have to queue and participation by bus operators in the control of such schemes.

Examples of all of these different types of bus priority can be found in both Great Britain and overseas but there is still much scope for extensions to the principle. In Great Britain, once a proposal has been accepted a statutory order will be prepared. The necessary signs can then be erected and observance will be enforced by the police. In the case of bus priorities, although the sign will refer just to 'buses' the vehicles which are authorised to take advantage are as specified in the Order and there is not necessarily consistency in this respect, not even within the same town. The word itself is open to interpretation and only the specific order will indicate whether 'buses' means vehicles operating in service on stage carriage routes (see Chapter 8), excursions and tours and vehicles working under contract and those running out of service. Even within the PSV category, therefore, there is no automatic definition of vehicles which may legally take advantage of bus priority measures. More than that, however, there are also other classes of traffic which might have bestowed upon them the right to use these special facilities. Examples are taxis, vehicles of the police and emergency services such as fire and ambulance and pedal cyclists. Clearly it would be a nonsense to deny access to the police acting in the interests of defending law and order or to the fire and ambulance services on the occasions of an emergency when there is some urgency in their mission (which is not always the case). Furthermore, it would be hazardous for cyclists not to use a 'with flow' bus lane, for example, where one is provided. When the total number of cyclists is small their presence on a bus lane is not likely to impede buses unduly and only if this mode of conveyance became much more popular (as in Holland, for example) would some better arrangements need to be made. Bearing in mind, however, the justification for bus priorities in the first place, it is, on the face of it, not easy to see a case for their use by taxis. A taxi takes up as much road space as a private car except that it does not need to park indiscriminantly. Similarly, express coaches, excursions and tours and private hire would seem to be outside the spirit of the thing. But a works bus might be an express carriage and a school journey might be under contract; it is very difficult to generalise.

Pedestrianisation

It is not only buses for which there is talk of priorities. Special facilities for pedestrians are becoming more and more fashionable. The concept really began to catch the public eye in 1963 when a working group led by Professor Sir Colin Buchanan produced its report *Traffic in Towns.** This report drew attention, among other things, to the undesirable effects of the conflicting and competing demands for limited road space, including vehicular and pedestrian traffic, with the resultant congestion, harmful effects on the environment and sometimes personal injury. The Radburn principle, which is the creation of residential pockets free from through traffic but with a system of footpaths entirely separate from vehicular routes and linking places generating pedestrian movement was quoted. This in turn led to thoughts regarding business and shopping areas, concluding with the view that there are advantages in these activities being undertaken in a completely traffic free atmosphere. The general theme of the report continued on traffic segregation with proposals on how it might be implemented.

Certainly it is pleasant to stroll and shop and perhaps rest awhile in a traffic free area. That is, free from noise and fumes and narrow pavements and sometimes crossing problems to get to the shops on the other side. Local politicians have their chance to impress upon the electorate their interest in people and the environment and planners have an opportunity to exercise their skills with trees and bushes, seats and ornamental lamposts, all in the alleged interests of creating a land in which it is fit to live. In real life, however, it is seldom possible to start from nothing with controlled planning at the outset. Any such new arrangements have to be superimposed on old established development. Traffic has to be diverted elsewhere, sometimes conveniently but often inconveniently. Sometimes the surrounding roads can accommodate the extra load but on occasions they cannot. To the bus operator, this in itself is bad enough, particularly if the revised route is longer and twisting, which so often is the case. But not only that. It has already been said that it is the duty of the bus operator to take people where they want to go and what is more, passengers want to be taken where they want to go, being right to their ultimate destination which is usually the shops and the commercial centre. Furthermore, longer routes will involve additional costs, the only return to the bus operator for which is loss of goodwill and a host of public complaints. Proper penetration of shopping centres, therefore, is a must if adequate facilities are to be provided and once again the bus operator has the task of making the case and convincing local councils accordingly. Pedestrianisation is ideal when it can be provided without creating other undesirable situations but a tortuous alternative route can, among other things, produce a greater safety hazard than ever the buses would be in the main shopping street. Falls inside vehicles are one of the more common accidents and a difficult route with sharp bends does much to increase these occurrences. Further reference to pedestrian and vehicle segregation is contained in Chapter 5.

Out-town Shopping Centres

Another concept, not catching on quite as quickly in Great Britain but popular in North America and gradually spreading across Europe, is the out-town shopping centre or 'hypermarket' as it is sometimes called. This is something which need not take up very much space in a book on bus operation as the bus undertaking is not the party which is principally affected.

Shopping areas of this kind do rather split the resources of the retail trade and if a sufficient amount of patronage is lost by shops in the established commercial centres, these areas could wither and eventually die. There are reasons, therefore, why applications for development of this kind are not always welcome and chambers of trade in particular might see detrimental repercussions. Nevertheless, such centres are highly convenient for those who wish to shop by car and that includes a lot of people. It is not the intention here to pronounce on whether vested interests should be allowed to deny the facility but if the concept did become established it could alter some bus route patterns. Like the shops, this might not always

**Traffic in Towns 1963;* HMSO

be to advantage as off-peak travel could be disturbed with traffic objectives diversified, assuming always that some people would wish to shop out of town and travel by bus to do so.

So concerned was the main department store in the centre at Fort Worth, Texas in the USA of the attraction of out town shops with ample parking that a tramway of over a mile in length was constructed to link a suburban 5,000 capacity car park with the basement of the shop. Free parking and free rides on the tram are available to those who wish to use them, regardless of whether they shop at the store concerned when they arrive.

Bus Stops

Bus stops might seem a somewhat obvious and minor part of bus operation to which the student is required to give his attention. On the contrary, it is much more involved than what at first might be apparent. Before bus stops are sited, policies must be determined. These are:

Fixed stops or buses allowed to stop at any reasonable point on request

At one time it was usual for buses to stop almost anywhere on request although trams generally had designated albeit frequent stopping places. Circumstances have now changed and in built-up areas, fixed stops are the rule. Nevertheless, in the more rural districts a fixed stop system is still unnecessary.

Distances between stops

This is a matter for discretion and there must be a balance between the convenience of frequent stops and maintaining the speed of the service. Historically, as noted above, buses, unlike trams, generally developed without very many fixed stops and even today there is a tendency for stops to be more closely spaced on those routes which were at one time worked by trams or trolleybuses. The Department of Transport recommended guidelines is 4 or 5 stops to the mile. Stops on opposite sides of a single two lane carriageway should be staggered, if possible by about 150 feet, and so arranged that buses pass each other before stopping and move off away from each other.

Compulsory or request stops

Undertakings which operate local town services usually have both compulsory and request stops. Compulsory stops are at the more heavily used locations where drivers are required to bring their vehicles to a halt regardless of passenger requirements. The remainder, being of the request type, need a hand signal to the driver from the intending passenger. Other undertakings, and particularly those which run into the more rural areas, use a universal type bus stop sign without any reference to request but nevertheless, operationally regard them all as request stops and generally observe them only when required.

For the convenience of passengers, stops need to be sited at popular traffic points and elsewhere at places where people will most likely have occasion to use them. This, however, might not be in the best interests of vehicular traffic circulation generally and might even be a safety hazard. As will be seen in Chapter 8, the ultimate authority for approving routes, etc, in Great Britain is the traffic commissioner. However, reliance is likely to be placed on the views of the highway authority and the police and bus operators will, therefore, wish to seek agreements with those bodies on matters concerning bus stops. Stopping places must not, for example, be placed immediately adjacent to road intersections, on narrow sections of road or on bends, etc, where it would be dangerous for other vehicles to overtake. At the more heavily used stops there should be adequate room on the pavement for people to queue and possibly for the erection of a shelter (see below). For queue control and vehicular congestion reasons there is a limit to the number of different services which can use any one stop and it is, therefore, sometimes necessary to group routes geographically on to two or more separate stops at the same point.

Very much a part of the bus stop topic is the provision of lay-bys. Any stationary vehicle is an impediment to free traffic flow and a bus waiting at a stop is no exception, particularly if it is one-man operated and the fare collection procedure is not of the most speedy kind (see Chapter 9). Once again, the agreement to and the construction of a lay-by is the responsibility of the highway authority and it is policy to provide this facility where practicable. To the bus operator it does remove a source of objection to one-man operation which thereby facilitates such conversions. Apart from that, however, the lay-by offers no great benefit from a bus operating point of view. The fact that other traffic might be delayed whilst buses stop in the nearside lane is not really the concern of the bus manager unless of course the situation became so serious that in the absence of a lay-by the stop would have to be removed. On the other hand, once in a lay-by, difficulty can be experienced by bus drivers in pulling back into the stream of moving traffic. As a rule of the road, priority to the bus when indicating an intention to make this manoeuvre would be helpful. A case where a lay-by is particularly useful to the bus operator is for stand purposes at the end of a journey. It is often a problem to find adequate terminal facilities, particularly in built up areas, and lay-bys are convenient in this respect.

Having determined the stopping arrangements, the erection of suitable signs is necessary. This, however, is more a part of publicity and will be considered in Chapter 7.

Shelters

Closely allied to bus stops is the bus shelter. There is

public clamour for some sort of protection from the weather when waiting at the kerbside and whilst it could be argued that the operator's responsibility for passengers is whilst they are actually on the bus, there must, nevertheless, be some sympathy with such requests. In any case it enhances the attractiveness of the service if people can wait (hopefully not too long) in reasonable comfort; shelters offer a site to display publicity and overall, there is no reason why operators should be opposed to the principle. On the other hand they cost money, they have to be maintained and they are targets for vandalism. It does not, of course, have to be the bus company who provides the shelters and very often it is not. As a public amenity they could be and are provided by local authorities and there are even cases where shelters have been donated by private individuals. An interesting alternative is the free erection and maintenance of shelters by commercial firms in return for advertising rights, expenditure being covered by advertising revenue. Whilst this would seem an admirable arrangement, in Great Britain at least, the erection of a structure which carries advertisements does require planning permission and the practise does tend to offend the environmentalists even though it is a way of providing a measure of comfort for people waiting for a bus. One possible disadvantage is that sites required for traffic purposes and those most suitable for advertising displays are not necessarily the same. Nevertheless, shelter provision by a third party can only be welcome. To the public, however, it does tend to be identified with the bus organisation who will always like to be consulted in connection with design and location. A poorly maintained shelter produces a bad image and the bus operator is criticised even though it might not be his responsibility. But good shelter facilities have the opposite effect and goodwill is engendered.

Shelter design takes many forms as will be seen from the illustrations and is to some extent dictated by the numbers of people that are likely to be involved and the space available. In Great Britain, old habits die hard and the practice of queueing, born 30 years ago in time of war and scarcity (and, in fact, made obligatory at the time when waiting for a bus by virtue of the Defence Regulations) is still observed today. Nobody would wish to alter this arrangement, particularly after experience in some other countries where the local populace is more precipitant and it is the strongest and the fittest who actually succeed in boarding. At the same time, the need to queue does have its effect on shelter design and where larger numbers congregate it is not a wooden hut or similar edifice which is required but a queue type shelter under which people can line up in traditional style and still have protection from the weather. One other factor which has some influence in shelter design is the type of vehicles which use the stops in question. The queue type shelter becomes a little complicated when buses of different designs serve the same queue. It will be seen from Chapter 10 that whilst boarding is now usually at the front, on some vehicles it is still at the rear. On others passengers may alight from a separate centre exit and if one is not careful, directly into a queue or the railings of a queue type shelter. But this is something which can be solved more easily by bus design than shelter design.

Bus Stations

Mention has already been made of the use of lay-bys for stand and terminal purposes. Even these are not necessary if side roads are available where vehicles can park without causing an obstruction. If a lay-by, therefore, is not an essential part of a terminal facility, far less is a purpose built bus station.

Reference is made in Chapter 5 to the government inspired machinery for town and country planning in

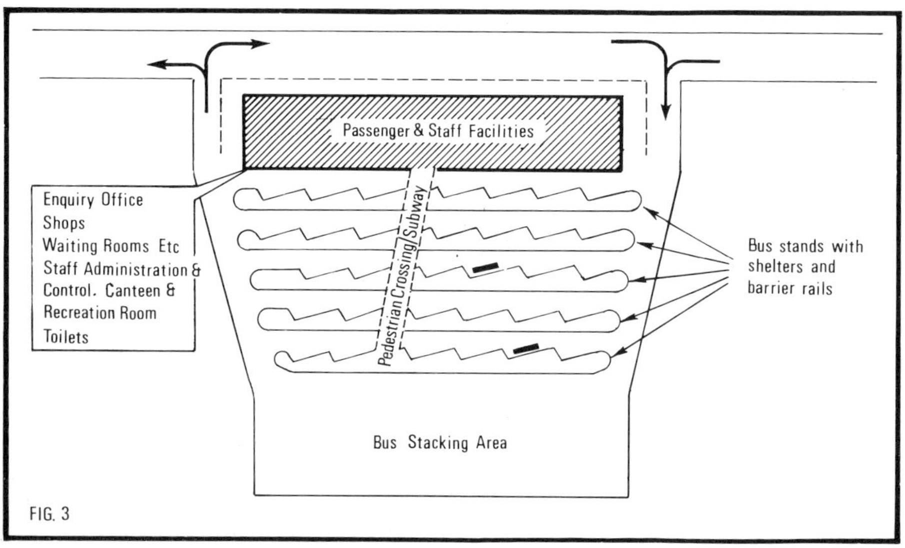

Left: **Fig 3. Sketch to illustrate the principle of a 'drive through' type bus station. In this example, the 'saw tooth' pattern for easy bus movement has been adopted. Note that the runways must be of sufficient width to allow buses to overtake others which are parked on the stands.**

Top right: **Fig 4. Sketch to illustrate the principle of a 'head on' type bus station. As in Fig 3 the 'saw tooth' pattern has been adopted. Whilst the design eliminates the need for passengers to cross the runways, the vehicles themselves must undertake reversing and conflicting movements.**

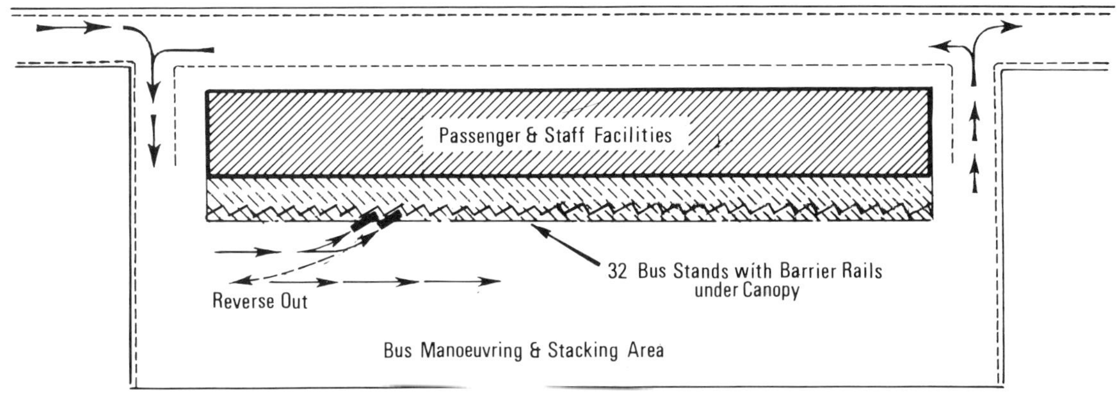

FIG 4

Great Britain and the formulation of structure plans by county councils and local plans by district councils. The preparation of local plans in particular gives a great opportunity to the planning fraternity to extol the virtues of the bus station with the supporting claim that it is something which no self-respecting town should lack. Impressive drawings can be prepared to impress on all through public participation just how bus minded the planners really are and that it is, after all, buses what people really want in spite of the pedestrianisation scheme round the corner! To avoid any unjustified criticism of environmental planning, however, it must be said that bus stations, although not crucial for successful bus operation, do have their uses providing the location is right. The big advantage is that there is hopefully a centralised terminal for all inter-urban and rural (as well as long distance) services. A series of different terminal points scattered throughout a town is always undesirable both for control purposes and passenger interchange. Once having established a bus station, then adequate arrangements can be made for vehicles to manoeuvre and stand, for passengers to queue, for all the supporting passenger and staff amenities and for supervisory and control facilities. Note, however, the important proviso that the location must be right. It has been said elsewhere that the bus must be afforded proper penetration of shopping and commercial areas and this does not mean into a bus station somewhere on the periphery. Furthermore, if such a bus station came as an alternative to kerbside stands in the centre but entailed a longer and devious route to reach it then both the operator and the users would be at a serious disadvantage. Longer routes mean more running time with the likelihood of more vehicles and staff which inevitably involves cost and passengers would have the inconvenience of having to walk from and to the bus. It follows that the ideal sites are where land is also most attractive for other commercial development. There is, therefore, a conflict of interests and prices are high. If the ideal is just not obtainable then there does sometimes have to be a compromise with the bus station a little off centre but subject always to satisfactory arrangements for ingress and egress. As an alternative a central site with the airspace above developed for commercial purposes might be acceptable.

Once having agreed the principle of a bus station, the design is for consideration. Clearly the number of stands must be determined and this will be governed by traffic demand and the number of services involved. Total departures is not a good guide as ideally medium frequency services or a series of services geographically grouped need a stand on their own to avoid a conflict of queues and a multi-user is only practicable where journeys are sufficiently widely spaced that neither queues nor vehicles are likely to clash. On the other hand, very frequent services might call for two (or even more) vehicles on the stand at any one time unless there is a separate parking area. If this is the case, space must be earmarked accordingly. There are two basic principles on which bus stations are designed, each with their advantages and disadvantages. The theory is explained by the drawings at Figs 3 and 4. Briefly, the first alternative comprises a series of island platforms. If passengers are to approach these platforms on the level then they must cross the vehicle runways and if the walkways are grade separated (either above or below) then it becomes necessary to negotiate stairs or escalators. This is a disadvantage but is balanced by the fact that vehicles can be driven progressively through the bus station compound without any manoeuvring or reversing movements. The alternative is a single platform with vehicles nosing on from a large circulating area. This provides maximum convenience for passengers but it does entail substantial manoeuvring with vehicles reversing out and in so doing crossing the paths of others coming in. The latter arrangement is more economical in terms of space but there are many examples of each basic design.

Another principle to be decided is whether a bus station should be combined with a bus garage. The answer can be determined only in relation to local circumstances but generally it is likely that it should not. Bear in mind that from a traffic point of view, the siting of a bus garage is less crucial than that of a bus station and to the passenger, the garage is really of no interest at all. If space is a problem, and at the ideal location it usually is, then the garage can be expected to be at some place elsewhere. Exactly where will be considered in the next sub-section. Exceptions, however, do arise, often in the smaller towns where more than one property holding could not be justified and no point is very far from the centre anyway. A possibility here is to use a large forecourt for passenger boarding and alighting purposes. Occasionally the garage itself is similarly used but for safety reasons, any practice which allows passengers on foot to mingle with garage activities is not ideal.

Bus Garages

It was acknowledged in the Introduction that people in the bus industry, as in most big businesses, represent many professions. Some are fundamental to the basic function of the industry whilst others assume more of an ancillary role although they are no less important for that. A 'busman' in this context is regarded as the operator and the commercial manager; in other words, the 'traffic man'. The engineer could well regard himself in similar vein and it is true that the design, construction and maintenance of buses is also somewhat fundamental. Without such support the operator would be ineffective. Nevertheless, this book is not being written by an engineer and there is no pretence of teaching engineering skills. A bus garage is primarily a place to service and overhaul vehicles and mechanical engineering is a science in itself. At the same time, managers and others who are not skilled in this respect do need a sound layman's knowledge of the subject as well as a good chief engineer and this side of things cannot therefore be completely disregarded. Furthermore, the operator (as distinct from the engineer) has some interest in bus garages in his own right if part of the premises is used for control, supervision and cash paying-in purposes as described in Chapter 11.

There are numerous policy decisions which must be determined at the garage planning stage as also must the role which the garage is to play within the organisation be decided. The main considerations are:-

Size

Whilst adequate facilities must be available for the entire fleet this in itself does not necessarily dictate the size of any one garage. What is the optimum size for a superintendent on the engineering side and a chief inspector on the traffic side to handle is largely a matter of opinion and different undertakings have different policies in this respect. It is not easy to generalise but provision for less than 40 vehicles could be regarded as rather small whilst a capacity for more than 200 too unwieldy. Geography also plays some part in determining size. Only a few vehicles might, for example, need to be housed at a small town location but being so far distant from a neighbouring centre, allocation elsewhere would be uneconomical or impracticable. To take the argument one stage further, it is at times appropriate to stable odd buses at a village to avoid a long empty run back to town and back again next morning. In circumstances such as this there is sometimes a case to have an 'out-station', being a small shed or even a piece of open ground able to accommodate one or perhaps two vehicles manned by drivers who live locally. Under this arrangement, staff bring back their buses to the out-station in the evening, probably sweep them out and collect them the following day, the vehicles being otherwise serviced at the parent garage.

It is the larger and more heavily trafficked urban areas where it is appropriate to consider alternative policies on garage capacities. Such decisions, however, are likely to have been taken long ago and it is never easy and often costly to reverse garage policies which have been followed over the years. That apart, there is at least a theoretical choice between a lesser number of larger garages or a greater number of smaller garages and it is not only the elusive optimum size which determines this. The function and location must also be taken into account and the fewer the garages are in number the more difficult it will be to satisfy the location requirements. On size alone, that is disregarding these other circumstances, it is suggested that a total capacity for about 120 vehicles is sufficiently large to properly exploit the potential of local garage managers whose traffic work is described in Chapter 11 but which at the same time avoids the organisational and operational complexities which a very large unit can bring.

The actual size of a garage in terms of area occupied is determined not only by vehicle allocation (that is, buses required for service plus an agreed percentage of spares) but also on the size of the vehicles in terms of length and width. It has already been seen from Chapter 1 that over the years buses have become bigger and the larger the vehicle, the fewer that can be accommodated in any given space. In this sense, however, size does not also mean capacity as subject to adequate headroom a double deck bus will occupy no more garage space than will a single deck of similar dimensions. In the 1930s the standard measurements of a bus were 27ft 6in × 7ft 6in. As regulations have been relaxed so sizes have been increased even to very long articulated vehicles and the following table showing approximate capacities by a selection of vehicle sizes of a garage which could accommodate 100 buses of the one-time conventional 27ft 6in dimension is of interest:

Size of bus	*Number of buses in garage*
27ft 6in × 7ft 6in	100
30ft 6in × 8ft 0in	82
33ft 0in × 8ft 2in	75
39ft 0in × 8ft 2in	63
57ft 0in × 8ft 2in (articulated)	44

These figures are essentially an approximation and much will depend on the design of the garage but they do give an order of magnitude and it is quite clear that length and breadth has a strong bearing on garage capacity and hence cost. On the other hand, as far as economics are concerned larger vehicles would hopefully also mean fewer vehicles and this is the other side of the equation.

Function

On the engineering side, vehicles need to be parked when not in use (which does not have to be under cover — this is an engineering expediency), washed, swept, refuelled and generally made ready for use on the following day, inspected as a routine, serviced (that is, greased, etc) at the required intervals, repaired as necessary and made good and overhauled periodically which will sometimes be a major overhaul. Not all garages need be equipped to undertake this work. There could be a centralised overhaul centre to take care of major overhauls and serious accident damage. Even if intermediate dockings and lesser services are to be undertaken at garages, every establishment still does not have to be so fitted. There could be dormitory sheds and parent sheds with the dormitory units used mainly for stacking at night and perhaps engineering work of a minor nature. Beyond that is the out-station to which reference has already been made.

Whilst still on the function of a garage, mention was made in connection with bus stations that on occasions it is sensible to combine the two and allow the garage or the forecourt to be used as a passenger terminal. Whilst operationally the use of the forecourt for this purpose is quite acceptable if the location is right, special care is necessary if the public is permitted to enter the precincts of the garage itself, particularly when buses are being shunted for parking purposes.

Location

From a physical point of view, a bus garage must have adequate access roads and freedom to use them. For a new construction, however, it is unlikely that the necessary planning permission would be granted if this was not the case. Operationally there are other reasons why the location of a garage is important. It must be

Below: **Fig 5. Diagram to show the basic requirements of a bus garage. This example shows covered parking accommodation for 180 buses with an adjacent workshop with pits for routine servicing and greasing and for mechanical, electrical and body repairs. Separate enclosures are available for chassis cleaning and painting and there is a workshop for brake shoes relining. Special facilities are necessary for stores, including tyres and fuel and there must be provision for waste oil. Fuel pumps and bus washing facilities are required near to the entrance. The administration block will include suitable accommodation for traffic supervisory and control staff including a paying in room and cash office. Welfare facilities incorporate a canteen and first-aid room and an outside car park.**

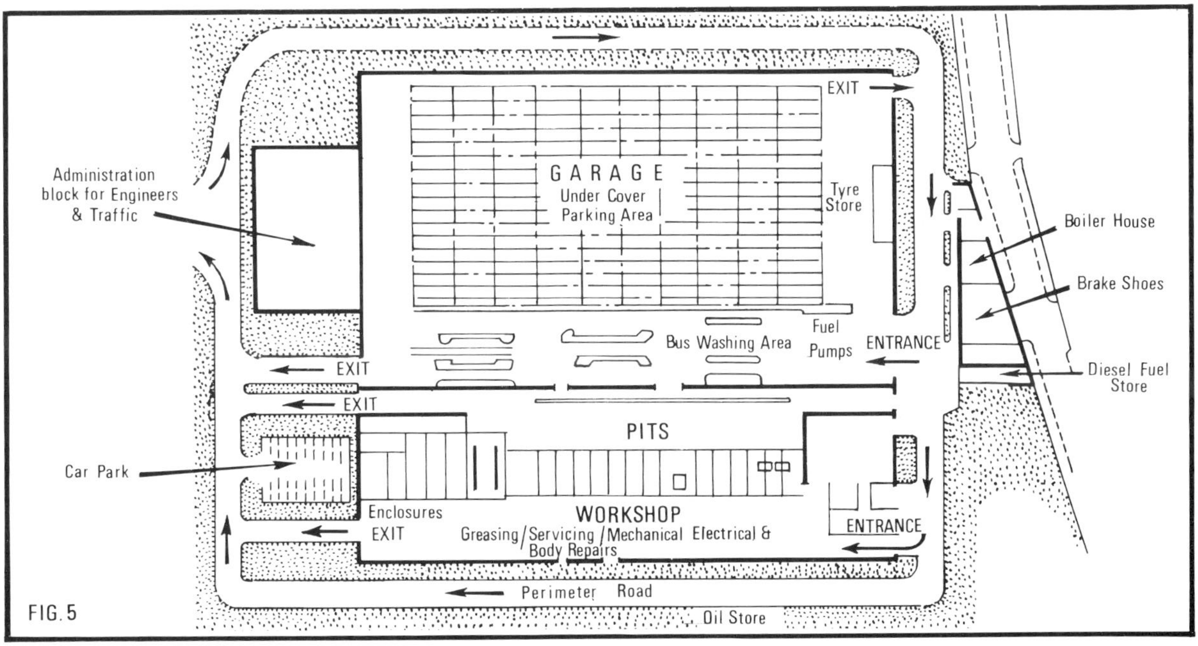

FIG. 5

strategically sited in relation to the bus route network if a lot of empty running is to be avoided and more will be said about that in Chapter 6. Bus garages provide work for a large number of people and for this reason it is an advantage if they are sited in an area where labour is most likely to be available. At the same time, a bus garage might not be popular with local residents on account of noise and the continual passing of heavy vehicles. There is also a divergence of views as to whether garages should be as near as possible to the centres or out in the suburbs of the larger towns. In this context there is the question not only of land values and accessibility but also of duty schedules and again this is a matter which will be further considered in Chapter 6.

Design

The design of a bus garage is conditioned by its size and function and whether facilities are required for traffic as well as engineering staff, which is usually the case.

As far as engineering facilities are concerned it must be decided whether some open-air parking is acceptable and then the number of pits and what equipment is necessary. Engineering technicalities are not for discussion here but the diagram at Fig 5 (p27) will offer guidance as it portrays a typical modern bus garage with facilities for undertaking any work up to major overhauls. This gives an indication of the range of equipment which is necessary but at this stage the subject passes from bus operation to mechanical engineering and thereby beyond the scope of these pages.

The facilities required by the traffic people are, however, very much a part of operation. They include offices for the control staff (there is a similar requirement by the engineering department), a cash office and a paying-in room for conductors and one-man drivers suitable also for the display of duty schedules and notices. Coupled with this are the welfare requirements of all staff employed at the garage regardless of the department to which they belong such as canteen or mess-room, recreation or games room, locker accommodation, washing facilities, first aid equipment, car park and other amenities for which the local trade unions will be eager to make representation. The arrangements for the collection, safe custody and disposal of cash, again a traffic function of a bus garage, will be considered in Chapter 11.

Fixed Track Systems

Tramways

As was shown in Chapter 1, the tram has been very much a part of the urban passenger transport scene. In the world-wide context it still is and no study on the subject can ignore it, particularly as the forthcoming energy situation could result in its numbers multiplying rather than further decreasing. The same could apply to trolleybuses but this is something for Chapter 12. Trams, however, are capital intensive and hence expensive animals. They need a specialised way which may or may not also be a part of the normal public highway. To that extent, therefore, discussion is appropriate for this chapter. References to the way and characteristics of trams (and trolleybuses) is contained in the contemporary book *Principles of Transport* and this study is intended only to summarise the salient features.

Tram lines may be laid either in a normal road or on a private right of way, in which case, the system becomes 'grade separated' to use a more recent but appropriate term. The provision of special tracks together with electrical equipment for power purposes is a costly affair, particularly when compared with the diesel bus whose only contribution towards the provision of its way is the annual vehicle licence and for all the extra money, a very inflexible form of transport has been provided. The statutory control of tramways is something for Chapter 8 and it is sufficient to say here that when considering the situation in Great Britain as far as tracks in the street are concerned, attention must again be directed to the Tramways Act, 1870.

A tramway undertaking whose line is on a private right of way is, of course, responsible for the entire cost of the land. At this stage the tram is only one stage removed from a light railway, in fact there is no clear delineation between the two. This in turn leads into what is now known as 'rapid transit'; a system of urban transport shortly to be considered. A similar title is also suitable for the upgraded tramway as the term 'light railway' is generally associated with a branch of the more conventional type of railway on which certain standards and legal requirements have been relaxed in return for specified operating restrictions. This sort of line is now fast disappearing and a more popular and perfectly apt description of an upgraded urban tramway system is 'light rapid transit'.

Suburban Railways and Rapid Transit

Classification and Interpretation

The public passenger transport needs of an urban agglomeration are often met by train as well as by bus, particularly if the area is large and thickly populated although the infrastructure of a railway is considerable and its capital cost formidable. To the extent that local needs are catered for, however, the railway is relevant to the subject under review even though this is not a railway text-book as such. For this reason, therefore, and only for this reason, some sort of imaginary line of demarcation must be drawn to decide where urban transport as a subject (which is what this book is about) ends and where main line railway operation as a subject (which is what this book is not about) begins. Just how blurred the distinction really becomes can perhaps be further appreciated by looking at the following modes and their progression from local bus to main line railway:

(a) Diesel bus
(b) Street tramway
(c) Segregated tramway
(d) Light rapid transit } both could have
(e) Rapid transit } rubber tyres
(f) Suburban railway
(g) Fast main line railway

Quite clearly the diesel bus is the subject of one study and the fast main line railway another. Modes (a) to (c) however are legitimate road passenger transport subjects, particularly if part of an otherwise segregated tramway system has its tracks in a normal road whilst modes (f) and (g) are obviously 'rail transport'. Modes (d) and (e) are arguably either a part of both or a part of neither but they certainly cannot be divorced from urban transport.

Looking at the situation world-wide, many of the larger urban areas have their own local railway facilities, often with lines underground, owned and operated by local autonomous bodies independently of any national railway network. The main line system could have local commuter facilities as well, in fact, more often than not this is the case. To take London as an example, the 'Underground' system of London Transport hardly needs introduction but the London suburban surface lines of the Southern Region of British Railways also constitute one of the most intensive railway systems in the world which caters for a similar type of traffic (but not to the same places). Nevertheless, it is here that the distinction must be drawn. Local commuter trains of a main line railway share common tracks, signals, stations and management with the longer distance main line fast services and also with freight. Their infrastructure and their operations must, therefore, be tied to main line practices and are thus beyond the scope of these pages. Only in the planning and commercial fields covered in Chapters 5 and 7 can their presence be recognised in this context. There is, however, justification for reference to the essentially local and independently operated systems which collectively now seem to be labelled 'rapid transit'.

Rapid Transit

Rapid transit is best described as a full scale heavy rail system or some alternative which has similar capabilities, which forms a completely self-contained network the operation of which, therefore, is not inhibited by conflict with any other traffic of the same or a different mode. Perhaps some of the best examples are to be found in North America with systems such as the Bay Area Rapid Transit of San Francisco and the rapid transit network of the Chicago Transit Authority. In Great Britain, the railway system of London Transport already mentioned is not completely self-contained although for traffic purposes some lines are. Other lines run over the tracks of British Railways at the extremities and any physical conflict can have serious repercussions on timekeeping. For this reason, new works have been undertaken over the years to segregate the different types of traffic. The flyover at Barking is an example. This structure replaced a flat crossing and before it was built, goods trains of British Railways had to cross the path of the LT passenger trains and delays were inevitable with repercussions right through to Ealing, etc on the opposite side of town. For a high density service, complete segregation is most desirable and that is why this feature is synonymous with 'rapid transit'.

The fundamental principles of the permanent way are discussed in *Principles of Transport*. Railways in urban areas may take the form of conventional surface lines, deep level 'tubes', shallow subways constructed by the 'cut and cover' method or elevated lines. All of these different types of way may be and are used to varying extents by both local and national railway organisations. One interesting site for a rapid transit line, and again North America produces good examples, is in the median strip of a motorway.

Once the civil engineering work has been completed and the track laid, a signalling system must be installed. Modern rapid transit lines have progressed a long way from the block working with semaphore type signals worked by hefty levers in a signalbox. Automatic signals activated by the trains themselves have long since been in use on many of these lines and modern technology has progressed further than that. Instead of lineside signals it is possible to transmit the necessary information direct to the driver in the cab. Beyond that, full automation is perfectly feasible with driverless trains. Stations could technically also be unmanned with automatic revenue control under the surveillance of closed circuit television.

These last few sentences have swept across a tremendous subject and if covered adequately would on its own embrace several volumes. The track bed or formation, if in a deep level tube, is of the most expensive kind. Add to this the track itself, sub-stations and other electrical equipment, automatic signalling, stations and the many incidentals which collectively make up railway infrastructure and the construction of a system of any magnitude will quickly run into many millions of pounds. When this is compared with the bus and its parallel costs which are the annual vehicle licence and a stop sign attached to a post at the kerbside with perhaps a simple shelter the differences are immediately apparent. On the credit side, however, there is not only speed of movement but also capacity and these are the great advantages of fixed track systems and which will need to be the subject of further consideration. Nevertheless, whilst this is a highly complex science which could overshadow all that could be said about road transport, this book is not to be complicated by railway technicalities. Just as mechanical engineering is not being dealt with, neither will be considered the finer arts of civil, structural, permanent way, signal or electrical engineering. This, together with the fact that rail rapid transit is only of somewhat marginal relevance to the subject under review and is much closer to railway operation anyway means that students seeking to advance their skills in these fields must look elsewhere for guidance. Similarly, new works engineers of rapid transit systems are not likely to want to be busmen as well. But the subject cannot be divorced entirely from urban transport. It has already been shown where the two merge together and whilst this is true in the analytical sense the literal interpretation is equally valid. The two modes do come together and good planning dictates more and more that they should. Bus is a natural feeder to rail and where it is used as such there must be a proper co-ordination of facilities. This is a matter for Chapter 5. But if road and rail services are to be co-ordinated, purpose built interchanges are desirable and at the very least there should be bus stops adjacent to the station entrance. The railway does, therefore, have to be given some consideration and in this context it does not have to be confined to rapid transit. Suburban stations of main line railways benefit equally from good interchange facilities.

Railway Stations

The justification for building railway stations for the use of local riders with the facilities which they contain such as bus interchange and car parks will be considered in Chapter 5. The essential features of the stations themselves, however, are for discussion here.

Whilst the extent of the facilities which are provided must depend on the numbers of passengers which use the station, the essentials are good foot and vehicular access from the main highway network, waiting point for taxis and private cars (for kiss and ride) near to the station entrance, bus lay-bys and car park where appropriate, covered booking hall, office for ticket issue, passenger enquiry and train control purposes, staff welfare facilities and passenger shelters on the platform. These may be supplemented by other amenities as the occasions demand such as a paper shop, etc, but this is more commercial policy than operating essential. If a station car park is to be provided there should be good footpath connection between the car park and the platforms. It is at this stage, however, that operational and commercial practices have a bearing on station design.

It is likely that that the railway under consideration in this context will have a double track and a relatively frequent service. Passengers will need to cross the tracks for one direction of their journey and for safety reasons will not be permitted to accomplish this at grade level. A subway or footbridge must therefore be provided unless there happens to be a road crossing the railway at the station site, in which case the road bridge (or underpass) can sometimes be used for this purpose. This does, however, create yet another complication. Access to platforms may be free or controlled depending on the revenue collection system. Exits will invariably be controlled for ticket checking purposes (this assumes the absence of an automatic system for revenue control). If the booking office is, for physical reasons, to be level with the tracks then the situation could arise whereby a passenger could arrive on foot or by car, cross the line to get a ticket and cross back again to board a train. Arrival passengers needing to pass through a controlled exit might have to cross the line to leave the station and cross back again (outside the station precincts) to the car park, bus stop or wherever they might wish to go. Such movements can be irritating and frustrating, particularly if, on alighting from the train, the next objective of the passenger lies just the other side of a fence. Such circumstances could be overcome by the provision of an additional entrance (such as a passimeter which is a free standing kiosk type ticket office combined with a barrier) which enables the passenger to purchase a ticket and pass through to the platform area in one movement. A second exit is also possible but like the extra booking office, additional staff are involved, which is costly. A balance must therefore, be struck between passenger convenience and staff costs and the ideal in the form of passenger ingress and egress is not always possible. Depending upon the contour of the land and particularly if the railway is in a cutting (and certainly if it is in tunnel) the booking office and barrier could be situated above the tracks with stairs leading off down to each platform (or down to one single island platform). In many respects this is the most acceptable solution where the levels lend themselves for this purpose although even here, if a car park is at track level, as it could well be, an up and over walk is necessary in each direction. If uncontrolled access is permitted at the inwards barrier, at least additional entrances could be constructed without entailing extra staff costs but they must be inwards only and passengers would need to be already in possession of a ticket. If it was possible for passengers to exit via the same route, fraudulent travel would be difficult to detect.

Such are the basic design problems associated with urban and suburban railway stations. Examples of different layouts are depicted at Figs 6 and 7.

Once the buildings have been established they must of course be embellished with the usual direction signs and other notices, etc. As is the case of the bus station, this is something for Chapter 7.

Modal Characteristics

Choice of Mode

The infrastructure as it applies to buses, which is the predominant subject of this book, has now been considered in some depth but in order that the urban

FIG. 6

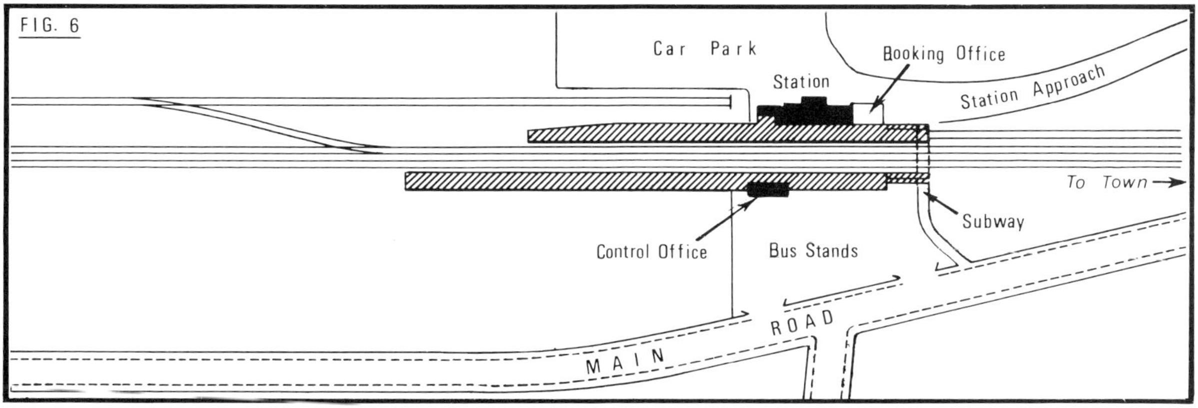

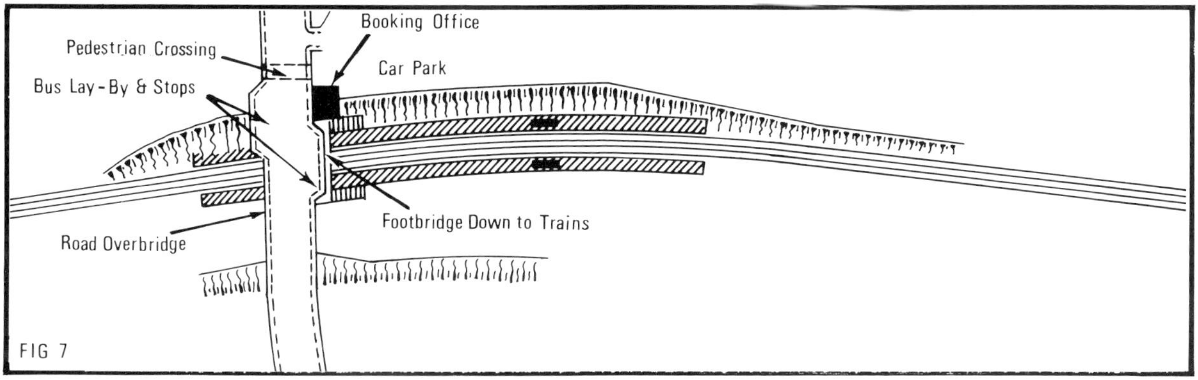

FIG 7

Top: **Fig 6. Diagram to show a possible railway station layout with road feeder facilities with tracks at road level.**

Above: **Fig 7. Diagram to show possible railway station layout with road feeder facilities with tracks below road level.**

transport picture should be complete, thoughts have been allowed to stray into trams and rapid transit and even main line railways. This is inevitable if the movement of people in urban and rural areas is to be dealt with adequately. Whilst, however, for short journeys, it is the diesel bus which overall carries most of the traffic, enough has been said to show that there is a choice. Alternatives to the diesel bus are trolleybuses, street trams, segregated light rapid transit (which may be on the surface, in shallow tunnels or elevated, perhaps even in the form of a monorail), heavy rapid transit (which again is found above, on and below the surface, including deep level tubes) and suburban lines of main line railways. In Great Britain, anything other than the bus for local journeys is very much the exception but elsewhere other modes can be found and Germany is a good example where all of the different types of systems just mentioned can be readily found. With the passage of time it seems almost inevitable that the oil situation will exert a strong influence on modal choice. Even now the relative economies of diesel oil and electricity varies between different places as a result of availability and local taxation policies which makes the latter more acceptable in some areas than in others. But there are also other reasons why the different modes have their particular attractions. Characteristics must, therefore, be examined which are both physical and financial. The physical factors are for consideration here whilst the financial effects are something for Chapter 4. It can nevertheless be said straight away that anything other than the diesel bus requires varying degrees of capital expenditure (and mostly heavy at that) for the specialised way which at the same time sacrifices the characteristic flexibility of the bus. There must, therefore, be strong reasons to justify that expenditure and those reasons, as already said, lie mainly in capacity.

The Case for Rapid Transit

The characteristic of the railway is that it is a bulk mover. A main line system has the potential to carry tremendous amounts in terms of passengers or freight over long distances. The same is true of urban transport and nothing can match a segregated rapid transit line to move the masses into and out of the centres of large conurbations at busy peak times. Inflation makes it impracticable to quote construction costs in a text book of this kind but even if this was not the case, physical features and the geology of the area make no two places alike as far as the construction of underground railways is concerned and hence costs vary very considerably. It is likely, however, that any new urban line will be at least partly underground, probably in deep level tube and the cost of this type of system is inevitably phenomenal. Any such project would undoubtedly be the subject of a cost benefit study but more to the point here, what any rapid transit line must have is a heavy traffic potential. The need for a segregated system is dependent on a range of circumstances and it is impossible to lay down a formula to indicate when one should be built. In broad terms, because of the obvious need to carry a lot of people, total population and population density have a strong bearing on the matter. To give a general idea, a total population of say 1.5million, reasonably compact and with a strong commercial centre to which the majority of business trips are focused could be the sort of area where an underground rapid transit system might be contemplated. This means that land use policy is an important factor in planning a rapid transit network.

Modal Capacities

Having established that the capital cost of a railway means that it will be constructed only when there is need for mass transit, there remains to consider the potential capacities of the different modes. But like setting down criteria and establishing costs of a rapid transit system, it is virtually impossible by any rule of thumb method to determine maximum capacities in terms of passengers per hour on any one type of system. Whatever the declared maximum there is usually room for one more. Another passenger could crush into a railway coach; another bus could find its place on the public highway. What follows, therefore, constitutes generalised observations more than scientific fact based on formulas compiled to interpret specific situations. The thoughts are presented only to give a measure of perspective and must be treated accordingly.

Diesel Buses and Trolleybuses

Although technically different, buses and trolleybuses have similar characteristics insofar as their passenger carrying ability is concerned. The point has already been made that buses share the public highway with all other vehicles, passenger and goods, which might care to use it. The amount of traffic which can be moved by a conventional bus service is not, therefore, determined by the qualities of the passenger transport service as such but by the highway on which it runs. Highway capacities are governed by such things as width of road and number of traffic lanes, general speed of traffic and obstructions to progress such as conflicting vehicle movements, traffic lights, pedestrian crossings, parked vehicles and the like. If a busy shopping street is compared with a motorway the differences become immediately apparent. It goes without saying that the capacity which a bus service can provide is governed by the size of the vehicle and the frequency. As far as vehicles are concerned, the capacity of a conventional type bus is finite, that is, it is limited to the number of seats plus a few standing which can easily be controlled. For a standard double-deck this is usually about 80, but articulated crush loading vehicles can carry more than this. To ascertain what is the maximum capacity which such a service can provide it is necessary to know how many vehicles can actually use the road in question and that is the figure which is elastic and depends on circumstances. If, for example, there was a 30-second headway or 120 per hour (and that is a lot of buses) then nearly 10,000 people could be moved in that hour providing they were evenly spread as any peak surges within that hour could not be accommodated. Apart from highway capacities, the provision of stops and facilities for queueing could also become a serious problem. A service of this level would be better with a segregated bus lane. If this in turn provided an exclusive uninterrupted flow, ie, grade separated junctions, etc, and if such a facility was provided for the full length of the route then it gets into the light rapid transit class (LRT does not have to be of the fixed track variety). The principle can be taken one stage further by the use of articulated buses which can accommodate up to about 150 people (under crush loading conditions) and, like the 80-seater double deck, still with just a one-man driver. This puts the theoretical potential capacity up to about 18,000 people per hour. This figure, however, like the previous one represents the extreme, they are not likely to be reached in practice and in the case of the articulated bus would at the same time produce a very uncomfortable way of travel. Again the traffic must be evenly spread although in practice traffic over a complete hour is not generally so obliging. There is usually a peak within a peak and the crucial factor is more what can be moved within the maximum quarter hour. To be realistic, in any one hour some capacity is invariably wasted and a sustained 30 second headway without some form of delay is optimistic. A practical talking figure for hourly capacities actually attainable, certainly on the normal public highway, might be more in the region of, say, 5,000 for double decks and 7,000 for articulated buses. This is substantially less than the theoretical maximum quoted but here there would be a little more room to accommodate short additional bursts of traffic. Furthermore, with the one-man articulated bus, fare collection problems arise. On the conventional double-deck the driver is either able to collect fares or check tickets in the way which is to be described in Chapter 9. Not so with the articulated bus and this is a feature which needs to be further considered.

Trams

A street tramway is perfectly feasible as is proved in a number of heavily trafficked urban areas in Europe and

North America. Whilst, however, the tram is at a serious disadvantage compared with the bus in terms of cost as will be seen in Chapter 4, it does have a greater capacity. Whilst the articulated tram, like its bus counterpart, can carry up to about 150 people, albeit in discomfort, the double-deck tram of Blackpool Corporation as depicted on page 101 has 100 seats. Together with a permitted 24 standing (which could probably be increased if necessary) its potential is not far short of that of the articulated vehicle but offers relative comfort for the majority to go with it. If the track is on a mainly segregated right of way with vehicle conflict only at controlled crossings and possibly on other short stretches where lack of space precludes any other arrangement, there would seem to be no reason why such trams should not be coupled in pairs with one driver. A double unit of this type running every 30 seconds would give a theoretical hourly capacity of about 30,000 people. However, like the buses, a regular 30-second service, even on a partially segregated system, is unlikely to be attained. With such fine precision, a slightly extended wait at a stop whilst passengers are boarding and alighting or even at traffic lights would result in a block back from which it is difficult to recover and would lead to yet wider gaps in the service. But based on a 60-second headway the theoretical capacity could still be 15,000 per hour and if this was accompanied by complete grade separation in the form of light rapid transit the figure becomes yet more realistic.

To digress slightly from capacities, one problem with articulated vehicles, be they buses or trams, is fare collection. The sheer weight of numbers makes pay as you enter a time absorbing process, be it to a driver or seated conductor and with crush loading a conductor cannot circulate through the vehicle. Alternative pre-paid or help yourself arrangements are, therefore, likely to be necessary with the attendant disadvantages as described in Chapter 9. The Blackpool arrangement for its latest type double deck tram is for one-man operation in the slack periods supplemented by a conductor in the peaks although even then, in terms of productivity, the arrangement is slightly less favourable than a one-man operated 80-seater bus.

Heavy Rapid Transit

To avoid getting beyond the scope of this book it is not proposed to discuss at length the potential capacities of heavy rapid transit. It is sufficient to say here that with such a system in being, completely segregated and grade separated, it represents the ultimate in mass transit. The movement of trains is governed by a signalling system, generally automatic, and by the judicious spacing of block lengths, 7 to 10-car trains can travel at speed between stations say a mile apart or even less with down to about a 90-second interval between them. A system such as this can provide for about 30,000 passengers per hour but the feature of heavy rail rapid transit is that it does have an overload capacity and hence the ability to meet sporadic heavy surges of traffic and the equivalent of 60,000 passengers per hour for short periods becomes physically possible and is certainly not unknown. The same fare collection problems do not arise as with high capacity buses and trams as with purpose built stations, controlled entry and exit can be enforced. This does, of course, sacrifice the casual but more frequent stops which are convenient to passengers in terms of length of walk to board the vehicle. Hence the need for systems of this type to be supported by feeder facilities.

3
Organisation and Management

Government and Politics in Relation to Transport

Central Government

The provision of a transport facility is a livelihood for those who are in the business. It is also a service to the nation as adequate means of moving people and goods from place to place is an essential ingredient for economic survival. The importance of transport in this respect is dealt with at length in *Principles of Transport*. At the risk of repetition, however, attention must again be drawn to the fact that although most transport services had their origins in commercial enterprise, in the 1980s, at least on the passenger side, it is not every type of operation which will produce an adequate return on the capital invested. If any railway service is still viable it is the longer distance inter-city train, not the heavily peaked commuter network and certainly not the rural branch lines. In road passenger transport, whilst there may still be money in long distance coaching, regular contracts, inclusive tours, excursions and the occasional private hire; except for a few routes, urban and rural stage carriage work is a different matter and when operators have to meet all of their costs out of revenue and still make a living they have to be very discerning indeed about the facilities which they offer. But to continue what was being said at the end of Chapter 1, because of the tremendous impact which transport has on community life, governments can no longer allow the provision of such essential services to be subject only to the law of commercial viability. What is being done about it is material for Chapter 7. The point here is that if there is a case for something more than a transport policy guided only by the economic forces of supply and demand then there must also be a supporting administrative machine to formulate and determine those policies.

In the event there are now very few governments which do not have some kind of policy (at public expense) for passenger transport. Even the United States of America where private enterprise, perhaps more than anywhere else, is still very much a way of life, is veering towards public ownership in urban transport with a policy of financial aid and the appropriate government department active in this field. Whilst, however, subsidies are a relatively new phenomenon, transport has long since been an industry which, on the operational side, has required a measure of government supervision, if only to ensure adequate safety standards and sometimes to regulate supply.

The outcome of the circumstances described is that governments will have departments within their administrations to which are delegated responsibility for policy and/or control of the various facets of transport. Great Britain is no exception and once again, the structure of the British government and in particular the parts which have transport responsibilities are detailed in *Principles of Transport*. This chapter will elucidate those areas of the British administration at national level (and also at local level) which formulate and control transport policy insofar as it relates to urban and rural passenger services.

In England it is basically the Department of Transport which interprets and administers transport policy as laid down by parliament. For the remainder of the United Kingdom, this, among other things, is the responsibility of the Northern Ireland, Scottish and Welsh Offices within their respective areas. The British government, in common with many countries overseas, does not directly manage transport undertakings, not even those in public (national) ownership. The operating organisations are autonomous bodies with their own managements and responsible to the appropriate government minister on broad policy matters. Policy control is effected through the statutes. The more important of the tranport issues involved and the methods of control are outlined in the table at Fig 8. In some cases, direct compliance with acts of parliament and supporting statutory instruments is required whilst in others, government appointed officers have direct responsibilities for quantity and quality control. For financial and planning matters there is an intermediary between operators and central government in the form of county councils who are able to determine their own local policies for submission to central government. It follows that government departments must be geared on the one hand to issue and enforce regulations in respect of operating practices as decreed by parliament and on the other to oversee and influence, particularly in financial terms, the policies of county councils.

As far as roads are concerned, whilst central government (in England the Minister of Transport) is the highway authority for trunk roads, for many purposes, local authorities are employed as agents and as was explained in Chapter 2, county councils are in any case the highway authorities for the non-trunk roads. In addition to the contact with central and local government as is indicated in Fig 8, therefore, bus operators must maintain an ongoing relationship with these bodies in view of their use of what is a common way.

Local Government

In Great Britain there is a two-tier system of local government with the country divided into large county (or, in Scotland, regional) authorities which are further sub-divided into smaller district authorities. As far as urban and rural transport is concerned it is the county councils which are responsible for such matters as strategic planning, transport planning, passenger transport, highways, traffic regulation and police. In England and Wales, however, in no case is a county council (or national government either for that matter) the operator of any transport undertaking. As will be seen later in this chapter, whilst the policy making bodies are parts of central and local government, implementation of the resultant policies and day to day management and control is in the hands of separate autonomous organisations.

An exception to the principle of divorcement of

Departmental Function	*Subject Matter*	*Method of Control*	*Chapter for cross reference*	*Government Dept (in England) primarily involved*
Operating	Bus routes and timetables	Traffic Commissioner	8	Transport
	Safety on railways, tramways and trolleybuses	Inspector of Railways	8	Transport
Engineering	Bus vehicle types and standards of fitness	Certifying Officer (through the PSV machinery)	8	Transport
	Safety on railways, tramways and trolleybuses	Inspector of Railways	8	Transport
Finance	Revenue support and capital grants for local passenger transport (for railways mainly in metropolitan counties) and highways	Transport Policies and Programmes of County Councils	4	Transport
	Revenue Support for local passenger rail services (mainly in non-metropolitan counties)	Public Service Obligation	4	Transport
Staff	Bus drivers hours of duty	Traffic Commissioner (through licensing machinery)	8	Transport
	Rights of employees	Industrial Tribunal	3	Employment
	Licensing of bus drivers	Traffic Commissioner	8	Transport
Planning	Public transport planning			
	Metropolitan Counties	Passenger Transport Plans of Passenger Transport Executives	5	Transport
	Non-metropolitan Counties	Public Transport Plans of County Councils	5	Transport
	Land use planning	Structure Plans of County Councils	5	Environment
	Policy for public and private transport and highways collectively	Transport Policies and Programmes of County Councils	5	Transport

Fig 8 Table to illustrate the method of control by central and local government over certain functions and interests of the providers of urban and rural transport.

management control from government is the one to which reference was made in Chapter 1. There is a substantial degree of local authority ownership in the bus business and in the UK there are 49 municipalities which actually own and operate local passenger transport with the undertakings trading as a department within the local government structure. But even here the principle remains as whilst transport policy is the responsibility of county councils, ownership and control of municipal bus fleets is vested in district councils. Section 1(1)(b) of the Transport Act, 1978, makes this point clear. District councils do, nevertheless, as owners and operators have their own policies as well.

Administration and the Political Influence

There is a division between political and professional control in the machinery which has been described. At one time there was very little political control (other than within the municipal bus undertakings) and the professionals ran their businesses in a speculative, commercial, competitive and expeditious manner with the maximum of service and the minimum of overhead costs in a climate which, to come back to the point made in Chapter 1, some people might prefer to see again. But the fruits of uncontrolled planning (or no planning at all) are, among other things, a desperate situation on the roads at busy times and difficult areas to serve effectively by public transport. Add to this the rising costs and falling traffics and public transport sometimes requires financial assistance if it is to run at all. When a company spends money it requires the support of its shareholders; when a government spends money it should have the support of the citizens, which means, in effect, their elected representatives. At this stage, therefore, the issue must become political. It is now, however, local government which is spending money on urban and rural transport. The Local Government Act, 1972, heralded a process of devolution which, as has already been noted, put responsibility for transport and related matters on to county councils. With county councillors required to make decisions of this kind came the need for a stronger support process through the offices of professional and technical staff and substantial administrative machines have, therefore, appeared at county level. These bodies have contact with the operators whose organisations must, in consequence, be geared accordingly and so the process develops. In the circumstances as described this is difficult to avoid but with bigger administrations one cannot help but think of a reversal of the old adage:

'Lesser fleas have little fleas put on their backs to bite'm,
Little fleas have bigger fleas and so ad infinitum.'

Structure plans and transport policies and programmes of county councils and the public transport plans of non-metropolitan county councils involve public planning and public spending. There must, therefore, be political decisions and the documents will reflect county policies although they are subject also to the influence of central government. On the other hand, traffic commissioners and the railway inspectors are government appointed officers and have responsibility for overseeing day to day operations. They also give decisions but in their own right. Their deliberations are technical and do not reflect political opinion.

In short, the providors of public transport are subject to government control at both county and national level and also by independent authority, some of which is political and some technical. Municipal bus undertakings go one stage further as their professional managements are subject to political control at district council level as well as to the machinery just described which applies equally to them. It is to this background that the structure and organisation of the British bus industry must be considered.

User Organisations

Users' organisations are fully considered in *Principles of Transport* and their impact on buses in Great Britain is very small. The transport users' consultative committees as constituted by Section 56 of the Transport Act, 1962 and amended by Section 55 of the Transport Act, 1968 have only limited relevance to urban and rural transport. As far as passenger transport generally is concerned, their responsibilities are, inter alia, to consider and, at their discretion, make recommendations, with respect to the services operated by British Railways other than fares and charges. A special procedure applies to proposed closures of railway lines and stations and this applies equally to the railways of London Transport (vide Section 25 of the Transport (London) Act, 1969). Briefly, where a line or station is proposed for closure and there is public objection, the TUCC will consider and report on any hardship which it is thought might arise and the closure will not be proceeded with without the approval of the minister. To this extent, therefore, the deliberations of the TUCC's have their influence on rural transport as it is so often the rural branch lines which are put up for closure. But this connection is with railways, not buses. On the bus side there is very little influence from users' committees. County councils have their transport responsibilities and policies and these bodies should represent the interests of the people at local level. Statutory provision for a users' committee in respect of bus services does however exist in London. Section 14 of the Transport (London) Act, 1969 establishes a users' consultative body for the purpose of considering and at its discretion making recommendations with respect to any matter affecting the services provided by the London Transport Executive, be they road or rail, other than matters concerning charges or railway closures, the latter being covered by the TUCC machinery.

The Structure of the Passenger Transport Industry

The companion book *Principles of Transport* covers in depth both the different forms of ownership which exist in the transport industry generally such as limited companies, public corporations, etc and details of those types of ownership which can be found in Great Britain.

When discussing forms of ownership, one of the fundamental distinctions lies between what is publicly owned and what is privately owned. Whilst at one time nearly all public transport was in private hands, for the reasons already explained, over the years public money has been spent to acquire either compulsory or voluntarily different parts of transport and the time has now been reached when the great bulk of local passenger services has become 'public property', that is, nationalised or municipalised. Whilst nationally owned undertakings can be operated directly by the government as a department of state, as noted elsewhere, this is not often the case. Some railway systems overseas are managed in this way but in Great Britain the more usual practice is to create separate autonomous bodies with those in charge accountable to the appropriate government minister and parliament on broad principles only.

In Great Britain the nationalised bus sector is in the hands of two what are, in effect, holding companies, the National Bus Company (in England and Wales) and the Scottish Transport Group (in Scotland). These bodies, both of which were created by the Transport Act, 1968 control a series of operating subsidiary companies which, to all outward appearances (apart from livery and symbol) are indistinguishable from the few remaining bus companies in the private sector. Also in public ownership are the municipal undertakings of the district councils to which reference has already been made, some with a history dating back to trams and the 19th century. Then there are the passenger transport executives (including the London Transport Executive) established in accordance with the principles embodied in the 1968 Transport Act. The privately owned undertakings, otherwise known as the 'independents' in the main work in the private hire, excursion and tour field, which is not relevant to this book. There is a very limited participation in long distance express services but, although small in relation to the whole, there is an 'independent' input to the stage carriage bus business in Great Britain. The continued survival of the small concerns is now following something of a two-way process. As the proprietors approach retirement, the fortunes of their businesses are often not attractive to their natural successors (assuming that they have any). They are, therefore, disposed of to an outside bidder who is usually the established operator, being either a National Bus or Scottish Bus subsidiary, a passenger transport executive or a bus operating district council. Such transfers are often acceptable as the major operator has at least a moral obligation to continue some sort of a facility and it is sometimes possible to effect economies through integration with the rest of the fleet. Conversely, in some cases rural services with what are now traditionally sparse traffics can be very expensive for the larger operators with their higher overheads and rigid staff agreements. Under these circumstances, the flexibility and easier working arrangements of the small independents lend themselves to this type of operation. Whilst, therefore, there is a process of acquisition by the larger groups, there is also a process of disposal according to the geography of the route in relation to the main network and to other local factors which either make for or improve economic efficiency. Nevertheless, the structure of the British bus industry is predominantly public ownership, either through central or local government. Within the public sector, some 50% of the vehicle fleet is in the ownership of NBC/STG, 37% is passenger transport executive (including London Transport) and 13% is local authority.* In broad principle the undertakings associated with local government tend to serve the densely populated urban areas whilst National and Scottish Bus very often operate the longer distance bus route networks as well as coaches and into the rural areas. If the private sector is taken into account then the split is publicly owned (all three groups together) 63% and privately owned 37% but for this purpose this information gives a misleading impression as the figures include vehicles in the predominantly contract and tour category which is not relevant in this context.

Ownership of the railway contribution to urban and rural transport is even more simple than the buses. The British Railways Board, providing as it does the national railway system has an extensive commuter business in the London area with smaller networks around some of the provincial towns such as, for example, in the metropolitan counties. Those rural branch lines which remain are also in the ownership of British Railways. These services are, however, an integral part of the main line system. The trains share common tracks, stations and equipment with long distance and freight traffic and operating techniques follow main line practices which fall outside the ambit of this book. More relevant are the self-contained or partially self-contained rapid transit type locally owned systems of which, in Great Britain, there are very few. The substantial London Transport network falls into this category, a small underground railway is owned by Greater Glasgow Passenger Transport Executive and Tyne & Wear Passenger Transport Executive has a system which is still in the course of construction. Whilst it is generally accepted that railways are now in public

*Source: *Transport Statistics — Great Britain;* HMSO

ownership, there are a few light railways and others which come within the private sector. Generally they cover disused British Railways lines and tend to be run on special occasions with part voluntary labour for the purpose of preserving steam traction. They do, however, sometimes provide a rural facility in the process. There are also a few narrow gauge lines, again with steam power and one interesting example, the Romney, Hythe & Dymchurch Railway in Kent actually has a contract from the county council for the conveyance of some 220 schoolchildren — a small but nevertheless useful contribution to a social need.

Trade Associations

A trade association is an independent body created for the purpose of giving guidance, information, assistance and support to its members. It acts as a 'clearing house' for the dissemination of technical information, seeks to protect the collective interests of its members, makes representations to parliament when relevant legislation is being considered and acts as the spokesman for the industry which it represents. There is a two-way process on the part of members who not only take benefit from the services provided but also contribute their own expertise without which such an association could not function. For purposes of administration it is normal for an organisation of this kind to form a series of specialist committees on appropriate matters with the participants drawn from representatives of senior management within the industry, suitably co-ordinated by a small permanent secretariat.

Associations of this kind are appropriate where there is a large number of separate organisations which together constitute 'the industry'. Whilst it is true that in road passenger transport, the individual units tend to be large with some very big combines there are also many small private operators particularly, as has been seen, in the coaching business. This is in contrast to the railway which, with a few exceptions, consists of one single operator for the entire country. A trade association for road passenger transport is, therefore, opportune and in Great Britain it is the Confederation of British Road Passenger Transport (CPT) which fulfils this role.

What has been said so far represents the national scene. But the principle can be and is extended to the international field to facilitate, for example, the exchange of information and formulation of agreements and economic policies between organisations of different countries. At this level, what has been said is equally appropriate for railways. As far as the subject matter of this book is concerned, there are two international associations which have relevance, namely the International Union of Public Transport (UITP) and the International Road Transport Union (IRU). The International Union of Public Transport represents the interests of those responsible for urban, suburban and inter-urban public passenger transport, which includes buses, trams, trolleybuses and metropolitan railways. Most of the major British publicly owned bus operators are members as is the Confederation of British Road Passenger Transport. The International Road Transport Union embraces the privately owned sector of road transport on both the passenger and goods side. The affiliated British association representing road passenger interests is the European Conference of British Bus and Coach Operators (ECBO) which was formed for that specific purpose and is now a specialist committee of the Confederation of British Road Passenger Transport.

Management

Having dealt with the organisation of the industry, it is now the organisation of management which is for consideration, or, in other words, the organisation of the individual units which together make up the industry. Organisation in this sense means the arrangement of the administration in order to ensure the satisfactory conduct of the business and in common with the other parts of this chapter it is a subject which is fully considered in *Principles of Transport*. The role of the policy making bodies has already been covered, consisting as they do of politicians in the public sector and shareholders in the private sector. At policy level there is a distinction between the two, the former paying more regard to social issues and the latter to economics, and their terms of reference are likely to be different. But both groups will employ professional managers (or corporate bodies) to run their businesses which they will do with the expertise and 'know how' acquired through years of study and experience. Their responsibilities are to supply the utility of place and to give their passengers a safe arrival, all within pre-determined policies and financial constraints. It matters little what might be the make-up of their policy making masters.

Internal Organisation

Centralised Control

The size of the operating unit is all important as it is this which determines to what extent the manager must delegate some of his work to others, thereby creating a chain of command and hence an organisational structure. An owner/manager of a fleet of, say, five buses might be able to write his own schedules, hire and fire his staff and generally control, supervise and administer the day to day running of the business. His 'office' might be a room of his own private house and he might do his own vehicle servicing whilst his wife 'keeps the books' in between her domestic chores. The parking lot could be his own back yard. Apart from a few drivers and possibly conductors, he might need a general hand to help keep the vehicles in an acceptable condition with heavier maintenance

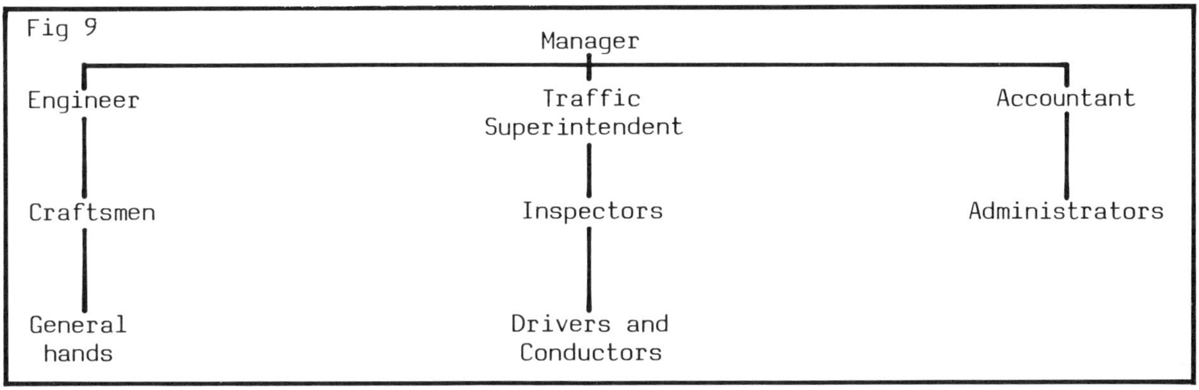

Above: **Fig 9. Skeletal chart to show the principal departmental heads and chain of command of a bus undertaking organised on a functional basis.**

arranged through an outside contractor. There would be minimal (if any) supervisory and clerical assistance but the services of a solicitor, an accountant, an outside builder and other specialists might be necessary from time to time. This is the reason why the overheads of a small proprietor are low in comparison with the larger concerns and hence their suitability for work in rural areas, as has been suggested.

Imagine now that the fleet expands to 20, 30, 40 or more vehicles. The time will come, legal requirements apart, when the volume of work gets beyond the capacity of one man with the minimum of help to undertake the more menial tasks. He will require some senior assistants to take charge of specific functions. The occasional major overhauls have become a regular job as there is now a continuous succession of vehicles which require attention of this kind. The outside contractor is, therefore, no longer economic as he himself is working to profit margins and it is beneficial for the bus company to do the work itself. Apart from capital expenditure on equipment and supporting facilities, therefore, a full time engineer is required, assisted by a foreman and mechanics according to the magnitude of the work. Route planning, time and duty schedules, route licensing, fares, publicity and staff consultation with an emergent and possibly active trade union element is another full time job for somebody. The financial side will by now have grown to the extent that a permanent professional input is crucial to this side of the business which could also absorb the administrative work necessary when considerable numbers of staff are employed. For this it would seem that three functional heads are indicated and in diagrammatic form, the organisation might appear as in the example shown at Fig 9.

This is the beginning of the functional or departmental system of the chain of command. Each functional head is responsible to the manager for his department and these officers are the only official links between the departments although in practice there will be day to day inter-departmental consultation between staff at lower levels. For example, when fares revisions are considered, traffic staff and accountants are both involved. If a vehicle develops a defect whilst in service both the inspectors and the engineering staff have action to take which must be properly co-ordinated if the service is not to suffer unduly. But the respective staffs are subject to the rulings of their functional chiefs and any clashes of opinion or procedure must, at least in theory, be referred to the top, across the 'functional bridge' and down again before progress can be made. Even the departmental heads might not reach agreement easily and it is only the manager in person who can give a ruling which is binding on all three. Whilst this is of little consequence in a relatively small unit, there is a stage when the system becomes cumbrous. That stage, however, has not yet been reached. The system represents a natural progression from the single handed proprietor and it is the most appropriate for the small and medium sized undertakings. With yet further growth, so additional staff have to be appointed. If any one department becomes unwieldy, it might be beneficial to divide the responsibilities into new departments. An organisation with 800 buses, for example, might perhaps look something like that shown in Fig 10 which lists the possible functions which could be contained within a department. For simplicity the chains of command within each department are not now shown.

At this stage there has been substantial growth but there is still a clear departmental style. The larger the system the more likely might be the possible administrative difficulties which have been described but at what stage the concept becomes unmanageable is a matter of circumstance and opinion. There are no rules which must be followed when determining an organisational structure except that whatever principle is adopted (and there is an alternative) it must be the one which enables the undertaking to work with the maximum of efficiency and economy and the exercise must not be confused with finding jobs for people. The needs of the service must be determined and suitable staff appointed. In other words, the

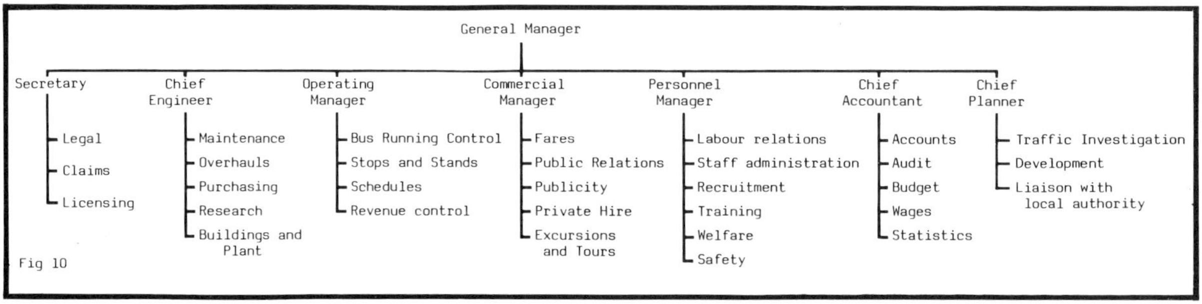

Above: **Fig 10. Diagram to show the responsibilities of departmental heads within a bus undertaking organised on a functional basis.**

administrative machine will seldom be right if existing personalities are taken as base and the structure built around their capabilities and aptitudes; but this is getting into the recruitment field.

De-centralised Control

An alternative concept in this study of organisational methods is the divisional system. This is a rather more recent and now a more fashionable approach to management control and is a principle in which government itself has taken a lead. The theory behind the concept is the devolution of power. It was said earlier in this chapter that government policies and directives are administered in England through departments which are in the charge of ministers, etc (departmental heads). Outside England administration is based not on departments but on geographical regions. In Scotland, Wales and Northern Ireland there are secretaries of state local to those areas but responsible for all of the functions which are departmentalised in England. They resemble 'divisional' heads which is the basis of the system. Reference was also made earlier to the fact that some responsibilities had been transferred from central government to county councils by the Local Government Act, 1972. In other words, the power of decision making was being transferred from the centre, not only geographically but in this case also to the levels nearer to where those decisions are actually implemented.

The principle can be and is applied to transport undertakings and in embryonic form, the chart at Fig 9 would instead follow the pattern of that contained in Fig 11.

With this system, the operating territory is divided into divisions (or areas or districts, it matters not what they are called) and a manager is appointed for each who reports direct to the general manager. The term 'manager' is significant. It implies that he is responsible for all of the day to day work within his division regardless of the function. In other words, he cleans and services the vehicles and ensures that they are available for traffic requirements, he recruits staff, he prepares his schedules, he controls the buses on the road (or trains on the railway) and is responsible for the necessary administrative work within his divisional headquarters. To do this he will need the support of senior assistants whose work could well be organised on a functional basis, such as an engineer, a traffic superintendent and a staff officer. But they will be very small units compared with a centralised headquarters responsible for the entire system.

Look again at the departmental structure as it was set out at Fig 10 for a theoretical 800-bus unit. It might now follow the lines of the chart shown at Fig 12 which suggests that there must be rather more to the headquarters organisation than might have been apparent from the outline sketch at Fig 11. One reason for this is that the undertaking as a whole will wish to trade as a single unit with a common policy and not as a series of distinct parts with perhaps different standards. Partly for this and partly in the interests of efficiency there are certain functions which are more appropriate for administration from the centre. If there are to be common standards and the undertaking is to speak with one voice, then the commercial manager will expect his fares officer, his public relations officer and his publicity officer to have responsibility for the entire system. Clearly the secretary would not find it convenient to divide his legal responsibilities and the work of the chief accountant will cover the undertaking as a whole. Similarly, efficiency might be lost if the chief planner lost the advantage of integration between divisions and had to recognise a series of 'independent' units. Major overhaul work, research and the purchase of supplies on the engineering side also attracts economies through centralisation. It follows that there still must be a sizeable centralised headquarters administration to determine policy and to undertake those functions which do not readily lend themselves to decentralisation. On the other hand, divisional managers must have a supporting administrative team if they are to discharge their responsibilities in a satisfactory manner.

Selection of an Organisational System

The advantage of the divisional system is that a senior manager with executive power is available 'in the field' as opposed to a 'base headquarters'. Decisions within the

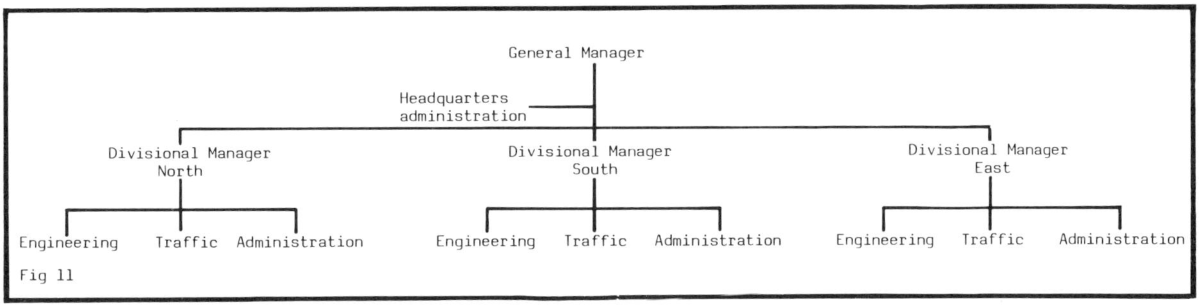

Above: **Fig 11. Chart to show the basic organisation of a bus undertaking utilising the divisional system.**

Below: **Fig 12. Diagram to show the responsibilities of chief officers of a bus undertaking organised on a divisional basis.**

broad policy framework can be given on the spot and the possible working disadvantages of the functional system as suggested at the outset and which magnify as the system grows larger are avoided. On the other hand, with administration as there must be at central and at local levels, an element of duplication creeps in.

It is at this point where opinions differ and why the determination of an organisational structure is so much subject to discretion at board level. Geography plays a part. If the network is large but far flung, if traffic concentrations are widely scattered with sparsely populated areas in between or if there is a series of physically separate units which do not easily lend themselves to complete operational integration, there is a much stronger case for decentralised control. A large national airline with an international network is a case in point. A national railway system is another, particularly, as is so often the case, it is an amalgamation of what was at one time a series of physically separate and independently owned railway companies. Perhaps 'line manager' would be a better term than divisional manager in this case. But bus undertakings do not usually fall into this pattern. Generally their operating territories are smaller and more compact and not of a sufficient size to make the functional system unwieldy. Even localised light rail or rapid transit systems lend themselves more readily to decentralised control with a manager responsible for each separate line.

Size and Scale

The purpose of this sub-section is to bring thoughts back to size and scale and the amount which one man can effectively manage. It is a follow on from the structure of the bus industry which, as far as Great Britain is concerned, was discussed earlier in this chapter. Many of the urban services are controlled by passenger transport executives (including the mammoth London Transport

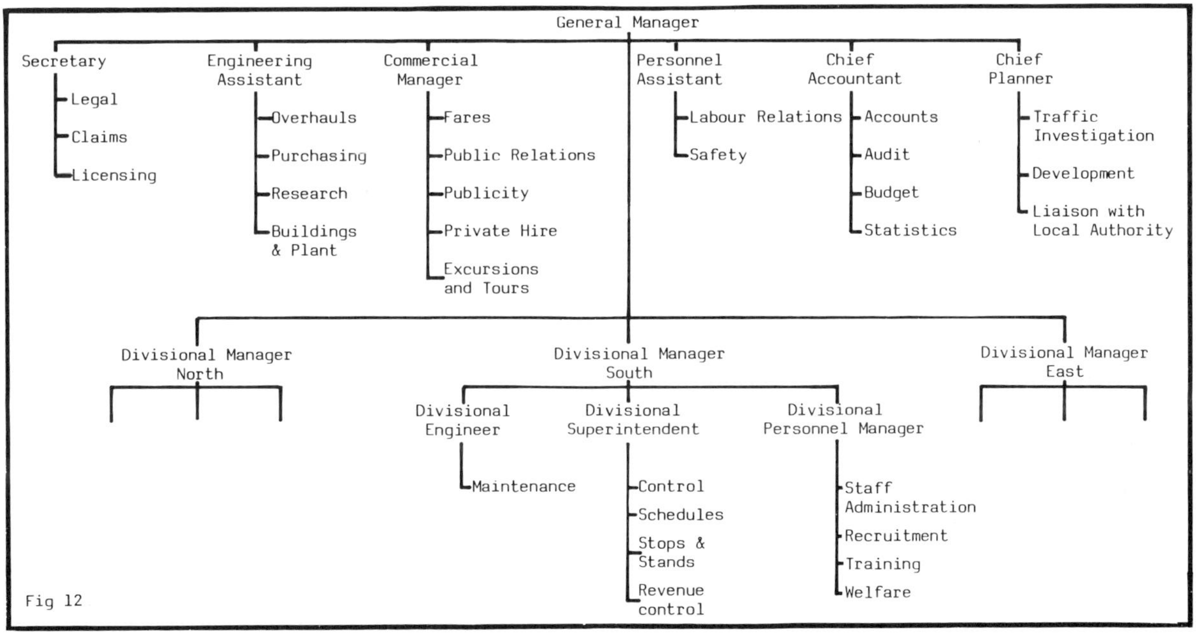

Executive) and district councils but the size of their undertakings are dictated largely by political boundaries and are, therefore, set and management efficiency must be geared to a pre-determined size regardless of other considerations. This is not the case, however, with the nationalised services. To take the National Bus Company as an example, the management board has not, for very good reasons, appointed an operating manager, chief engineer, etc, with direct functional and day to day working responsibility for every bus service in England and Wales. Even the structure of the company is not planned in this way. Business is conducted through a series of subsidiary operating companies which are legal entities in their own right. This in itself is devolution of control and each has its own internal organisation drawn up on the principles as just described. Most of these subsidiary companies have their roots in the developing era of private enterprise and under new management have survived in what is now little more than name only. The point of importance here however is that these companies have developed, in themselves perhaps through a process of acquisition, to an optimum point where benefit can be taken from the economies of scale but not beyond what a manager can properly manage or where the overhead costs become disproportionate and diseconomies set in. This criteria in itself offers quite a range and the optimum size is again a matter of conjecture. Disregarding the purely coach operating concerns, the National Bus Company for example has some 31 bus-operating subsidiaries. Of these, the arithmetical average of vehicles per company after allowing for those jointly managed is about 600 with a range of 1,166 in the ownership of London Country Bus Services to some 166 of Cumberland Motor Services. The median of the range is 571. These figures are an indication of the range between which what might be regarded as an optimum size remembering that, although, as already said, the respective operating areas have historical connections, subsequent adjustments and amalgamations can and in some cases have been made by NBC.

Conclusions on Organisation and Size

It has been shown that the internal structure and organisation of an enterprise recognises, among other things, the amount which it is considered that one man can successfully manage although the size of an undertaking is not necessarily dictated by this restraint as some transport undertakings must of necessity serve a large area. In private industry there is also some very large scale enterprise. In transport, Greyhound Lines which provides long distance coach services throughout the United States of America and beyond is an example as also are the international oil companies. But the internal structures must take size into account and with very large combines there is little doubt that devolution of authority in some form must be considered. At what stage, however, absolute control from the centre ceases to be practicable must depend on personal preferences. It is the opinion of the writer that decentralisation is better avoided if at all possible. If that 800-bus unit, a suggested organisation for which was depicted at Fig 10, served a compact operating area it is submitted that the departmental system with centralised control should be practicable. Decentralisation not only introduces an element of duplication of administration, it also tends to put the functional heads within each division responsible to two masters, being to their respective divisional managers and also to those in charge of their function at headquarters.

The point was made however that there are no rules as such to determine what the chain of command should be. The departmental and divisional systems represent the basic theory. The resultant structure will be geared to one or the other or perhaps to a blend of both. Decentralisation within a department is not unknown. A 'divisional superintendent' for example might carry responsibility for operating matters within his division, being directly responsible to a functional head. Such an arrangement could however represent the worst of both worlds as there would be duplication of work without any compensating benefit.

Staff Administration

Introduction

The title of this sub-section covers what has become in Great Britain an involved and far reaching issue. It is a very important part, not only of bus operation but of industry generally but as transport is a large employer of labour, and this applies to rail as well as to road, staff matters are now tending to occupy what might be regarded as a disproportionate amount of a manager's time. Until quite recently, the chief officers of the various functions as just described were usually able to handle the staff side of the business. Between the functions, it is the operating department which has the largest payroll but even here the traffic manager, divisional superintendent or whatever his title was generally able, subject to the size of his unit, to handle personnel matters with only the minimum of assistance. Today, the volume and complexity of staff work has grown to the extent that it has become a specialised subject in itself. So much so that in large undertakings a person with particular knowledge of the subject and probably with a sizeable supporting staff is necessary to deal with the complex day to day issues which arise. Staff administration now has rather less significance in the operating syllabuses of the professional examining bodies as there are separate subjects which cover the many ramifications of this important topic. For these reasons, this book will remain silent on the teachings of this branch of management. It does not mean however, that the student can remain ignorant of the subject as it impinges on other work which is more directly related to operations. This chapter would not, therefore, be complete without at least a reference to the issues involved.

Industrial Relations

Good staff relations are essential if there is to be good service. It is worthwhile, therefore, to look briefly at recent trends and to put into perspective any shortcomings and difficulties which could be a source of discontent to both employers and employed.

Over the years the trade union movement has become progressively stronger, backed by a wealth of social legislation. Several acts of parliament have established a variety of rights for individuals in employment. Most of these rights are now contained in the Employment Protection (Consolidation) Act, 1978 which brought together in one enactment previous legislation which covered redundancy payments, contracts of employment, trade union and labour relations matters and protection of employment. Additionally there are other acts which also bestow rights on employees, the main ones being the Equal Pay Act, 1970, the Sex Discrimination Act, 1975 and the Race Relations Act, 1976. With such extensive rights now conferred on employees, the British government has seen fit to set up a series of industrial tribunals to deliberate and give directions on any complaints which might arise. These tribunals are independent judicial bodies of whom the chairmen are legally qualified and both parties at a hearing (being the employer and employed) may be legally represented if they so wish.

Whilst this may be congenial for employees, it does nothing to help run buses and trains. However, whilst the transport industry in general has a history of security of employment, it also has a history of long hours and relatively low wages. It might also be said that for many years, life for the transport worker (as, no doubt, for many others) was hard and somewhat uncompromising with the result that a sense of mistrust and hostility was engendered between employers and employed which is not easily eradicated. The record of management is not without blame in this respect. But even if some harsh decisions were made, it must be emphasised that the goodwill of a service is dependent on standards. The service must be reliable if it is to be any good at all. Buses must run in accordance with advertised times, which means that they do not run early, nor must they be subjected to unnecessary delay. The correct destination blinds must be displayed. Uniformed staff need to be courteous and smart in appearance and drivers should not smoke whilst on duty, particularly with the now open cabs which permit the objectionable effects to penetrate the interior of the vehicle (it is illegal anyway). All uniformed staff should be effective public relations officers. Any shortcomings such as have been mentioned (and there are plenty) will do more than anything else to accelerate the erosion of traffic and without proper discipline, service will be lacking and goodwill lost. It is submitted that managements should produce rules and procedures for efficient running which are practical in their implementation, that they should not be impeded by trade unions in so doing and that staff should work to those rules. It is unfortunate that some members of some trade unions seem to have a different interpretation of 'working to rule'.

Managers do, therefore, have their reasons for wishing to impose a strict code of discipline but the legislation referred to certainly does not assist them in doing it.

Another standard is that charges should not be excessively high but, disregarding subsidies, fare levels depend on working expenses which in turn, to a large extent, depend on wages. Whilst the writer accepts absolutely that a fair day's work deserves a fair day's pay, it is his view that restrictive practices and other measures which enforce inefficient schedules and produce inflated wages for idle time make no contribution at all to the interests of either the nation, the travelling public or, in the long run, to the staff themselves. Agreements as are now sought by trade unions, particularly in respect of duty schedules, are, nevertheless, becoming more restrictive and hence more costly. This is why 'productivity' has become a fashionable term in labour relations but the legislation referred to makes productivity impossible to enforce without agreement and sometimes difficult to negotiate.

The foregoing has but briefly touched upon the complexities of labour relations in Britain today. Because transport is a labour intensive industry it is something which must enter into the daily lives of all those who have a responsibility for the running of buses and trains. Part of the staff function involves a knowledge of current legislation (which is always liable to change). Another part — man management and human relationships — calls for a natural gift, the absence of which no amount of technical know-how can compensate. But this is a book on how to run buses, not how to manage staff and the matter will not, therefore, be developed further. There are other parts of the staff function which again are not part of operations and these, therefore, will also have only brief mention.

Administration

Having discussed the basic issues of the staff function, there are other more routine matters which usually fall within the scope of this department. Records must be kept of all staff and internal administration must be dealt with. Promotions, etc, require advice to the wages section (probably a part of the finance function), entitlement to uniform calls for notification to the supplies section (which might be a part of the engineering department) and management is likely to require statistics in respect of staff utilisation. Such examples could continue. Administration is also necessary in respect of certain other activities within the staff officer's domain, references to which follow. This comes back to the point that the larger the undertaking, the greater is the internal administration, particularly within the present legal framework. A big house has many servants and more servants are required to serve those servants — and so it goes on — and it all adds up to greater overhead expenses. Care must be taken to avoid the production of unnecessary information by departments anxious to justify their existence. There is always the danger of reports and statistics being produced to be received by staff at the other end whose sole job is to file them, the paper being stored until it is finally destroyed.

Recruitment and Training

Recruitment of staff is something which is normally undertaken by the respective employing officers within the overall policy of the undertaking as applied through the recruitment section. This is another example where two separate functions meet with the staff people ensuring that an appointment is appropriate and within an authorised establishment, checking references, etc whilst the actual employing officer will need to satisfy himself regarding the suitability of the applicant for the job. Having recruited staff, there is a difficulty in some areas of retaining them and the turnover, particularly in the case of platform staff, is sometimes heavy. The most unpopular aspect of this work is the socially inconvenient shifts and weekend working. This, of course, is an essential and unavoidable feature and not something which management can do very much about. But the fact that there is both unemployment and unfilled vacancies for bus drivers and conductors at the same place at the same time suggests that there can perhaps be too much welfare in the welfare state. A bus company cannot match the competing attractions of unemployment pay and supplementary benefits backed with a little casual work here and there.

Turning to the training side of the section, most people employed in transport are at least semi-skilled and training is, therefore, an essential feature. Vocational training includes schools for, in particular drivers, conductors, inspectors and on the railway signalmen and many other grades which require specialised tuition. The actual work of training is generally carried out by the undertaking's own staff especially appointed for the purpose and an appointed bus driving instructor may be authorised to examine and certify drivers as competent to hold a driver's licence. Budding engineers normally follow the apprenticeship schemes of their particular trades. Also the responsibility of the training officer are the many different types of courses which are available for general background training and geared to the various levels of management. This category of staff is also encouraged or required to study for the examinations of the appropriate professional bodies.

Welfare

The welfare input to the transport business is something which has developed over more recent years, particularly amongst the larger undertakings. Not being a sociologist, the writer does not propose even to attempt to consider the many personal and domestic problems encountered by staff and how they could effect their standard of work, let alone to suggest how they might be solved. The employer of a large workforce, however, might well be advised to have somebody on hand who can deal with such matters.

One of the better known functions and one which is usually classified as a part of welfare is the provision of canteens. This is a very useful facility, particularly as so many employees are on shift work with the odd hours of work which that entails. It is important that somewhere is available for rest and refreshment at reasonable prices during periods of meal relief and a subsidised canteen service does meet a need in making what can be sometimes rather difficult working conditions more tolerable.

Welfare facilities are really something which are provided by management as a good employer over and above the agreed conditions of service even though probably not now introduced without staff consultation. In this enlightened age, however, some of these arrangements for staff welfare have become legal requirements. An example is safety.

Health and Safety

The Health and Safety at Work etc Act, 1974 is in addition to and only partially replaces hitherto existing health and safety legislation. It also extends its scope as it applies not only to employers but also to those self employed and to employees. The main aims of the Act are to secure the health, safety and welfare of people at work; to protect other persons against any risks arising out of the activities of those workpeople and to control the storage and use of dangerous substances and their emission into the atmosphere. As the legislation involves the entire workforce, staff as well as management have a legal responsibility to achieve high standards of safety.

The requirements of the 1974 Act are extensive and provision is made for the appointment of safety representatives and establishment of safety committees within the various workforces. The general duties of employers to their employees are contained in Section 2. One of the most pertinent in this context is the requirement to provide and maintain as far as is practicable a working environment which is safe without risks to health and with adequate welfare arrangements. Suitable training must be given as necessary.

Conclusions

The foregoing has opened the door but has made no attempt to walk through and explain or teach on the many facets of staff work. Enough has been said, however, to make it clear that a transport manager must be adept in human relations. He also needs an encyclopaedic knowledge of statute law as it relates to employers and employed quite apart from all of the other controls as are described in Chapter 8 which includes the ever growing contribution from the European Economic Community. He must be able to find his way through the entanglements of the negotiating procedures, bearing in mind that some governments are always ready to give power and backing to the trade union movement whilst at the same time offering to employers guidelines on the ceiling of wage awards and other benefits. Having tended to all this, it is to be hoped that the manager can find some time to run his trains or his buses in accordance with the staff agreements which he has negotiated, to the standards and with the fares which his passengers find acceptable, all within his predetermined financial constraints.

4
Finance

Introduction

As is the case with mechanical engineering, finance and accounting is an essential part of the job of running buses and trains. But it is a profession in its own right and important as it is as far as the science of transport is concerned, finance is a separate and, in this sense, ancillary discipline. For this reason there is no pretence here to try and teach this very specialised subject. The purpose of this chapter is to examine the financial issues rather than the accounting methods. It is a subject which has assumed greater significance over recent years with the gradual transition from commercial viability to social service. There is a need to see how revenue is obtained (being partly from fares but now also partly from public funds) and the machinery which has been established to deal with this matter. Parliament must, of course, be involved in such issues and the procedures which are to be outlined relate to British law, being to some extent unique to the United Kingdom.

Revenue

Although very pertinent to this chapter, revenue is also considered in various other places in this book as the subject impinges on several facets of operation. Suffice to say for the moment that whatever services are provided costs will be incurred and those costs must be recovered, either from fares or from some other source. Revenue obtained through fares, either on or off the vehicles, must be collected and the various methods of doing this are considered in Chapter 9. Having received the money, proper arrangements must be made for its security and banking and this is covered in Chapter 11. To maximise revenue, facilities must be as attractive as possible and this is a matter for Chapter 7. Any shortfall must be made up in the form of a subsidy, something again considered in Chapter 7.

If revenue is insufficient to cover direct working expenses, that is, not enough to pay the drivers' wages or buy fuel, then the undertaking would cease trading very quickly. If these costs could be met but there was insufficient to cover overheads then again business could not continue and it would still eventually go into liquidation. If all costs including interest on loans could be covered but there was nothing left to remunerate shareholders then those concerned would still be encouraged to dispose of their assets and reinvest in a more lucrative industry. This is how private enterprise must work and there is a clear incentive to combine economy with service and give the maximum in return for the least if patronage is to be encouraged and a living is to be made. The principle is not altered by public ownership. The British Railways Board, National Bus Company and Scottish Transport Group (by Section 41 of the Transport Act, 1968) the passenger transport executives (by Section 11 of the same 1968 Act) and the London Transport Executive (by Section 7 of the Transport [London] Act, 1969), are required to pay their way. This means that revenue from the fare box together with any revenue support which might be forthcoming must cover costs.

To follow on from what was said in Chapter 3, transport in urban and rural areas, even if not viable, can be a social necessity. If this is the case, then a political decision to give revenue support from public funds is likely and in the UK county councils have power to do this through the transport policy and programme machinery.

Transport Policies and Programmes

The final section of Chapter 1 drew attention to the growing need to subsidise public transport and concluded on the note that the 1968 Transport Act brought with it, among other things, provision for subsidies under certain circumstances for local passenger services, be they road or rail. Very briefly, machinery was set up as follows for such assistance to be given where considered necessary:

Section 13

Passenger transport authorities able to issue precepts for the levying of rates to meet deficits arising from the provision of services by passenger transport executives in passenger transport areas.

Section 20

A responsibility for passenger transport executives to support financially local railway passenger services through the passenger transport authority and the precept machinery of Section 13. (The application of this Section is permissive on the minister but in the event it has been applied to all passenger transport executives).

Section 32
Assistance towards the purchase of new buses. This has amounted to up to a 50% grant on vehicles to be used for stage carriage work and of an approved type. One of the conditions has been suitability for one-man operation which has, therefore, excluded rear entrance vehicles and this requirement has influenced the design of buses now in use in Great Britain.

Section 33
Grants towards the duty charged on fuel used by buses on stage carriage services.

Section 34
Authority for county councils to support financially rural bus and ferry services. The minister was also empowered to make grants to county councils for approved cases and in the event, the Department of the Environment, which was the department responsible at the time, generally considered only those services where revenue did not fall below 50% of the direct operating costs.

Section 39
Authority for the minister to make grants to British Railways for the retention of loss making services which had a social value. This necessitated service by service costing by BR for submission of grant-aid applications.

Section 56
Infrastructure grants at the discretion of the minister for the provision, improvement or development of facilities for public passenger transport.

Much of this legislation has now been swept away by the Local Government Act, 1974 whereby certain specific grants for transport have been abolished and replaced by a new system which incorporates within a single process payments for the provision of: Public Transport; Highways; Traffic Regulations; Parking Places.

This is a logical development from Sections 202 and 203 of the Local Government Act, 1972 which puts a duty on metropolitan and non-metropolitan county councils respectively to develop policies which promote the provision of efficient and co-ordinated systems of public transport and the authority to support them financially. These new powers supplemented their highway and traffic regulation responsibilities which they already had and county councils are, therefore, now able to make comprehensive approaches to the inter-related and now total transport requirements within their respective areas. Gone are the specific grants (though not the need for them) for infrastructure (Section 56), rural buses and ferries (Section 34) and local railways in passenger transport areas (Section 20) as also are the principal road grants under Section 235 of the Highways Act 1959. Instead there is a unified system covering both current and capital expenditure. Part of the money hitherto used for specific grants has been absorbed into the needs element of the rate support grant. The remainder is distributed annually as a transport supplementary grant to those county councils whose programme of estimated expenditure as accepted by the minister exceeds a prescribed threshold. The minister also decides on the basis of the accepted estimates the element of the likely total borrowing for which block loan sanctions will be authorised.

In determining the allocation of transport supplementary grants and loan sanctions the minister will have regard to the progress being made by county councils towards their obligations as imposed by the 1972 Act. To enable decisions to be reached, county councils are required to produce annually, statements of their transport policies and costed programmes for giving effect to them. These documents are known as transport policies and programmes or, in more familiar terms, TPPs. They contain statements of transport objectives and strategies over 10 to 15-year periods and five-year expenditure programmes, rolled forward annually. They cover proposals for investment in public transport, roads and parking; pricing and operation of public transport and parking and maintenance, traffic management and environmental and safety measures of the road network. They also contain statements of past expenditure and physical progress and the extent to which the objectives and policies are being met. TPPs must be compatible with structure and local plans but this is now running into Chapter 5.

This system of block grant is of no small interest to operators of public transport. As far as public transport operators are concerned, the TPP machinery covers the following categories of expenditure by county councils.

(a) Contributions towards the cost, incurred in the provision of public transport facilities by operators including publicly (ie nationally and municipally) owned undertakings, passenger transport executives [including London Transport], private bus operators and British Railways under Section 56 of the 1968 Act.
(b) Direct expenditure by councils on facilities such as bus stations, shelters, interchanges, bus lanes, etc.
(c) Contributions of metropolitan county councils towards expenditure by PTEs under Section 13 of the 1968 Act and Section 202 of the 1972 Act.
(d) Expenditure by a council in connection with public transport under Section 203 of the 1972 Act.
(e) As far as London is concerned, contributions by the Greater London Council to London Transport or to British Railways if for passenger transport purposes under Section 3 of the Transport (London) Act 1969.
(f) Contributions by councils for the support of rural bus and ferry services under Section 34 of the 1968 Act.

(g) Contributions by metropolitan county councils to passenger transport executives for the support of local railway services under Section 20 of the 1968 Act.

It will be of interest to bus managements that all forms of ownership, be they public or private, are eligible for support and that county councils do need to discuss their proposals with operators. Of the main features of the 1968 Act which made provision for some forms of financial aid as were listed earlier on in this chapter, it will be seen that Sections 13, 20, 34 and 56 have now been accounted for by the TPP procedure. Section 39 is a railway item still to be discussed which leaves grants under Sections 32 and 33 (new bus grants and fuel rebate) still outside the TPP machinery. The new bus grant is, in any case, due to be phased out by 1984.

Railways

Financial support of railways in Great Britain has been partly covered by the TPP procedure just described. Passenger transport executives have been given responsibility to consider and support at their discretion and subject to county council approval all local lines within and up to 25 miles beyond the boundaries of their passenger transport areas. The resultant payments which the executives make to British Railways is reimbursed by county councils through the TPP machinery. Non-metropolitan county councils have no specific obligation to support railways although they have powers to do so but they are certainly not the mainstay of the passenger network. Remember it was Section 39 of the 1968 Act which gave authority to the Minister to support at his discretion specific lines. These became known as the local grant-aided services as distinct from inter-city routes. Section 39, however, was repealed by Section 3 of the Railways Act, 1974 and to encroach on to Chapter 8, the same section, by so doing, empowered the minister to impose on the British Railways Board obligations of a general nature with respect to the operation of the whole or any part of its passenger network. This is known as the public service obligation. In short, therefore, British Railways will run whatever it is required to run and will be compensated for any deficits incurred in so doing. This revised arrangement conforms with the transport regulations of the council of the European Communities and Section 14 of the Transport Act, 1978 requires those obligations not to exceed £1,750 million without special authority.

This, then, is how British Railways is reimbursed for running an uneconomic but socially desirable passenger business. The freight side is regarded as being viable in its own right. But herein lies the first problem of implementation. Passenger transport executives, for example, will support (assuming they support anything) only the local passenger services. However, as was said in Chapter 2, it is quite likely that those trains will share the tracks, stations and lineside equipment with longer distance inter-city trains and perhaps goods trains as well. There is also a single management and one set of overhead expenses. By some means, therefore, these common costs have to be apportioned if, in this case passenger transport executives, are to pay their rightful share. Immediately exercises of this kind are encountered and particularly when costs have to be apportioned, an important principle arises. It is one thing to allocate costs according to the extent of use and so calculate the total expense of running any one service. But quite a different thing is how much of those costs would be saved if the service did not operate. In the case of a shared route the answer is likely to be only the direct costs, being the train crew, the fuel and perhaps the train itself. The track and all of the lineside equipment would remain as also would the overheads although nothing would be used as intensively.

This is now introducing the marginal cost theory and the running of PTE sponsored trains over tracks used also by non-PTE traffic is a case in point. To follow up on this example, if PTE sponsored trains did not run, all of the indirect costs might remain. It is for consideration, therefore, what elements of costs should be charged to an outside party (in this case a PTE). The same principle arises if a bus is let out on private hire on say a Sunday afternoon. Should the organiser be charged only the actual costs incurred, bearing in mind that the bus itself, the garage and all that goes with it is there in any case but not otherwise used, or should the full apportionate costs be charged with the danger that the business might be lost? It is, after all, only using assets which are already available. On the other hand, what can be the logic of not charging the full costs? The hirer is enjoying the benefit of the bus which has to be bought, licensed, etc, and in this sense, there would seem to be no reason why he should have the free use of it.

More is to follow about marginal costing but enough has already been said to show that with common use of tracks by different types of traffic there can be no easy solution to this question of allocation of costs. A national railway system does not split easily in this way (in fact, it does not really split at all) and whatever the basis of costing, the result must be theoretical. Formulas have been devised which have already changed once during the lifetime of passenger transport executives. Greater cognisance is now given to the marginal cost principle than was the case when PTEs were first introduced.

Route Costing

So far this chapter has centred on the statutory background for financing the deficits incurred by public passenger transport in Great Britain. It has done little more than list rules as decreed by parliament and it all relates to British law. Apart, therefore, from illustrating at least one method of applying subsidies, there has been little of real interest to overseas students. But they can take heart, the tenor is about to change. What is now to follow has no reference to legal niceties but instead covers a certain product of the finance function which is a most useful tool for those responsible for route and timetable planning. It is the profit or loss statement of each individual route.

The Purpose of a Costing System

There are limitations to what the financial accounting system of a business can provide to enable a firm to be run effectively. Financial accounting falls short on two counts; it gives a historical picture and deals only with the costs of the business in total. This is insufficient for forward planning. It is, of course, true that for fare fixing purposes, total revenue must exceed total costs if the business is to survive but even then, as has just been seen, as far as stage carriage services are concerned, economic circumstances are such that some of the revenue often has to come in the form of a subsidy. Route costing is not concerned with the preparation of data necessary for price fixing. Total costs and average costs per mile are obtainable through normal financial accounting and fares can be set on this basis. It is only in the case of private hire and guaranteed journey operations where neither the service nor the fare need be pre-determined or to a standard scale that each individual job can be separately costed for rate-fixing purposes. Unless, however, a bus or coach undertaking operates only one route, management will need to know the financial viability of each individual service just as a manufacturer needs to know the profitability of each separate product. If it does not, then any changing fortunes of a particular service cannot be identified and the consequent lack of or application of the wrong remedial action would result in an inevitable deterioration of the financial situation.

The subject of route costing has been examined by the Chartered Institute of Public Finance and Accountancy (CIPFA). The resultant recommendations provide a uniformed basis for information to be supplied to county councils in connection with their responsibilities under Sections 202 and 203 of the 1972 Act and for a common approach to be made in the preparation of TPPs.

Classification of Costs

For costing generally, expenses can be classified under four main headings:

(a) cost of materials used directly in the manufacture of goods or provision of a service.
(b) cost of labour directly associated with (a)
(c) other expenses associated with goods or service.
(d) expenses which cannot be directly identified with or attributed to the goods or service.

The first two are variable and are known as direct costs. The third can be regarded as semi-variable whilst the fourth category is usually known as overheads. All four make up total costs. Translated into bus operating terms, the more important of the various expenses may be classified as under. The list of items is by no means exhaustive:

Variable: Drivers' and conductors' wages and expenses
Fuel
Tyres
Servicing of vehicles.

Semi-variable: Vehicle depreciation including spares
Vehicle maintenance
Vehicle licences
Fare collection equipment
Supervisory and traffic staff salaries and expenses
Publicity.

Fixed: General administration including salaries and costs of management and administrative staff
Rent and rates
Legal costs
Maintenance of buildings and plant.

The categorisations are suggested as the most appropriate but they must not be regarded as inviolable. The classifications can alter according to circumstances and the time periods involved. Variable costs relate directly to the service provided and if the particular buses did not run then these expenses should be saved. This is certainly true of fuel and tyres and if vehicles are serviced on a mileage basis, the same reasoning would apply. It is also a fair assumption that if the service did not run, drivers and conductors would not have to be paid. However, staff are generally employed on a guaranteed weekly wage basis and if savings are to be made, any reductions would need to be sufficient to actually save duties and not just to produce shorter spells of work. Turning to the semi-variable costs, if the complete service was withdrawn, the vehicles would be saved, unless, of course, they worked on other routes as well. Nevertheless, assuming that buses did become redundant, they might not be disposed of immediately although they certainly would not have to be replaced when they became time expired. Similarly, publicity costs might be reduced in due course. Whilst overall publicity would still go on, roadside timetable display would no longer be required. Conversely, additional vehicles and publicity are likely to be required when new services are introduced. Inspectors and traffic staff employed in the direct operation of the buses, such as staff controllers and schedule compilers, will vary in numbers according to the quantum of service provided and any substantial changes will have fairly short term effects. On the other hand, the management team and general administration, the costs of offices, other buildings such as garages and the associated equipment and all other such expenses known collectively as the overheads, would still go on regardless of service changes. Even then, however, there would come a time when, if the trends were significant, the overhead expenses would be affected. The size of the administration would, in the long term, require adjustment, new garages might be required or some might be closed as the case may be. One small point here on the subject of the relationship of costs with mileage operated is worth noting in passing. In terms of timetable compilation, supervision, publicity and public relations, an infrequent service could cost more than a frequent one and it would certainly not cost less. With wide headways, each journey has a specific purpose and inconvenience and even hardship might arise if the full service failed to operate. A few journeys of this type might occupy as much time of the people mentioned as would a frequent all day route. But on the other (and major) items, costs would, of course, be less.

Costing Method

So much for the classification of costs. They now have to be apportioned route by route. As far as the direct expenses are concerned, fuel and tyres present no problems as their costs are based on mileage and the mileage is known. Drivers' and conductors' wages and vehicle servicing, which is also mostly wages, is rather different as they are based on time. Certainly the number of hours worked on a given route could be calculated and multiplied up by the rate per hour but this takes no account of a basic guaranteed weekly wage, penalty payments and other costs such as allowances for superannuation and national insurance contributions, sick pay, holidays, uniform, etc. The position becomes yet more complicated if, as is so often the case, platform staff work on more than one service in the course of a duty and the same difficulty arises with all of the semi-variable and fixed costs. They all have to be apportioned route by route on either a time or mileage basis.

Receipts have to be dealt with similarly and here again complications can arise. Whilst cash received by conductors on the bus was at one time relatively straightforward, it is now becoming more difficult to get this information for reasons which are explained in Chapter 5. Furthermore, some theoretical allocations to services have to be made in respect of revenue received in the form of, say, a general subsidy to either maintain a group of routes, to hold down the level of fares or for travel concessions for elderly people, season tickets valid on more than one service, etc.

Once these allocations have been made, the total costs can be set against the total revenue for each service and its financial state determined on a daily, weekly, four weekly or annual basis. To bring each service to a common denominator, all of the figures may be divided by the mileage operated to produce costs, receipts and profit or loss per mile, route by route.

Interpretation

Contained in Chapter 6 is a schedules exercise based on six imaginary services. To quote some equally imaginary but nevertheless realistic figures, an individual route result statement based on the mythical Newtown garage might look something like as is shown in the table at Fig 13. The figures bear a little examination and to do this it is helpful to glance ahead to Chapter 6 to see what sort of services are involved. The timetables and vehicle runnings are set out at Figs 23 and 24. Service 2/A is the mainstay of the network and earns enough surplus not only to cover itself but also to compensate for the combined losses of the remainder. This is an example of cross subsidisation which the bus industry has long since practised and is a reason why the more lucrative routes are jealously guarded by operators through the licensing system to the extent that they are able. If another small operator appeared on the scene he would be interested only in service 2/A and whilst some profit might be made in so doing, traffic would be abstracted and it would, therefore, be at the expense of the established undertaking which in turn could no longer support the unprofitable part of its network. Overall, therefore, passengers would suffer, which goes to show that competition is not always a good thing. But this is digressing. Notwithstanding the highly profitable service 2/A, the system as a whole shows a very meagre profit and prudent management would wish to do something about it if possible.

Looking again at the schedules exercise in Chapter 6, sure enough service 2/A has a regular 15-minute service throughout the day. In other words, it has a consistently good traffic without the need for heavy peaking. Service 1 covers a different type of area where there is a high car ownership. Only a bus every 30 minutes can be justified here except that in the peaks four buses in the hour are required but in the evenings it drops to a 60-minute frequency. This means that vehicle utilisation will not be as good and the buses which work the extra mileage in the peaks will be considerably underutilised. They are, in fact, running numbers 3 and 4 and a look at their scheduled work confirms the point. What this means, therefore, is that the same vehicle costs will be spread over much less mileage (and less revenue). This makes the service results unfavourable in comparison with service 2/A, and in purely financial terms, the route loses money and something must be done. However, ignoring the disturbance to traffic aspect, it could be assumed for this purpose that withdrawal would save the variable and the semi-variable or, in other words, the avoidable costs. This

Route Number	*Costs*				*Receipts*	*Net surplus* (+) *or deficit* (−)
	Variable	*Semi-variable*	*Fixed*	*Total*		
	£	£	£	£	£	£
Mondays to Fridays						
1	4,625	2,158	694	7,477	7,028	−449
2/A	11,242	4,309	1,312	16,863	18,258	+1,395
3	178	169	44	391	221	−170
4	34	122	29	185	52	−133
5	355	343	101	799	470	−329
6	72	139	34	245	104	−141
Total	16,506	7,240	2,214	25,960	26,133	+173

Fig 13 Specimen route results of the services depicted in the schedules exercise in Chapter 6.

means that in the period quoted above a figure of £4,625 plus £2,158 or £6,783 would be saved but the receipts which amount to £7,028 would be lost. Assuming therefore, that the overheads would remain, this course of action would make the undertaking worse off to the extent of £245. This suggests that if fixed costs cannot be reduced then any contribution towards them, which is the excess of receipts over the avoidable costs is better than nothing. To make a worthwhile saving would be to reduce the peak commitment but another glance at bus running 4 shows that this vehicle also works journeys on service 4. If those journeys had to be maintained then any reduction of the service 1 work would result only in crews and vehicles lying idle for longer periods than they already are with minimal savings (tyres and fuel). The other low mileage buses, being runnings 10 and 11 cover services 3, 5 and 6 which are confined to works and school journeys and because of this they show up badly and they would have a very high cost and deficit per mile. If the peak hour extras on service 1 had a different route number and were costed separately they would produce a similarly adverse result but the basic service would be improved and maybe become even profitable, although the total would, of course, be the same. The results of these individual route statements are, therefore, influenced by the numbering system. If services 5 and 6 were re-numbered 2B and 2C respectively and costed within a single route 2 group, the result would show a profit, albeit a lower one. Two loss making services would have been deleted from the books. But this is only playing with figures and that is one reason why it is important to interpret the results correctly.

It was said when discussing costing methods that if the different cost figures produced where divided by the mileage of the route concerned to indicate all such costs on a mileage basis, true comparisons could be made as there would then be a common base. By this means, a situation might be revealed which need not necessarily be detected from the figures as they stand. For example, high crew costs per mile indicate an inefficient duty schedule, high vehicle costs per mile indicate slack in the vehicle runnings, high peaking, etc.

There is one other feature in cost statements which must be recognised. Some services run daily, others on weekdays only and there are those which run on Mondays to Fridays or perhaps even just on Sundays. Whenever they run, the maximum vehicle requirement for urban services is likely to be in the Monday to Friday peaks and the vehicles, fare collection equipment and all of the overheads will be geared to accommodate the maximum level of service which prevails at this time. There is a different type of traffic with different demands and hence different levels of service required on Mondays to Fridays compared with Saturdays and Sundays. Furthermore, premium payments are likely to be made to staff on Sundays and perhaps on Saturdays as well. In planning timetable changes, management will need to see separate results for these days and over recent years Sunday traffic has been particularly vulnerable to abstraction by the private car. If separate figures are to be prepared then it is for note that as vehicles etc must be available for the Monday to Friday peak maximum requirements, they will be there in any case on Saturdays and Sundays regardless of whether they are used. If the Monday to Friday service is to bear the full vehicles costs then the theory is valid. If, however, those (fewer) vehicles which continue to run daily bear only five sevenths of their total costs on Mondays to Fridays, then M-F costs will cheapen but a proportion must be borne on Saturdays and Sundays. This leads in to marginal costing.

Marginal Costing

The marginal cost of running an extra journey or a new service, which is the actual additional cost which would be involved in putting it on or, conversely, what would be saved by taking it off has already been touched upon. There is a big difference between properly allocated costs and marginal costs but it is sometimes appropriate to bear in mind the marginal cost aspect. Consider what the extra cost would be of putting on one more bus or one more service or even one more journey. In the latter case the marginal cost might only be fuel and tyres if there is enough slack in the schedules. Think also about what could be saved in real terms if a service or a journey was withdrawn. Again, in the case of the latter, it might well be only fuel and tyres and it might need only one or perhaps two passengers on the bus to cover that. Both the arguments and the use of marginal costing must, however, be approached with caution. In the short run it may be justified (eg partly utilised vehicle) but in the long run all costs must be covered and to ignore fixed costs completely will court disaster sooner or later.

Referring once again to the schedules exercise in Chapter 6, services 4 and 6 are special school services and they incur deficits. A possibility here is to ask the local education authority to meet the cost of these journeys. If the services were withdrawn the buses concerned would still be required for work on service 1 (running number 4) and service 5 (running number 11) and it is unlikely, therefore, that any actual costs would be saved except fuel and tyres. The marginal costs of these services are, therefore, very small and are likely to be more than covered by revenue. The question then is what should be charged for the service. The writer considers that there is every reason to support the view of the Chartered Institute of Public Finance and Accountancy that whilst accepting that there should always be an element of flexibility to allow for special circumstances, as a general policy, figures should reflect a full allocation of costs. The main reason given is that all costs must be recovered by some means and it is only possible for any one service to make less than its proper contribution to overheads if other services contribute more. Route costing is a long term planning tool and it is important, therefore, that all costs are properly accounted for and any variation from this practice should be done only as an exception based on carefully considered commercial policy.

The problems and effects of marginal costing have already been discussed with reference to railways. The difficulties of allocated bus costs as just described are compounded on the railway with the common use of track and equipment, not only by different services but by different classes of traffic. The application of marginal costing to bodies like passenger transport executives who pay for local train services could have a dramatic effect on costs. The subject has become particularly contentious where the railway must retain and maintain its track and equipment in any case regardless of the operation of any local trains. Instances can arise where such services are withdrawn because of their high allocated, albeit artificial, costs, which means that justifiable savings cannot in practice be realised. Nevertheless, the principles propagated on the bus side should remain regardless of the mode but with emphasis on flexibility and the need to consider also the merits of each case.

Modal Costs

Introduction

Reference was made in Chapter 2 to the characteristics and capacities of the different modes. It was said at the time that it was impracticable to quote actual costs of construction of any fixed track system in view of the substantial variance due to local conditions and the fact that with the effects of inflation they would become rapidly dated anyway. Nevertheless, for comparison purposes, some sort of guide is desirable and although it is the policy of the writer only to deal with general theory, to get some measure of the situation it is helpful in this particular context to examine and interpret the published accounts of three specific undertakings, each of which is, as far as Great Britain is concerned, unique in its way, being that

London Transport operates buses and underground railways
Blackpool Corporation operates buses and electric trams
Douglas Corporation operates horse trams

A classification and weighting of the relevant working expenses appears at Fig 14 in the case of the London Transport Executive and at Fig 15 in the case of the transport departments of Blackpool and Douglas Borough Councils.

Comparison of Bus and Rapid Transit

The figures incorporated in Fig 14 are derived from information contained in the report and accounts of the London Transport Executive for the year 1978. In order to produce a common denominator for comparison purposes, total costs have first been converted to mileage figures (ie per bus mile and per seven-car train mile) and then translated (both bus and train) into factors of 100 based on the bus figure.

It will be seen that the total cost per mile of running a seven-car train is about $4\frac{1}{2}$ times greater than that of a bus (within the same operating territory) mainly because heavy expenditure is involved in the maintenance of the way in the case of the train compared with the relatively minimal cost of vehicle licences in the case of the bus. On the other hand, from statistics which also appear in the Executive's report referred to, it can be ascertained that the bus has accommodation for, on average, 74 people whilst a seven-car train carries about 850. This latter figure assumes full loads with some standing passengers travelling in reasonable comfort. During the height of the peak trains can carry up to 50% more passengers for

	Road per bus mile	Rail per train mile
DIRECT OPERATING AND MILEAGE COSTS		
Staff costs	57.3	143.0
Fuel and power	2.8	51.6
Tyres	0.8	—
Vehicle licences	0.2	—
Servicing rolling stock	2.7	7.8
	63.8	202.4
ANCILLARY OPERATING AND TRAFFIC COSTS		
Station cleaning	—	9.2
Ticket equipment and tickets	0.4	5.1
Training operating staff	1.1	4.8
Support services	1.2	4.7
Rates	0.6	4.5
Insurance and compensation for accidents	0.6	1.1
Police	0.3	1.5
Promotional advertising	0.4	3.4
Revenue support for other bus operators	0.3	—
Miscellaneous	1.5	4.8
	6.4	39.1
MAINTENANCE		
Rolling stock	17.6	48.0
Stations, garages and other buildings	1.6	20.9
Tunnels, bridges and other works	—	9.5
Permanent way	—	23.1
Signals and communications	—	23.4
Lifts, escalators and pumps	—	7.2
Support services	0.8	4.6
Rates	0.2	0.3
	20.2	137.0
GENERAL MANAGEMENT AND ADMINISTRATION	3.7	20.5
DEPRECIATION AND RENEWAL OF ROLLING STOCK, LIFTS AND ESCALATORS, BUILDINGS, PERMANENT WAY AND OTHER STRUCTURES	5.9	54.0
Total expenditure	100.0	453.0

Fig 14 Comparative Mileage Costs of London Transport Buses and Trains with the total Bus Figure based on 100. Note: These figures do NOT represent pence per mile./*Source: Annual Report and Accounts, 1978* London Transport Executive

short distances or, in other words, a total of 1,275. (To digress for a moment back to Chapter 2, with trains at 90-second intervals able to carry up to 1,275 each, there is a theoretical capacity of 51,000 per hour and this, therefore, is a practical demonstration and backing of the figures discussed). It follows that whilst the mileage cost of a seven-car train is some $4\frac{1}{2}$ times more than the bus, its capacity is nearly 12 times greater and this is without any extreme crush loading. This, of course, is reflected in revenue, provided always that the traffic is there to be carried. The message then is clear. If the potential is there, heavy rapid transit has much to commend it, if it is not, it is an expensive luxury. The pattern and density of traffic in the Greater London area is such that the pulse of the metropolis could not beat without its local railway networks but it also explains why other British transport

	Diesel bus per bus mile	*Electric tram per tram mile*	*Horse tram per tram mile*
TRAFFIC OPERATIONS			
Staff Costs	62.1	73.4	80.9
Traffic revenue control	7.4	7.4	4.5
Traffic equipment of routes	1.0	1.7	—
Other expenses	0.3	0.2	0.3
	70.8	82.7	85.7
SERVICING VEHICLES AND ROUTES			
Heating, lighting and cleaning depots	0.5	1.0	0.5
Cleaning and servicing vehicles	3.1	5.0	2.1
Cleaning, salting and sanding track	—	1.0	—
	3.6	7.0	2.6
FUEL AND POWER	5.0	8.4	73.2
TYRES	1.0	—	—
LEASING	0.4	0.4	—
REPAIRS AND MAINTENANCE			
Permanent way	—	26.7	0.3
Electrical equipment of line	—	11.7	—
Vehicles	12.0	31.9	10.4
Buildings and fixtures	—	0.2	7.3
	12.0	70.5	18.0
VEHICLE LICENCES	0.4	—	0.2
RENT AND RATES	0.4	2.7	2.1
MANAGEMENT AND GENERAL EXPENSES	6.4	9.3	29.2
Total Expenditure	100.0	181.0	211.0

Fig 15 Comparative Mileage Costs of Diesel Buses and Electric Trams of Blackpool Corporation and Horse Trams of Douglas Corporation with the total Blackpool Bus Figure based on 100. Note: These figures do NOT represent pence per mile./*Source: Annual Accounts 1978/79* of Blackpool Corporation and Douglas Corporation Transport Departments. These documents were supplied by those undertakings.

authorities outside London are likely to be slow to invest in heavy rapid transit.

Comparison of Bus, Electric Tram and Horse Tram

On the same principle as has just been adopted for comparing the different modes within London Transport, Fig 15 shows the relationship between diesel buses and electric trams at Blackpool and horse trams at Douglas with the Blackpool buses based on 100. Unlike the previous example, two separate undertakings are involved, which is unavoidable and will influence comparisons. Nevertheless, the figures are sufficiently useful to justify examination. Furthermore, because of different cost groupings and method of presenting accounts, cost headings and percentage apportionments in respect of the Blackpool buses are not directly comparable with those contained in Fig 14 in respect of the London buses. It is for this reason that the information is not all contained in the same table. As in the case of buses and trains in Fig 14, the buses and electric trams in Fig 15 are within the same undertaking and the figures are illuminating. The total costs per mile of the trams are some 80% higher than the buses largely because of the cost of the specialised way but the potential capacity of a tram could be up, to, say, 50% greater than that of a bus. Also in this instance there is some scope to reduce staff costs on the trams by one-manning.

Moving on to the horse tram figures, allowance must be made for the fact that they refer to a completely separate undertaking. However, as it is now only Douglas Corporation which uses animal power on a regular basis there are no other figures with which to compare and Douglas itself operates no other mode (its buses have passed to Isle of Man National Transport). The accounts are at least presented in a similar style to Blackpool and notwithstanding the differences, the information is worth considering.

Of particular interest are the figures in respect of motive power and it becomes immediately apparent that there is nothing particularly economic about horses. Admittedly the mileage costs are accentuated by the fact that the trams run only during the six summer months whilst the horses must be fed and cared for throughout the year. But even after allowing for this, as a form of motive power they are not cheap. The following extract from the accounts of Douglas Corporation Transport Department for the year 1978/79 showing costs per mile as far as 'power' is concerned broken down into various parts are of interest:

	Cost per tram mile (p)
Provender	13.9
Stable wages	20.9
Grazing	16.5
Saddlery	2.5
Shoeing	4.9
Stable expenses	1.8
Stables lorry	2.8
Veterinary surgeon	2.1
	65.4

On the credit side in this particular year there was stud appreciation (0.3p) and sale of manure (0.5p). Had the trams run throughout the year instead of for only six months, then, if the same horses worked through, the cost per mile would have been proportionately less. However, at Douglas, horses work for only four months per year, the remaining eight months being spent on grazing pastures.*

Horse power saves oil but these figures show that in terms of finance, it has little to commend it and the vehicles do, of course, also lack capacity and speed.

**Douglas Corporation Horse Trams — The First 100 Years;* Douglas Corporation.

5
The Planning Process

Introduction

Planning is an all-embracing term. Reference was made in Chapter 3 to the different functions within a transport organisation and it will be recalled that planning was one although it is only the larger undertakings which have a separate planning department. The primary functions must, of course, all plan ahead. The engineer must plan his future fleets and where to house them, the accountant will prepare his budget estimates and the operator will consider service revisions to keep abreast with ever changing demands. A well run undertaking should at least do this even though some might still work from day to day, meeting (or failing to meet) problems and circumstances as they arise. But this is all short term planning and calls for no specialist planning department.

Attention was drawn in Chapter 1 to the connection between transport and land use. As part of the discourse on the development of passenger transport, it was appropriate to note the undesirable operating conditions which have been created in some areas as a result of haphazard and uncontrolled growth. The remedy is organised planning and mention was also made in Chapter 1 of the natural resistance in some quarters towards this trend which is seen as placing yet one more restriction on personal liberties. Nevertheless, population grows whilst the total land mass does not and in a country such as Great Britain with a relatively dense population some sort of orderly development which makes the most of limited resources is desirable.

The result is that over the past decade there has, in Great Britain, been an abundance of legislation with its associated green papers, white papers, departmental circulars, government guidelines, statutory instruments and other directives, much of which has been responsible for keeping local government busy in the preparation of various plans. There has also been a call for land use and related transport studies. This has brought forth a need for town and country planners whose work is not part of the subject matter of this book except to note where the products of their labours have repercussions on the providers of public transport.

There is also a newer breed, the public transport planner. He uses what has now become a conventional planning technique which was imported from the United States in the 1950s. It is not proposed to consider this aspect of planning in depth but an indication of the way in which the subject is tackled is nevertheless useful background information for operators and there must, therefore be a brief mention.

The process involves first the definition of the area to be studied and its division into geographical zones for analysis purposes. Account is taken of the existing public transport system which is detailed for computer analysis. Within each zone a series of nodes are created which collectively form a network, the nodes representing the centres from which all trips (by public and private transport) are generated or are attracted to. The next stage is to produce a series of models which simulate the way in which people behave under varying sets of conditions and what their responses would be to changes in basic assumptions. To do this, trip generation figures are compiled which estimate the total number of trips there would be into and out of each zone. From this is developed a trip distribution over the whole network and trip matrices (one for public and one for private transport) prepared which indicate the number of trips passing between each of the zones. The division between public and private transport is referred to as 'modal split'. All of this work is based on data produced in respect of a base year; at the distribution stage there will be revised numbers of trips and different modal splits according to the different assumptions fed in for the design year in question. To assess what the future modal splits might be, a weighting factor is used, the most important inputs of which are the travel time whilst actually on the move and in the case of public transport walking, waiting, changing, etc, together with a monetary cost. Trip assignments are then compiled which relate the specific number of trips to each main road in the case of private transport or to each bus route or railway line in the case of public transport. Alternative policies are by this means evaluated to show the effect of building a new road or providing a new train service or bus route. Different options produce different predictions, all of course worked up on the basic data plus the range of assumptions which have been used.

This transport planning process is a specialist technique and not something which is a supplementary job for the operator although bus and railway managements are able to provide a valuable input to such studies. However, 'theoretical planning' for want of a better term and the methodology of the supporting computer simulated exercises as has been briefly described is a subject which, for more detailed study, is better left to other works. To the operator, it could still seem that notwithstanding the degree of sophistication that this planning process has attained, the fact must remain that much of the input is based on assumptions and that what comes out of a computer can be no more accurate than what is put in. Bus and railway managements might, therefore, sometimes be excused for putting faith in their own instincts and intuitions when considering development projects for public transport and if they do they could on occasions be at variance with what the planners predict.

In view of the foregoing, reference to long term planning will here be confined to the statutory machinery for controlling, among other things, the land use concept together with the requirements which have a direct bearing on local bus and rail services. Much more elaboration will be given to 'operational planning'. This looks at service development in the shorter rather than the longer term (this year, next year rather than sometime, never, 10 years hence or the turn of the century) and which is something closer to the operator's work. This is not to decry the principle of long term planning which can only be built up on facts as are available plus the application of trends and assumptions and other outside influences, known or estimated with the whole being constantly updated with the passage of time. Whether responsibility for shorter term traffic planning is actually allocated to the planning function as discussed in Chapter 3 is a moot point. As, however, the more immediate service changes not only can but must be based on hard fact rather than circumstantial evidence, the work could be undertaken by the traffic branch of the operating department.

Statutory Planning Documents

Structure Plans

The reader was introduced to the connection between transport and land use in Chapter 1 and brief reference was made to structure plans in Fig 8. It is not proposed to trace the history of the planning process which has led to the legislation as it exists today. Nor is it intended to discuss the heavy planning responsibilities which are currently placed on county and district councils beyond the point where they have repercussions on the activities of bus and railway managements. The planning requirements of local authorities in Great Britain, however, are now such that no student of transport can remain ignorant of them regardless of how adept he might be in operating techniques.

To the local planning authorities, it is the Town and Country Planning Act, 1971 which is the legislative background to the present requirement to produce development plans. County councils are required to produce structure plans for their respective county areas which have three functions, being:

(a) to state policies and general proposals for the use of land, which includes the improvement of the environment and traffic management and guidance for development on issues of structural importance.
(b) to interpret national and regional policies in terms of physical and environmental planning.
(c) to provide the framework for local plans which are considered below.

The second function (b) represents the stage where national and regional policies are integrated with those of the counties and is expressed in terms of land use, the environment and the transport system. The county planning authorities are required to concentrate on issues which are of key structural importance and these are likely to include at least the location and scale of employment and housing and the transport system, which embraces roads and private transport as well as public transport. With transport as one of the key issues, the written statement of structure plans must deal with this aspect in depth. The relevant circular from the Secretary of State* to county councils acknowledges that transport policies form an integral part of overall development policies. In so doing, the structure plans provide a framework not only for local plans but also for transport policies and programmes (see below).

Of particular note to bus and railway managements is an indicated need to reflect the policies and financial constraints of the rail and bus operators. Quite clearly there must be a close liaison with county planning officers.

Local Plans

The main function of local plans, which are normally but not necessarily prepared by district councils, is to develop the policy and general proposals of the structure plans and to relate them to precise areas of land. Once again, therefore, public transport managements are involved and the planning authorities have a statutory requirement to give adequate publicitity to their work and opportunity to those people who may be expected to want to make representations to do so.

Transport Policies and Programmes

As was seen in Chapter 4, the purpose of transport policies and programmes produced annually by county councils is to enable central government to reach decisions on finance issues. Nevertheless a brief reference to TPPs is also appropriate here as their preparation

*Department of the Environment Circular 55/77; HMSO.

requires county councils to set out their transport objectives and strategy and the resultant documents must, therefore, by definition reflect and record planning policies. The contents of TPP's must be compatible with structure plans and local plans to which reference has already been made and the submissions are, of course, of no small interest to the providers of public transport.

Public Transport Plans

Passenger Transport Areas

Recorded in Chapter 3 were the various types of passenger transport undertakings which operate in Great Britain, one of which was the passenger transport executive. The concept of PTEs was introduced by the Transport Act, 1968 with which came four passenger transport areas. Within these areas, PTEs were constituted which, for operating purposes, had vested in them all of the existing local municipally owned buses, trolleybuses (there were some at the time), railways and ferries. Subsequently, by virtue of the Local Government Act, 1972 the boundaries of the passenger transport areas were made co-terminus with the new metropolitan counties and additional PTEs were born. The important point in this context, however, is that PTEs have a planning responsibility. They do, in fact, have two basic but distinct functions. One is operating the services which they acquired. The other is planning for all public passenger transport, regardless of the operator and including bus, train and ferry, within their respective areas. More will be said about the planning process later in this chapter. Reference is made in Chapter 8 to the statutory powers (or lack of them) which PTEs have to discharge their responsibilities as decreed by parliament. However, to get back to the point of this paragraph, PTEs were required to prepare policy statements jointly with passenger transport authorities (the policy making bodies consisting of elected representatives) within one year of their formation and passenger transport plans within two years of their formation.

These development plans prepared for designated passenger transport areas differ from other statutory plans in several ways. Being prepared by passenger transport executives, they are the work of organisations which are also the operators of some of the services which are the subject of the plans although admittedly in their role of public transport planning authorities. Another major difference is that the PTE development plans do not call for any specific consultation with outside bodies in the course of their preparation although the policy statements already referred to will have indicated the nature of agreements with other operators and the machinery for securing co-ordination with the planning policies of local authorities. A third feature is that these plans are 'one off'. In other words, they are prepared as soon as possible at the outset of the formation of the PTE and, unlike the plans prepared by the county and district planning authorities, there is no provision for updating. As, therefore, the most recent passenger transport executives were formed in 1974, reference to these plans is now somewhat academic unless, of course, further passenger transport areas should be declared in the future.

Non-Metropolitan Counties

The requirement for development plans for passenger transport areas vide the Transport Act, 1968 has since been extended by the Transport Act, 1978 to embrace the whole of Great Britain. The 1978 Act requires the county councils of all non-metropolitan counties to prepare public passenger transport plans in respect of their areas.

Although in no case is a county council (metropolitan or non-metropolitan) an operator within its own right, non-metropolitan counties co-ordinate the activities of those who do provide the services. However, unlike passenger transport executives, non-metropolitan county councils are not specifically charged with responsibility for railways. The 1978 Act and the powers and duties which it gives to non-metropolitan county councils are, therefore, more of interest to and concern of the managements of bus undertakings, be they nationally owned, municipally owned, privately owned or even PTE owned if an executive runs its buses beyond the boundary of its own passenger transport area. There are differences between transport plans prepared by non-metropolitan county councils and those of the PTE's, the most important being that non-metropolitan county plans are updated annually in respect of each ensuing five-year period and in the course of preparation there must be consultation with bus operators, district councils and other bodies who might be concerned.

Policy for the Inner Cities

Referring back to the general planning responsibilities of national and local government, there is one other edict of the British government which is of interest to bus operators. Concern has been expressed at the decay of the inner areas of many of the large towns in the UK and a white paper *Policy for the Inner Cities** published in 1977 set out a series of policies to be followed in order that they might be revitalised. It was noted in the white paper, among other things, that if the objectives are to be achieved commerce and industry in the inner areas must be efficiently serviced by transport and local authorities were asked to consider improvements such as traffic management schemes and parking facilities as part of their normal programme. The need for attractive bus

**Policy for the Inner Cities*; Cmnd 6845, HMSO.

facilities was also stressed which could mean service revisions. To this end it was suggested that consideration should be given to more cross-town services, thereby making it easier for people to travel locally within and across central areas. The white paper referred to was subsequently backed by the Inner Urban Areas Act, 1978.

Modal Split

Public and Private Transport

Reference was made in Chapter 2 to the private car in relation to bus priorities where it was recognised that people want cars and that politicians are not likely to be anxious to impose restraints without very real justification. To do so would be an unwarranted intrusion into personal liberties and would in any case jeopardise the future support of the electorate. Bus and railway managers themselves are probably also motorists. Their staff certainly are as witness the requirement for car parks at garages and depots. In their professional capacity, however, busmen would like to be rid of the congestion on the roads which cars create. On the other hand, and this point was also made in Chapter 1, they would not wish all of the 'drive to work' fraternity to leave their cars at home and seek conveyance by bus. This would place an impossible strain on peak hour resources and the additional heavy surges of traffic would also be costly to accommodate. If the cars once left at home were used by wives in the daytime instead of the bus, the diseconomies would be compounded with even more accentuated peaks. Financial stability calls for a levelling out of the peaks and it is extra traffic in the slacker periods when vehicles and staff are already available which is constantly sought.

To summarise, therefore, the case has been made for bus priorities. Cars delay buses and abstract their traffic but in urban areas some of that abstracted traffic would not be economic to carry anyway. In short, there are times when the bus needs preferential treatment over the car but only in very selective circumstances would it wish to annihilate it. Looking at the overall transport picture, ie, including also the highway input, there might well be a case to accept the cost of a heavy peak on the buses as there could be adequate compensation through the elimination of some of the expenditure on roads together with all the related problems. In this case, however, there are as has been seen political reasons why this principle is not likely to be pushed too far. Nevertheless, at least in theory the concept does support the principle of buses and highways being funded through a common set of accounts.

At this stage it is worth considering exactly what is public and what is private transport and like the progression from bus to train, there is a stage when distinction becomes blurred. Consider the following:

(a) Private car
(b) Contract hired car
(c) Hired car with driver
(d) Taxi
(e) Car sharing, social car scheme or 'jitney'*
(f) Demand responsive bus
(g) Bus

At the extremities of the scale — (a) and (g) — there is no doubt in which camp they lie; (d) to (g) all 'ply for hire' but the writer does not accept that this is necessarily the definition of public transport whilst (c) is also often a freely available facility and all except (a) represent services which are provided for the public at large to move around without the need to actually purchase a vehicle. Those in classifications (a) and (b) produce the same parking problems but those in (a) to (e) are all extravagant in road space whilst on the move. Once a taxi (d) has been engaged, the occupant is just as much a part of private transport as is the owner driver or the passenger in a chauffeur driven car. It is submitted that the borderline comes with the demand responsive bus (dial-a-bus), being a mini or midi bus carrying passengers within a defined area but in accordance with their specific requirements. Nevertheless, there is controversy on what can be regarded as public and what as private transport just as there is no universal definition of a bus as was discussed in Chapter 2 in connection with bus priorities. The writer suggests that highway and planning authorities should for their purposes classify the taxi, in fact everything from (a) to (e) as private transport and formulate their proposals accordingly. The only real justification which the author can see for the inclusion of the taxi in the public transport sector apart from the absence of parking problems is when it assumes the role of a feeder to long distance transport. In the knowledge that taxis are available at the extremities of the journey a person might be willing to travel by public transport throughout (say train). In the absence of such a facility he could well elect to go all the way by car.

Road and Rail

It has been stated that when roads become overloaded it is helpful if people can be persuaded to turn from private to public transport. This was said in the context of car to bus. From a traffic management point of view it is even more advantageous if there is a shift from road to rail and railway administrations never cease to advertise this fact (provided always of course that for commuter services

*A slang term to describe a large taxi style vehicle which follows bus routes on an unscheduled basis and picks up passengers as required. The practice is prevalent in some urban centres overseas, Mexico City and Tel Aviv in Israel being examples. The nearest approach in the UK is a shared taxi.

somebody else meets the deficit). Nevertheless, it is recognised that the railway can have an important part to play in urban transport; governments accept to varying degrees the benefits which accrue from expenditure in this way and as far as Great Britain is concerned, provision was made in the 1968 Transport Act for the railway contribution to urban transport to be taken into proper account. To encroach a little on to Chapter 8, it is Section 20 of the 1968 Act which, subject to implementation by the minister, places a duty on passenger transport executives to review and if considered desireable to support and develop local railway services within designated areas.

Railway Development

The reasons why a dense railway network was built up in the 19th century was explained in Chapter 1. In due course many of the local lines (and some of the longer distance ones as well) became heavily uneconomic and in 1963 Dr (now Lord) Beeching produced proposals for eliminating most of them. Many of these recommendations were implemented with the result that although in some cases the tracks and the formation are now lost for ever, being swallowed up by new development, others remain in either a derelict state or are used for freight purposes only. However, circumstances have changed somewhat since Lord Beeching did his work as whilst railway operation has not become any more economic, roads have become more and more overcrowded. In terms of cost benefit there is now a case to consider the resuscitation of certain lines where predictions suggest that they would have a traffic value if only to relieve the pressure on the highway system and avoid some of the heavy capital expenditure and environmental repercussions which would otherwise follow. The classic example is at Toronto in Canada where, under the auspices of the Government of Ontario, a main line railway has been upgraded and a frequent local commuter train service provided, extending some 59 miles across the metropolis, in order to attract some people out of their cars and thereby moderating demands on the adjacent highways. In Great Britain similiar circumstances led, as has already been noted, to the 1968 Act and in particular to Section 20. PTEs have now had their powers for about 10 years with the result that in places such as Liverpool, Birmingham and Glasgow new life (and money) has been injected into the local railway systems and new or restored facilities have emerged.

The chain of events necessary when reviewing local railway networks to decide which sections, if any, are suitable for retention and development may be summarised as follows:

(a) Assess future traffic potential:
   This must take account of proposed land use developments. Information could be supplemented by household surveys to test public attitudes towards future travel habits.

(b) Examine alternative methods of serving the corridor:
   As far as public transport is concerned, the alternatives would probably be bus or express bus.

(c) Ascertain whether the parallel roads are likely to become overloaded:
   If there is likely to be a highway problem (which might also mean a bus problem) in the area, the case for the railway would be that much greater.

(d) Examine the practicalities and the extent of the railway facilities that could be provided:
   This exercise will involve consideration of track capacities, bearing in mind any existing traffics. Also to be considered would be the provision of station car parks for park and ride and any repercussions on the surrounding bus route network, bearing in mind the need for feeder facilities. Other limited new works might be desirable such as revised track arrangements, connecting links, new stations, etc.

(e) Evaluate the cost of the railway service:
   This is a complicated process as the railway infrastructure is likely to be shared with long distance traffic and goods trains. Reference to this aspect was made in Chapter 4.

(f) Undertake a cost benefit study:
   Even if a new or augmented train service carries heavy loadings, the chances are that it will still produce a financial deficit. On the other hand, savings elsewhere, particularly on highway expenditure and other benefits which might accrue to the area such as increases in land values and rateable values could justify the project and these externalities, therefore, need to be evaluated.

Very briefly, this is the planning process necessary before a railway line is developed. Under certain circumstances it might be necessary to go beyond the upgrading of a suburban main line and look at the extension of or provision of a new rapid transit type system. In Great Britain this is, in fact, the case in London and Newcastle respectively and there are many centres overseas where new systems of this kind are being developed.

Operational Planning (Buses)

Services Provided

Operational planning is very much a borderline issue between the planning process and commercial practices. The standard of service provided and the criteria for service provision which is to be considered shortly in this chapter certainly reflects commercial policy. Furthermore, the operating department cannot be divorced from this issue as that is where responsibility lies for implementing the proposals and the chances are that it is the operating manager, being the employing officer, who will have to agree the resultant time and duty schedules with his platform staff. Nevertheless, that is an organisational problem. For this purpose, here is a convenient point at which to consider shorter term planning which must be preceded by a brief review of the types of services which are provided.

The legal definition of different types of service as is explained in Chapter 8, ie stage, express and contract carriages, does not necessarily constitute an accurate description in commercial terms of the types of services provided. To produce yet another order of progression, the following will illustrate in traffic (as opposed to legal) terms the different groups of services which collectively constitute a road passenger transport network:

(a) Local town services
(b) Special works and school services
(c) Orbital services
(d) Rural services
(e) Inter-urban services
(f) Local limited stop services
(g) Long distance express services

These different types of services cater for as many different types of traffic and the distinctions are more apparent in some areas than in others. A small town might not even be large enough to support separate local services, what short distance traffic there is being catered for by inter-urban services. On the other hand, a very large urban (plus suburban) agglomeration could produce some long and complex local routes and the inter-urban facilities, ie facilities to neighbouring urban areas, probably on the other side of a tract of open country, become at least limited stop but often closer to the long distance express category.

Although even a small pocket of population might support an odd bus running around locally, it is not until a built-up area reaches upwards of, say, 40-50,000 people that a discernible network of town services begins to emerge. At this stage, the local system tends to become more self-contained (although not necessarily under separate management) and passengers become selective between the short and the longer distance services. This distribution of traffic is often encouraged by protective minimum fares, at least in the out-town direction on the inter-urban (trunk) routes, a practice which is considered further in Chapter 7. Town services may be: radial, ie terminating at the centre and proceeding outwards like the spokes of a wheel; cross-town, ie linking places on the opposite extremities of the built-up area but routed via the centre; and orbital, ie circular or part circular services without touching the centre. Superimposed on these regular services are likely to be special facilities for works and schools which do not conform to the regular pattern and which run in accordance with specific rather than general requirements.

Cross-town routes have particular relevance in this study of urban transport. They are advantageous compared with separate services which radiate out from the centre in that they provide a useful facility for people who wish to travel either within but across the central zone or from the outer suburbs through to the other side, even if only for a short distance. In other words, it becomes possible to have a direct bus between many more pairs of points, thereby providing a more attractive and useful service. Operationally there are disadvantages as will be considered in Chapter 11 where it will be seen that for control purposes there is an advantage in routes which do turn in the centre. A compromise would be to run only a short distance to the opposite boundary of the central zone; an idea which the writer does not support.

Consider the diagrams below showing services converging at a Town centre from six separate neighbourhoods. In (i) all turn at the centre, in (ii) they are linked to run across the town and in (iii) they are projected to give a limited cross-centre facility. The advantages and disadvantages are:

(a) It is clear that in the case of example (iii) additional

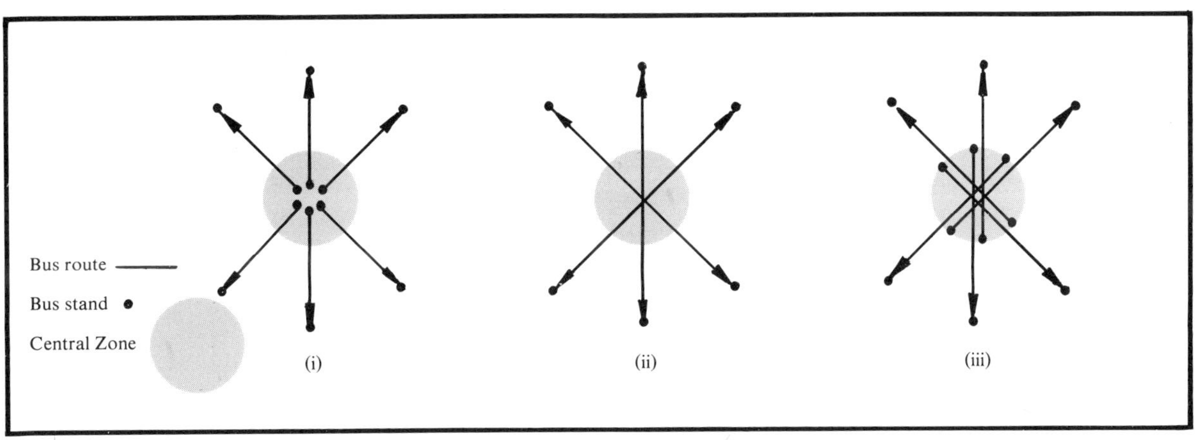

mileage is incurred in the most heavily congested part of the town and this is likely to be unacceptable on the grounds of traffic congestion, particularly as the resultant facilities would be inferior to that provided by example (ii).

(b) The extra mileage of (iii) would involve additional schedule costs in the form of vehicles and staff, again with inferior facilities compared with (ii). On the other hand, example (ii) saves stand time in the centre which is 'dead' time and can, therefore, only reduce schedule costs, not only compared with (iii) but also with (i) as well.

(c) Example (iii) does not remove the disadvantage of (i) that standing space must be found in the busy central area where space is likely to be scarce anyway. Example (ii) requires no such facility.

Certainly for local services in a closely knit urban area, cross-town services provide a useful facility and have much to commend them.

A rural service is one which is usually regarded as radiating outwards from an urban centre into the surrounding countryside to serve various villages and hamlets. Rural communities may also be served by the main trunk inter-urban routes depending on geography and whether a village happens to be conveniently located for this purpose. It is quite usual for the trunk routes to make limited deviations for this purpose but there needs to be a balance between the demands of the through and the intermediate riders. Other devices for serving sparsely populated areas take the form of postal buses and other vehicles designed for the carriage of both goods and passengers, community buses, etc. These different types of operation are considered later in this chapter and also in Chapter 7.

En route diversions of trunk routes to serve what would otherwise be isolated rural communities are more likely to be tolerated if through traffic is also catered for by a faster parallel limited stop service using a direct route. Urban limited stop services are also not unknown, being designed to cater for blocks of traffic which regularly travel between given pairs of points. Not only is a faster journey time more attractive to passengers, it is also more economical in terms of vehicles and staff if more trips can be worked in the same overall time. This is particularly valuable in the peaks when any saving of vehicles and crews has a marked effect on total operating costs. In practice, however, there are also disadvantages which again is a matter for Chapter 7.

The final classification, being the express services or, in other words, the coach business, caters for the longer distance rider, usually on a pre-booked basis, with vehicles expected to have a higher standard of comfort. Even here, some services are faster than others and it is those routes which utilise the motorway network which have the greatest premium on speed. However, although this category is strongly allied to the bus industry and many coaches have common managements with the buses, use the same bus/coach stations and often the garages, coach operation as such constitutes neither urban nor rural transport and the particular peculiarities of this type of operation falls outside the scope of this book.

Criteria for Service Provision

The criteria which determines what, where and how much bus service will be provided is rapidly changing. Remember what was said in Chapter 1. Transport was pioneered by private enterprise. Speculative bus and railway managements set up in business and earned their livelihood by providing facilities which the people needed. They created demands and they met demands. The more responsible elements within the bus industry accepted that they were providing a service which was essential to the new found life of the community and they offered comprehensive facilities within what they had come to recognise as their operating territories. Some routes were profitable, others were not, but overall there was a financial surplus. The criteria for service provision was clear; the undertaking as a whole had to pay its way. Within this overall constraint maximum facilities were provided, distributed according to need whilst endeavouring to ensure that nobody was unreasonably isolated. Up until the 1950s it was possible to give a service by allowing these economic forces of supply and demand to follow their course. Traffic managers were able to use their discretion and everybody could be satisfied as much as the public ever can be satisfied on matters of this kind. But times have changed. It is not now always possible to support the weaker routes out of those which are profitable. Subsidies are necessary and once this happens, then gone is the economic indicator and gone also is the long established criteria for service provision. Its need, however, has by no means gone but what is to take the place of judgement by commercial viability remains a very big but unanswered question. The problem is not as much one for the operator as for the third party which provides the subsidy and which in Great Britain is county councils. The operator, regardless of the form of ownership, must still pay his way and in the absence of subsidies, unprofitable routes just have to be withdrawn. But the elected representatives who spend public money to support public transport require some sort of measure in order to determine the level of service which should be provided. It is to this body of people that the criteria for service provision has particular interest.

If public transport is to be partially paid for out of rates and taxes then those ratepayers and taxpayers resident in the more sparsely populated areas will not respond kindly to a refusal to provide a service on the grounds that there will not be a sufficient number of users to justify it. The greater proportion of revenue support in relation to cash collected from fares, the stronger will any resentment become and the maximum dilemma would arise should a free service with no fares charged at the time of travel ever be introduced. The theoreticians will no doubt seek a formula to determine whether or not any specific request for a bus service should be met, what level of frequency should be provided and whether the existing pattern is right. The production of such a formula, however, produces a host of imponderables although the need for some sort of guidance on service provision when one side of the equation (ie revenue) is no longer an adequate measure must, nevertheless, be acknowledged.

A basic criterion is, of course, demand, but if the only consideration is to maximise passenger miles then the more thinly populated areas where loadings could never be heavy would not qualify for a service. Once a facility is instituted, however, demand, if only by trial and error, can set the frequency, but only down to a certain level, below which the timetable could become too unattractive to be worthwhile. Also for consideration is the route network and its density, particularly in urban areas. It is for decision, for example, if the overall vehicle provision and hence the quantum of service is set, whether a large number of different roads within a residential district should be covered by relatively infrequent services or whether a lesser number of roads should have much higher frequency services.

All of this indicates a need for some pre-determined standards. Consider the following parameters:

(a) Distance which a person may be expected to walk to a bus stop.
(b) Minimum frequency.
(c) Minimum load factor.
(d) Length of wait if first available bus has no accommodation.

If (a), (b), (c) and (d) could be quantified then surely at least some standards will have been set and hence progress made towards determining criteria for service provision. The evaluation of these factors, however, can only be subjective as different people will have different interpretations on what might be regarded as reasonable. The British government has issued guidelines* which includes one of these aspects. It is suggested by the minister that housing estates should be designed so that the maximum walking distance to a bus stop is 400 metres which represents a walking time of about five minutes.

It is not sufficient, however, just to quantify these suggested four component parts as they have a bearing on each other, one can influence another and furthermore, standards may have to vary according to circumstances. The distance to walk to a bus might be acceptably (and usually has to be) longer in the country than in town or perhaps longer if the terrain is flat but not so far if it is very hilly and a higher load factor might be expected in the peaks than at midday or in the evening. Items (a) and (b) throw back to network densities already mentioned. Minimum acceptable frequencies certainly vary between urban and rural areas. The town dweller is not timetable conscious, at least for local journeys. He wants only to walk to the bus stop and wait for one to come. He does not want to walk very far and he does not want to wait very long and this means for the first vehicle which has available accommodation. The writer is of the opinion that the suggested maximum 400 metres walk could prove over generous in application even in urban areas as it might produce a very dense network, in which case, either frequencies or load factors would fall below acceptable levels. Consider the diagrams at Fig 16 which illustrate a hypothetical road layout in a housing estate with alternative possible bus routes. Option (i) provides for maximum coverage; option (ii) shows maximum concentration on a centre spine road. What is an acceptable load factor has not yet been considered but for the time being, suppose

Below: **Fig 16. A hypothetical road layout in a housing estate with alternative possible bus routes.**
Note: Every household would be within approximately $\frac{1}{4}$ mile of a bus in option i and within about $\frac{1}{2}$ mile in option ii but the frequency of the service in option ii would be three times that of option i.

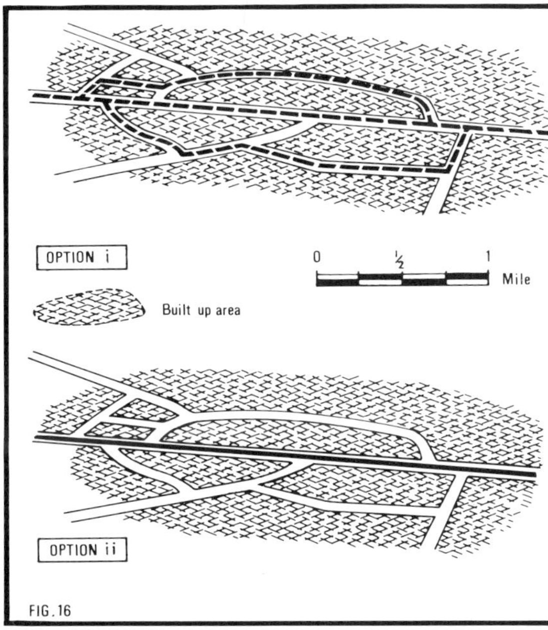

Bus Operation in Residential and Industrial Areas; Department of the Environment Circular 82/73, HMSO.

that whatever it is, the traffic generated by the local residents is sufficient to support six buses per hour or, in other words, a 10-minute headway on the one route as shown in option (ii). If alternative (i) was adopted, the resources would be fragmented and instead of a 10-minute headway on one route there would be three separate routes each with a 30-minute frequency. In this case, it is certainly true that some people would not have to walk as far to and from the bus but it is submitted that the resultant frequencies could be unattractive, passengers would have to be timetable conscious and in the event of late running or cancellations stop selection would become a matter of chance and intending passengers might see a bus pass, perhaps only a few yards away, but not at the point where they are standing. There could also be selective inadequacies (for example, waiting for the next bus because it goes nearer to home and then there is no room on it) and timetables could give rise to complaints (such as, who is to be favoured with the last bus out of town).

All of this suggests that the writer is somewhat critical of those systems which cover as many roads as possible with a lot of relatively low frequency services. But there is, nevertheless, a limit on how far one can go the other way; the limit being the distance which a passenger might be expected to walk to the bus.

Consider now factor (b), the minimum acceptable frequency, which is allied to but nevertheless distinct from factor (d) which is what might be regarded as an acceptable wait for the first bus with available accommodation. Common with factors (a) and (c), the standards adopted are bound to be influenced by the density of population in the area concerned but assume for the moment that the services in mind are running through high density residential districts. The question is, how frequent should the buses run to qualify as an acceptable facility, that is, a service which is convenient to use without pre-planning. At busy periods, frequency is not the only consideration; what is more important is how long a person must wait before he is actually able to board. This comes back to the distinction between peak and off peak periods. As far as the all day service is concerned, if an acceptable standard is to be maintained then the frequency should not fall below a certain minimum even if, arithmetically, all passengers could be accommodated with a wider headway. It is in the peaks when additional buses must be provided and when load factors are acceptably higher that the maximum wait becomes critical and sets yet another standard.

There remains to consider factor (c), being the minimum number of people that should be on a bus, below which its justification becomes a matter of doubt. Once again, there is a distinction between peak and off peak periods but there are further complications. The normal traffic pattern of an urban bus service which radiates out from a town centre is a general pick-up of passengers progressively through the central zone, a maximum point not far beyond the periphery of the centre and a gradual set-down right through to the outer terminal. It would seem that the place to measure loadings is at the maximum traffic point but even this will not give the complete answer as demand could justify only some of the runnings proceeding through to the extremity of the route with others turning short. Another feature is that some journeys will be popular; others might be very lightly used, but if they were not operated the minimum frequency criterion would not be met. Loadings will, therefore, probably need to be averaged out over all journeys before a satisfactory conclusion can be reached.

This, then, is the more practical background to setting the criteria for service provision. Little of what has been said so far, however, will assist those responsible for spending public money in deciding just what sort of a service they should support. Furthermore, there is still another standard, so far not discussed in this context but one which has a considerable bearing on subsidies, and that is fare levels. This is something which also impinges on Chapters 4 and 7 which deal with the various methods of determining subsidies and the commercial aspects of rate fixing respectively. The three factors (standard of service, amount of subsidy and fares) are inter-dependent and their respective values cannot be set in isolation. If standards are determined for any two then the level of the third is automatically fixed. If those providing a subsidy wish to set the amount of such assistance and set the fares then they must accept the level of service which can be provided. If they wish to set the amount of subsidy and the level of service then the resultant fares must, together with the subsidy, cover costs. If the service and the fares are set, then the net deficit must be met whatever it might be. Those responsible for meeting the bill can only get what they pay for. They have, therefore, to balance what they want against what they are prepared to pay and to do this they must determine their own criteria according to needs and preferences. But still the big question remains — how to quantify those needs and preferences.

One reason why there is no readily available answer to this problem is that even now the question is not often posed. Most existing bus networks, even the heavily subsidised ones, are still very much as they were built up in the days of commercial enterprise. There may have been a few route and timetable adjustments to take account of changing patterns and levels of demand but apart from that, things remain as they always were and even if new criteria was introduced it would not be easy to implement as people are creatures of habit and seldom take kindly to change without very good reason. Such considerations come mainly when in the absence of revenue support, services come up for withdrawal or where a rural area is intensively developed and there comes into being a large new housing estate or a new town to be served for the first time. Under these circumstances it is appropriate that there should be some criteria for service provision.

Suppose now that an attempt is made to quantify the suggested factors (a) to (d). Begin with some arbitrary price tags which look about right. It has already been suggested that there will have to be different standards for urban and rural areas. For a working example, therefore, concentrate on urban areas (suburban would be a better term as that is where most people live) which could be defined as those which have a population density of, say, not less than 10,000 per square mile. For territory of this type, on weekdays (the situtation is likely to be different on Sundays) the following standards might be reasonable:-

(a) Half a mile to walk to a bus.
(b) Minimum regular frequency not less than every 12 minutes.
(c) Minimum load factor 25% increased to 95% in the peaks if there is more than a 12 minute service.
(d) An actual wait in the peaks of up to 10 minutes if and after the first bus has departed full. (This assumes that buses are on time and are not delayed by traffic and are 'bunching'.)

These are suggestions only. The next step is to see whether they are practical in application. Implementation on these lines could result in over provision and excessive cost and it would be helpful to have an overriding governing factor. One possibility lies in total population figures. In Great Britain in 1977 a population of some 54.3 million was served by about 46,000 buses* which averages out over the country as a whole at about one bus for every 1,200 people. This of course is only a guide but it is a good guide. Those concerned will wish to fix their own levels and demand will in any case be influenced by fare scales and by car ownership, both of which vary from area to area. Even so, buses per unit of population does give a basis on which to start. If this figure, whatever it might be but for the present say 1,200, becomes a fifth dimension (e) superimposed on (a) to (d) above, the criteria would then become sufficient to develop a realistic exercise. In other words, services meeting the criteria laid down in (a) to (d) could be designed within the overall constraint of (e). The likelihood is that at the first attempt things will not work out that way and one or more of the specifications will have to be relaxed, being more buses or lower standards, determined, as has already been indicated, according to local circumstances and preferences. It must be reiterated, however, that a network exercise such as this is really only feasible when planning for a new town or the like although the standards as determined should be suitable for application when changes are required within established systems.

Transport Statistics — Great Britain; HMSO. This is an arbitrary figure calculated by accounting for all buses and coaches in the public sector and discounting all in the private sector which will approximate a bus total but exclude coaches.

Route Planning

Route planning was partially covered by the previous sub-section which dealt with the criteria for service provision and where the difficulties involved in keeping rigidly to a pre-determined standard were seen. The subject will be considered here not from the angle of placing everybody within a short walk of a bus but planning a route which for the passengers achieves maximum benefit for the greatest number of people and for the operator attracts as many people as possible on to the bus.

Consider again the types of service provided as listed (a) to (g) earlier in this chapter. All are designed with specific traffic flows in mind. Most services follow a fairly progressive route between a pair of terminal points although this is not essential. What is important is that in taking people where they want to go, too many other passengers are not involved in riding on a bus which follows an unnecessarily circuitous route which is both irritating and time consuming. Routes can, however, be of the devious kind as, for example, those which follow the course of an arc, if there are alternative direct facilities for through passengers who are not therefore required to travel the long way round. Other services may follow a circular route or adopt loop workings at terminals. It was noted earlier that a full service is not always required right through to the end of the journey. This point is often met by the introduction of bifurcations at the outer ends where routes split in the form of a fish tail giving a choice of less frequent services to different places. These different route patterns are considered in greater detail in Chapter 6.

Except for the orbital and special services, most routes are likely to penetrate the centre of at least one town and this can perhaps be regarded as the key to route planning. Consider the places to which most people want to go; shops, commercial centres, places of employment, places of recreation, etc, or, in other words, the traffic magnets. Remember also the role of the bus as a feeder to train. This is something which the student will find difficult to forget as road/rail co-ordination and the systems concept is now a very fashionable planning approach, being hailed by some almost as the panacea for all transport ills. Certainly the bus is an essential and effective feeder to rail but it also has its own established traffics and large numbers of passengers should not be inconvenienced if only an occasional person wishes to transfer to a train. At times there is a case to divert a route via the station but such consideration can be, like the computer analysis sytem, very much a desk exercise, the findings of which are not, in the event, always substantiated by passenger use. Operators need to be circumspect when introducing devious routes for special purposes. Sometimes occasional journeys are so diverted to serve such as railway stations, works or schools where there is an established and heavy demand which is quite acceptable but the practice can become confusing to both passengers and staff if taken too far.

Next consider the traffic affinity between major centres. There is likely to be a movement to and from neighbouring towns and the resultant inter-urban services can often perform a dual role by catering for both intermediate and through riders. This introduces an important concept in route planning. It has already been said that radial services pick up in the centre and then gradually set down in the environs with perhaps only a very few people riding right through to the end of the journey. Even if the bus started with a full load, the chances of seats becoming vacant on the way and not being refilled are virtually certain. A similar process takes place in reverse when travelling towards town. The routes with traffic magnets only at one end must have a 'thin end' at the other with seldom the chance of good loadings all the way. On the contrary, services which have traffic magnets at each end are more likely to start picking up again as the first batch of passengers begins to alight. To that extent, therefore, inter-urban services have a natural advantage in terms of passenger loadings and they are often the mainstay of many of the provincial networks.

Another important aspect of route planning is any physical difficulties such as weight restrictions in the form of sub-standard roads or overbridges, height limitations caused by underbridges, trees, etc, narrow or tortuous roads or any other factor which might preclude the operation of a standard type bus. It also pays to ensure that the roads concerned have been adopted by the local highway authority. If they have not it is politic to obtain an indemnity from the owner (probably a private developer) against any damage to the surface which buses might cause before a service is inaugurated. A recent and more deliberate obstruction to buses and one to which reference was made in Chapter 2 is the now fashionable concept of segregating pedestrians from vehicular traffic or, in other words, pedestrianisation. It was said that it might be very nice for shoppers to wander in a traffic free environment decorated with ornamental street furniture but those same people do not take kindly to walking further to the bus stop with heavy baskets. Neither do through riders appreciate a twisting, longer and more costly route if that is what it means in order to avoid a closed street. Certainly the bus is a large vehicle and it is inevitable that there are limitations on where it can run but the artificial restriction of pedestrianisation is something which could be avoided. There are numerous examples where shopping streets are restricted to buses only and the Government Circular *Bus Operation in Residential and Industrial Areas** indicates that official policy is quite open to such an arrangement. It is one way of ensuring that the natural advantages of the bus are not lost. It is not surprising, therefore, that bus managements press for an extension of this practice when proposals for pedestrianisation are produced which involve serious disturbance to established routes without any satisfactory alternatives.

Stops and stands are also important issues to be determined and here the operator is to some extent in the hands of the local highway authority. The subject was considered in Chapter 2. In areas of new development, bus stop sites are often predetermined, hopefully after consultation with bus managements, but generally there is a common objective by all concerned which is for vehicles to stop in the most convenient places for passengers subject to physical considerations. Once again, however, there seems to be a desire by planning authorities backed by government policy to segregate pedestrians from vehicular traffic as witness the networks of footpaths which appear in some of the newly developed housing estates. Whilst it is no problem for the bus operator to stop at points suitable for these footpaths and what happens to passengers after they have alighted is not his responsibility, the writer does consider it unfortunate that such policies are being pursued which could in due course well lead to requests from passengers for buses to stop elsewhere. Touching now on Chapter 12, the fact of life that violence, robbery and other undesirable behaviour is increasing should be recognised. Many women are now nervous of using narrow and lonely footpaths and in the years to come it might be quite unsafe to do so as it is in parts of the USA today. To avoid this, some pedestrians are already taking unauthorised routes which sometimes involve walking along and crossing roads, including those which are used by buses, which are not designed for that purpose.

It is the opinion of the author that unless applied very selectively, segregation of foot and vehicular traffic in whatever type of area, be it commercial, residential or industrial, will, in the long run and for various reasons, make no net improvement to either convenience or personal safety and as a matter of general policy there is a case for some rethinking.

These, then, are the principles which need to be observed in route planning. It is clear that the operator is not the sole arbiter of where his buses will run. Neither can he expect to be as he is only one of many users of a shared way and he is not the highway authority. But there are ways in which planning authorities could assist. Of particular importance is the fundamental requirement that buses should be afforded proper penetration into commercial, industrial and residential areas and such

**Bus Operation in Residential and Industrial Areas*; Department of the Environment Circular 82/73 HMSO.

access should not be prejudiced by traffic management or pedestrianisation schemes. The priorities must be right and this applies in more senses than one.

Special Services

The types of services discussed so far are those which provide continuous all day facilities for general purposes and cater for the predominant traffic flows. Special services cater for specific traffics which require something different to what the basic network provides. They are introduced when there is sufficient demand to warrant the provision of buses solely for this purpose and the routes either serve places which do not otherwise have a bus or they permit a through journey to be made which otherwise could be undertaken only by changing vehicles. Routes of this type run mostly to factories and schools.

Rural Services

It was the rural services which were first hit when the fortunes of the bus industry began to deteriorate in the 1960s. It was also the rural services which were the subject of study by one of the earlier government appointed committees and which subsequently reported (the Jack Report) as referred to in Chapter 1. Again it was the rural services which first qualified for financial assistance; Section 34 of the Transport Act, 1968 made provision for this although what actually constituted a rural service was never specifically defined. Today it is still the rural services which are most in need of outside assistance and the criteria for service provision has a particular application for this type of operation. The bodies which meet the deficits (in Great Britain the county councils) must again determine standards but unless an astronomical amount of money is to be spent in moving empty seats along country lanes then, whatever the locals might think, very different standards have to be set compared with what might be applied in urban areas. In rural districts the criteria for service provision is much more directly related to specific needs and the degree of hardship which would arise if no service at all was provided. Country dwellers (at least those without private transport) have long since adjusted their way of life around occasional bus journeys which might run only once or twice a week although even this limited provision is likely to be costly.

Particularly apposite to rural services is the reference to thin ends made earlier in this chapter. A route which on leaving town gets into the country, serves a few hamlets and finishes up on the edge of a field never ever had much chance of commercial viability, even if it did run only on market days and bank holidays. Remember what was said in respect of inter-urban services. They have infinitely better opportunities and the rural areas which are located astride or close to such routes can be served much more economically. It is the places which lie away from these main arteries which pose the problem and it is the ways and means of serving these otherwise isolated rural communities which are for discussion here.

The particular difficulties associated with the provision of services for rural areas arise from the paucity of the population which means that demand can never be consistently good. Even if a work or shopping bus might carry some people there is unlikely to be a demand sufficient to make proper use of vehicles and staff throughout the day. Traffic cannot easily be spread as workers, shoppers and schoolchildren as groups, village by village, are all likely to require transport at about the same time. The problem of the peak is just as real in the country as it is in the town.

If rural services are to be provided, then once again it must be decided what can be regarded as reasonable facilities. Works traffic will need to be catered for five days per week and shoppers perhaps twice a week, say market day and Saturday. Schoolchildren create a problem but one which must be shared by local education authorities. The need for maximum economy in operation is paramount for work of this kind and various methods of achieving greater efficiency are often advocated although they are not always practicable.

The first seemingly obvious step is to eliminate the conductor and introduce one-man operation which in many cases has, in all probability, long since been done. Even so, an odd journey might sometimes fit into a space in the crew schedule and if so there would be every justification to work it this way. The next consideration is the timetable and the route. To get as much work as possible out of one bus and driver some staggering might be necessary with the result that the times will not be ideal for everybody but there is a limit as to how much can be done here. There is, however, likely to be a greater tolerance in the country areas of circuitous routes designed to serve as many villages as possible on a single journey. If the alternative is nothing at all these passengers might well accept a longer ride if in the end they are taken to where they want to go. Perhaps the greatest clamour for economy lies in the type of vehicle which is used on country routes, that is if the constant criticism levelled at operators when double deck buses are seen working on rural services carrying negligible traffics is anything to go by. But the student must not allow himself to be misled in this way. Certainly, a 12-seater minibus is cheaper to buy and will use less fuel, remembering always that the smaller van type vehicle will have a shorter working life than a larger conventional type bus. However, the driver will require a standard wage regardless of the type of vehicle he is driving and crew costs (even if a one-man driver) are always the largest element of overall expenditure. But the real test is adequacy in terms of capacity. Certainly for most of the time loadings could be depressingly low but at some point in the working day it is likely that there will be a sudden burst of traffic, perhaps on a school journey or at a factory break when all of the accommodation of the large bus will be taken up, albeit for only a short distance. There are few bus runnings where this situation is not experienced and immediately it happens the use of the large bus is justified. It would be quite uneconomic to use it only for such sporadic occasions and then substitute it for a smaller vehicle at other times. It would be equally uneconomic to keep the smaller bus and duplicate at the pressure points. By far the cheapest way is to keep the one bigger bus and use it all of the time. Having said that, there is, nevertheless, a place for mini and midi buses and that place comes in cases where either there is no heavy influx of traffic as described or when, for physical reasons, a larger vehicle cannot be used and this could apply to some of the country lanes in the more remote areas.

To make it easier for small vehicles to be used as service buses the British government has in recent years relaxed certain of the licensing regulations. Details of the various ways in which small buses may be operated without the need to conform to the full licensing procedure are contained in Chapter 8. One outcome is the community bus which, subject, inter alia to the driver being a volunteer, may be authorised by traffic commissioners without recourse to the standard licensing procedure. The inauguration of such schemes requires local initiative and the availability of volunteer drivers but where this is possible, otherwise isolated communities could have a service. Another practice sometimes adopted is the use of dual purpose vehicles carrying both passengers and parcels. One stage further and there is the post bus whereby vehicles used for the delivery of mail, which must run in any case, are also used for the conveyance of passengers. The system is not widespread as so often the delivery routes are too circuitous even for a rural bus and the Post Office must let mail take precedence over the needs of passengers, which also means that times might not be the most convenient. Nevertheless, there are places where such a system is practicable, in which case a useful facility can be provided.

Statistics

Statistics of various kinds are required by all branches of management in the day to day conduct of the business. The engineer will want to know, for example, how many miles his buses will run for each gallon of fuel, how frequently breakdowns occur, how many miles are lost due to engineering causes, etc. Similarly the operating manager will seek information on miles lost through staff and traffic reasons, etc. All of this information is readily obtainable. Those responsible for service development require information on the number of passengers carried and financial viability, route by route, as it is the information produced by the examination of the trends of these figures when comparing one period with another which is the first indicator that something might need attention. Although details of passenger loadings are not always readily available, information regarding cash taken by conductors and one-man drivers is and the total divided by the mileage, service by service, produces statistical data in terms of receipts per mile (RPM). Up until recently this information was a valuable tool for short term traffic planning but with the increasing use of season tickets and the like it is gradually becoming useless.

Whilst a blanket subsidy to maintain services and hold down fares will affect revenue collected by platform staff and hence produce lower RPM figures, for statistical purposes this is not serious if such revenue support is applied evenly across the system and a common albeit cheaper scale is applied to all passengers. For various reasons, however, which are partly political and partly operational, this is now tending not to be the case. Politically there is a call for cheaper fares for certain classes of people, notably the elderly. There is also political support in some areas for 'anywhere' type period tickets which are also acceptable operationally as they facilitate one-man operation. Once this happens, the accuracy of the RPM has gone as it no longer reflects the number of people who are using the service. Passengers who pay nothing at all at the time of travel are not recorded and if some pay less than the normal fare then again cash receipts cannot be translated into traffic volumes. Furthermore, if a farebox type fare collection system is used as is described in Chapter 9 (this is another way of overcoming problems of one-man operation) and buses move from one route to another in the course of a day, cash collected cannot be allocated to specific services. In any case, conductors' waybills are not as explicit as they were at one time and all of these factors militate against the production of a record of route receipts which are of sufficient accuracy to be of any value.

When the RPM barometer becomes suspect or useless, some alternative data is required if services are to be properly developed and that alternative can only be passenger loadings. But just as the RPM cannot be calculated when circumstances as described prevail, neither can this information be obtained from ticket sales if some passengers do not buy tickets on the bus at the time of travel. The alternative is to count physically. To do this will give total passenger journeys but to obtain passenger miles then the numbers boarding and alighting at each point must also be known. To obtain this information manually in respect of each passenger on high density services is unrealistic; the cost would be tremendous and beyond contemplation even if the necessary manpower could be obtained. This must immediately reduce the exercise to a sample. However, to keep costs within reasonable limits, the sample must be a small one but the smaller the sample the less reliable it becomes. It might, in fact, have to be reduced to something like once or twice a year and then maybe only on the less frequent services could on bus point to point loadings be recorded. On the busier frequent routes passing loads at the maximum traffic points might have to suffice which, for traffic planning purposes, is something less than ideal. In the light of these circumstances it is worth reflecting on how many bus managements know with any degree of accuracy how many passengers they are carrying, in total or service by service, and how many could refine those figures to passenger miles. Depending on circumstances such as fare collection methods and travel concessions, the answer might be not very many. But how many managements would admit that they do not know how many passengers they are carrying? The answer again is not very many. Their reticence is understandable and in any case they all actually produce these figures; they appear in published statistics. The answer of course is that they are estimates — but estimates based on what and how accurate are they? Such figures as are available are adjusted according to local circumstances. It will be known how many pre-paid anywhere and elderly persons tickets are issued. Some special sample census might help to establish how many rides per week and where are made per ticket. Different types of ticket issuing machines produce varying amounts of statistical data and fleet figures must be built up on whatever information is available. And the fleet figure might be somewhere near the mark but it is hardly an adequate basis on which to start to think about timetable changes.

All of this only poses the problem, it does not answer it. What is needed is some means which produces passenger loading figures and people left behind, journey by journey, stop by stop, at least for a period in the summer and another in the winter and more frequently if possible, all without incurring excessive cost. This information properly summarised will indicate where there is over provision and where strengthening is necessary. The only other source of information is inspectors' observations as mentioned in Chapter 11. Electronic equipment is being developed which records the numbers of passengers boarding and alighting at each stop and it is perhaps something like this which will eventually have to replace the information extracted from conductors' waybills.

6
Schedule Compilation

Introduction

This chapter is about the compilation of time and duty schedules and following the principle outlined in the Introduction to the book, most of the information will relate to buses. Reference to railways will be made only where principles differ between the two modes.

Scheduling falls into two parts, being that which applies to vehicles and that which applies to the staff who man them, ie, the drivers and conductors. It is the vehicle schedules which must first be prepared and it is here that the compiler must maintain a close liaison with his counterpart who determines service requirements. The latter performs more of a commercial function which is considered in Chapter 7 as is the publication of the timetable after it has been prepared. Not only must the compiler be advised regarding the quantum of service and any set timings for specific purposes which might be necessary; he must also be informed regarding the scheduled speeds, which is a subject of Chapter 11.

It is the predetermined schedules which govern the utilisation of vehicles and staff, both of which are very expensive items. An inefficient schedule would cost the undertaking a great deal of unnecessary money and it is imperative that the assets be used to maximum advantage. At the same time there is nothing to be gained by padding out the timetable with journeys of no traffic value only to keep buses moving. Idle time on the part of drivers and conductors is also waste time because they will be entitled to a full day's pay regardless of what they do, which brings in the point that duty schedules must conform to conditions as agreed with the trade union.

The schedules department, assuming that the undertaking is of a sufficient size to warrant a separate function for this purpose, is sandwiched between what is fed into it from the commercial, operating and staff sides and the implementation of its endeavours on the road by the operating staff. For the reason already stated, much of the financial prosperity of an undertaking depends on the skill of the schedule compilers in getting the most out of the least. This applies particularly to duty schedules where there is likely to be a much greater range of alternatives and it is with experience that optimum solutions can be produced. Nevertheless, however much ingenuity might be exercised, if the parameters are set it could be that even the best possible schedule is extremely wasteful. It is under these circumstances that compilers might seek a reconsideration of the specification and a balance must then be struck between service requirements and schedule efficiency.

It is not easy to describe and explain in textbook style the art of schedule compilation. Different undertakings have different approaches to the subject; their method of working varies just as does the way the finished product is presented. Duty schedules in particular are not only very closely associated with staff agreements, the process of preparation and implementation is also one of the main topics of staff consultation. Trade unions have a particular involvement on this issue and schedules do certainly affect the working life of their members as much as anything else. At the same time trade unions tend to be parochial. Whilst, therefore, there are basic principles which can be explained here, the detail becomes more a matter of custom and practice and that is why the successful schedule compiler relies as much on experience (and that means local experience) as on book knowledge. There is, however, one breakaway from established practice and that is schedule compilation by computer. Such a process has been in the course of exploration and development since the early 1960s and some of the larger organisations do now actually prepare their schedules in this way. The same basic principles must, of course, apply, but they are programmed into a computer instead of being interpreted manually. What has been said in a few words, however, has meant years of research and experiment and it is not part of this book to become involved in the finer arts of computer programming.

Timetable Preparation

The type of service most appropriate for consideration here is that which runs regularly all day at set frequencies (which may, of course, be varied according to the time of day). The essential ingredients for drawing up such a timetable are:

(a) The required quantum of service, which may be end to end or with augmentation over certain sections and which is likely to vary according to the day of the week.

(b) The speed schedule (which will include intermediate timing points for operating and publicity purposes and which could vary between different periods of the day).

(c) Minimum layover periods at each end of the route and any intermediate hesitation points plus any built in recovery time at the termini.

(d) Any special instructions such as specific departure or arrival times either as a general requirement or for particular journeys such as factory breaks or connections with other services.

(e) First and last journeys.

Armed with this information, preparation can proceed. The important feature as far as timetable efficiency is concerned is the variable at (a) in relation to (b) plus (c). To put it another way, the relationship between (a) and (b) will determine the length of the layover at (c) and the shorter this is (down as far as the declared minimum) then the less will be the stand time, remembering always that vehicles do not earn money when their wheels are not turning.

The following formula is important:

$$\frac{\text{Journey time} \times 2 + \text{stand time}}{\text{service frequency}} = \text{number of vehicles required}$$

In other words, the return journey time plus the stand time must be a multiple of the service frequency. It is the stand time which is the variable and it is this which determines efficiency. To take an easy example, if the single journey time is 26 minutes, the frequency is every 30 minutes and the agreed stand time plus recovery time is 15% of the running time (which would make it eight minutes split between the two ends) then, in accordance with the formula:

$$\frac{26 \times 2 + 8}{30} = 2 \text{ buses}$$

The stand time of eight minutes is the bare minimum, there is 52 minutes wheel turning time in every hour and nothing could be more efficient than that.

Imagine now that the running time was not 26 minutes but 31 minutes. The figures would then be:

$$\frac{31 \times 2 + 10}{30} = 3 \text{ buses}$$

As the numerator must be a multiple of the denominator and the only variable is the stand time (now 10 minutes), this figure must become 28 to give:

$$\frac{31 \times 2 + 28}{30} \text{ or } \frac{90}{30} = 3 \text{ buses}$$

If the stand time is split equally at each end, then the bus would run for 31 minutes and then stand for 14 minutes, which would be very wasteful. If the vehicle had to remain manned whilst on the stand, then the waste would be compounded. In fact the three buses could give a 24-minute frequency at no extra vehicle (or staff) cost, viz:

$$\frac{31 \times 2 + 10}{24} = 3 \text{ buses}$$

Whether a 24-minute headway would be acceptable, bearing mind that the times are not standard for each hour but can be repeated only in every alternate hour is another matter, but this does lead into a working practice which is usually adopted at the formative stage. If it is accepted that the times need to be repetitive, and that means that the service frequency is a factor of 60, then, apart from first and last journeys and those which mark a change in frequency, only the 'specimen hour' needs to be indicated (ie 'and then at the following minutes past each hour'). This means that it is the specimen hour which is first considered by the traffic department when the specification is being prepared. It should be noted, however, that the more frequent is the service, the less will be the effect of the relationship between running time and timetable efficiency. When a headway gets down to as little as, say, five minutes, wheel turning time can be maximised regardless of the journey time.

Consider now some living examples. The specimen timetable of service 84 shown at Fig 17 represents a local town service and illustrates a straightforward 20-minute frequency. With a journey time of 15 minutes and five minutes layover at each end, then, by use of the formula, it is clear that two buses are required. Overall, the timetable provides for 75% wheel turning time and 25% stand time. Being a short route, vehicles have to turn more frequently and it is inevitable that the actual work content cannot be as high as on the longer services which travel for more lengthy periods of time without the need for a time allowance for terminal working. The next example at Fig 18 (service 480) shows a more complex specimen hour and one which the required number of vehicles cannot be calculated by recourse to the formula. However, as the timings show the complete workings during the course of one hour, the totals of the running times and stand times for each direction must be a multiple of 60. For convenience, stand times have been appended in brackets and it will be found that the total figures are as follows:

Journey times

to Valley Drive (total of 6 journeys)	345 minutes
to Erith (total of 3 journeys)	213 minutes
to Dartford (total of 3 journeys	144 minutes

NEWARK · BARNBY-IN-THE-WILLOWS

Service **83**

Wednesdays			Saturdays	
NEWARK, Bus Station	0900	1200	1250	1700
Barnby Crossing	0905	1205	1255	1705
Isolation Hospital	0908	1208	1258	1708
BARNBY-IN-THE-WILLOWS	0915	1215	1305	1715

Wednesdays			Saturdays	
BARNBY-IN-THE-WILLOWS	0915	1215	1305	1715
Isolation Hospital	0922	1222	1312	1722
Barnby Crossing	0925	1225	1315	1725
NEWARK, Bus Station	0930	1230	1320	1730

32/165

NEWARK TOWN SERVICE
GRANGE ROAD · YORKE DRIVE

Service **84**

Route: From Grange Road via Churchill Drive, Elizabeth Road, Eton Avenue, Windsor Avenue, Albert Street, Beaumond Cross, Carter Gate, Appleton Gate, Queens Road, North Gate, Lincoln Road, Strawberry Hall Lane, Yorke Drive.
From Yorke Drive via Strawberry Hall Lane and above route reversed to Elizabeth Road, Hawton Road and Grange Road.

Weekdays only

	NS	NS	* NS	S	*																
GRANGE ROAD	0703	......	0830	......	0850	0910	0930	0950		10	30	50		1910	1930	1950	2030	2110	2150	2230	2307
Elizabeth Road/Churchill Drive	0706	......	0833	......	0853	0913	0933	0953		13	33	53	mins.	1913	1933	1953	2033	2113	2153	2233	2310
Beaumond Cross	0710	......	0837	......	0657	0917	0937	0957	then	17	37	57	past	1917	1937	1957	2037	2117	2157	2237	2314
Church Walk	......	0801	0839	0839	0859	0919	0939	0959	at	19	39	59	each	1919	......	1959	2039	2119	2159	2239	......
Railway Bridge ⇌	......	0805	0843	0843	0903	0923	0943	1003		23	43	03	hour	1923	......	2003	2043	2123	2203	2243	......
YORKE DRIVE/FOSSE EST.	......	0807	0845	0845	0905	0925	0945	1005		25	45	05	until	1925	......	2005	2045	2125	2205	2245	......

	NS	NS	NS	S							†									
YORKE DRIVE/FOSSE EST.	.....	0810	0830	......	0850	0910	0930	0950		10	30	50		1910	1930	2010	2050	2130	2210	2250
Railway Bridge ⇌	......	0812	0832	......	0852	0912	0932	0952		12	32	52	mins.	1912	1932	2012	2052	2132	2212	2252
Church Walk	.....	0816	0836	......	0856	0916	0936	0956	then	16	36	56	past	1916	1936	2016	2056	2136	2216	2256
Beaumond Cross	0653	0818	0838	0838	0858	0918	0938	0958	at	18	38	58	each	1918	1938	2018	2058	2138	2218	2258
Elizabeth Road/Churchill Drive	0657	0822	0842	0842	0902	0922	0942	1002		22	42	02	hour	1922	1942	2022	2102	2142	2222	2302
GRANGE ROAD	0700	0825	0845	0845	0905	0925	0945	1005		25	45	05	until	1925	1945	2025	2105	2145	2225	2305

CODE
NS—Not Saturdays.
S—Saturdays only.
*****—Via Portland Street when Schools open.
⇌—Adjoining or near Railway Station.
†—Monday - Friday The 1630 hours departure Yorke Drive/Fosse Estate will depart at 1625 hours and proceed via R.E.M.E. Works, arriving Railway Bridge at 1632 hours.

32/63

Erith – Gravesend Valley Drive
via Dartford and Northfleet

London Country 480

Mondays to Fridays

Erith *Bexley Road Cross Street*	0834	....	....	0854	0904	....		24	....	44	....	04	....		1524	....	1544	....	....	1604	....	1624	....	1644	....	....	1704
Slade Green Station ⇌	0841	....	....	0901	0911	....		31	....	51	....	11	....		1531	....	1551	....	....	1611	....	1631	....	1651	....	....	1711
Crayford *Jolly Farmers*	0844	....	....	0904	0914	....		34	....	54	....	14	....		1534	....	1554	....	....	1614	....	1634	....	1654	D	....	1714
Crayford *Bridge*	0848	....	....	0908	0918	....		38	....	58	....	18	....		1538	....	1558	....	....	1618	....	1638	....	1658	1703	....	1718
Dartford *Bus Garage*	↓	0905	0910	↓	↓	0935	Then	↓	55	↓	15	↓	35		↓	1555	↓	1610	1615	↓	1635	↓	1655	↓	↓	1715	↓
Dartford *Westgate Road* ⇌	0856	0906	0911	0916	0926	0936	at	46	56	06	16	26	36		1546	1556	1606	1616	1626	1626	1636	1646	1656	1706	1711	1716	1726
Horns Cross *Bull*	0908	0918	0923	0928	0938	0948	these	58	08	18	28	38	48		1558	1608	1618	1623	1628	1638	1648	1658	1708	1718	1723	1728	1738
Swanscombe *George & Dragon* ⇌	0915	0925	0930	0935	0945	0955	minutes	05	15	25	35	45	55	UNTIL	1605	1615	1625	....	1635	1645	1655	1705	1715	1725	....	1735	1745
Northfleet *Leather Bottel*	0920	0930	0935	0940	0950	1000	past	10	20	30	40	50	00		1610	1620	1630	....	1640	1650	1700	1710	1720	1730	....	1740	1750
Northfleet *Bus Garage*	0922	0932	0937	0942	0952	1002	each	12	22	32	42	52	02		1612	1622	1632	....	1642	1652	1702	1712	1722	1732	....	1742	1752
Gravesend *Stuart Road* ⇌	0924	0934	....	0944	0954	1004	hour	14	24	34	44	54	05		1614	1624	1634	....	1644	1654	1704	1714	1724	1734	....	1744	1754
Gravesend *Clock Tower*	0927	0937	....	0947	0957	1007		17	27	37	47	57	07		1617	1627	1637	....	1647	1657	1707	1717	1727	1737	....	1747	1757
Denton *Milton Ale Shades*	0931	0941	....	0951	1001	1011		21	31	41	51	01	11		1621	1631	1641	....	1651	1701	1711	1721	1731	1741	....	1751	1801
Valley Drive *St. Albans Close*	0936	0946	....	0956	1006	1016		26	36	46	56	06	16		1626	1636	1646	....	1656	1706	1716	1726	1736	1746	....	1756	1806
Valley Drive *Mackenzie Way*	0942	0952	....	1002	1012	1022		32	42	52	02	12	22		1632	1642	1652	....	1702	1712	1722	1732	1742	1752	....	1802	1812
								[7]	[7]	[7]	[7]	[7]	[7]														

Valley Drive *Mackenzie Way*	0859	0909		19	29	39	49	59	0(		1459	1509	....	1519	1529	1539	1549	....	1559	1609	1619	1629	1639	1649	....	1659
Valley Drive *St Albans Close*	0905	0915		25	35	45	55	05	15		1505	1515	....	1525	1535	1545	1555	....	1605	1615	1625	1635	1645	1655	....	1705
Denton *Milton Ale Shades*	0910	0920		30	40	50	00	10	20		1510	1520	C	1530	1540	1550	1600	....	1610	1620	1630	1640	1650	1700	....	1710
Gravesend *New Road Co-Op Stores* ⇌	0915	0925	Then	35	45	55	05	15	25		1515	1525	1530	1535	1545	1555	1605	....	1615	1625	1635	1645	1655	1705	....	1715
Northfleet *Bus Garage*	0919	0929	at	39	49	59	09	19	29		1519	1529	1534	1539	1549	1559	1609	....	1619	1629	1639	1649	1659	1709	....	1719
Northfleet *Leather Bottel*	0921	0931	these	41	51	01	11	21	31		1521	1531	1536	1541	1551	1601	1611	....	1621	1631	1641	1651	1701	1711	....	1721
Swanscombe *George & Dragon* ⇌	0926	0936	minutes	46	56	06	16	26	36	UNTIL	1526	1536	1541	1546	1556	1606	1616	....	1626	1636	1646	1656	1706	1716	....	1726
Horns Cross *Bull*	0933	0943	past	53	03	13	23	33	43		1533	1543	1548	1553	1603	1613	1623	1628	1633	1643	1653	1703	1713	1723	1728	1733
Dartford *Market Street*	0943	0953	each	03	13	23	33	43	53		1543	1553	1558	1603	1613	1623	1633	1638	1643	1653	1703	1713	1723	1733	1738	1743
Dartford *Bus Garage* ⇌	0947	↓	hour	07	↓	27	↓	47	↓		1547	↓	1602	1607	↓	1627	↓	↓	1647	↓	1707	↓	1727	↓	1742	1747
*Crayford *Bridge*	....	1002		....	22	....	42	....	02		....	1602	....	....	1622	....	1642	1647	....	1702	....	1722	....	1742	....	....
Crayford *Jolly Farmers*	....	1006		....	26	....	46	....	06		....	1606	....	....	1626	....	1646	D	....	1706	....	1726	....	1746	....	....
Slade Green Station ⇌	....	1009		....	29	....	49	....	09		....	1609	....	....	1629	....	1649	....	....	1709	....	1729	....	1749	....	....
Erith *Bexley Road Cross Street*	....	1020		....	40	....	00	....	20		....	1620	....	....	1640	....	1700	....	....	1720	....	1740	....	1800	....	....
				[8]	[4]	[8]	[4]	[8]	[4]																

Top: **Fig 17. Specimen timetable of a rural service and a self-contained town service.**
Reproduced by permission of the Lincolnshire Road Car Co Ltd

Above: **Fig 18. Timetable extract of a service to show a slightly more complex specimen hour.**
Reproduced by permission of London Country Bus Services Ltd

Stand times	
at Valley Drive	42 minutes
at Erith	12 minutes
at Dartford	24 minutes
	——
Total	780 minutes
	——

The number of vehicles required is obtained by dividing 780 by 60, which is 13.

It could be that the service specification is such that the resultant timetable could never be efficient. With only one variable, being the stand time, it is this figure which has to be adjusted to complete the cycle; it can only be adjusted upwards and the result could be an excessive layover. If the journey time could be altered, there would be alternative permutations and efficiency might well be improved. It is unlikely that the speed schedule could be altered but the route pattern might be. Whilst the actual route followed might not lend itself to change there is the chance that two services of similar frequency might be linked or buses might interwork between different routes, that is, alternating from one to another. Such arrangements greatly enhance the prospects of better timetable efficiency and the timetable extracts which appear at Fig 19 are an example.

Below: **Fig 19. Specimen timetable showing services where vehicles are interworked.**
Reproduced by permission of the South Yorkshire Passenger Transport Executive

SHEFFIELD CITY SERVICE — **ONE MAN Service**

CITY · LONGLEY · SANDSTONE ROAD — 1

Via Waingate and Nursery Street **outwards**; (**inwards** via Chatham Street, Corporation Street, West Bar and Snig Hill); Pitsmoor Road, Barnsley Road, Firshill Avenue, Firshill Crescent, Shirecliffe Road, Longley Avenue West, Norwood Avenue, Longley Lane and Longley Hall Road; journeys terminating at Longley returning via Longley Hall Road and Longley Lane; Longley Lane, Barnsley Road, Stubbin Lane, **Firth Park**, Bellhouse Road, Primrose Avenue, Bracken Road, Wincobank Avenue, Jenkin Road and Sandstone Road.

Monday to Friday

CITY, Castle Street	0655	0725	0753	0825	0849	0925	0945		05	25	45		1525	1601	1625
Firshill Crescent	0706	0736	0804	0836	0900	0936	0956	then at these	16	36	56		1536	1612	1636
LONGLEY, Longley Hall Road	0716	0746	0814	0846	0910	0946	1006	minutes past	26	46	06	until	1546	1622	1646
Firth Park, Bellhouse Road	......	0751	......	0851	......	0951	......	each hour	...	51	...		1551	......	1651
SANDSTONE ROAD	......	0759	......	0859	......	0959	......		...	59	...		1559	......	1659

SANDSTONE ROAD	0640	......	0740	......	0840	......		...	40	...		1440	......	......	1540
Firth Park, Bellhouse Road	0647	......	0747	......	0847	......	then at these	...	47	...		1447	......	......	1547
LONGLEY, Longley Hall Road	0652	0722	0752	0818	0852	0912	minutes past	32	52	12	until	1452	1512	1528	1552
Firshill Crescent	0659	0729	0759	0825	0859	0919	each hour	39	59	19		1459	1519	1535	1559
CITY, Castle Street	0713	0743	0813	0839	0913	0933		53	13	33		1513	1533	1549	1613

SANDSTONE ROAD · CITY · GRAVES PARK — 34
UPWELL STREET · CITY · NORTON — 38
SANDSTONE ROAD · CITY · MILLHOUSES — 39

Services 34 and 39 via Sandstone Road, Jenkin Road (**from City** via Wincobank Avenue, Wincobank Road, Shiregreen Lane and Wincobank Avenue), Newman Road, Merton Lane, **Wincobank**, Fife Street, Barrow Road, Tyler Street and Holywell Road; **then all Services** via Upwell Street, Upwell Lane, Grimesthorpe Road, Cyclops Street, Margate Street, Grimesthorpe Road, Hunsley Street and Petre Street; **or** via Upwell Lane, Hunsley Street and Petre Street: (**from City** via Botham Street, Cyclops Street, Margate Street, Grimesthorpe Road, Hunsley Street, Carlisle Road, Carlisle Street East and Upwell Street; **or** via Hunsley Street, Carlisle Road, Carlisle Street East and Upwell Street); Ellesmere Road, Spital Hill, **The Wicker**, Waingate, Fitzalan Square, Flat Street, Pond Street, Central Bus Station **Platform A**, Paternoster Row, Furnival Street, Eyre Street, Bramall Lane, Havelock Bridge, Myrtle Road, Prospect Road, Richards Road (**inwards** via Spencer Road), Gleadless Road, **Heeley Green**, Gleadless Road, Carrfield Road, Meersbrook Road, Carfield Avenue and Upper Albert Road; **Service 34** via **Hollythorpe Rise** and Thorpe House Avenue, returning via Lees Hall Road, Thorpe House Road and Hollythorpe Rise, then via Norton Lees Lane and Derbyshire Lane to **Graves Park**; **Service 38** via Norton Lees Lane, Scarsdale Road, Chesterfield Road, **Woodseats**, Meadowhead, Norton Parkway, Norton Lane, Henley Avenue and Cloonmore Drive; **Service 39** via Norton Lees Lane, Scarsdale Road, Chesterfield Road, **Woodseats**, Abbey Lane, Beauchief, Abbeydale Road South, Abbeydale Road, Springfield Road and Hastings Road.

Monday to Friday—*continued*

Service No.	*39*	*34*	*39*	*38*		*39*	*34*	*38*		*38*	*34*	*39*	*34*	*34*	*34*
SANDSTONE ROAD	0806	......	0845	......		06	...	...		......	......	1406	......	......	......
Wincobank, Fife Street	0813	......	0852	......		13	...	...		......	......	1413	......	......	......
UPWELL STREET, Reform Chapel	0823	0843	0902	0903		23	43	03		1403	......	1423	......	1443	......
Margate Drive	0826	0846	......	0906		26	46	06		1406	......	1426	......	1446	......
CENTRAL BUS STATION	0845	0905	0920	0925	then at these	45	05	25		1425	1435	1445	1455	1505	1515
Heeley Green	0855	0915	......	0935	minutes past	55	15	35	until	1435	1445	1455	1505	1515	1525
Hollythorpe Rise, Thorpe House Ave.	......	0921	......	......	each hour	...	21	...		......	1451	......	1511	1521	1531
GRAVES PARK	......	0933	......	......		...	33	...		......	......	......	......	1533	......
Scarsdale Road Bottom	0902	......	......	0942		02	...	42		1442	......	1502	......	......	......
NORTON, Cloonmore Drive	......	......	......	0957		...	...	57		1457	......	......	......	......	......
MILLHOUSES, Hastings Road	0918	......	......	......		18	...	...		......	......	1518	......	......	......

Service No.	*34*	*34*	*38*	*34*	*39*	*34*	*34*	*38*	*34*	*39*		*34*	*38*	*39*		*34*
NORTON, Cloonmore Drive	......	......	0802	......	......	......	......	0903	......	......		...	02	...		......
MILLHOUSES, Hastings Road	......	......	......	......	0821	......	......	......	......	0921		...	...	21		......
Scarsdale Road Bottom	......	......	0813	......	0833	......	......	0914	......	0933		...	13	33		......
GRAVES PARK	0749	......	......	......	......	......	0849	......	......	......		49	...	...		1449
Hollythorpe Rise, Thorpe House Ave.	0754	0804	......	0824	......	0837	0854	......	0930	......	then at these	54	...	...		1454
Heeley Green	0800	0810	0820	0830	0840	0843	0900	0921	0936	0940	minutes past	00	20	40	until	1500
FITZALAN SQUARE	0815	0822	0835	0842	0855	†	0915	0936	0948	0955	each hour	15	35	55		1515
Margate Drive	0828	......	0848	......	0908	......	0928	0949	......	1008		28	48	08		1528
UPWELL STREET, Reform Chapel	0836	......	0856	......	......	......	0936	0957	......	......		36	56	...		1536
Wincobank, Fife Street	......	......	......	......	0920	......	......	......	......	1020		...	...	20		......
SANDSTONE ROAD	......	......	......	......	0933	......	......	......	......	1033		...	...	33		......

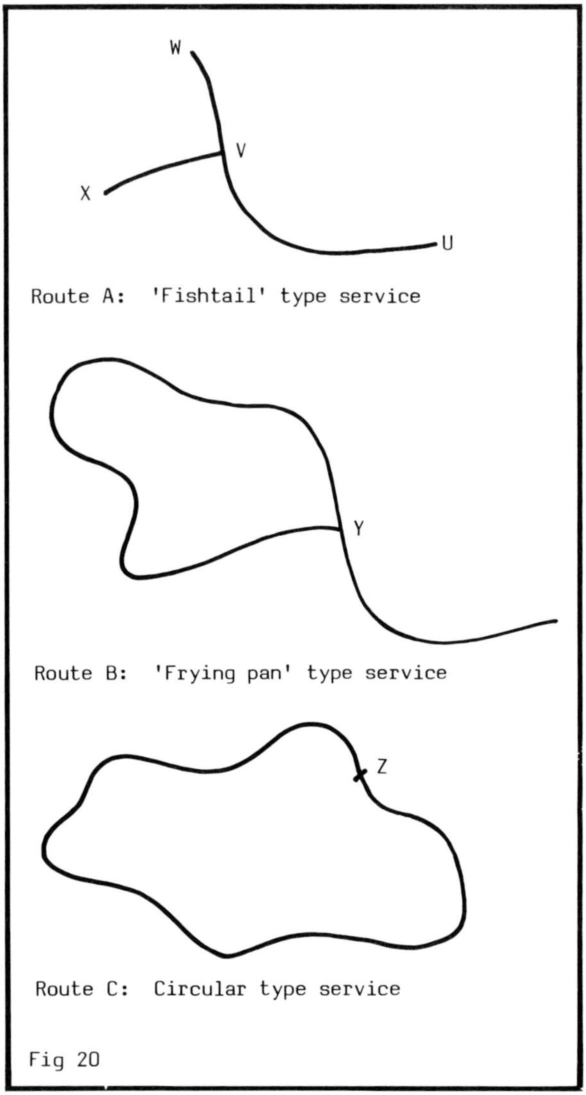

Left: **Fig 20. Specimen routes to illustrate different timetable patterns.**

Looking first at Service 1, whilst the short workings are reasonably efficient standing on their own, the through service to Sandstone Road is not. Similarly with the 34/38/39 group, services 34 and 38 are reasonably efficient on a self-contained basis, but service 39 is not. If, however, services 1 and 39, at least for vehicle running purposes, are interworked and buses exchange their route allocation at Sandstone Road, utilisation is much improved. Taking the through journeys on service 1 and service 39 together, the situation for a complete cycle becomes:

Journey times	34+72+72+33	=211
Stand times	7+ 3+ 7+12	= 29
Total		240

Divided by 60 this indicates a need for four buses.

All that has been said so far relates to services which follow a progressive route, reverse direction at the outer terminal and return the same way. A slight variation on this is the 'fishtail' type service as depicted at route A in Fig 20. In this example, the full service runs between points U and V but bifurcates at V with probably alternate journeys serving different places at W and X. Providing the running times to each point are similar then the principles regarding timetable preparation as already described remain. But if one leg is substantially shorter than the other and an even headway is to be maintained on the main spine, then an excessive layover will be incurred at the end of the shorter of the two unless the difference in journey time is sufficient to approximate to a multiple of the service frequency. The following illustrates the point:

U	1.10	1.40	2.10	2.40	3.10	3.40
V	1.30	2.00	2.30	3.00	3.30	4.00
W	1.35		2.35		3.35	
X	↓	2.35 →	↓	3.35 →	↓	4.35
X		1.40		2.40		3.40
W	1.40		2.40		3.40	
V	1.45	2.15	2.45	3.15	3.45	4.15
U	2.05	2.35	3.05	3.35	4.05	4.35

In this example, the journey times beyond V are five minutes to W and 35 minutes to X and the difference is sufficient to maintain schedule efficiency.

If the ends of the 'fishtail' are linked to form a continuous route, so forming a loop working or 'frying pan' type service as depicted at route B in Fig 20 a rather different situation arises. The size of the loop will determine whether buses need to traverse it in both directions. If it is reasonable to ask a passenger who uses the first stop on the loop beyond the junction at point Y to travel the long way round one way (subject, of course, to no fare surcharge) then there is advantage in going one way only. Resources do not then have to be split and a more concentrated service is possible at the stops in the one direction. It is likely that all stand time will be given at the single terminal, which means that on the 'handle of the pan', the timings in one direction are governed by those on the other and there is no opportunity for adjustment. If a hesitation period is given somewhere on the loop, it can only be to the inconvenience of passengers who need to override that point.

One stage beyond the loop working is the complete circle as shown at route C of Fig 20, so often advocated by those outside the industry but so rarely having any real traffic value. It is the radials to and from the centre which usually attract the passengers, not the orbitals which tend to keep on going without ever getting anywhere. There are notable exceptions but only when there are sizeable neighbourhoods or industrial areas between which there is a particular traffic affinity. To return to running schedules, if the journey time of route C from z back to z is an exact multiple of the service frequency, then the vehicles will keep going without any hesitation, giving 100% utilisation. Certainly this is super efficiency in scheduling terms but there would be no recovery time to correct late running; on present day standards it would be highly unpopular with the staff and so in practical terms the arrangement would be something less than satisfactory. In any case it would be fortuitous if the running time was an exact multiple of the service frequency and if it was not and repetitive timings were to be maintained then time would have to be lost somewhere. This could only be at a point en route, to the irritation of passengers on board.

Time Schedules

This discourse on timetable preparation has so far concentrated on the basic all day services. This, however, is only one part of the subject. Even on these routes it is likely that augmentation is required during the peaks when the timetables might depart from standard timings. But other services of a more specialised nature also come in at these times, often for works and schools but also, perhaps, as variations to the regular routes. There can be no general pattern here on which to calculate vehicle requirements. Such supplementary services have to be superimposed on the basic runnings and worked in the most expeditious way to meet local requirements. It is likely that these extra peak hour buses will do more interworking between different routes, often travelling 'dead' (ie out of service) after finishing on one and taking up service on another. Specific timings are often important and occasionally it is necessary to resort to dead running on the non-essential sections in order to get a faster run and thereby enable a particular commitment to be met. This is not, however, something which should be practised unless:

(a) the extra speed is crucial either for physical or duty schedule reasons, or
(b) the section concerned is not part of an authorised bus route.

Most journeys will carry at least some traffic and it is pointless (and irritating to intending passengers) for an empty bus to pass people waiting at stops without a very good reason. From a revenue point of view, a bus working dead earns no more than one which is stationary on a stand but the cost is there just the same. A similar type of service, ie odd journeys at specific times, but one which does not run at the same periods and hence caters for a different clientele is that which meets the shopping needs of the rural populace of hamlets outside the main towns. A typical example also appears at Fig 17 (Service 83) which has journeys only on Wednesdays and Saturdays, being market days. Although two journeys are provided in each direction only one is likely to carry many passengers as the movement is from the country into town and then back. In territory of this kind it is inevitable that the base of the bus is at the opposite end of the route to that of the passengers and a return journey must be made for each single effective trip. For a route of only 15 minutes running time this is not particularly serious but if it becomes longer and the journeys more numerous then waste is then a greater cause for concern. This is the reason for the out-station concept referred to in Chapter 2.

The most convenient way of allocating vehicles to services which have only sporadic journeys is to diagram all of the bus runnings on a time basis as depicted in the specimen time schedule which will be described shortly.

A Schedule Exercise

Preparation

Whilst timetable presentation is quite straightforward and examples of printed specimens have been shown, to explain the preparation of time and duty schedules, rather more material than this is necessary. A small imaginary network has, therefore, been devised on which to base a theoretical schedules exercise and is illustrated on the pages which follow. A fictitious presentation is necessary as for the sake of clarity and to bring out various features the operating unit used as an example is unrealistically small with the timetables designed primarily to illustrate principles. In real life, schedules are bulky documents, and in any case there is no standard method of preparation. For various reasons, therefore, it would not be practicable to include an actual example. Even if it was, the detail would obscure the issues involved. The explanatory material falls into eight parts, being:

Map of routes	(Fig 21)
Speed schedules	(Fig 22)
Draft timetables	(Fig 23)
Vehicle runnings	(Fig 24)
Time schedule	(Fig 25)
Duty allocation	(Fig 26)
Duty schedule	(Fig 27)
Duty roster	(Fig 28)

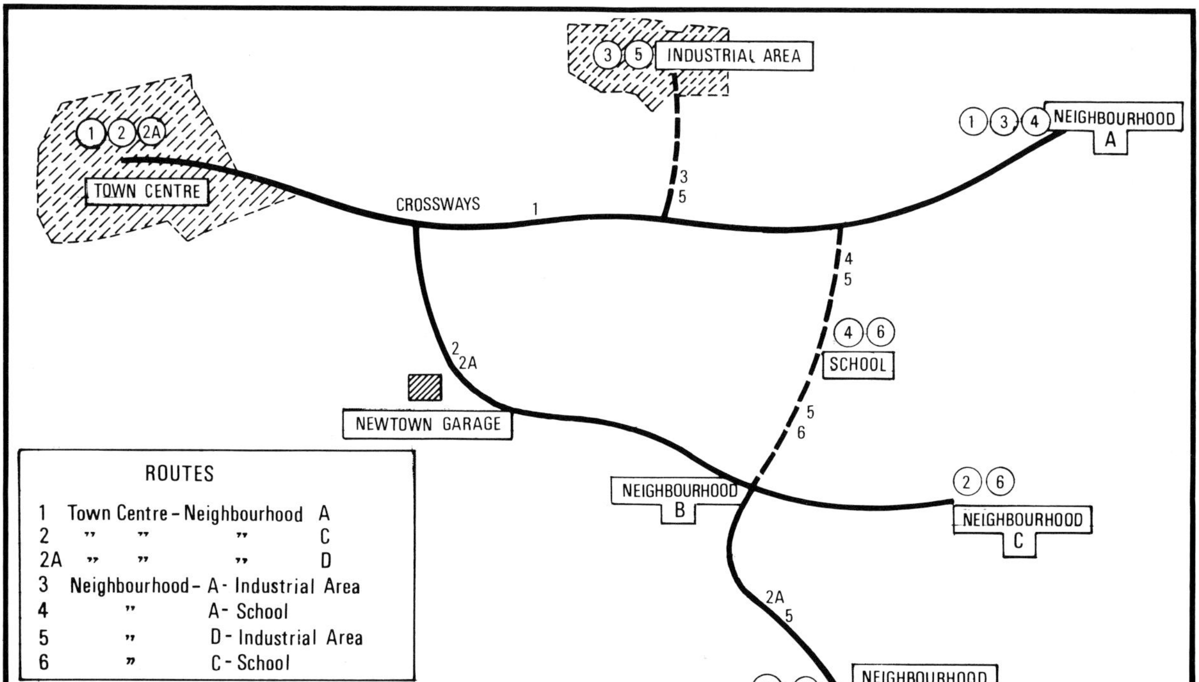

Fig 21. Map of Routes for Schedule Exercise.

Speed schedules

	minutes	*miles*	*mph*
	Route 1		
Town Centre			
Crossways	8	1.6	
Neighbourhood A	17	3.4	
School	5	1.0	
	15	3.0	12.0
	25	5.0	12.0
Walking time			
Crossways to garage	10		
	Route 2		
Town Centre			
Crossways	8	1.6	
Garage	2	0.4	
Neighbourhood B	14	2.8	
Neighbourhood C	10	2.0	
	34	6.8	12.0
	Route 2A		
Town Centre			
Crossways	8	1.6	
Garage	2	0.4	
Neighbourhood B	14	2.8	
Neighbourhood D	9	1.8	
	33	6.6	12.0

	Route 3		
Neighbourhood A			
Industrial Area	14	2.8	
	14	2.8	12.0
	Route 4		
Neighbourhood A			
School	7	1.4	
	7	1.4	12.0
	Route 5		
Neighbourhood D			
Neighbourhood B	9	1.8	
School	5	1.0	
Industrial Area	10	2.0	
	24	4.8	12.0
	Route 6		
Neighbourhood C			
Neighbourhood B	10	2.0	
School	5	1.0	
	15	3.0	12.0

Fig 22 Speed Schedules for Schedule Exercise

Everything which follows in respect of this exercise must be read in conjunction with these specimens.

The map, speed schedules and timetables represent the basic data and are included to illustrate what has already been explained and to provide a foundation on which to build time and duty schedules. In this exercise routes 1 and 2/2A form the all day services. Route 1 is deemed to serve an area of fairly high car ownership which means that whilst a 15-minute headway is needed in the peaks, a half-hourly service is adequate at other times coming down to hourly in the evenings. Certainly this sort of service goes contrary to minimum standards as was suggested in Chapter 5 in connection with the criteria for service provision. Nevertheless, it is typical of many areas and, more importantly in this context, introduces the schedules complexities of a disproportionate number of vehicles required in the peaks only. Route 2 serves a different type of area which calls for four buses per hour all day with a bifurcation near the extremity to form a fishtail to two other residential areas. Routes 3, 4, 5 and 6 comprise isolated works and school trips consisting only of morning and afternoon journeys. The speed schedules produce average speeds of 12mph to be reasonably realistic. The timetables represent the sort of specifications which might be submitted by a traffic department. The vehicle running and time schedules show how the non-standard timings of routes 3, 4, 5 and 6 have, in some cases, been interworked with the runnings of the basic services although the allocation of extra vehicles has also been necessary. Only the Monday to Friday operation has been tabled. Different traffic requirements are likely for Saturdays and Sundays but for this purpose it would be pointless to proceed laboriously through a complete set of schedules for different days of the week. On the assumption, however, that this information is also available, there is now sufficient data to compile a duty schedule and roster for a week's work.

Duty Schedule

Reference has already been made to the acquired art of the duty schedule compiler. He spends his working life selecting pieces of the time schedule jigsaw puzzle and assembling them to produce workable schedules which:

(a) are acceptable to management in that they make maximum use of staff within the various parameters (which is the very antithesis of what the platform staff are likely to seek).

(b) conform to the statutory limitations on drivers' hours referred to in Chapter 8.

(c) comply with trade union agreements (which are often more rigorous than the statutory limitations) and are acceptable to the trade union representatives. (Conformity with an agreement has, unfortunately, proved to be no guarantee of acceptance and apart from pay, duty schedules are perhaps one of the most common causes of disputes in the industry.)

It is emphasised that the example which follows is but one method of compilation and presentation. To keep the figures as realistic as possible for readers in Great Britain, the British drivers' hours regulations have been kept in mind but it must be appreciated that the purpose of the exercise is not to demonstrate the implications of such restrictions. Neither does the final production constitute a 'model schedule' or purport to give what might be in practice the optimum solution whilst meeting the requirements of (a), (b) and (c) above. Only the very simplest staff agreement has been observed. This elimination of the trimmings will, however, hopefully make the stages of compilation that much clearer and thereby enhance the value of what is no more than a text book exercise.

In the preparation of this specimen duty schedule the imposed restraints are simplified compared with actual practice and are:

Abridged drivers' hours regulations, being:

Maximum continuous driving	$5\frac{1}{2}$ hours
Minimum required break	30 minutes
Maximum driving in a day	10 hours
Maximum on duty in a day	16 hours
Minimum daily rest	10 hours (but $8\frac{1}{2}$hours three times a week)
Minimum rest days	2 per fortnight

Important note: The above does not constitute the entire drivers' hours requirements and must NOT be interpreted as such.

Staff agreement (all one-man operated services)

Sign on time	15 minutes
Sign-off time	15 minutes
Minimum turning plus stand time (other than dead workings)	3 minutes
Working week	40 hours over 5 days
Spreadover limitations	
9hr 1min to 10hr	up to 10% of whole
10hr 1min to 11hr 30min max	up to 5% of whole

It is now necessary to return to the time schedule and select pieces of work which, when put together, comprise a driver's (and conductor's) duty within the required constraints. It is helpful here to mark on the running schedule each time that the bus passes the crew relief point. In this case the crew change point is at the garage for all except route 1 which, apart from the when working journeys to and from the garage, is at Crossways. There is an agreed 10 minutes walking time between Crossways and the garage. Drivers are required to sign on and off at the garage and they are paid walking time for the meal break as well in order that they can take advantage of canteen facilities. As the different parts of the bus runnings are covered, so they are underlined covering first the early and late journeys and then filling in the middle. The job is finished when the entire bus runnings are so covered. For purpose of illustration the possible crew relief times and the duty allocations have been superimposed on a second copy of the time schedule (Fig 26).

It will be seen from Fig 25 that the total daily (Monday to Friday) runnings of all 11 buses amounts to 131hr 31min. A working week of 40 hours over five days means eight hours per day, but with an allowance of 15 minutes for signing on and 15 minutes for signing off (or 30 minutes per day) there is a theoretical driving day of only $7\frac{1}{2}$ hours. The $7\frac{1}{2}$ hours goes into the total of 131hr 31min, 17+times. On a strict time basis, therefore, 18 duties would cover the work. However, in both the morning and evening peaks, 11 buses are on the road simultaneously and unless the same drivers can cover both peaks, there must be 11 sets of duties for the morning and another set of 11 for the evening or, in other words, 22 overall.

The last bus to leave the garage in the morning is running number 4 at 7.25 and the first bus to finish in the evening is running number 10 at 5.37. With the 30 minutes signing on and off time, this gives a total

1 Town Centre—Neighbourhood A

(TC)	Town Centre	*	*	*	*	7.23	7.38	7.53	8.08	8.23	53	23	4.23	38	53	08	23	6.23	6.53	53	10.53
(CW)	Crossways	6.31	6.46	7.01	7.16	7.31	7.46	8.01	8.16	8.31	01	31	4.31	46	01	16	31	6.31	7.01	01	11.01
(A)	Neighbourhood A	6.48	7.03	7.18	7.33	7.48	8.03	8.18	8.33	8.48	18	48	4.48	03	18	33	48	6.48	7.18	18	11.18

Neighbourhood A	6.55	7.25	7.40	7.55	8.10	8.25	8.40	8.55	25	55	4.25	‡ 10	25	40	55	6.40	6.55	25	10.25	11.25
Crossways	7.12	7.42	7.57	8.12	8.27	8.42	8.57	9.12	42	12	4.42	27	42	57	12	6.57	7.12	42	10.42	11.42
Town Centre	7.20	7.50	8.05	8.20	8.35	8.50	9.05	9.20	50	20	4.50	35	50	05	20	+	+	50	10.50	+

* Departs garage 2 minutes earlier

\+ Arrives garage 2 minutes later

‡ 6.10 pm dep to Crossways and Garage only

Additional Journey

Neighbourhood A to garage 5.18pm

Journeys on Service 2

8.38am TC to Garage
9.08am TC to Garage

4.25pm Garage to TC
4.53pm Garage to TC

2 Town Centre—Neighbourhood C
2A Town Centre—Neighbourhood D

(TC)	Town Centre							7.16	01	16	31	46	10.46	11.01
(CW)	Crossways							7.24	09	24	39	54	10.54	11.09
(G)	Garage	6.11	6.26	6.41	6.50	6.56	7.11	7.26	11	26	41	56	10.56	11.11
	Neighbourhood B	6.25	6.40	6.55	7.04	7.10	7.25	7.40	25	40	55	10	11.10	11.25
(C)	Neighbourhood C	6.35		7.05			7.35		35		05			11.35
(D)	Neighbourhood D		6.49		7.13	7.19		7.49		49		19	11.19	

Neighbourhood D		6.55		7.25		55		25		10.25		10.55		11.25	
Neighbourhood C	6.39		7.09		39		09		10.09		10.39		11.09		11.39
Neighbourhood B	6.49	7.04	7.19	7.34	49	04	19	34	10.19	10.34	10.49	11.04	11.19	11.34	11.49
Garage	7.03	7.18	7.33	7.48	03	18	33	48	10.33	10.48	11.03	11.18	11.33	11.48	12.03
Junction	7.05	7.20	7.35	7.50	05	20	35	50	10.35	10.50					
Town Centre	7.13	7.28	7.43	7.58	13	28	43	58	10.43	10.58					

Additional Journeys

Town Centre to Garage 8.38am
9.08am

Garage to Town Centre 7.25am
4.25pm

Neighbourhood D to Garage 5.32pm

spreadover of 10hr 42min, but according to the staff agreement of this imaginary outfit, no more than 5% of the duties may have spreadovers of this length. In this case this means one duty. On this basis, therefore, the 22 duties can be cut to 21 and this is what has been done, the resultant split being:

up to 9 hours	18
9hr 1min to 10hr	2 or 10%
10hr 1min to 11hr 30min	1 or 5%
	21

There is an average work content per duty of 6hr 53min. As, however, there would be a guaranteed eight hours pay per duty, this is not particularly efficient but such are the diseconomies of the peaks. Duties could, of course, be saved by imposing more onerous conditions. They could also be saved by leaving short pieces of work to be covered locally by unscheduled voluntary overtime. If some of the low mileage peak hour buses remained unscheduled and were covered in this way there might be a considerable saving in duties and a higher average work content for the remainder. But overtime would involve a premium rate and might even incur penalty payments as

Left & Below: **Fig 23. Draft Timetables for Schedule Exercise.**

3 — Neighbourhood A—Industrial Area

(A) Neighbourhood A	7.06	7.11	7.41		
(IA) Industrial Area	7.20	7.25	7.55		
Industrial Area	7.23			4.36	5.01
Neighbourhood A	7.37			4.50	5.15

4 — Neighbourhood A— School

(A) Neighbourhood A	8.58
(S) School	9.05
School	4.15
Neighbourhood A	4.22

5 — Neighbourhood D—Industrial Area

(D) Neighbourhood D	7.16	8.41		4.36
(B) Neighbourhood B	7.25	8.50		4.45
(S) School	7.30	8.55		4.50
(IA) Industrial Area	7.40	-		5.00
Industrial Area	8.05	8.14		5.05
School	8.15	8.24	4.02	5.15
Neighbourhood B	8.20	8.29	4.07	5.20
Neighbourhood D	8.29	8.38	4.16	5.29

6 — Neighbourhood C—School

(C) Neighbourhood C	8.40
(B) Neighbourhood B	8.50
(S) School	8.55
School	4.10
Neighbourhood B	4.15
Neighbourhood C	4.25

Fig 24

Bus Running 1

1	6.29G	6.48A	6.55A	7.20TC
	7.23TC	7.48A	7.55A	8.20TC
	8.23TC	8.48A	8.55A	9.20TC
	9.23TC	9.48A	9.55A	10.20TC
	10.23TC	10.48A	10.55A	11.20TC
	11.23TC	11.48A	11.55A	12.20TC
	12.23TC	12.48A	12.55A	1.20TC
	1.23TC	1.48A	1.55A	2.20TC
	2.23TC	2.48A	2.55A	3.20TC
	3.23TC	3.48A	3.55A	4.20TC
	4.23TC	4.48A	4.55A	5.20TC
	5.23TC	5.48A	5.55A	6.20TC
	6.23TC	6.48A	6.55A	7.14G

Bus Running 2

1	6.59G	7.18A	7.25A	7.50TC
	7.53TC	8.18A	8.25A	8.50TC
	8.53TC	9.18A	9.25A	9.50TC
	9.53TC	10.18A	10.25A	10.50TC
	10.53TC	11.18A	11.25A	11.50TC
	11.53TC	12.18A	12.25A	12.50TC
	12.53TC	1.18A	1.25A	1.50TC
	1.53TC	2.18A	2.25A	2.50TC
	2.53TC	3.18A	3.25A	3.50TC
	3.53TC	4.18A	4.25A	4.50TC
	4.53TC	5.18A	5.25A	5.50TC
	5.53TC	6.18A	6.25A	6.50TC
	6.53TC	7.18A	7.25A	7.50TC
	7.53TC	8.18A	8.25A	8.50TC
	8.53TC	9.18A	9.25A	9.50TC
	9.53TC	10.18A	10.25A	10.50TC
	10.53TC	11.18A	11.25A	11.44G

Bus Running 3

1	6.49G	7.08A	3 7.11A	7.25IA
DEAD	7.28IA	7.37A	1 7.40A	8.05TC
	8.08TC	8.33A	8.40A	9.05TC
2	9.08TC	9.18G	4.25G	4.35TC
1	4.38TC	5.03A	5.10A	5.35TC
	5.38TC	6.03A	6.10A	6.29G

Bus Running 4

2	7.25G	7.35TC		
1	7.38TC	8.03A	8.10A	8.35TC
DEAD	8.38TC	8.55A		
4	8.58A	9.05S		
DEAD	9.08S	9.17G	4.03C	4.12S
4	4.15S	4.22A	1 4.40A	5.05TC
1	5.08TC	5.33A	5.40A	6.05TC
	6.08TC	6.33A	6.40A	6.59G

Bus Running 5

2	6.11G	6.35C	6.39C	7.13TC
2A	7.16TC	7.49D	7.55D	8.28TC
2	8.31TC	9.05C	9.09C	9.43TC
2A	9.46TC	10.19D	10.25D	10.58TC
2	11.01TC	11.35C	11.39C	12.13TC
2A	12.16TC	12.49D	12.55D	1.28TC
2	1.31TC	2.05C	2.09C	2.43TC
2A	2.46TC	3.19D	3.25D	3.58TC
2	4.01TC	4.35C	4.39C	5.13TC
2A	5.16TC	5.49D	5.55D	6.28TC
2	6.31TC	7.05C	7.09C	7.43TC
2A	7.46TC	8.19D	8.25D	8.58TC
2	9.01TC	9.35C	9.39C	10.13TC
2A	10.16TC	10.49D	10.55D	11.18G

Bus Running 6

2A	6.26G	6.49D	6.55D	7.28TC
2	7.31TC	8.05C	8.09C	8.43TC
2A	8.46TC	9.19D	9.25D	9.58TC
2	10.01TC	10.35C	10.39C	11.13TC
2A	11.16TC	11.49D	11.55D	12.28TC
2	12.31TC	1.05C	1.09C	1.43TC
2A	1.46TC	2.19D	2.25D	2,58TC
2	3.01TC	3.35C	3.39C	4.13TC
2A	4.16TC	4.49D	4.55D	5.28TC
2	5.31TC	6.05C	6.09C	6.43TC
2A	6.46TC	7.19D	7.25D	7.58TC
2	8.01TC	8.35C	8.39C	9.13TC
2A	9.16TC	9.49D	9.55D	10.28TC
2	10.31TC	11.05C	11.09C	11.33G

Bus Running 7

2	6.41G	7.05C	7.09C	7.43TC
2A	7.46TC	8.19D	8.25D	8.58TC
2	9.01TC	9.35C	9.39C	10.13TC
2A	10.16TC	10.49D	10.55D	11.28TC
2	11.31TC	12.05C	12.09C	12.43TC
2A	12.46TC	1.19D	1.25D	1.58TC
2	2.01TC	2.35C	2.39C	3.13TC
2A	3.16TC	3.49D	3.55D	4.28TC
2	4.31TC	5.05C	5.09C	5.43TC
2A	5.46TC	6.19D	6.25D	6.58TC
2	7.01TC	7.35C	7.39C	8.13TC
2A	8.16TC	8.49D	8.55D	9.28TC
2	9.31TC	10.05C	10.09C	10.43TC
2A	10.46TC	11.19D	11.25D	11.48G

Bus Running 8

2A	6.56G	7.19D	7.25D	7.58TC
2	8.01TC	8.35C	8.39C	9.13TC
2A	9.16TC	9.49D	9.55D	10.28TC
2	10.31TC	11.05C	11.09C	11.43TC
2A	11.46TC	12.19D	12.25D	12.58TC
2	1.01TC	1.35C	1.39C	2.13TC
2A	2.16TC	2.49D	2.55D	3.28TC
2	3.31TC	4.05D	4.09D	4.43TC
2A	4.46TC	5.19D	5.25D	5.58TC
2	6.01TC	6.35C	6.39C	7.13TC
2A	7.16TC	7.49D	7.55D	8.28TC
2	8.31TC	9.05C	9.09C	9.43TC
2A	9.46TC	10.19D	10.25D	10.58TC
2	11.01TC	11.35C	11.39C	12.03G

Bus Running 9

2	7.11G	7.35C	7.39C	8.13TC
2A	8.16TC	8.49D	8.55D	9.28TC
2	9.31TC	10.05C	10.09C	10.43TC
2A	10.46TC	11.19D	11.25D	11.58TC
2	12.01TC	12.35C	12.39C	1.13TC
2A	1.16TC	1.49D	1.55D	2.28TC
2	2.31TC	3.05C	3.09C	3.43TC
2A	3.46TC	4.19D	4.25D	4.58TC
2	5.01TC	5.35C	5.39C	6.13TC
2A	6.16TC	6.49D	6.55D	7.28TC
2	7.31TC	8.05C	8.09C	8.43TC
2A	8.46TC	9.19D	9.25D	9.58TC
2	10.01TC	10.35C	10.39C	11.03G

Bus Running 10

1	6.44G	7.03A		
3	7.06A	7.20IA	7.23IA	7.37A
	7.41A	7.55IA		
5	8.14IA	8.38D		
5	8.41D	8.55S		
DEAD	8.58C	9.07G		
DEAD	3.53G	4.02S		
5	4.05S	4.16D		
DEAD	4.17D	4.35IA		
3	4.36IA	4.50A		
DEAD	4.51A	5.00IA		
3	5.01IA	5.15A		
1	5.18A	5.37G		

Bus Running 11

2A	6.48G	7.13D		
5	7.16D	7.40IA	8.05IA	8.29D
DEAD	8.32D	8.37C		
6	8.40C	8.55S		
DEAD	8.55S	9.04G	3.58G	4.07S
6	4.10S	4.25C		
DEAD	4.28C	4.33D		
5	4.36D	5.00IA		
5	5.05IA	5.29D		
2A	5.32D	5.55G		

well. Nevertheless, it could be cheaper to do it this way. Voluntary overtime does, however, introduce an element of unreliability and banning overtime is a favourite tactic for industrial action. For the larger and more impersonal undertakings it is a practice which is not particularly recommended. More will be said about this in Chapter 11.

Note that there are no entries in the column for allowances in the written up duties (Fig 27). It is likely that some duties will carry penalty payments such as for starting before or finishing after certain times, working on Saturday afternoons and Sundays (ie unsocial hours) and time for a meal break in excess of one hour, for example, could be paid for. In short, different duties have different earning powers over and above the flat rate. Overall this duty schedule is not a particularly onerous one. There are spells of five hours continuous driving which might result in union representation. If this was the case then in duty 1, for example, bus 5 could be relieved at 10.48am instead of 11.11am. Duty 11 could take over bus 5 that much earlier and still have an adequate meal break. This has not been done as duty 1 already has the lower work content of the two, but it would nevertheless be possible.

Of significance in connection with duty schedule compilation, and this is a continuation of a point made in Chapter 2, is the siting of the operating garage. With the relatively short but high frequency services used in the illustrations, the connection between garage location and schedule efficiency does not have the same impact but there is still an affinity between the two. In order to achieve maximum work content of a duty, the agreed spells, be they the driver's hours regulations or as

Left: **Fig 24. Vehicle Runnings for Schedule Exercise.**
Below: **Fig 25. Time Schedule for Schedule Exercise.**
Bottom: **Fig 26. Duty Allocation for Schedule Exercise.**

Fig 25

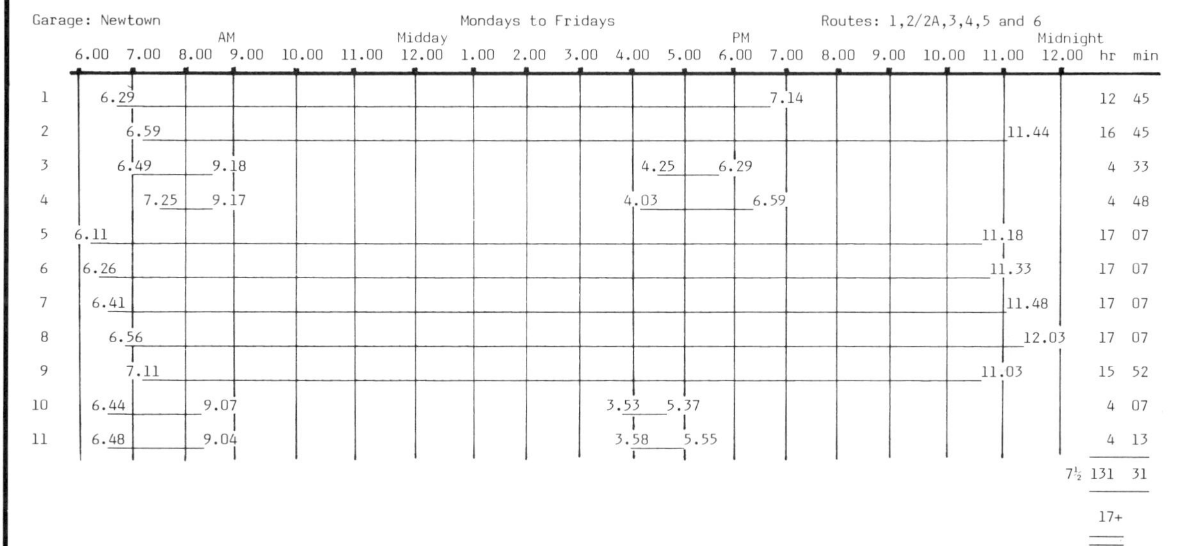

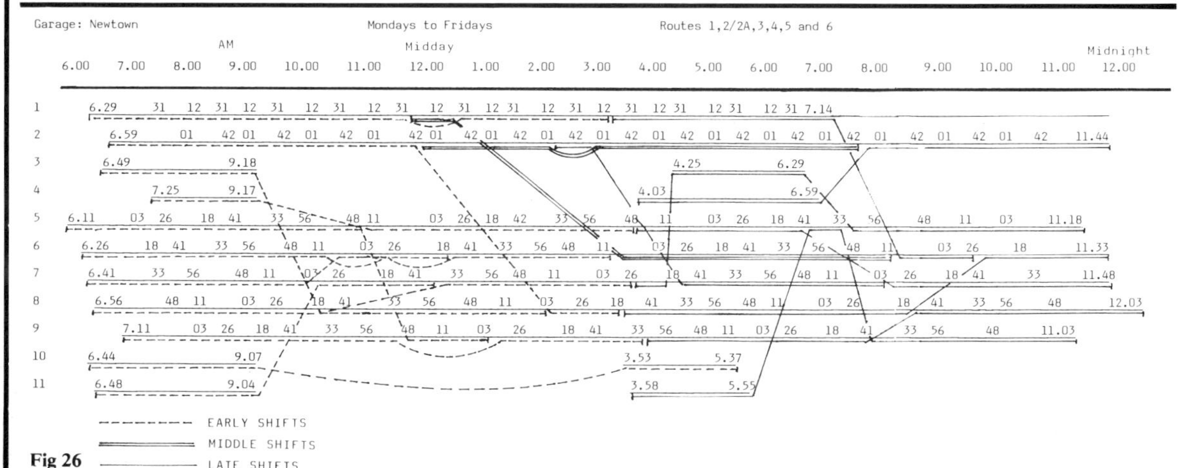

Fig 26

Fig 27. Duty Schedule for Schedule Exercise.

Duty No	Sign on hr min	Route No	Bus Running	Duty Start hr min	Finish hr min	Sign off hr min	Time Worked hr min	Total Spreadover hr min	Allowances
Mondays to Fridays									
1	5.56	2/A	5 9	6.11G 11.48G	11.11G* 1.03G	1.18	6.45	7.22	
2	6.11	2/A	6 6	6.26G 11.26G	10.11G* 12.41G	12.56	5.30	6.45	
3	6.14	1 Walk Walk 1 Walk	1 1 	6.29G 11.31CW 12.21G 12.31CW 3.12CW	11.31CW 11.41G* 12.31CW 3.12CW 3.22G	3.37	8.43	9.23	
4	6.26	2/A	7 6 6	6.41G 10.11G 12.41G	10.03G 11.26G* 3.11G	3.26	7.45	9.00	
5	6.29	3/5	10 10	6.44G 3.53G	9.07G* 5.37G	5.52	4.37	11.23	
6	6.33	5/6 2/A	11 7	6.48G 10.03	9.04G* 12.33G	12.48	5.16	6.15	
7	6.34	1 2/A	3 8	6.49G 10.18G	9.18G* 2.03G	2.18	6.44	7.44	
8	6.41	2/A	8 7	6.56G 12.33G	10.18G* 3.26G	3.41	6.45	9.00	
9	6.44	1 Walk 2/A	2 8	6.59G 11.42CW 2.03G	11.42CW 11.52G* 3.18G	3.33	6.38	8.49	
10	6.56	2/A	9 9	7.11G 1.03G	11.48G* 3.33G	3.48	7.37	8.52	
11	7.10	1 2/A	4 5	7.25G 11.11G	9.17G* 3.48G	4.03	6.59	8.53	
12	11.06	Walk 1 Walk 2/A	 1 6	11.21G 11.31CW 12.31CW 3.11G	11.31CW 12.31CW 12.41G* 8.11G	8.26	6.50	9.20	
13	11.17	Walk 1 Walk Walk 1 Walk	 2 2 	11.32G 11.42CW 2.01CW 2.51G 3.01CW 7.42CW	11.42CW 2.01CW 2.11G* 3.01CW 7.42CW 7.52G	8.07	8.10	8.50	
14	1.36	Walk 1 Walk 2	 2 7	1.51G 2.01CW 3.01CW 4.18G	2.01CW 3.01CW 3.11G* 8.03G	8.18	5.35	6.42	
15	2.47	Walk 1 2/A	 1 6	3.02G 3.12CW 8.11G	3.12CW 7.14G* 9.26G	9.41	5.57	6.54	
16	3.03	2/A	8 6	3.18G 9.26G	8.18G* 11.33G	11.48	7.37	8.45	
17	3.11	2/A 1 2/A	7 3 5	3.26G 4.25G 7.33G	4.18G 6.29G* 11.18G	11.33	7.18	8.22	
18	3.18	2/A	9 8	3.33G 8.18G	7.41G* 12.03G	12.18	8.23	9.00	
19	3.33	2/A	5 7	3.48 8.03G	6.41G* 11.48G	12.03	7.08	8.30	
20	3.43	5/6 2/A	11 5 9	3.58G 6.41G 7.41G	5.55G* 7.33G 11.03G	11.18	6.49	7.35	
21	3.48	4/1 Walk 1	4 2	4.03G 7.32G 7.42CW	6.59G* 7.42CW 11.44G	11.59	7.38	8.11	
Saturdays									
30									
31									
32									
33									
34									
35									
36									
37									
38									
39									
40									
41									
42									
43									
44									
45									
46									
47									
48									
49									
Sundays									
60									
61									
62									
63									
64									
65									
66									
67									

negotiated locally, should fit conveniently into return journey or part journey times of the services concerned. Take, for example, a route from A to C via B with a throughout running time of 1hr 25min and which passes near garages Y and Z as in the following diagram:

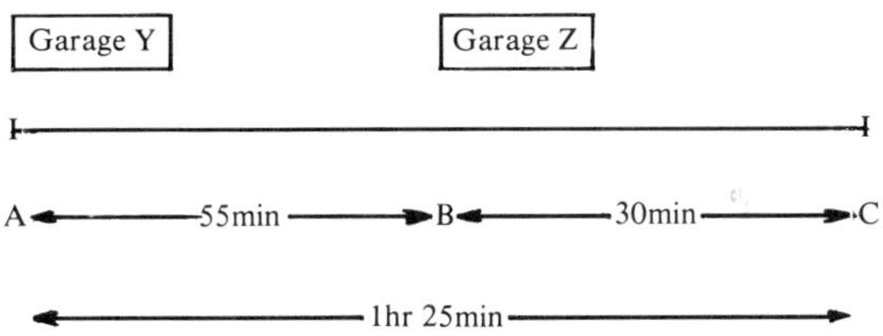

If crews were allocated to Garage Y and took charge of their vehicles at A, a round trip to C would take 2hr 50min plus stand time at C. Two round trips to C would take 5hr 40min plus two periods of stand time at C and one at A, which would exceed the maximum permitted spell of continuous work. Unless, therefore, other work was available on a shorter route from Garage Y, the crew could do no more than one return trip before coming off for a break. The second spell of duty would, in the absence of any work on another route, again be one trip to C. This would produce a duty with a total work content of 5hr 40min plus stand time. The agreed conditions of service, however, will undoubtedly call for a guaranteed daily wage equivalent to about eight hours work, in which case, in this example (and ignoring stand time) 2hr 20min would be paid per man per day for no work at all.

Consider now the position as it would be if staff were attached instead to Garage Z. The route would not now consist only of a single 'block' of 2hr 50min but one of 1hr (30min×2) B to C, another of 1hr 50min (55min×2) B to A and others consisting of any combination of these two. A duty comprising B-C-A-C-B (3hr 50min) in both the first and second spells would produce a duty of 7hr 40min which might well be within the terms of the agreements, again disregarding for this purpose the additional time necessitated on layover at the termini and time taken to sign on and take over the vehicle and to sign off and pay in cash for which there must be due allowance.

In the specimen schedule exercise, if the operating garage was so sited that the crew relief point was at the town centre, then the only available spells of duty would have been 57 minutes on route 1 and 1hr 12min on route 2/2A. In this particular case blocks of this length would be reasonable enough for duty schedule compilation, but a glance again at the time schedule at which the passing times of the crew relief points have been appended (Fig 26) will show that a far greater range of permutations is available. The chances of maximising

Garage: Newtown
Routes: 1, 2/2A, 3, 4, 5 and 6

Duty Roster

Rota Number	Sun	Mon	Tues	Wed	Thurs	Fri	Sat	Total work for week
1	-	14 5.35	14 5.35	14 5.35	-	1 6.45	30 7.50	31.20
2	60 7.50	1 6.45	1 6.45	1 6.45	1 6.45	-	-	34.50
3	-	-	21 7.38	21 7.38	21 7.38	21 7.38	49 7.50	38.22
4	-	9 6.38	9 6.38	9 6.38	-	10 7.37	47 7.50	35.21
5	66 7.50	19 7.08	-	-	9 6.38	9 6.38	39 7.50	36.04
6	-	17 7.18	17 7.18	17 7.18	17 7.18	17 7.18	-	36.30
7	-	11 6.59	11 6.59	-	11 6.59	11 6.59	37 7.50	35.46
8	-	16 7.37	16 7.37	16 7.37	-	INST 8.00	38 7.50	38.41
9	62 7.50	7 6.44	7 6.44	7 6.44	7 6.44	-	-	34.46
10	-	-	19 7.08	19 7.08	19 7.08	19 7.08	40 7.50	36.22
11	63 7.50	3 8.43	-	-	6 5.15	6 5.16	46 7.50	34.55
12	-	18 8.23	-	11 6.59	14 5.35	14 5.35	35 7.50	34.22
13	-	4 7.45	4 7.45	4 7.45	4 7.45	4 7.45	-	38.45
14	-	-	18 8.23	18 8.23	18 8.23	18 8.23	41 7.50	41.22
15	64 7.50	15 5.57	-	-	8 6.45	8 6.45	36 7.50	35.07
16	-	-	8 6.45	8 6.45	5 4.37	7 6.44	44 7.50	32.41
17	-	20 6.49	12 6.50	6 5.16	-	2 5.30	34 7.50	32.15
18	61 7.50	2 5.30	2 5.30	2 5.30	2 5.30	-	-	29.50
19	-	-	20 6.49	20 6.49	20 6.49	20 6.49	48 7.50	35.06
20	-	6 5.16	6 5.16	-	13 8.10	INST 8.00	43 7.50	34.32
21	-	13 8.10	13 8.10	13 8.10	-	13 8.10	31 7.50	40.30
22	65 7.50	10 7.37	10 7.37	10 7.37	10 7.37	-	-	38.18
23	-	-	15 5.57	15 5.57	15 5.57	15 5.57	45 7.50	31.38
24	-	5 4.37	5 4.37	5 4.37	-	5 4.37	32 7.50	26.18
25	67 7.50	21 7.38	-	12 6.50	12 6.50	12 6.50	-	35.58
26	-	8 6.45	3 8.43	-	16 7.37	16 7.37	42 7.50	38.32
27	-	12 6.50	-	3 8.43	3 8.43	3 8.43	33 7.50	40.49

Above: **Fig 28. Duty Roster for Schedule Exercise.**

efficiency and at the same time meeting staff agreements etc are, therefore, that much better. As an example, the point made about the five-hour spell in duty 1 and the adjustment with duty 11 took advantage of the passing times at the changeover point of bus 5 being only 23 minutes apart. A crew change point part way along a route gives greater flexibility but geography is nevertheless also important. In the examples the fact that the garage is not on the direct line of route 1 carries a disadvantage in that it necessitates 10-minute penalty payments in terms of walking time on each occasion that a crew is relieved.

Duty Roster

Having prepared the time and duty schedules, the final task of the schedules section is to prepare a duty roster. It is this document which details, in effect, who will work what and as, in this example, the agreement calls for a five-day week, where the rest days will be. A specimen duty roster is appended as a follow-up from the duty schedule (Fig 28).

The exercise as progressed so far has indicated a need for 21 duties on each day Monday to Friday. As said at the outset, it is not proposed to cover the same ground again for Saturdays and Sundays but for this purpose let it be assumed that there are 20 duties on Saturdays and eight on Sundays, all with a work content of 7hr 50min. The number of duties per week, therefore, is:

Monday-Friday	21×5	105
Saturday		20
Sunday		8
Total		133

As each driver works a five-day week the total number of staff required is 133 divided by five, which calls for either 26 with three duties not covered or 27 with two duties to instructions without any scheduled work. This means that in the case of a 26-week roster (ie 26 drivers in regular scheduled employment) three duties would have to be covered locally by spare staff (if any) or by overtime or rest day working or, if a 27-week roster, two spare duties would be available to cover absences, approved or otherwise. In the example the latter alternative has been selected.

The preparation of the duty roster is best done by first filling in on the skeleton the rest days with, in this case, 27 lines. There must be two rest days per week (per line) and as far as possible, staff might like to have them consecutively. If drivers drop down one line each week, a Friday/Saturday rest one week and a Sunday/Monday the next gives four days off together. They might also prefer an early in front of the rest days and a late after. The more popular roster is a week of earlies, then rest followed by a week of lates although it does not always work out as neatly as that. Services are now often very much thinner on Sundays which means that there must be a preponderance of Sunday rests. A similar situation cannot, of course, apply to Mondays, which means that some split rest days cannot be avoided. Care must be taken to ensure that an adequate period of rest is available should a driver work a late turn followed by an early. In the example, the actual time worked is shown as well as the duty number. Many duties, however, will have allowances and penalty payments according to local agreements and in practice it might be convenient to indicate the monetary value (if any) of each duty over and above the eight hours flat rate.

Application to Railways

All that has been said so far has reference to buses. The same procedure can, however, be applied to trolleybuses and really also to trams; except that if there are long lengths of single track timetables would have to take account of the location of passing loops. Even with railways the principles as described remain but there are added complications on the timetabling side. Whilst the railway is the sole user of its own specialised way and is not, therefore, subject to delays caused by other traffic, it is to some extent 'self-congesting' as although the speeds of different classes of trains vary, if there is only one set of tracks they cannot pass each other except when special facilities are provided, which is usually only at the larger stations. Although this book is concerned only with local passenger services, on a main line railway system they are often required to share the tracks with faster long distance passenger trains and slower goods trains and even with these three basic classifications there are varying speeds and conflicting traffic movements. It follows that if all of these different categories of trains are required in the same periods then the timing of one must influence the timing of the others and the maximum speed is governed by that of the slowest. Commercially the backbone of any national railway system on the passenger side is its network of fast long distance trains which stop only at the main stations in the larger towns. These express trains are sometimes timed to connect with each other at important provincial interchange centres (Birmingham is an example) and any adjustments at one point could have repercussions on other timings even hundreds of miles away. The movement of freight is also valuable to the railway as it is an important revenue earner. The public service obligation does not apply to the carriage of merchandise, hence such traffic as is accepted is part of a viable enterprise in a competitive market and the trains

Right: **Fig 29. Specimen train diagram over a section of a hypothetical stretch of line between stations A and N. The specification is one fast train per hour A to N, one semi-fast A to N stopping intermediately only at H and two local trains stopping at all stations as per the timetable extract as shown. A simple double track is provided throughout except that four tracks plus refuge sidings and hence passing facilities for trains travelling in the same direction are available at H. The steeper the line diagram the faster is the speed of the train. In this example where there are repetitive timings in each hour, X represents the fast, Y the semi-fast and Z the stopping trains. If the line was single track then both directions would have to be shown with, for the other way, line diagrams proceeding upwards from left to right across the page. Trains could, of course, pass only where suitable facilities are available which, in this case, is at H. The actual spacing between trains is dependent upon the signalling arrangements and block lengths. Note that if a special train had to be superimposed with an average speed of, say, only 20 to 25mph, the paths available would be very restricted but the dotted line is a possibility. By graphical presentation in this way train paths can be plotted with conflicting movements becoming immediately apparent. In this example the track is heavily utilised and very little space is available for any more trains. It also follows that the service could be easily disrupted as apart from the passing facility at H, any delay (and this is always possible, particularly with local trains stopping at all stations) could only hold up those trains in the rear. The same style of working sheets can be used for bus schedules but in this case there is not the need to detect and eliminate the points of physical conflict.**

FIG. 29

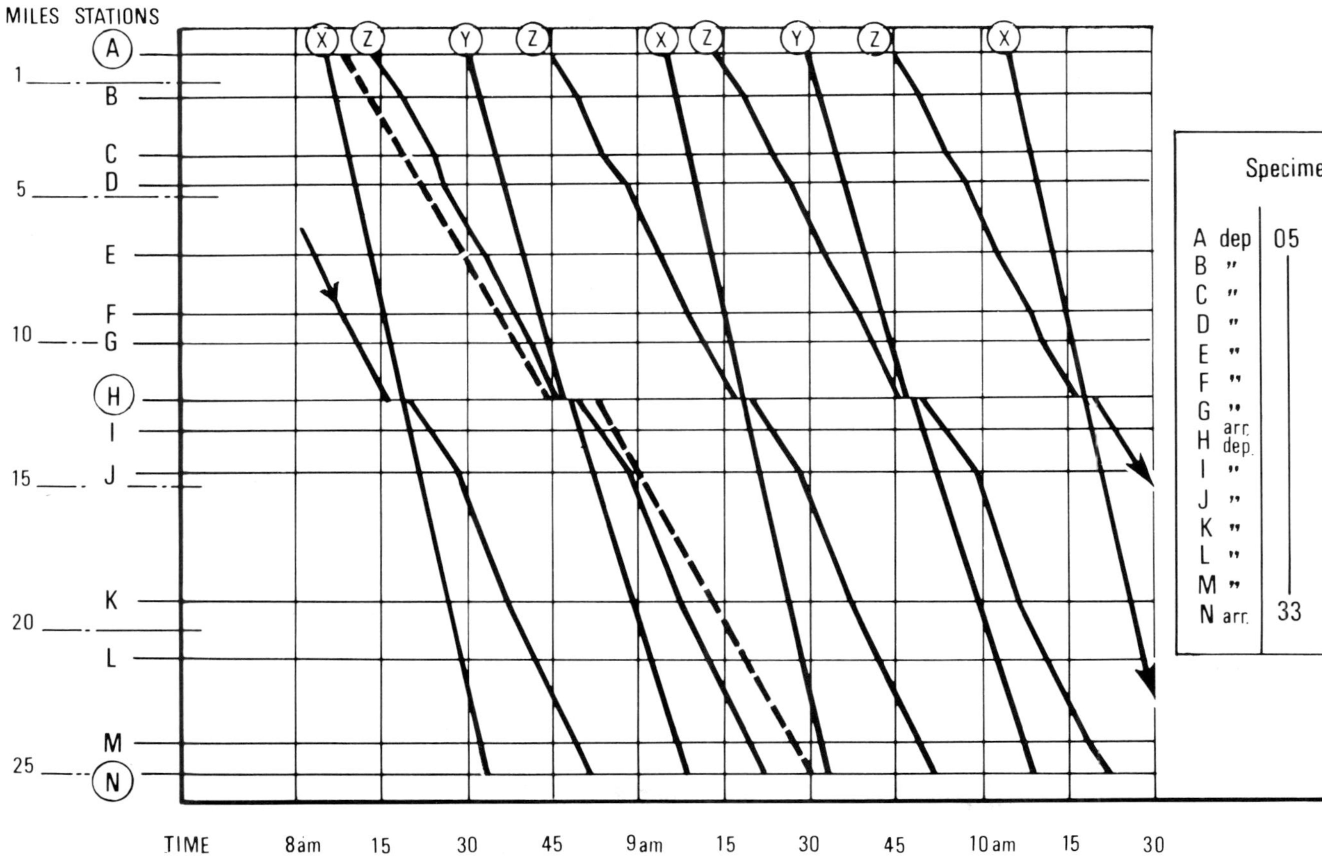

Specimen Hour

A dep	05	14	30		44
B "		19			49
C "		24			54
D "		27			57
E "		33			03
F "		38			08
G "		41			11
H arr.		46	47		16
H dep.			49	50	20
I "				53	23
J "				58	28
K "				07	37
L "				12	42
M "				19	49
N arr.	33		09	22	52

must be afforded adequate facilities. On the other hand, specific timings are not in this case as vital which means that there is some scope to avoid conflict with the more particular requirements of passenger traffic.

In fact, not all freight trains are of a regular nature. In Great Britain, British Railways classifies its trains as either 'mandatory' or 'conditional'. The purpose of this is to distinguish those which must always run from others which are not so committed on account of the unstable nature of the traffic offering. Generally, all passenger and parcel trains are mandatory as are all regular wagon load, block or company trains. It is the irregular block or company trains and much of the local trip working such as to steelworks and collieries which by nature do not operate with daily regularity which are termed conditional. Superimposed on all of this is the empty stock and perhaps also light locomotive working necessary for positioning purposes but which nevertheless involves track occupation just the same as anything else.

The relevance of this information to urban and rural passenger transport could be questioned and in some respects the answer is none. On the other hand, enough has been said to show that on lines where there is mixed traffic the local passenger services are only one consideration in terms of track occupancy. Furthermore, bearing in mind that outside the large heavily populated urbanised areas (and in Great Britain this is London and the south-east) local stopping trains are a small and highly unremunerative (disregarding revenue support) part of the business, it is understandable if railway administrations do not always regard them as first priority. This means that where there is a heavy user of common tracks the local trains might not always be able to run at the ideal times or even at the ideal frequencies. It also means that notwithstanding the point made earlier that there is much to be said for repetitive 'clock face' timetables, where there is a heavy mix of traffic and paths are not easy to find, this is not always possible. There is also the conflict between local needs and connections with long-distance trains and even here the views and priorities of local and national operators might well be different.

For various reasons, there can be no simple preparation of a timetable based only on passenger need and the economics of running time/service frequency affinity as was done in the case of buses. For ease and clarity of presentation, all trains which share a common track must be plotted on a diagram which will immediately indicate potential conflicts and available paths. The example which is illustrated at Fig 29 shows possible train movements over a hypothetical stretch of line. On this imaginary section there is only one pair of tracks throughout (ie, one line in each direction) with limited passing facilities as shown but it is relatively heavily used by all three classes of traffic. Diagrams of this type are built-up in accordance with traffic requirements but, unlike the buses, there is this ever-present added dimension of the need to avoid conflicting movements. This exemplifies the lower degree of flexibility which is characteristic of fixed-track systems.

It is circumstances as described which make it operationally undesirable to mix two or more classes of traffic on the same track if there is a heavy movement of any one and this narrative now becomes a follow-up to what was said in Chapter 2 with regard to rapid transit. The definition of a system which bears that descriptive title was quoted in that chapter as a self-contained network, the operation of which is not inhibited by conflict with any other traffic of the same or a different mode. If this is the case, then the difficulties as described with suburban trains superimposed on a main line system will not arise unless, of course, there is a requirement to run a few semi-fast trains within the rapid transit network itself on a 'skip stop' arrangement. This apart, there is then really no need for the timetable compiler to diagram trains in the conventional railway style as if they all travel at the same speed this would result in a series of parallel lines without any message to convey. Furthermore, if the lines are self-contained then there are no movements of potential conflict and the only limitations are:

(a) track capacity to the extent dictated by the speed (including acceleration and deceleration) of trains and the signalling system which governs minimum headways (being the interval between trains) as was discussed in Chapter 2.

(b) track availability for trains to stand at reversing points either intermediately or at a terminus.

To elaborate on item (b), study the following diagram which shows a single terminus with a scissors crossover and an island platform.

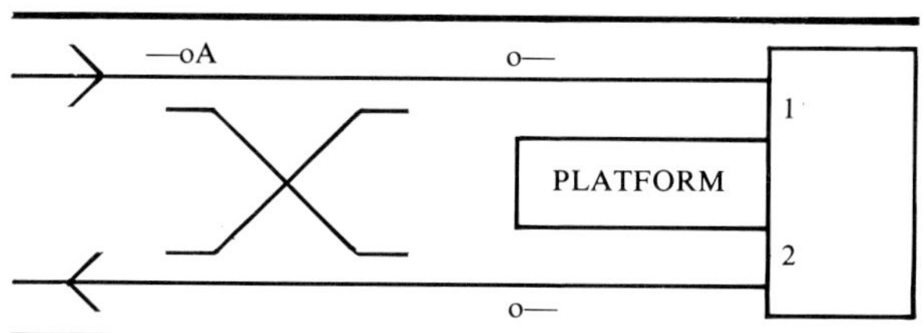

Visualise the first train entering platform 1 followed by a second train coming into Platform 2. Before the third train can arrive the first train must have left. If it has not then the third train will be held at the approach signal (—o) A. This in turn would hold back all trains to the rear and on a high frequency service chaos would quickly result. In circumstances such as this frequencies are very much governed by terminal allowances. Relief could, of course, be afforded by the provision of an extra platform, but the cost could be considerable even for a surface line and in the case of an underground railway, well nigh prohibitive.

What should now be apparent is that the railway timetable compiler must have a more intimate knowledge of the limitations of the way than is needed by his counterpart on the buses. Furthermore, the many conflicting interests of the various traffic and track limitations often make suitable paths difficult to find and perhaps even more difficult to alter. This gives very little room for manoeuvre when it comes to allocate train crews and whereas slight timetable adjustments might be made to improve the efficiency of bus duty schedules, it could become highly complex to introduce further dimensions into train diagrams. Administratively, therefore, there is less affinity between the functions of time and duty schedule preparation on rail as there is on road.

It is from the train diagrams that working timetables are prepared which contain information for staff of all movements including empty stock working. The final stage is the public timetable which eliminates what, for this purpose, would be unnecessary and highly confusing information.

USE
Fry's Pure Cocoa
LONDON GENERAL OMNIBUS COMPANY LIMITED
LIVERPOOL STREET STATIONS
STARCH GREEN SHEPHERD'S BUSH
NOTTING HILL, OXFORD ST. HOLBORN, BANK.
AAX
LONDON GENERAL OMNIBUS COMPANY LIMITED.
BAYSWATER

St GEORGE'S Ch
Suchard
271
860
271

Left: **Horse bus of the London General Omnibus Company of the 1890s in Goldhawk Road, London, W. Although drawn by two horses, these buses had seats for only 26 passengers. By this time the early 'knifeboard' type seats on the upper deck (being two rows of longitudinal seats back to back facing outwards) were giving way to 'garden seats' (pairs of seats facing forward with a centre gangway); an arrangement which has now stood the test of time.** *London Transport Executive*

Below left: **Horse tram of the London Tramways Company of the 1890s in Camberwell Depot, London, SE. Less tractive effort is required to haul a vehicle which has smooth steel wheels running on smooth steel rails and this tram has accommodation for 46 passengers. As a matter of interest the photograph was taken prior to acquisition by the London County Council in 1899. The Tramways Act, 1870 gave to local authorities the power to purchase tramways but not to work them themselves. Powers to operate horse trams had, however, in this case already been conferred on the Council in 1896.**

Below: **Whilst in the latter part of the 19th century passengers by road generally had available to them only the services of the horse, the railway was not so inhibited. This Beyer-Peacock steam locomotive of the District Railway in London was built in the 1860s and offered a far superior form of transport than what could be provided by buses and trams. It was for this reason that a multiplicity of railway lines were developed far beyond what could have been justified had the petrol engine become available before steam. But the line depicted in the illustration has not suffered dereliction and closure. The train is standing in West Brompton station which is now part of the Wimbledon branch of the District Line of the London Transport network. The photograph was taken in 1876.**
London Transport Executive

23
NON-STO

BELGRAVIA HOSIERY Co
PRINTER ACCOUNT BOOK MAKER
COURT HAIR-DRESSER
SEAYEARS
COSTUMES
LEWIS HART
BEDDOES
CASH DRAPERS
WARWICK St WILTON Rd
VICTORIA STATION
GROSVENOR PLACE
PARK LANE
MARBLE ARCH OXFORD ST.
Pears'
Soap
GOLDERS GREEN
EBURY BRIDGE
SHAFTESBURY
Mr ROBERT COURTNEIDGE'S
THE CINEMA STAR
2
B 620
LE 9173

Left: **Although it was steam which nurtured the railway, electricity as a form of motive power came relatively early in the history of mass transit. Electrification of railways and tramways developed around the turn of the century and in 1905 the District Railway (control of which had by this time passed to the Underground Electric Railways Company of London Limited) withdrew its steam trains. Here is depicted 1905 electric stock of the District Line which follows the North American style open type coaches as distinct from the separate compartment type which at the time was the more usual British practice.** *London Transport Executive*

Below left: **A landmark in standardisation of bus design came in 1910 when London General introducted its B type, three of which are shown here in Belgravia, London, SW. Note the similarity of the body with that of the horse bus. The source of power (by now a 30hp petrol engine) remained forward of the driver and the body which boasted 34 seats was still placed at about the same height from the ground. It is of passing interest that the service numbers and routes of the buses which appear in this photograph are still in operation today apart from extensions at the extremities as the suburbs have developed. Route planning and traffic investigation there must be, but passengers tend to resent disturbance of their travel habits. Change is sometimes necessary but there must never be change for change's sake.**
London Transport Executive

Top right: **The next stages in the evolution of the bus were a covered upper deck, pneumatic tyres and a windscreen for the driver. These refinements came to most of Great Britain in the early 1920s but the illustration shows the NS type of London General which was not fitted with pneumatic tyres until 1928. London was somewhat behind the provinces in these respects because of police restrictions regardless of the fact that the bus was designed specifically to accommodate these features. With a lower centre of gravity a covered top became possible and with the driver beside instead of behind the engine there is greater carrying capacity. This particular type seated 50 passengers.**
London Transport Executive

Bottom right: **This E/1 type tram of London Transport was adopted as standard by its predecessor operator, the London County Council in 1907. Compared with the B type bus as depicted it was superior indeed but this photograph was taken in 1937 and some of the class were still to see another 15 years' service. Seen here at Mitcham Lane, Streatham, London, SW, apart from a fresh livery, there is little actual change in external appearance since its first introduction. Certainly it had been refurbished when the livery was altered and many of the cars of this type were destined for another refurbishment before they were finally phased out. Nevertheless, whilst compared with the B type bus of 1910 the LCC trams with their totally enclosed upper deck had a standard of comfort almost ahead of their time, their long life put them at a disadvantage in comparison with subsequent generations of buses which first reached and then passed them in terms of comfort.**

Left: **Interior view of the upper deck of a London Transport (ex-LCC) tram of the type depicted. What was acceptable in 1907 was inadequate in the 1950s but the potential comfort of the tram as a mode of transport must not be judged accordingly. Even so, if seats continue to be slashed at the present alarming rate then 80 years on in 1987 there will have been progression from wood to fibreglass with little improvement in the degree of comfort.**

Below: **This Commer char-a-banc of 1922 is another example of the 'toastrack' style seating. Without a centre gangway maximum seating becomes possible.** *National Bus Company*

Right: **The one time conventional railway carriage was a development of the 'toastrack' concept with no central gangway but with access from each side to what at this stage had become pairs of bench type seats facing each other forming separate compartments. This example was on the Metropolitan Line of the London Transport system prior to electrification through to Amersham when the style gave way to open type stock with sliding doors.**
London Transport Executive

Below right: **This single deck Leyland PS2 of Birmingham City Transport (a predecessor of the West Midlands Passenger Transport Executive) was new in 1950 and gave sterling service in its day. But with a separate driver's cab and forward (as opposed to front) entrance, it was not ideal for one man operation. This particular model had 34 seats.**

431
LONDON
TRANSPORT
431

27
JOJ 247

Above: **Evidence which suggests that trams could be equally as attractive and comfortable as buses lies in this picture of one of the last types ever to be produced in Great Britain until the recent development in Blackpool. This tram was delivered to Sheffield Transport Department in 1950 but was destined for a life of barely 10 years before the system was finally abandoned.**
South Yorkshire Passenger Transport Executive

Left: **The various stages of evolution of the bus from horse to diesel have been illustrated with a natural progression culminating in the front engine, half cab, forward entrance vehicle. But just as the upper deck was projected over the driver's cab in the 1930s to give more accommodation, so, if the half cab became a full front and the entire length of the vehicle made available as floor space, the payload would be yet further increased. With a single deck this could be achieved by placing the engine under a higher base. With a double deck this is not practicable and in 1958 with the introduction of the Leyland Atlantean the whole concept of double deck bus design changed. The new standard became front entrance (ie, in front of the front wheels) and engine at the rear with (on normal British dimensions) up to 78 seats. This Bristol VR of the Eastern Counties Omnibus Company which is constructed on the same**

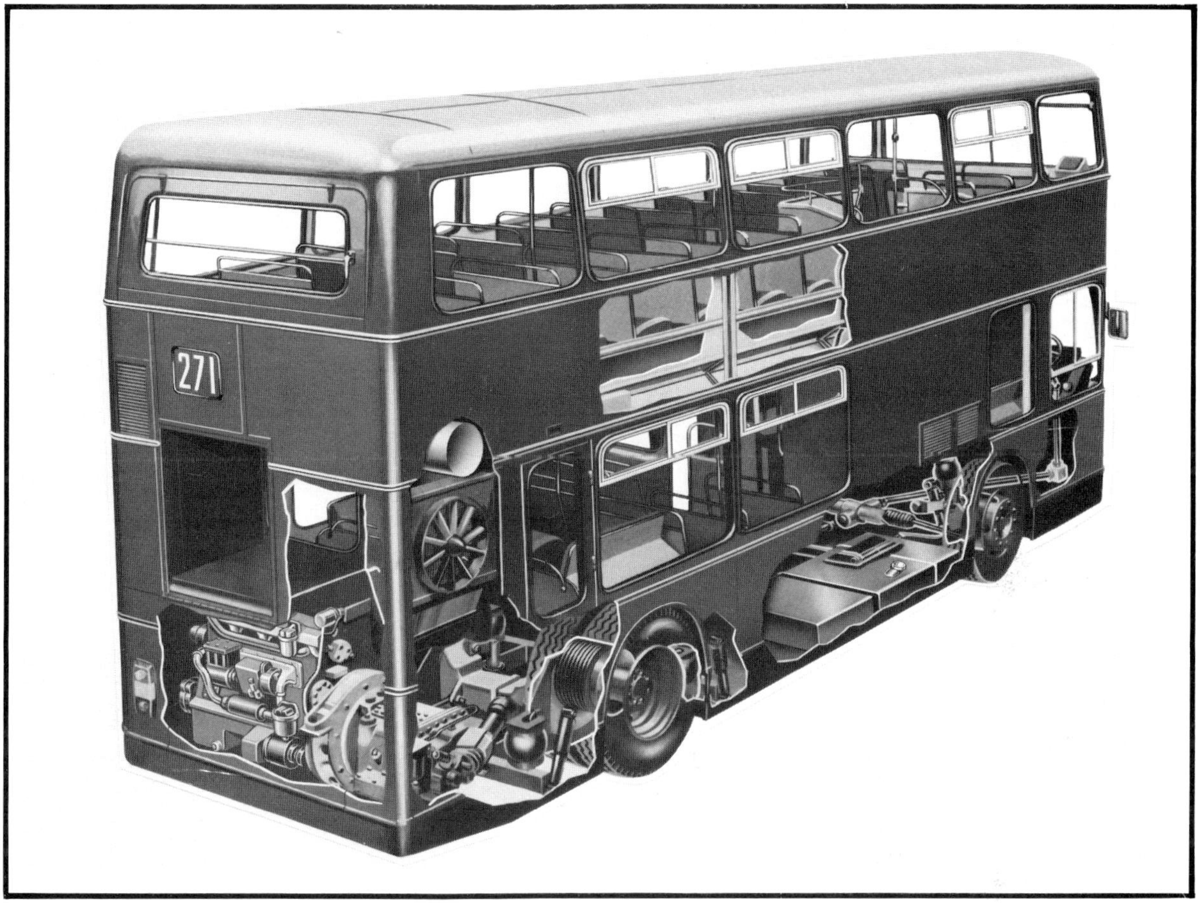

principle and which is illustrated here is typical and is seen in service in Great Yarmouth. The design is eminently suitable for one-man operation.

Above: **Cutaway of a Leyland Titan integral double-deck bus showing layout of major components and automotive details.**
Leyland Vehicles

Right: **As with most of the now conventional designs, a centre exit is an optional extra although there has been much controversy over this arrangement and few undertakings are now specifying vehicles of this type. The bus illustrated here of the former Birmingham City Transport undertaking was pictured in 1969.**

12
ALUM CHINE

4
POOL FARM ESTATE
AND COTTERIDGE
PAY AS YOU
ENTER
BON 451C

Far left: **The ubiquitous bus — a vehicle of the Trent company negotiates a narrow road in the village of Bradwell in Derbyshire.**

Left: **Although the cover over the upper deck came in with great acclaim in the 1920s as a new dimension in passenger comfort, the open top is still an attractive feature under certain conditions. A very limited number of open top vehicles are, therefore, in service and this Daimler Fleetline of Bournemouth Corporation is seen at Southbourne on its seasonal coastal route. Some undertakings have vehicles so designed that a semi-permanent cover can be fitted to the upper deck thereby permitting use throughout the winter months.**

Below left: **Although with single decks there is not the same justification for an engine at the rear the option is available and this single deck Fleetline was delivered to Birmingham City Transport in 1965.**

Top right: **An alternative to the double deck as a means of increasing accommodation is the long articulated bus — very useful where tall vehicles are precluded for physical reasons but where road space is such as not to produce traffic problems. This articulated vehicle is seen in Karl Liebknecht in East Berlin adjacent to Alexanderplatz S-bahn station.**

Centre right: **Another means of increasing passenger accommodation within a limited headroom is the half decker. With conventional single deck style forward, a rearrangement of the floor levels at the rear permits a partial second deck. This vehicle was pictured at Hameln in West Germany.**

Bottom right: **On routes which serve the more remote areas it is economical to convey goods as well as passengers. On the longer journeys accompanied luggage is also much in evidence and to avoid the need to encroach on the passenger accommodation, accompanied or unaccompanied baggage, etc may be conveyed either on the roof or in a trailer. Here is seen a long distance bus of South African Railways approaching an interchange point near Mount Ayliff in the Transkei, southern Africa.**

4 Knaves Hill
UNITED COUNTIES
Bedfordshire County Council
PKX 272R

HEX 683N

Above far left: **A joint service by United Counties and Bedfordshire County Council provides a local facilitiy in Leighton Buzzard. This small bus offers a useful transport facility.** *National Bus Company*

Above centre: **Articulation with a difference and a style more familiar with road hauliers is this separate tractive unit and semi-trailer which is one of the standard designs which operates in the larger towns in India. The vehicle is 40ft long and has seating accommodation for 100 passengers. The example shown here is in the ownership of the Bombay Electric Supply and Transport undertaking and is seen operating in Bombay.**

Left: **Ford 12-seater mini-bus seen working on one of the first community bus services. The project is sponsored jointly by Norfolk County Council and Eastern Counties Omnibus Company.**
National Bus Company

Above: **In rural areas where bus traffic is very light it is economic if practicable to combine the carriage of passengers with goods or mail. The villages of Crundale, Solestreet, Godersham and Thruxted around Canterbury in Kent provide just such territory and a postal bus service was introduced in 1972. The Bedford Utilabus shown here in the village of Petham can carry up to nine fare-paying passengers at the same time as mail is delivered and collected. The Royal Mail Post Bus has a distinctive livery with red bodywork and yellow roof and lettering.**
Post Office Copyright Reserved

Right: **One of the remaining trolleybus networks with the one time conventional British style double deck trolleybuses is that of the Johannesburg municipality in South Africa. Pictured here in 1976, the hardware is becoming time expired and the system will be unable to remain operational for many more years without renewal but in the absence of the backing of a trolleybus manufacturing industry, replacement brings forth problems. Nevertheless, the oil situation has brought pressure to retain electric propulsion and the future of this sytem must remain a matter of conjecture.**

Left: **Bus priority at Great Yarmouth in Norfolk. This vehicle of Great Yarmouth Corporation Transport Department is still able to observe an important boarding point and is about to make a right turn and thereby avoid an otherwise lengthy circulatory working which all other traffic is required to observe.**

Below left: **As far as road passenger transport is concerned, trams are unique in that they may be either single or double ended, meaning that they can be adapted for driving in either direction. Trams so equipped require no special reversing facilities other than a crossover if on a double track. Doors must, however, be provided on either side and the arrangement affects the design of the seats. Braunschweig in West Germany is an example where single ended trams are in operation and where terminal loops are therefore necessary at the terminals. This photograph shows a tram which has just negotiated such a loop at Wesserstrasse in the outer suburbs.**

Below: **Another view of a Braunschweig tram, this time before negotiating the terminal loop at Wessertrasse showing the offside (without access facilities) and non-driving end.**

Above: **The 100-seat double-deck vehicle pictured here is a rebuild by Blackpool Corporation Transport Department into what might become the prototype of the next generation of British trams. Double ended with each end based on an Atlantean bus design (which includes an entrance/exit and stairway which is in contrast to the original central entrance and stairway) one-man operation becomes possible.**
Blackpool Corporation Transport Department

Right: **One of the few monorails which takes a legitimate place in an urban transport system is that of Wuppertaler Stadtwerke AG at Wuppertal in West Germany. Here a car is seen leaving one of the stations on the 8-mile line.**

Top: **An example of a 'drive through' type bus station at Newport, Isle of Wight. This design has the advantage that vehicles do not have to reverse on to or off a stand but the resultant platform arrangement means that access must either be grade separated (which involves the use of steps which are costly and unpopular) or passengers must cross the bus runways. To the left can be seen a stacking area for vehicle layover purposes which is a useful facility if sufficient land is available. The first priority in site selection must, however, be convenience in relation to traffic objectives and if bus stacking space is not available then this facility will have to be provided elsewhere, perhaps at a local garage if there is one. This would, of course, involve some extra cost in empty running.** *National Bus Company*

Above: **Circulating area of the bus station in Barnsley, South Yorkshire, of the Yorkshire Traction Company. This arrangement does allow passengers to board and alight without crossing vehicle runways but it also involves a reversing movement for vehicles across the path of incoming buses. For safety reasons, therefore, it might sometimes be considered desirable to have a pointsman on duty to control the reversal of buses away from the stands.**

Top: **Bus stopping area at Rennes in France. This is a neat example of a form of bus priority where the original highway has been utilised for bus stands and other traffic uses diversionary roads which also serve car parks.**

Above: **In the smaller towns, a separate bus garage and bus station cannot always be justified. In this example at Great Yarmouth in Norfolk a small forecourt of the local garage is used as a bus stand and an adjacent enquiry/booking office has been provided. For reasons of space it is in this instance also necessary to use part of the enclosed garage area for bus stand purposes.**

BUS STOP
REQUEST

Top left: **Bus stop and shelters of the EGGED bus co-operative in the Negev Desert south of the Dead Sea in Israel.**

Left: **A bus shelter incorporating the 'Amstad' seat design. This arrangement takes up less space than the conventional type seat as the traveller is 'perching' instead of sitting and is hence in a more upright position whilst still being able to take the weight off his legs. When not in use the seat swivels to an upright position thereby avoiding obstruction to pedestrians.**
Amstad Systems Limited

Above: **An example of a bus shelter erected primarily for advertising purposes. This 'Adshel' shelter incurs no cost to the bus undertaking or local authority as the shelter is provided by the contractor in return for advertising rights.**

Right: **Typical standard British bus stop sign of the nationally approved design.**

1473-63

Top left: **Bus stop at Tetouan in Morocco. Outside the influence of the western world queuing does not come naturally but the conductor (who in this instance is seated at the rear of the bus) is usually quite tolerant about standing passengers.**

Left: **Doors are fitted to the entrances/exits of buses in the interests of safety and they have achieved a substantial reduction in boarding and alighting accidents. They also enable the temperature inside the bus to be better controlled. With one-man operation, doors are essential. But to passengers they are often irksome as they preclude boarding and alighting between stops. Where doors are not provided (as on the majority of London buses) passengers enjoy the benefits (at their peril) as well as the disbenefits and if every passenger who now boards or alights intermediately had instead to do so at authorised stops, journey times could well be lengthened.**

Top: **On occasions it is more economic for buses to be stabled at a rural outstation overnight rather than return to the garage. This example shows two vehicles of Eastern Counties standing on private ground at Loddon near Norwich after having covered late journeys into the village the night before.**

Above: **In the less developed countries the bus often carries a wide variety of accompanied baggage. At this bus stop and interchange point at Nuanetsi a dual purpose vehicle of Rhodesia Railways has just discharged passengers who are now awaiting the arrival of a bus on another service.**

21
WRU 276

Top left: **Bus is able to provide the door to door facility whilst rail caters better for the trunk haul. The former is therefore an important feeder for the latter but the ideal can be reached only if proper interchange arrangements are available. With an island platform such as is illustrated here steps up and then down are unavoidable if the road is on the same level as the rail. Nevertheless a covered way is provided in this example of a station on the rapid transit system in the suburbs of Boston, USA.**

Left: **The one time conventional type trolleybus could not be reversed as easily as other road vehicles which are not encumbered by dependence on overhead wires. Normally a turning circle was provided but this was possible only where the road layout was suitable. An interesting reversing point for trolleybuses was on the Bournemouth system at Christchurch where vehicles were driven on to a turntable and manhandled by the crew.**

Above: **Collection of fares on one-man buses can be very fast or very slow according to the ticketing system and the aptitude of the passengers. In use here is a Setright ticket machine but what really takes the time is when passengers do not know the fare, do not know where they are going or do not have the correct money. With one man buses passengers must pay as they enter without fuss and without discussing the transaction at the same time.**
National Bus Company

Right: **The farebox is the ultimate in speed of fare collection on one man buses and has maximum security whilst on the road as the money is deposited in a locked vault. On this particular bus a flat fare was in operation, tickets were not, therefore, necessary and passengers were required to produce the correct coinage.**
South Yorkshire Passenger Transport Executive

Contro
SMB

INTRODUCTION

Setright Roll Ticket Registers are in use all over the world, on buses, in sports, entertainment and leisure centres. Chosen for reliability, they give years of economical, trouble-free service.

Robustly designed, they are easy to operate, simple to read and give a continuous record of cash flow.

The standard register prints up to 99 stages or 32 stages and 24 hours, the date, day and month, a 3 figure serial number, the machine number and up to seven different classes of ticket.

It also has a 5 figure total ticket counter, total cash counter, a multi journey validation slot and punch cancellation device.

Optional extras include a fixed type bar which can be used to print the operator's name, two counters which can be used to record the number of tickets issued in any given class, a statistical counter which can be used to record the number of tickets issued for one selected fare value in one selected class, or any single fare value regardless of class.

Setright Roll Ticket-Registers substantially reduce the amount of clerical work required as all relevant information can be readily obtained from the register. This automatically ensures complete revenue control.

Blank paper rolls are utilised in Setright Registers to ensure cheaper tickets and ease of administration. Rolls can be fitted in minutes even on a moving vehicle. The inking ribbon will print up to 50,000 tickets before it needs replacing. This generally necessitates the machine being opened about once every three months depending on usage.

THE LONG RANGE SMB

For inter urban and inter city bus networks, the Long Range SMB is a reliable, flexible and efficient ticket register which adapts easily to either long or short journeys. The Long Range SMB can issue a maximum of 200 different fare values in increments of 1 unit or multiples to a maximum of 199-50.

THE SHORT RANGE SMB

The Short Range SMB has provision for 23 different fare values and is ideal for shorter bus routes where only a restricted number of fare stages have to be catered for.

It records fare stages in increments of 1 unit or multiples up to a maximum of 23 units.

① Class
② Fare
③ Boarding Stage (99 max.)
④ Day
⑤ Month
⑥ Class
⑦ Total Tickets
⑧ Class
⑨ Cash

Extended Range
SMB Model

Setright roll ticket registers.
Control Systems Limited

ystems
nge

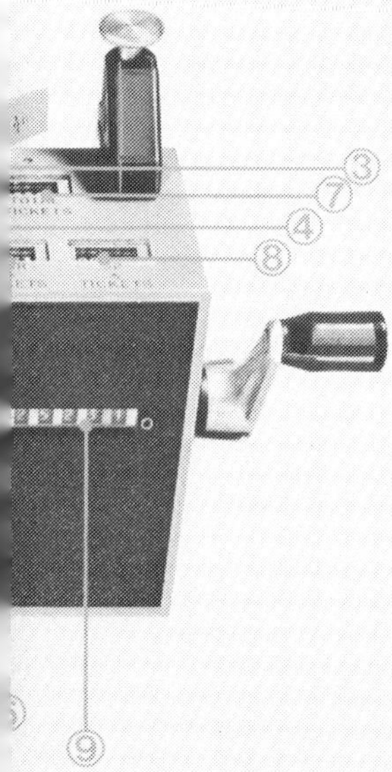

ight Motorised
Ticket Register
short range SMB Model

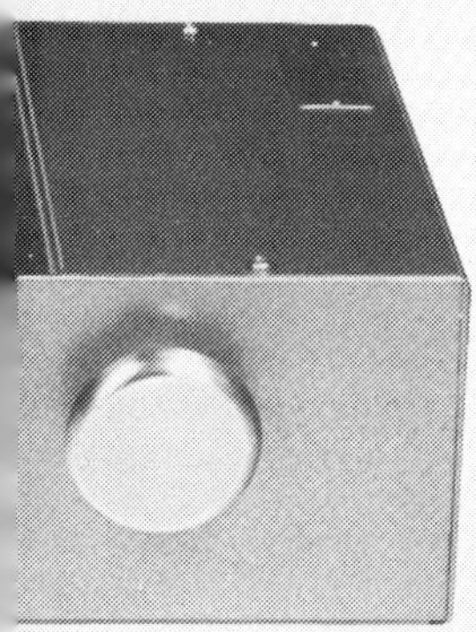

THE EXTENDED RANGE SMB

This incorporates all the cost and reliability features of earlier versions, and is designed for operators of long distance bus routes, recording any fare up to 999 values with the decimal point in any desired position.

The Extended SMB issues up to seven classes of ticket with 99 or 32 stages or trips as well as other variables such as time codes.

The machine is easy to operate and is robustly built to withstand use in buses operating on poor road surfaces.

THE MOTORISED UNIT

All Setright Roll Ticket Registers can be adapted to fit a motorised unit which can be set up near the driver to help speed ticket issue. This effectively cuts down on passenger boarding times and contributes to a more efficient bus service. The unit is specifically designed to help speed service on one-man-operated buses.

It is operated by push button and works from a 12 volt or 24 volt vehicle battery or from the mains on 110 or 120 volts. The register can be detached at any time from the unit and operated manually by fitting a clip-on handle.

1. Operators Name
2. Fare
3. Stage 0–9
4. Stage 0–9
5. Date
6. Month
7. Machine No.
8. Serial No.
9. Machine No.
10. Class

Long Range
SMB Model

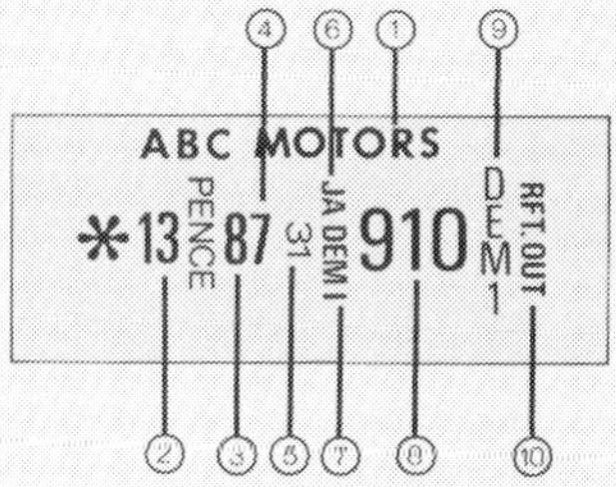

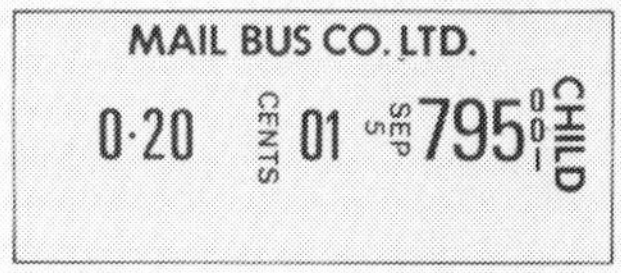

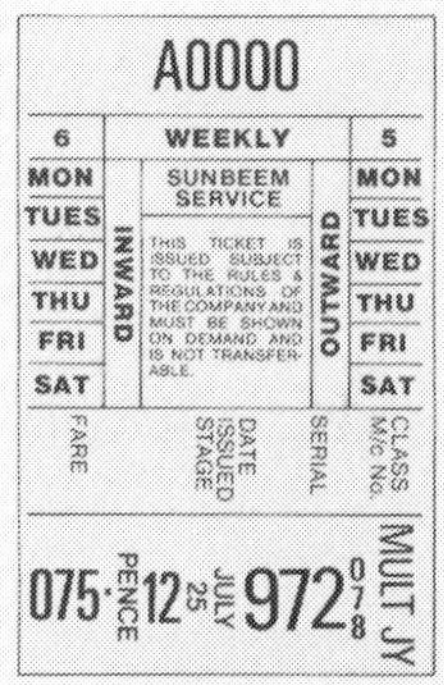

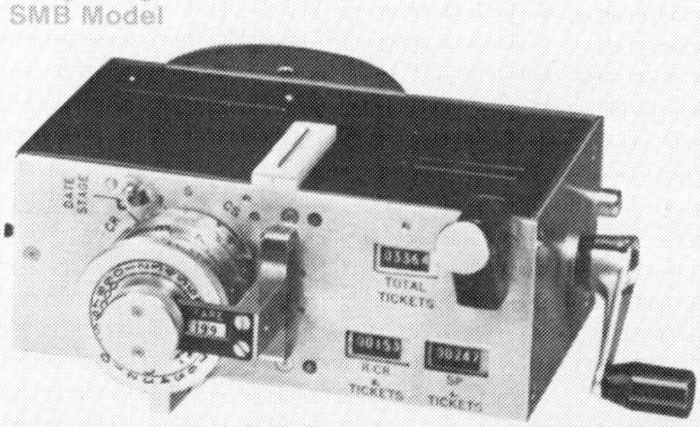

the international answer . . .

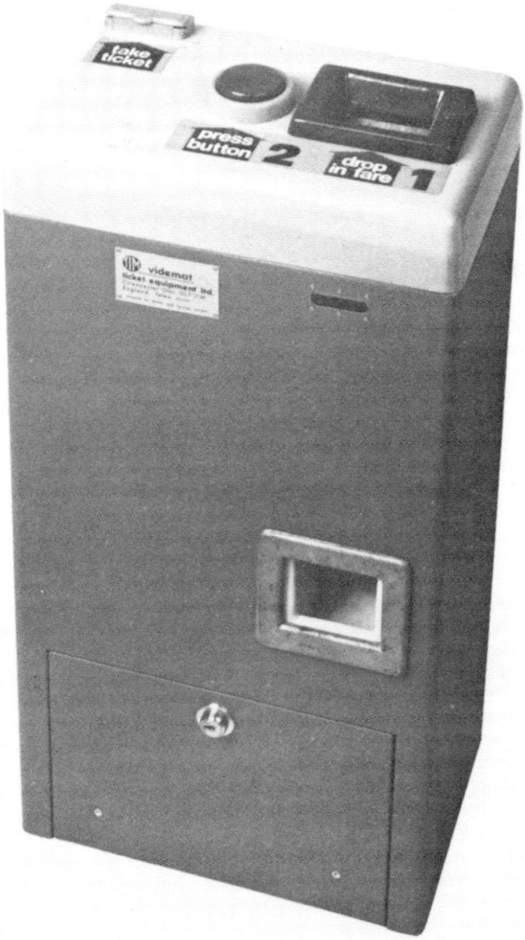

TIM *Videmat* is the most advanced form of passenger self-service in the world.
Gone are the traditional coin slots and individual rejectors causing delays, limitations and complexity for the passenger. Instead, this revolutionary new machine is extremely simple to operate, and infinitely flexible in its acceptance of any combination of coins. For example, from the moment the passenger inserts say, three coins, a ticket is produced in 1.9 seconds.

The secret of *Videmat* versatility is simplicity: a large hopper enables any selection of coins to be inserted in one handful, without ever jamming;

foreign objects accidently dropped into the hopper are rejected without mechanical stress;

an actual reproduction of each coin appears on the ticket itself, together with all necessary control data;

changes in fare prices or even currency can be accommodated without any machine modification.

This totally new method of fare collection and ticket issue provides complete flexibility in establishing fare prices in any country, and its machinery is extremely reliable and simple to maintain.
In short, TIM *Videmat* is the complete international answer to fast, efficient passenger self-service.

In order to ensure the correct sequence of passenger operation the *Videmat* is available in either right or left hand loading versions.

it's so simple . . .

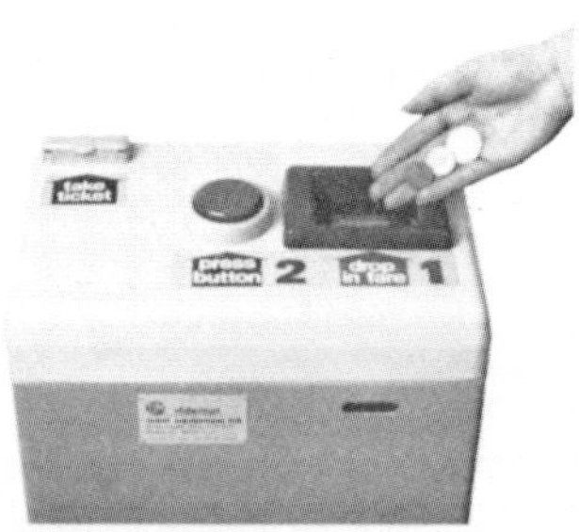

money in

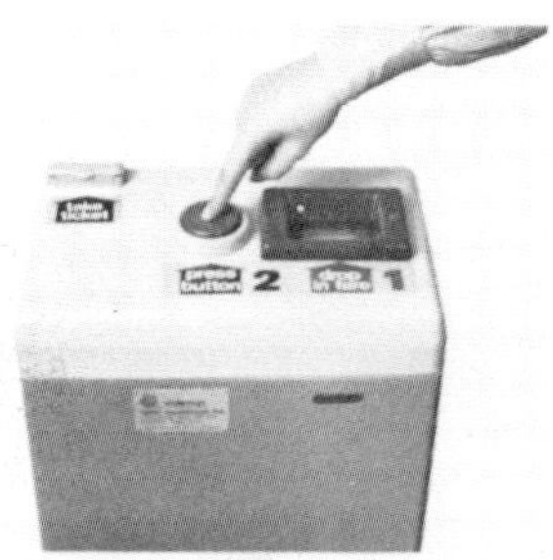

press button

take ticket

Above & right: **The Videmat self-service ticket vendor.** *Emidata*

general information

new style fare printing . . .

Environment
TIM *Videmat* will operate in the following conditions: humidity of 90%; temperature of -10° to $+40^{\circ}$C; voltage from 18V to 30V on nominal 24V supply; and normal vibration levels expected in a bus.

Maintenance
The *Videmat* is constructed on a modular basis for easy replacement of parts. After suitable training the maintenance of the equipment is of a routine nature as laid down in comprehensive service manuals.

Machine life
This is estimated to be ten years at 1,000 tickets per day between major overhauls.

Electrical
All circuitry is solid-state and fully protected, with no radio or TV interference. Machine logic is based on integrated circuits, and the standard machine contains only two circuit boards.

Possible variants
If it is desired to install the machine under the control of the driver, a remote operating button can be supplied.

Protected by British and Foreign patents.

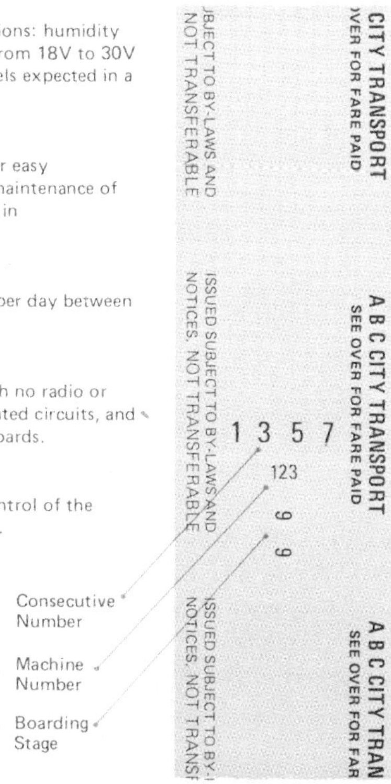

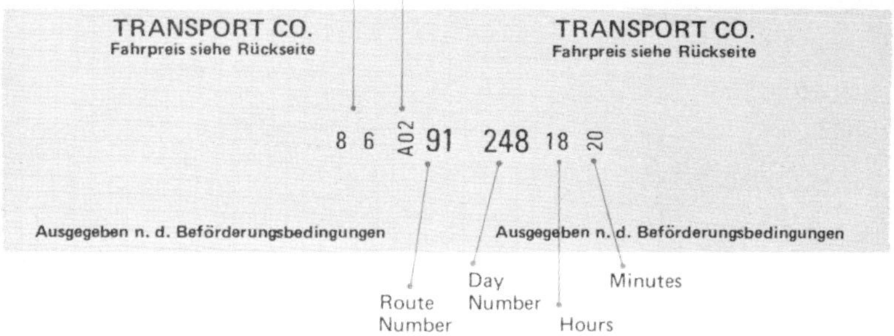

EMIDATA
Ticket Equipment Division

Love Lane
Cirencester
Gloucestershire GL7 1UF
Telephone: Cirencester 4161. Telex. 43120

EMI

(05.08.77)

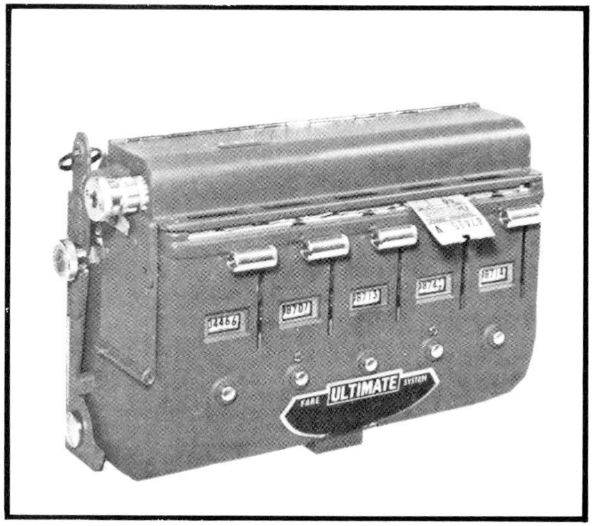

Left: **The Almex Model P self-service ticket vendor.** *Almex*

Above: **The 'Ultimate' portable ticket-issuing machine.**
Control Systems Limited

Below left: **One method of reducing time spent at stops on one-man operated buses is two streams of boarding. This example at Sheffield in South Yorkshire shows passengers intending to pay the driver boarding on the left and those using the self-service arrangement (in this case the Videmat) on the right. Note the centre-exit with passengers alighting simultaneously. The advantage of the centre exit, however, is negligible. Even in this picture passengers can be seen standing on the upper deck waiting to alight which means that the area around the staircase is impassable to those who are boarding and who can, therefore, only block back at the front of the bus until their passage is clear.**

Top right: **In the USA fareboxes are in universal use for security reasons and change cannot be given, hence the notice at the entrance.**

Right: **Although maximum security is crucial in the USA, across the border in Mexico robbery and violence is not quite such a way of life. This trolleybus driver in Mexico City, in 1970, was quite happy to accept cash, provide change (occasionally on a help yourself basis) and leave his float on an open tray**

Exact fare required —
Driver has NO change
Exact fare required —
Driver has NO change
Exact fare required

AS YOU ENTER
BUSAF

Top left: **In Tel Aviv, Israel, where the tempo of life is fast and resources are not wasted, manual ticket issue by one-man drivers is satisfactory and change is given as required.**

Far left: **With the driver seated inside the bus and accessible by passengers he is in a somewhat exposed and vulnerable position, particularly as he is in possession of cash. Trials have already been made with protective screens but at this stage have not proved popular with staff. The time may come, however, when screens become a necessary accessory and this example in Cape Town, South Africa shows a bus working in an area where this is already the case.**

Left: **The cash transaction at the time of boarding is a potential source of delay to one man operated buses, particularly when changegiving is involved. Pre-purchased tickets speed the process and a ticket dispensing machine is seen here at the kerbside of Lauentzien Strasse in West Berlin.**

Above: **One bus and 15 other vehicles appear in this picture and more were present but outside the range of the camera. Of the traffic which is visible, the bus alone was carrying nearly three times the number of people than all of the rest put together. If all of the bus passengers also became motorists then the effect on congestion can be imagined. Private transport is extravagant in road space and here lies the justification for bus priorities.** *National Bus Company*

Right: **Parts of the centre of Exeter have been pedestrianised but shoppers have not been denied access to buses at the places where they need them and neither has the bus been put on to a costly and irritating devious alternative route.** *National Bus Company*

Fountain Restaurant

Left: **An interesting example of a bus contra-flow facility in Naples, Italy. At one time this was a two-way road with trams on a separate reservation. A traffic management scheme made the road one way only but for buses what would have been a circuitous route was avoided by paving the appropriate tram track and allowing buses to share the reserved way with the trams.**

Below left: **A special contra-flow bus lane in Piccadilly, London.**

Right: **It is most useful for supervision purposes if the scheduled running number of each bus can be easily identified by road staff but surprisingly few undertakings adopt this practice. It has however always been the policy of London Transport to display running numbers.**

Below: **School train of the Romney, Hythe and Dymchurch Railway at New Romney Station.**
Romney, Hythe & Dymchurch Light Railway Company

Way out
Highbury & Islington

Top left: **An interior view of an electric suburban commuter train of the type as shown below.** *British Railways Board*

Left: **An electric suburban commuter train arriving at Highbury & Islington station in London which is in tunnel.**
British Railways Board

Above: **Whilst the underground station depicted opposite is built to accept stock of the standard British loading gauge, most of the London Transport tube tunnels are of a smaller bore. Although the track gauge is the same, London Transport tube trains must conform to a much smaller loading gauge and a typical LT train is here seen entering Swiss Cottage tube station.** *London Transport Executive*

Right: **Interior of a London Transport tube train. The smaller loading gauge means a lower floor level which necessitates wheel arches penetrating the interior. This in turn requires a longtitudinal seat layout except in the centre of the coach.** *London Transport Executive*

Right: **A local electric multiple unit train of Indian Railways seen south of Marine Lines Station in Bombay approaching Churchgate. Seen in the morning peak, commuter traffic is heavy and the urban railway network relieves pressure on the parallel roads. Standing space is at a premium and it can be seen here that a little more room can be made available by not closing the doors!**

Below: **Although there may be only one or two trains per day, in rural Africa, where there is a railway the villagers rely heavily on this form of rural transport. Here is seen a mixed goods and passenger local train of Rhodesia Railways picking up passengers at Gwanda station to take them in to Bulawayo.**

7
Commercial Practices

The Commercial Function

The commercial manager is responsible for promoting and selling the service. His particular designation, how he fits into the organisation and his relationship with other functions were considered in Chapter 3 and are not important in this context. The smaller bus undertakings are unlikely to have a separate commercial department. The work involved is then normally part of the responsibility of the operating side although it is quite distinct from the day to day task of actually controlling movement. In fact, under these circumstances it is common practice for this function to become known instead as the traffic department with the traffic manager or traffic superintendent in charge of both running and selling the service. In popular jargon, marketing is now a frequently used term for the same subject. The writer feels that when 'market' is used as a verb, it is more appropriately applied to merchandise than to a service. Nevertheless, the fact that the subject has had sufficient thought and attention to bring about a re-christening is not a bad thing. The subject which the name describes is something more than sales or publicity as this activity attempts only encourage and help people to use what is there. True traffic promotion (or marketing) adopts a rather different approach. It first seeks what the people want and what they are most likely to use. Market research (another comparatively recent term) techniques are used and publicity is the natural supporting follow up. The principle of this is, of course, very good. It is right and proper that passengers should be provided with what they want. On the other hand, such exercises take time and money and there must not be heavy expenditure just to prove something which any experienced traffic man should know in any case.

As far as urban and rural areas are concerned, bus services are normally of the stage carriage variety. It is the commercial or traffic people who must supply the raw material for schedule compilers to turn into workable programmes for implementation on the road by operating personnel. The schedule process has been explained in the previous chapter (Chapter 6) and in a sense, therefore, this, being stage one, is for consideration first. Not being presented in this way, however, is not illogical as whilst the schedule compiler requires his own skills to work on the information with which he is supplied, it is to advantage if the traffic staff also have some elementary knowledge of scheduling principles. This will enable them to prepare realistic specifications, which is the subject under discussion now.

Just as the schedules staff work to the requirements of the traffic department, the latter is, in turn, developing the policy which has been laid down at the basic planning stage. This was covered in Chapter 5 and the final sections of that chapter which covered operational planning lead directly into what is now being considered.

Facilities

Types of Services

Route planning and timetable specifications are developed from the basic parameters as determined by the criteria for service provision. Unless, however, the system becomes essentially a social service with a high percentage of income coming from places other than passengers at the time of travel, it is unlikely that there will be a pre-determined and laid down set of standards which has to be rigidly followed. It will be there but more likely subconsciously in the manager's mind and commercial decisions will be made accordingly as the different issues present themselves. Whatever the background, however, there will be a policy on route patterns, service frequencies and load factors and it is on this that the network will evolve.

The different types of service are listed (a) to (g) in Chapter 5. Factors to be considered are:

(a) Route
(b) Frequency
(c) Timetable
(d) Stops
(e) Stands
(f) Type of vehicle

Each is important and none can be considered in isolation. One has a bearing on another and all will be influenced by general policy. Much of this will be based on preferences and opinions. The treatment of this particular topic is, therefore, to some extent subjective by nature. The thoughts which follow will reflect the commercial practices of some undertakings and not others. Those who work differently will have their reasons, even though the author might not necessarily agree with them.

The relationship between route network and service frequency is fully considered in Chapter 5. There might also, however, be a relationship between the route and the type of vehicle. In a country (and Great Britain is in mind) where available headroom on public roads of 16 ft 6in is accepted as a national standard, the writer is of the opinion that that advantage should be fully exploited by bus operators. A double deck bus can carry either a larger payload than its single deck counterpart, which means it is more economical, or, depending on the design of the single deck, the double-deck will carry a similar number but in much greater comfort. In other words, the double-deck will give everybody a seat whilst the single-deck will be a standee type crush loader. To follow this principle through, the author is suggesting that as a basic principle, all services should be worked by double deck vehicles unless there is some special reason why this should not or cannot be done. On very short inner-city services, passengers are unlikely to wish to climb to the upper deck and crush loading does not really matter for such short distances. Even so, it is of note that this type of operation when tried in central London was not exactly an overwhelming success and what might be accepted on local railways (underground or otherwise) is not similarly tolerated on buses. Custom and practice may be one reason but the fact that steel wheel on steel rail gives a smoother ride which makes standing less arduous is certainly another. The other reason in support of single deck buses is physical obstruction and here it is for consideration whether a diversion to avoid a height or weight restriction is justified. Much depends on any alternative routes which might be available. It is interesting to note in this context that there are some single deck routes today which were double deck at one time, that is, many years ago when buses had open tops. A covered top bus inevitably increases its height and it cannot, therefore, go everywhere that its predecessors went. A low bridge, for example, could often be negotiated by an open top bus providing the passengers did not stand up — and that in their own interest they seldom did. The conductor, of course, had to be excused from collecting fares outside at the crucial time. All a little hazardous perhaps, but conductors were regarded as being rather more expendable then than they are today.

Whatever the policy, bus routes must be devised so as to provide the greatest good for the greatest number. Most people put some value on the availability of a public service, even though they may want it only when their car is not available and preferably the route covers the next road rather than their own but it must be only a short walk away. As far as stops are concerned, certainly not outside their own house; several doors away at the very least. What this is really saying is that route determination does sometimes have complications even after an otherwise ideal way through has been found. This applies particularly to residential neighbourhoods on the outer fringes.

The foregoing applies to all types of services be they town, rural, inter-urban or even those provided for specific rather than general purposes. They all run to a pre-determined and published timetable from point to point at standard speeds. For special circumstances, variants must be considered. Possibilities include guaranteed journeys, limited stop services (which is why stops were mentioned as one of the considerations) and customer orientated anywhere to anywhere or fixed point to anywhere, frequently referred to as dial-a-bus. All are devices to give more attractive facilities and/or reduce costs and hence improve viability.

A guaranteed journey is a method of providing a service for which there is a specific demand but which would otherwise be quite uneconomic. It could apply, for example, to an additional journey on an established service, perhaps before the first or after the last bus. The idea is that the vehicle would operate as a normal service bus with normal fares charged and available for anyone to board who might care to do so. The only difference is that the guarantor would underwrite any shortfall between costs and receipts, which means that the greater the number the passengers the less would be the subvention. It is an alternative to a contract.

A device which might reduce costs and give a more attractive service at the same time is the provision of limited stop journeys. The theory of this principle is sound although unfortunately the practical arrangements are difficult and often not a success. It could be a special service or just selected journeys with distinctive blinds of an otherwise normal stopping service which run fast. If the running time is less, there is greater productivity. If the saving is sufficient to move a greater number of people say by working an extra trip with the same resources, then there is an economy. At the same time, the facilities should become more attractive. In the event, however, things do not always work out like that and that is why the practice is not widely adopted. With traffic congestion the level that it is (and it is at its worst at the very time that the limited stop journeys will be wanted, being in the peaks) speed is often dictated more by the general traffic flow than the need to stop for passengers. If this is the case, then the faster timetable is not realistic and there is no great benefit. But there is something much more fundamental than that. Whilst, certainly, there are some stops which are much more heavily used than others, it is customary for there to be pick-ups and set-downs at frequent points all the way along the route. Indeed, it is this door to door facility which is a characteristic of the bus and which gives it an advantage over other modes. There is, therefore, the very real possibility of buses with empty seats passing stops where people are waiting and if they have to wait long, the writer regards this as a very bad operating tactic. The resources of most undertakings are strained in the peaks. Queues form and waits are sometimes extended. If, under these circumstances, any buses (express or otherwise) are running around (that is, in the appropriate direction) with surplus capacity, then, as a general principle, it is the view of the writer that something is badly wrong and the runnings need a rearrangement.

Demand Activated Systems

It was said in Chapter 1 that the tram played a significant role in urban development. Residential and commercial areas flourished along its fixed routes and there was a self-perpetuating process whereby public transport both controlled development and created traffic sufficient to support a frequent service. But the private car has changed all that. No longer need the dormitory areas be centred around public transport routes. The journey can be made by car no matter how diverse the travel requirement might be. Of course, this has led to problems in other directions; congestion, cost of road space, need for car parks, plight of those without cars and now forced economy in the use of fuel. Hence the new approach in Chapter 5 that public transport should be a function of land use. Nevertheless, residential districts have already grown up in the more affluent areas both in Great Britain and overseas, particularly in North America, where either development is too dispersed or there is no adequate through road which means that it is difficult or impossible to provide a viable public transport service.

It is places such as this where the dial-a-bus concept (a colloquial but perfectly apt term used to describe a special demand responsive bus service) might be suitable. The principle is that a mini or midi bus would be made available between any pair of points within a defined zone upon receipt of a telephone call. Alternatively it could run to and from a central point (shops, local railhead, etc) on a many to one/one to many basis. In this case, only the forward journey would need to be by prior arrangement. A control office is, of course, essential with two way radio between controllers and drivers and optimum routes must be devised immediately requests are received to minimise both excessive mileage and passenger waiting times. It has been established that in the right places, a service of this kind is popular and serves a useful purpose. The question of viability, however, is another matter. The economics of small buses was discussed in Chapter 5 and the dial-a-bus concept cannot alter the situation. Indeed, the higher mileage involved in order to meet specific requirements can only worsen the position. Another factor for consideration, however, is the effect on the public transport system as a whole. If the bus is used as a feeder to rail then it might encourage people to go this way instead of by car. If a free car park at the station is provided and passengers use their own cars it might be cheaper, but once in the car, they might be tempted to stay in it all the way to town. Conversely, dial-a-bus could abstract traffic from normal bus services which might otherwise be more profitable. If, for the reason already stated, it is impossible or very costly to provide normal buses to what could be fragmented development then this is a practical alternative and it is the nearest approach to the convenience of the private car. It is this latter situation where thoughts could most usefully turn to a demand responsive system.

Specialised Vehicles

It is Chapter 10 which is concerned primarily with vehicle design and the subject is, in any case, more akin to the operating and engineering functions. Certainly, the body design could influence the popularity of the service and capacity has a strong connection with economy. The writer has already expressed a preference for double-deck vehicles. Reference to vehicles in this context however, is not to discuss basic designs but to consider any adaptions for specific purposes.

The provision of services in rural areas was discussed at some length in Chapter 5. One possibility in territories where demand is particularly light is the combination of passengers with goods in the same vehicle, the goods being parcels, mail or general merchandise. This calls for the provision of specially constructed bodies or perhaps a trailer. The practice is more common overseas than in the UK, although even here there are a few examples of this type of operation. Generally, however, services of this kind overseas are of an interurban nature. An example of this type of operation in Great Britain is the specially adapted post bus which does, in selected cases, carry passengers to what would otherwise be isolated communities.

Excursions, Tours and Private Hire

Excursions, tours and private hire do not generally play a large part in urban and rural transport. If a town has a particular commercial or historical interest, short guided tours might be arranged with a charge inclusive of admission to buildings. On the private hire side, most of it is likely to be regular contract work such as conveying schoolchildren to playing fields, swimming baths, etc. But on a wider field, there is always the chance to utilise vehicles at times when they would not otherwise be required for longer distance day excursions or for hire by a private party. This could, of course, develop into big business with extended tours embracing a week or more covering anywhere in Great Britain or even the mainland of Europe with hotel and other expenses all contained in an inclusive charge. A tour of this kind can be very remunerative as, unlike a regular stage or express service where the vehicle is not necessarily in continuous operation and the advertised journeys must run even if there are only a few passengers, the touring coach is fully utilised all of the time and it would not be operated in the first instance if it was under subscribed. There are, of course, complications as whilst the operator is responsible for giving satisfaction, much of the success depends on outside people such as hotel proprietors and others over whom he has no direct control. Furthermore, if the business is to be viable and prices kept at an acceptable level, resources in terms of vehicles must be kept fully employed. Intensive utilisation of this kind does, however, produce difficulties in the event of unavoidable delays which can happen, particularly on foreign tours. But this is a separate subject and outside the terms of reference of this book. Also, if a tours programme develops to this extent, the work becomes very specialised and distinct from bus operation as such. This is why some companies deal exclusively in tour work and those bus undertakings which do cater for this type of traffic generally organise the activity within a separate department. The point being made here is that the odd excursion, tour or private hire is useful business for bus undertakings. A request for a quotation could always be refused if a vehicle did not happen to be available at the time it was wanted.

Ancillary Services

Parcels

Reference has already been made to the carriage of passengers on a parcels service in remote areas where demand is insufficient to support a separate facility. This is the exceptional case. What is more usual is for parcels to be conveyed on passenger services. Trains of a main line railway system invariably do this, the term parcels including newspapers and mail. With station staff and guards, there are built in means of dealing with this traffic and a special compartment is provided on passenger rolling stock for this purpose. The same circumstances, however, do not necessarily prevail on rail rapid transit systems. Here the density of passenger traffic is likely to be too heavy to permit the provision of space either on trains or on station platforms for parcels and the guard could not cope with such duties. It is unlikely, therefore, that unaccompanied parcels will be carried on railways of this type. Buses lie somewhere between these two extremes. On town services again there is no scope for unaccompanied parcels but on the less heavily used inter-urban and rural routes, some operators have developed quite a considerable subsidiary business in this traffic.

Systems have grown up based on a series of collection and delivery points being either the company's own enquiry offices or suitable shops appointed as agents. Consigners deliver their parcels to and consignees collect them from these agencies. A scale of charges is likely to be based on weight without the application of a distance complication although this could also be taken into account if required. Conductors would call at these agencies to collect and deliver. Alternatively, consigners could hand packages direct to conductors who would collect the fee and issue a special parcel label in the form of a receipt. One half of this ticket would be attached to the parcel and the other half handed to the consigner. Similarly the consignee could meet the bus rather than utilise the services of the agency. Over recent years, however, the increase in one-man operation has inhibited the operation of a parcels service in all but the very rural areas. Drivers cannot easily leave their vehicles to collect and deliver parcels, particularly as they have cash and tickets in the cab. In any case, for them to look after parcels when there are heavy surges of traffic on double deck buses is expecting rather a lot, just as it is of the intending passengers who would have to wait for the driver to attend to this duty before they could board. Nevertheless, where operating conditions are right it has been possible to preserve a useful facility which at the same time earns additional revenue at little extra cost.

Left Luggage

Provision for passengers to deposit their luggage for short periods is a facility which has been provided at some railway stations and some bus stations for many years. It is not a service which is likely to bear a high charge and can, therefore, really only be provided in conjunction with some other activity, such as a parcels or lost property office. A more recent innovation is the provision of lockers activated by coins in a slot. Unaccompanied baggage, however, is becoming a serious security risk and the small amount of additional revenue which is forthcoming is of doubtful justification if there is no other parcels traffic on the premises.

Catering

The provision of a restaurant, cafeteria or snack bar is a popular and hopefully remunerative sideline at the more important passenger transport terminals. A national railway system generally carries its own catering service and provides facilities at its more important stations. Whilst this service along with restaurant cars on trains is aimed at inter-city travellers, the station buffets are, of course, equally available for local riders and the catering business is, in itself, a going concern. Most bus undertakings are also involved in catering, either directly or through an outside contractor, as it is becoming more and more the accepted practice to provide staff with subsidised canteen facilities. Bus crews are often scheduled for meal reliefs at central bus stations in which case there is a need to provide a staff canteen. It is then but a small step to provide separate facilities for passengers all based on the same kitchen. Even if there is no link-up between staff and passenger amenities, ownership of a bus station does give the opportunity for entry into the property business with the possibility of letting spaces for small shops. Restaurant facilities could quite easily be provided by an outside caterer in this way and it is a useful source of additional income.

Other Miscellaneous Activities

All that has been mentioned so far refers to facilities which are subservient to the main business of carrying passengers. In providing such conveniences, goodwill is promoted with some additional revenue to go with it. Transport undertakings do, however, often engage in other activities. The larger ones might have a separate consultancy business which is of particular value to overseas clients. The smaller firms frequently run their buses alongside a garage repair business and petrol filling station, possibly also with self-drive cars and even mini-buses for hire. Bus undertakings, both large and small might run travel agencies, quite lucrative in themselves but sometimes producing the ironical situation of providing booking facilities for not only their own services but also for those of their competitors.

Commercial Advertising

One further way in which a public transport undertaking can earn revenue other than through selling transport is commercial advertising. The exteriors of road vehicles and the interiors of buses, trams and trains provide valuable advertising sites, the announcements on which will be seen and read by hundreds of thousands of people. Railway stations, bus shelters and other public places in the ownership of public transport undertakings also offer potential revenue earning possibilities in this way. Some administration is, of course, involved although the entire job could be placed in the hands of a contractor. Some will say, and the author accepts the point, that commercial advertising has an aesthetic disbenefit. This is particularly so in the case of the complete overall advertising in which some buses are dressed. But in hard times money must come from somewhere. The more that is earned through advertising the less will need to come from public funds — money which people have paid in rates and taxes — and environmentalists or no, any saving in taxes must be a welcome relief. It is important that advertisements are kept in good condition — this helps to keep up appearances — and for this reason they are sometimes painted on by signwriters instead of using paper stickers.

Another possibility is audible advertising accompanied by piped music. Although anxious to get in all money which is offering, some passengers could react strongly at being forced to sit amidst noise of this kind. It is, therefore, the opinion of the writer that the possible ill-will so engendered by this arrangement could off-set any advantages which might be forthcoming. Furthermore, in Great Britain it is of doubtful legality. Regulations exist which control the conduct of drivers, conductors and passengers* (which, to digress, students should acquaint themselves with). One of the requirements is that passengers will not when on a vehicle distribute advertising material and another is that they will not operate a noisy instrument. Should the piped music plus advertising, therefore, ever be challenged it might be interpreted as being contrary to the requirements of these PSV regulations.

Fares and Charges

In a commercial setting it is the responsibility of the fares and charges officer to fix his rates at a level sufficient to cover costs and service capital in accordance with the financial structure and requirements of his undertaking. If by political necessity or whim there is a declared social need to bolster up the system with monetary support then clearly not all of the costs will have to be recouped through fares but there could, nevertheless, still be a target according to whatever dictates may have been issued. Further reference to this aspect will be made later in this chapter. Whilst, therefore, the different methods of charging as are to be described are certainly valid when economic fares are required, the principles could also be applied when part of the revenue appears in the form of a subsidy. First, however, must be considered the economic theory of rate fixing in a competitive market.

A logical base on which to fix charges is cost plus profit. This is something which can be and is done by, for example, the smaller road haulage undertakings when asked to quote for a specific job. Apply the same concept to large scale enterprise and it becomes impracticable to cost individually any one item. The sheer magnitude and complexity of a national railway system to take another example clearly makes it impossible to identify in a meaningful way the extra cost involved in the carriage of one particular consignment. An alternative method is to charge not on the cost of the service but on the value of the service (that is to the customer) and the principle of charging what the traffic can bear is something which is steeped in railway history. At the same time, the concept is ever present, consciously or sub-consciously, in people's minds and this applies to their own personal movements as well as when they are seeking transport for their goods. Furthermore, this thinking applies regardless of the mode and as far as the users are concerned, the bus passenger will be just as interested in its effects as will be the person who is sending merchandise by rail.

To expand a little on transport economics, note that the function of transport is to move goods or passengers from where they are to where their relative value is greater or

*Public Service Vehicles (Conduct of Drivers, Conductors and Passengers) Regulations, No 619, 1936 (as amended), HMSO.

where they would prefer to be. In the case of people this could be for a variety of reasons of an economic or personal nature such as travel between home and work, the places being dictated by house prices and district appeal on the one hand and availability of work and salary levels on the other; or for shopping where prices might be cheaper or there might be a wider range of goods to justify travel, or even for pleasure where the cost is set against some alternative pursuit. Although this process will not be undertaken by the individual with mathematical precision, it is nevertheless very real. For example, a man might be prepared to spend £1 per day in travelling between home and work. He might not be prepared to spend £10 a day. It follows, therefore, that somewhere between these two points — the point where it is no longer 'worth it' — and that means were he is beginning to spend more than he is getting in return, he will have no alternative but to change his habits. The options open to him might be to move his home, change his job, walk, buy a bicycle or whatever. If no option is open to him and hardship arises or if the adoption of one of the options, say, becoming a private motorist, carries a disbenefit to the community at large, then there is a case for political intervention with subsidies but that is another matter. The point being made here is that on economic factors alone there is a limit (undefined) above which fares cannot go. If they do, then less and less people will use the service and it has to be withdrawn.

The parameters for rate fixing, therefore, are at the lower limit, revenue must be sufficient to cover costs and at the upper limit must not be above what the traffic can bear. These limitations should, as far as possible, be applied collectively taking one journey with another and one service with another. To meet the needs of the operating territory as a whole, some cross subsidisation is likely but in the final accounts the undertaking must remain solvent.

There are various methods which may be adopted for the formulation of a charges scheme just as there are means of collecting those charges, which is the subject of Chapter 9. Fare fixing is a commercial activity but fare collection on the bus or on the train is an operating responsibility. The former can, however, materially help or hinder the latter depending on the method and scale adopted and the two functions should not, therefore, be considered in isolation.

Basic fares may be determined in accordance with any of the following principles:

(a) Rate per mile.
(b) Rate per mile with a taper (ie the longer the journey the lower the mileage rate)
(c) Flat rate.
(d) Flat rate within a geographical zone.
(e) Flat rate within a time zone.

Superimposed on this could be special concessions designed either to maximise revenue or to facilitate fare collection.

Dealing first with the basic structure, option (a) which produces a graduated scale of charges is simple in theory but does not always lend itself to rigid application. It is for consideration whether fares would be charged to the nearest whole mile, half mile, quarter mile or whatever. Also, suitable fare stage points must be selected. In the case of the railway this is pre-determined by the presence of stations and similar circumstances could apply to limited stop bus services. With normal bus services, however (as with trams and trolleybuses) stops are frequent, they cannot all be fare stages and there is a choice. Stage points could nevertheless still be frequent or they could be widely spaced and this is one of the differences between a fine scale and a coarse scale. The coarser the scale the greater is the likelihood that the correct fare will be charged and a coarse scale is a help with one-man operation. The siting of fare stages is also important regardless of mileage. If a fare expires at a little used stop just short of a popular setting down point, overriding can be anticipated. Geography as well as distance, therefore, should help to determine stage points. One other difficulty in adhering strictly to a rate per mile policy is if two or more services link pairs of towns via different routes. The combined timetables would be designed so as to provide an adequate facility for through traffic. Such provision would be satisfactory subject to a spread of traffic and by the law of averages, other things being equal, this would happen. If, however, there was a difference in mileage with a corresponding difference in fares, the chances are that traffic would not spread. Instead, the shortest route would become overloaded because it was the cheapest and there would be surplus accommodation on the other but which could not be altered because of intermediate traffic. The solution is to equate the fares but this can only mean that either the shorter route is priced at a higher scale (which might not be desired) or that fares on the longer route become substandard. Once substandard fares are introduced, however, there must be care not to introduce anomalies. An anomalous fare is one which, by the process of re-booking, enables the journey to be made at a cheaper rate than the advertised through fare. To avoid this, one substandard fare, particularly if on an intermediate section of route, can hold down another and a ripple effect is created. Consider the following example where fares are based on a standard 6p per mile with a stage every half a mile (see diagram).

In the specimen farechart (i) (which is an example of a fine scale), 3p is charged for each half-mile fare stage but for some reason the fare between Stage D and Stage G, which is worth 9p, is held down at 6p. This, however, causes anomalies. The correct fare between

Farechart (i)

Stage A								
3	Stage B							
6	3	Stage C						
9	6	3	Stage D					
12	9	6	3	Stage E				
15	12	9	6	3	Stage F			
18	15	12	6	6	3	Stage G		
21	18	15	12	9	6	3	Stage H	
24	21	18	15	12	9	6	3	Stage I

Farechart (ii)

Stage A								
3	Stage B							
6	3	Stage C						
9	6	3	Stage D					
12	9	6	3	Stage E				
15	12	9	6	3	Stage F			
15	12	9	6	6	3	Stage G		
18	15	12	9	9	6	3	Stage H	
21	18	15	12	12	9	6	3	Stage I

Stage D and Stage I, for example, is 15p but by re-booking at Stage G it could be done for 12p and there are numerous other similar instances. To avoid these anomolies there is a ripple effect on the other fares and the resultant farechart is as shown at specimen (ii). In farechart (i) the anomaly is circled. In farechart (ii) the fares reduced by the ripple effect are circled. One further point before leaving the rate per mile system and that is to facilitate collection, it is helpful if fares could be reasonably compatible with coins of the realm. Reference is made in Chapter 9 of the time consuming process of giving change and in Great Britain, for example, a fare scale of 5p, 10p, 15p etc would be ideal. Of course, this cannot always be and in times of inflation, even if it is attained, it will be only until the next fares revision. What really should be avoided, if at all possible, are fares like 5½p, 10½p etc. It is also of note that in British currency fares of 8p and 9p require at least three coins for the correct fare but as passengers often pay for more than one person and the fact that fares tend to change (upwards) rather frequently anyway the ideal become impossible. Even so, if help yourself coin in the slot machines are in use it is something which cannot be disregarded.

The tapered scale — option (b) — has similar characteristics to the true mileage scale and is the system which is in most common use in the UK. One justification for a taper is that it can be argued that the major cost lies in providing a vehicle for somebody to board with all the overheads and administration which that entails. The distance travelled has slightly less significance. If, in support of this theory, an imaginary split in the fare is applied to distinguish between a standard boarding charge and a mileage charge then the taper will appear. The specimen farechart (ii) above has actually had a taper forced into it for a different reason. The system does give a means of relief to the longer distance rider and it might, therefore, encourage travel and overall it can be regarded as quite a sensible commercial practice. However, for urban and rural transport, where journeys are not likely to be particularly long, the impact is not great.

Option (c), being a flat fare is the simplest of all both to prepare and to implement and is the very antithesis of the graduated system. It consists of just the boarding charge, no more, no less, and for that money, the passenger can go as far as the bus or train goes. If he has to change vehicles then he pays another boarding charge (unless a transfer facility is available) and if the fare is compatible with a coin in current circulation, nothing could be easier. Statistics are also easily obtained. For passengers carried just divide the total revenue by the flat fare. It is a practice which is very common in North America but is less widely adopted elsewhere with only isolated examples in Great Britain.

The great disadvantage of the flat fare is that the longer distance passengers get a cheap fare whilst the short distance riders are penalised and could be discouraged from travelling. Those passengers who can complete their journeys only by means of two short trips on two different buses are at a disadvantage and it is here that a transfer facility is particularly welcome. Furthermore, such a facility could avoid demands for a direct service which might be costly to provide. Whilst it need not necessarily be the case with local urban and rural services, for longer inter-urban routes the flat fare is likely to become impracticable. Even in the large conurbations it produces serious inequalities to the extent that it cannot be tolerated and it is the zonal system — option (d) — which achieves a degree of compromise between the flat fare and the graduated scale.

As its name suggests, the zonal system involves the division of the operating area into two or more fare zones which might take the form of a series of concentric circles radiating outwards from the centre, although there could, of course, be any suitable geographical base. In its simplest form, there is a flat fare within each zone and passengers travelling in two zones, for example, pay twice. This puts a burden on those passengers who wish to travel only a short distance into the second zone and a still greater burden on those whose journey is short but crosses a zonal boundary. Again, the North Americans are used to this system and it works well with fareboxes even without tickets as will be considered in Chapter 9.

Option (e), being the time system, is sometimes found in Europe. It is, in effect, a flat fare for a defined period, say 45 minutes and involves the issue of a ticket from a special machine which is capable of recording the time. It has the advantage of allowing free transfer between vehicles without any further recording but would seem a little hard on passengers travelling on vehicles which are delayed through traffic congestion or for any other reason.

A further aspect of rate fixing is a premium fare for a superior service. The classic example on the railway is the provision of first class accommodation. If adequate second class capacity can still be provided and there is a clientele which is prepared to pay a higher fare for this purpose then it is good commercial practice to arrange accordingly although whether the passengers concerned get value for money is sometimes questionable. Very occasionally buses can be found with a separate compartment for superior class travel, particularly in the developing countries overseas but what has a greater potential on buses is to apply higher fares on premium type services such as those of the faster limited stop variety. It depends again on what the passengers are prepared to pay and it must certainly not result in empty seats with a parallel stopping bus becoming overloaded.

Passenger resistence is an important factor when considering charges and has particular significance when preparing fares revisions. It is for this reason that the additional yield cannot be predicted by a straight arithmetical calculation. An allowance must be built in for those passengers who decide either not to travel, to travel less frequently or to make shorter journeys. For example, a 10% fares increase might produce a net yield of only 7%, but this is just a suggestion; a more precise estimate must depend on local circumstances and the type of traffic involved. Those making essential journeys will remain captive for a little longer. In other words, the elasticity of demand has a strong bearing on the matter. It is also important when considering special promotional fares as will shortly be seen.

Closely allied to higher fares are minimum fares which are sometimes applied on certain sections of longer distance services. The purpose of this is to protect passengers for whom the service is intended from being crowded out at the main boarding points by short distance riders who have alternative facilities available to them. It is, of course, only necessary to do this in the out town direction as on the inwards journey the passengers who are being protected are already on the bus. Such application is entirely a matter of local circumstances. It could hardly be justified if, for instance, it meant empty seats whilst local passengers had an extended wait but to apply the system to isolated journeys in the peaks does tend to be confusing.

Traffic Promotion

Sales Promotion

In one sense, traffic promotion is still very much a part of fares and charges as traffic can be promoted by the availability of special cheap fares. The subject, however, goes further than that as it embraces also the provision of special promotional services but first will be considered cheap fares, that is cheap fares as a commercial venture and not as a political decision for social reasons.

Sales promotion through the pricing mechanism is a practice which is widely followed in the retail trade and just as business can be stimulated by attractive offers so can passengers be encouraged to use buses and trains by the availability of travel bargains. Vacant seats on public transport services are highly perishable. Once the journey has been completed they have gone for good and can never be sold. If those empty seats can be filled, however, there is additional revenue without any significant increase in costs. On the other hand, if the offer of an attractive facility results in the available accommodation becoming over-subscribed and the service has to be strengthened or the net result is that existing ordinary fare paying passengers instead become cheap fare paying passengers, the exercise would not be an economic success. Once again the elasticity of demand is involved and in this case any special facilities are directed at those whose demand is elastic, being those who do not have to travel but who might be encouraged to do so. It is the job of the commercial manager to plan any such schemes with these factors in mind. The principles involved apply equally to road and rail but in practice any cheap fares scheme might be different in view of the fare collection process ranging from a clerk in a booking office on the railway to a driver in the cab of a bus and the fact that extra traffic is more likely to be accommodated on a railway train at least in the off peak, without the need to put on anything extra. In the case of a bus, schemes must be simple in application; indeed it is helpful if any such concessions have the added advantage that they facilitate fare collection on the road.

The sort of promotional fare schemes which might be offered with the mode in which they are most likely to be adopted are shown opposite.

As far as buses are concerned, most of the facilities mentioned require the sale of tickets off the vehicle and prior to travel. If this is done, then the driver has only to check the ticket and sometimes there is a machine even to do that. In any case, a cash transaction at the time of boarding is avoided which will materially help to make it possible to convert to one-man operation. Much play is

(a) Day returns, sometimes confined to the off-peak.	Usually on the railway but sometimes on buses.
(b) Season tickets between any two defined points.	Usually on the railway.
(c) Day tickets for unlimited travel within a defined area.	Usually on buses.
(d) Period tickets for unlimited travel within a defined area.	On railways and buses. There are examples of such tickets being valid on the services of most operators, both road and rail.
(e) Weekly 10 journey tickets.	Sometimes on buses.
(f) Prepaid tickets or multi-journey tickets.	Sometimes on buses.
(g) Special rates for family or party.	Usually on the railway.
(h) Free transfers.	Usually applied automatically on the railway but could be difficult to administer for single journeys on the buses.

made today to identify the holder with the ticket in his possession by the inclusion of a card containing a photograph usually at the passenger's expense. All this is to help enforce the 'not transferable' regulation which prohibits a multi-journey ticket being used by anyone other than the person who bought it. The author fails to see the importance of this. One ticket has been paid for and one seat is occupied and whether it is the same or somebody else's posterior on that seat can have little effect on costs. Very occasionally it might make the ticket more attractive, say if the wife works on days and the husband on nights, but such cases are few and hardly worth the elaborate safeguards. Certainly if a queue of people are boarding with season tickets which are not subject to journey cancellations a person who has boarded could hand out his ticket to another person in the queue but in the opinion of the writer this is trivial and there are some misguided priorities here. Concessionary or free tickets issued on a personal basis to elderly people or staff, for example, are, of course, quite another matter.

The issue of pre-paid tickets means that sales points must be established and agents might seek commission which would be over and above any discount already given on the ticket. It is inevitable, therefore, that cost will be involved but the resultant easier operation is one of the compensating factors.

Traffic Development

Another way to stimulate demand is by the introduction of new facilities such as special services or even excursions and tours as has already been mentioned. These measures might encourage people to travel and the staff responsible must keep themselves fully acquainted with public fancy and be prepared to adjust their services as occasions demand. Even in Great Britain where the emphasis is now on co-ordination rather than competition there is still potential traffic to be attracted from the private car and other recreational pursuits by the provision of new services and facilities.

Traffic promotion can be likened to a manufacturer of say patent food products who introduces a new line or a special reduced price with the object of boosting sales. Before doing so he will carefully assess probable demand for his new commodity bearing in mind that (a) there is likely to be some initial production cost in the form of special machinery etc, and (b) the sale of the new product could prejudice sales of existing products, if only for a time. In the short term it is possible that overall the influence of these factors might worsen the manufacturer's overall position, but if his enterprise is successful, then in the long run he will have increased his sales sufficiently to justify the initial expense. The provider of transport is in the same position. The 'traffic development' section (or whatever title it may have) is an important part of the organisation and its task is not easy. Competition from private transport is very real and it is essential that ways and means of attracting new custom are fully investigated.

Surveys

On bus or train loadings as recorded by supervisors or staff appointed for that specific purpose are one thing but special investigations into not only the requirements of the passengers but the potential demands of the local populace as a whole is another. This is the meaning of market research. It is of no small importance that the services provided are in accordance with what the people want and there must be genuine attempts to ferret out those needs. It is not sufficient just to daub on a new name such as 'marketing' to an old established function and with lip service thus done, take no further real interest in the matter. This is a world of change and a dynamic management must constantly trim, adjust and supplement as the case may be. As long as it is somebody's job to do this, it does not really matter what he is called.

The basis of a survey of this type is usually pre-printed questionnaires which ask for complete details of the passenger's overall journey or, in other words, origin and ultimate destination. They can be distributed on the vehicles but that only catches existing passengers. A household survey is more representative but the magnitude of the task must confine the information to a sample. Such surveys could take the form of a personal interview with answers to questions filled in on the spot or cards could be completed by householders at their leisure and returned through the post in pre-paid envelopes. Questions will, of course, be designed in accordance with whatever project might be in mind but if people are to answer and if what they say is to be meaningful, there must not be too many questions and they must be short, to the point and free from ambiguity. Preferably the answers should be one of several alternatives which requires only a tick in an appropriate box. As not everybody will answer, and this applies particularly to postal surveys, the resultant evidence will be only a sample of a sample. Nevertheless, it is still likely that a mass of information will become available for processing. The individual responses will need to be put into a summarised form before they can be properly considered and a computer is appropriate for work of this kind. This of course must have a bearing on the design of the original questionnaire and specialised techniques have been developed. Smaller undertakings which do not employ staff with particular qualifications and training in this field might, therefore, find it more convenient to engage the services of an outside firm which undertakes this sort of work on the occasions when specific projects are in mind.

Selling the Service

Publicity

Publicity can be either indirect or direct. Indirect publicity is provided automatically by the efficiency of the undertaking itself, by the degree of service afforded by its staff, by the sight of vehicles well maintained in a suitable livery of smart appearance and by the mere existence of bus stops. Also, special reports in the local and national press or trade journals and the display of films etc can do much to further the interests of the service.

It is, however, the direct publicity with which this subsection is particularly concerned. Direct publicity is produced to stimulate demand and to make known new facilities to which traffic must be attracted if it is to be profitable. Advertising must also be used to publicise existing facilities, which is done in two ways. First and most important is the publication of timetables and maps. The issue of a system map is the ideal way of conveying to the public the extent of the services and the value and interest of the map is enhanced if it is true to scale and contains other more general features as opposed to a diagrammatic plan of the routes concerned. A production along these lines is in popular demand. Having reached the masses it does bring home to all who may care to see the existence and details of the public transport system, even if the map was not acquired originally for that purpose. Most transport undertakings do in fact publish a map of some kind of their services in many cases as an insert contained in their timetable booklets. One of the best examples is that produced by London Transport in respect of its bus routes. On a sheet of paper measuring no more than $25\frac{1}{4}$in by 21in conveniently folded for pocket use is contained all of the bus routes including those of other operators and the names of the roads served within an area of approximately 1,200sq miles and also showing place names, route numbers with terminal points, all railway lines which are open for passenger service, parks and open spaces etc, all with remarkable clarity. If a system of this magnitude can be plotted successfully in such a concise form, few undertakings should experience difficulty in this respect and the resultant publication has substantial advertising value.

Even more desirable (except possibly where services run at very frequent intervals) is the issue of a timetable. No matter what the form of transport, users must be able to ascertain by easy reference the exact times of operation and for this purpose, the availability of a timetable is essential. The tables themselves should be presented clearly to be readily understood by the layman unfamiliar with operational techniques, supported by an index to places served. At this point the writer is at odds with possibly the majority in the passenger transport industry in expressing his dismay at the 24-hour clock system of presentation which is so dear to the hearts of publicity officers and the like. A public timetable is for passengers to read and readily understand. Why they should be subjected to a mental arithmetic exercise before ascertaining the time of the next departure is beyond comprehension. Many people cannot do this calculation and others who think they can get it wrong. It is ironic that in North America where long distance services do cover a 24-hour day they adhere to the 12-hour clock in their timetables as does the British Broadcasting Corporation in *Radio Times*. If there was light type for AM and heavy type for PM, everybody would understand. In the case of bus timetables it is usual for most routes or groups of routes to be presented separately as are the specimens at Figs 17, 18 and 19 but railway timetables are sometimes compiled on a line basis. This has the advantage that all journeys covering the same ground are covered within one table irrespective of their ultimate destination, whereas with separate tables for each route, any one journey could necessitate reference to several pages. Individual bus routes are however generally identified by route numbers, information which could be obtained from a map as suggested above if not already known and difficulty should not therefore arise. Because of the complexity of most bus systems, individual services cannot easily be summarised into composite tables on an area basis as on the railway, which has a predominance of

Table 152 | **Mondays to Fridays**

London to Chessington, Epsom, Kingston, Twickenham, Shepperton and Hampton Court

											B						A	D					E	
		[2]		[2]			[2]		[2]		[2]	[2]		[2]			[2]	[2]	[2]		[2]		[2]	
London Waterloo 156, 158	d	16 16	16 22	16 26	..	16 30	16 34	..	16 36	16 41	16 42	16 46	16 52	16 54	..	16 56	16 57	17 02	17 04	17 06	17 06	17 12	17 12	..
Vauxhall	d	16 19		16 29					16 39			16 49		16 57					17 07		17 09			
Clapham Junction	d	16 23		16 33			16 41		16 43		16 49	16 53		17 01				17 09	17 11		17 14		17 19	
Earlsfield	d	16 26		16 36					16 46			16 56		17 04							17 17			
Wimbledon 156	d	16 30	16 33	16 40		16 41	16 46		16 50	16u52	16 55	17 00	17 03	17 08				17 14	17 17		17 20		17 25	
Raynes Park	d	16 33		16 43			16 49		16 53		16 58	17 03		17 11				17 17	17 20		17 23		17 28	
Motspur Park	d								16 55		17 00							17 20			17 26		17 30	
Malden Manor	d								16 59												17 29			
Tolworth	d								17 01												17 32			
Chessington North	d								17 05												17 35			
Chessington South	a								17 07												17 37			
Worcester Park	d										17 03							17 23					17 33	
Stoneleigh	d										17 06							17 26					17 36	
Ewell West	d										17 08							17 29					17 38	
Epsom 180	a										17 12							17 33					17 42	
New Malden	d	16 35		16 45			16 52					17 05		17 13					17 23					
Norbiton	d	16 38					16 55					17 08							17 26					
Kingston	d	16b44					16 57					17b14							17 28					
Hampton Wick	d	16 45					16 58					17 15							17 30					
Teddington	d	16 48					17 01					17 18							17 32					
Strawberry Hill 146	d	16 51										17 21												
Twickenham 146	d	16e59										17e29												
Richmond 146	d	17 03										17 33												
London Waterloo 146	a	17 30										17 58												
Fulwell	d						17 04										17 25		17 36					
Hampton	d						17 08										17 29		17 40					
Sunbury	d						17 12										17 33		17 44					
Upper Halliford	d						17 14										17 35		17 46					
Shepperton	a						17 18										17 38		17 49					
Berrylands	d			16 48										17 16										
Surbiton 154, 158	d		16 39	16 52		16 49				16 58			17 09	17 20		17 12				17 22		17 28		
Thames Ditton	d			16 56										17 24										
Hampton Court	a			16 58										17 26										

main trunk routes with relatively few bifurcations. A specimen of a main line summary table appears at Fig 30, being an extract from the published timetable of British Railways. This particular table covers all of the lines thickly marked on the railway system map at Fig 31. Students must familiarise themselves with these methods of presentation.

A secondary feature to timetables and maps is the issue of advertising material in either poster or leaflet form regarding special facilities, cheap fares, scenic routes, etc. There is scope for considerable initiative in the preparation of this literature but valuable as it may be, the work and expense of production must not be accorded priority over the timetables for which there is every justification to sell below actual production cost.

So much for the direct advertising of available facilities. An alternative method of inducing people to travel is by advertising places served, with footnotes indicating how to get there by public transport. Again there is considerable scope for publicity of this nature. Booklets or leaflets could be prepared covering such topics as historic buildings with hours of opening, details of popular exhibitions, sporting events, popular resorts, etc, with a view to stimulating travel. As in all business, the product must be advertised if it is to sell and any monopolistic tendencies do not lessen this need. A public transport undertaking which operates under conditions of so-called monopoly has still to compete with private transport and

Above: **Fig 30. Specimen timetable presentation of a group of local railway services covering a geographical area.**
Reproduced by permission of the British Railways Board who will not be responsible for any inaccuracy contained in this timetable.

Below: **Fig 31. Outline map of the south-western section of the London suburban system of the Southern Region of British Railways with the lines covered by the timetable page reproduced at Fig 30 indicated in thick black.**

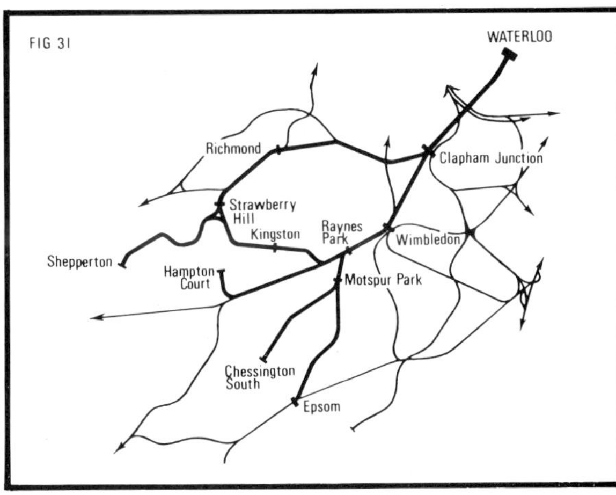

for the optional traveller (ie when the demand is elastic) with other forms of relaxation such as television which encourages them to stay at home.

Another important function of a publicity department but unfortunately not always recognised as such is the provision of signs and the outward display of other written material. It is good advertising to adopt a standard short title for the undertaking (which might be slightly different to the legally registered name), written in a distinctive style and supported by a house symbol for use on all printed matter, on vehicles and property and for all outside display purposes. Over the years, fleet names in all branches of transport have become well known household terms. Many are based on geographical locations; a few on the colour of the fleet. In Great Britain examples such as Royal Blue, Grey Green, Chocolate Express, Red and White, Green Line, Black and White, Yelloway etc, come readily to mind although some have long since vanished and others no longer wear the livery which their name suggests. It is of note, however, that most of these names mentioned refer to longer distance coach services where traffic is more of an optional nature and the degree of competition that much greater. Perhaps there is a connection here with the need to generate public interest and goodwill demanding rather more than a service known only by a geographical reference or the name of the proprietor. It is the opinion of the writer that a company image, providing it is a good image, is important and the identity of the undertaking should instill confidence in the passenger. It is suggested therefore, that the policy of co-ordination, so persistent in Great Britain today, can be taken too far if it is allowed to overspill into the publicity arena. It is not only in the retail trade that a brand name stands for something and where it is the label rather than the contents which sells the bottle. If a comprehensive map or timetable is produced advertising a co-ordinated but faceless product (or service) there is the danger that it will lose public appeal. The need for revenue support is very real (and the effects on commercial practices of political involvement will be considered later in this chapter), but even so, if the enthusiasm of some co-ordinating bodies prompt them to do just this (ie to produce a co-ordinated albeit faceless product), then in the opinion of the writer, it is unfortunate. County councils seem to like the practice and some are actively encouraging it for reasons which are not always clear. County boundaries pay no regard to traffic watersheds and for bus timetable purposes have no significance. A publication produced on an operator basis could well be more appropriate. But managements themselves cannot escape criticism. There is now a tendency, which the writer regards as equally ill conceived, to publish a series of timetables, comprehensive or otherwise, covering a number of relatively small local areas. Those same undertakings will perhaps issue day or period tickets valid anywhere on their systems but their policy on the dissemination of information makes it either impossible or, if a set of timetables is offered for sale, very expensive for would-be passengers to plan an itinerary.

Whilst on the subject of brand names, the author again sees countless examples of what he regards as misplaced enthusiasm in this respect by the recent proliferation of descriptive titles given to specific or groups of services. Few ever stick and they do nothing to sell the service. Publicity might implore people to go by 'Wonder Rail' or 'Rapid Ride' or whatever fancy name tag might be dreamt up but the passengers still see themselves as travelling by train or bus as the case might be. They are likely to identify only the name of the operating company which comes back to the point that, in the opinion of the writer, this is the name which should be sold and not a particular facility.

Public Relations

The larger the undertaking, the more distant does top management tend to become from both its customers and its staff. The resultant staff problems were discussed in Chapter 3. It is essential that this difficulty is overcome because should management appear to the rank and file as some remote mythical body, team spirit and sense of loyalty will be lost, which can, among other things damage good staff relationships. Similar problems arise in respect of the customers. Management must take steps to guard against the danger of actions becoming stereotyped and public protest lost in bureaucratic officialdom. Nevertheless, it must be recognised that in a large undertaking it is difficult to preserve the personal touch and it is the job of the public relations officer to maintain the goodwill of the undertaking which he represents. He is the medium through which management speaks to its customers and customers speak to management. The customers' interests are his interests and it is his responsibility to bring public opinion to the notice of other sections of management responsible for shaping policy. But it must be remembered that good public relations does not end with the establishment of a specialised department at headquarters. All staff, be they for example a railway station manager or a bus inspector, are ambassadors in their own right and the appointment of a public relations officer in no way lessens the responsibilities of other staff in this respect.

A branch of public relations activities calling for special mention is the press section. All transport undertakings, particularly the large ones, are frequently 'in the news' in the national and local newspapers, both of which can and do influence public opinion regardless of the accuracy of their announcements. Lack of first hand information usually leads to a misinterpretation of policy and misrepresentation in the press makes bad publicity. Bad news sells better than good news and unjustified criticism is more likely to be avoided if newspaper editors are given adequate and authentic advice. The publication of such information has a dual purpose, particularly if it relates to the introduction of new facilities as a suitable column in the press has news value to the publisher and advertising value to the operator. It is the special job of the press officer to maintain friendly contact with editors and keep them fully informed of current events as they effect the undertaking by the preparation of special press handouts. It is the image which counts and it is the job of the public relations officer as well as the publicity officer to help to create and preserve it. If the engineers or the operators fall down then the task becomes difficult; it is always easier to bring a good service to public notice than it is to explain why it is not a good service. Nevertheless, some explaining has to be done, particularly if policies are not likely to be received with general acclaim. Staggering of hours, bus priorities and other such measures which contribute to efficiency or economy take a little bit of public education if opinion is to be directed the right way. The reasons must be pursued through the media, in correspondence and at public meetings. This is not likely to be done satisfactorily without a public relations department even if in a small undertaking the function happens to be one of the many responsibilities of the traffic manager.

Political Influence

Commercial Implications

Whatever the context, politics tends to creep in and although the reasons for its implications with public transport were considered at some length in Chapter 3 it is once again a very pertinent issue in this discussion on commercial practices.

To illustrate just how dependent local public passenger transport is on revenue support from public funds, a report for consultation, being the first stage of a public transport study* produced by Cheshire County Council is a good example. In this document, seven possible county wide bus networks were depicted ranging from the existing with appropriate revenue support through to what would remain if there was no financial support at all. The networks at each end of the scale (ie existing and no revenue support) are reproduced at Figs 32 and 33. An exercise such as this does, of course, involve estimates of costs which include wages and hence fare levels in a non-

*Public Transport Study, First Stage — Policy options and implications for Revenue Support; Cheshire County Council.

Below: **Fig 32. Existing bus route network within the County of Cheshire as it is able to be with revenue support.**
Information compiled by and reproduced by permission of Cheshire County Council

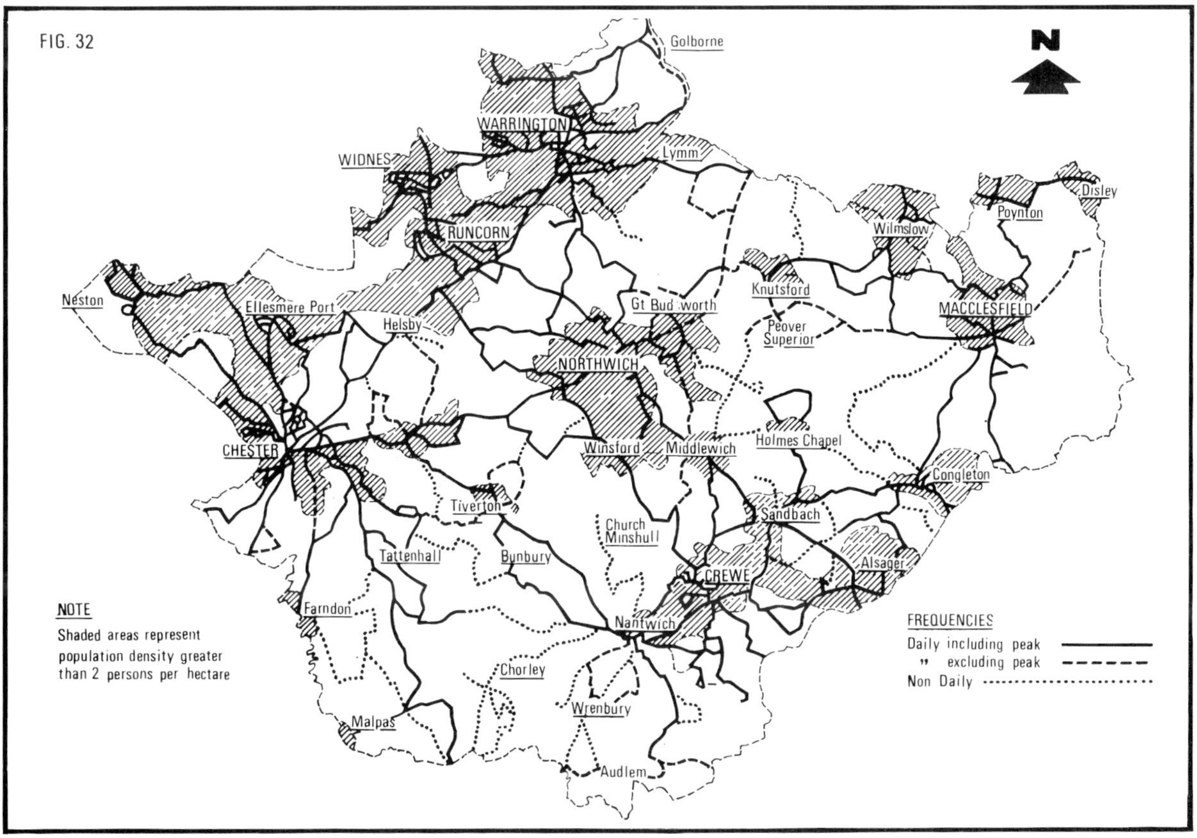

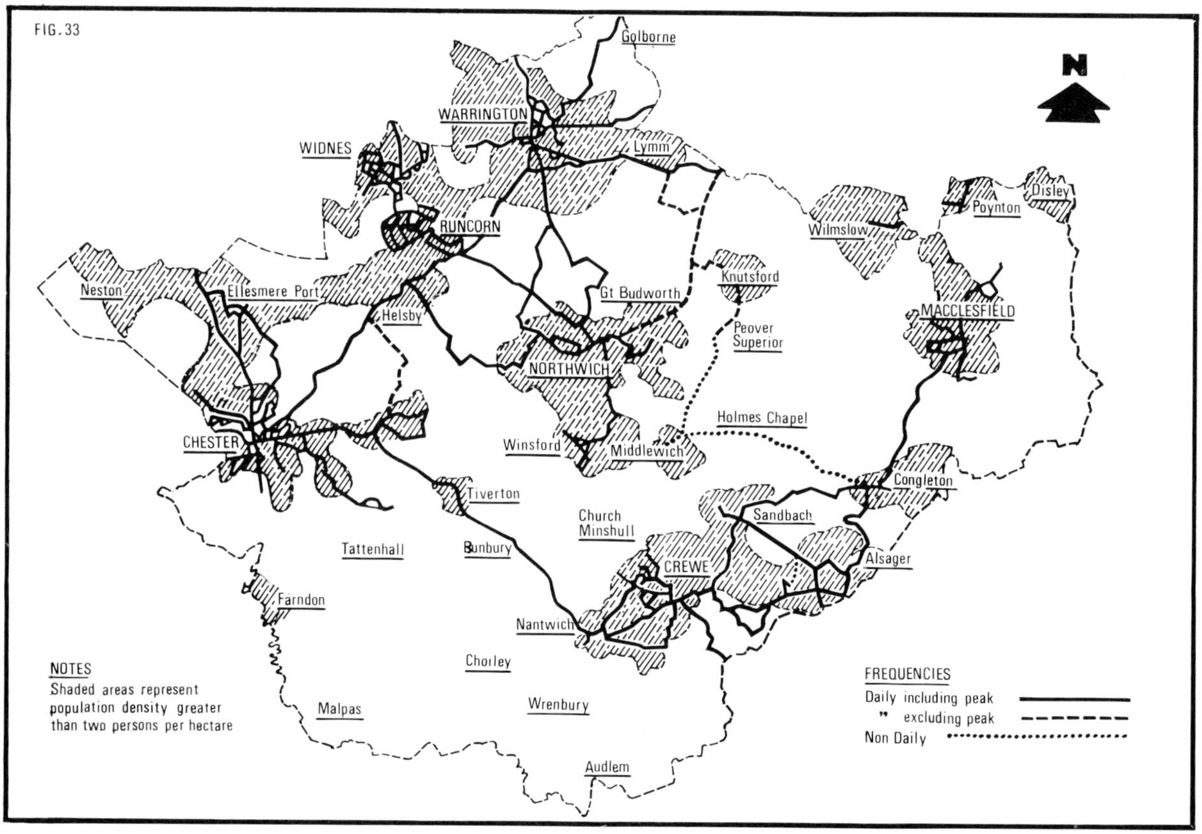

Above: **Fig 33. Bus route network within the County of Cheshire as it would likely be without revenue support.**
Information compiled by and reproduced by permission of Cheshire County Council.

subsidy situation. There is always some passenger resistance to fares increases and in practice, therefore, even the services as indicated might not be practicable. Nevertheless, in presenting such networks it does illustrate what might be provided for a particular sum of money but the maps themselves give no indication of the volume of services. For this reason, certain supporting statistical information is necessary.

Whilst the network shown for the final no support option is not definitive, it gives an indication of the sort of reductions which might perhaps have to be faced. Cheshire County Council suggested that the mileage of road covered might be reduced by 56%, the total bus mileage operated reduced by about 41% and some 12% of the people who at present have access to a bus might lose that facility as the chances are that there would no longer be a service passing through the main centre of their parish. Furthermore, what buses that were left could become inadequate, meaning that people would abandon them and this would lead to yet further withdrawals.

This is but one exercise conducted by one county council and is included here only to illustrate how dependent buses are in some areas on outside support. Even in the commercial sense, therefore, this situation cannot be ignored. But receipt of money from public funds must not bring with it into the industry a feeling of complacency or sense of false security. Managements must remain dynamic. At the same time it is equally important that traffic promotion and the development of prestige and goodwill is not inhibited by any policies of those who provide the subsidies.

In the UK up until comparatively recent times, the classic example of a commercial undertaking being managed directly through a government department was the Post Office. But in 1967, a white paper* envisaged its divorcement from direct government control and reorganisation as an autonomous public corporation. (In the event this change was implemented by the Post Office Act, 1969) The white paper set out the scale of the business and went on to stress the need for commercial enterprise. Extracts from paragraphs 2, 3 and 35 read as follows:

'Trading operations on this scale must be managed on commercial lines if they are to be efficient.'

**Reorganisation of the Post Office;* Cmnd 3233, HMSO

'Its present structure and methods are those of a Department of State. These have been evolved primarily for the formulation and execution of government policy and are geared to the discharge of ministerial responsibility to Parliament. They are unsuited to the running of the postal, telecommunications and remittance services.'
'Traditionally, the Post Office has followed the organisational pattern of a central government department. This pattern is not appropriate for the successful management of a large service industry.'

The principle is a general one and the publicly owned sector of British transport was already organised into autonomous bodies. The theory applies to local government just as much as national government and that is one reason why, as is explained in Chapter 8, the Transport Act 1968 created passenger transport executives as entities distinct from local government with its own customs and practices. Not only is a department of local government by its very nature not geared to manage a commercial enterprise, a local council is a politically dominated body. Regardless of its bearing to the left or to the right, democratically elected as it may be, a body such as this will never be acceptable to all of the people. Some will be hostile and, in the opinion of the writer, this cannot be a good basis on which to run a business. Whilst, therefore, the monetary lifeline which the policies of some councils bestow is valuable indeed, again, in the opinion of the writer, it is unfortunate if politics comes also to the sales counter and thereby frustrates efforts to build on that support to generate goodwill and stimulate public acceptance of what could be an expanding service. To repeat what was said earlier, it is the operator who is in the best position to create a good image and stimulate goodwill and if he is to stay in business, revenue support or no, then that he must do.

There is one other political influence which has a strong link with commercial practice and that is on the level of charges. The basis of charging has already been considered and the cost of travel has a strong bearing on the number of passengers who use the service. It has been seen that it is self-defeating to charge more than the traffic can bear but this in itself is dependent on the purpose of the journey and the person who is making it. The cheaper the fare the more people will be attracted to ride, although seldom would the extra traffic so generated be sufficient to justify commercially any general lowering of fares. But it could, nevertheless, be a political expedient that more people should ride and if adequate compensation is forthcoming, then the operator can be expected to charge lower fares as required. In any case, he is not likely to demur as it can only mean more business for him. If, however, the process is taken to its ultimate conclusion with no fare at all being charged at the time of travel, the bus (or the train) would then become a purely social service paid for out of taxation either nationally or locally. Although apart from isolated services, special cases or groups of people, there are at present no examples of a free fare system of any significance, the idea has been mooted in various places. If it ever came it would have a profound effect on operating practices and does, therefore, require a mention in a work such as this. Although in a sense this is somewhat inconsistent with commercial practices, discussion in this context is appropriate in view of its close association with charging practices and revenue receipts. Before so doing, however, there is one other side to the revenue support issue which should be considered, and that applies not to the receiver being the operator, but to those who authorise such an arrangement.

Revenue Support

All that has been said so far has been geared to the commercial viewpoint of a bus (or railway) undertaking. Whilst the need for revenue support has been acknowledged it has been suggested for operational and customer relation reasons that independent transport managements should not only remain but should be seen to remain and be in complete control of their businesses, thereby preserving their local identities and public goodwill. But at the same time it must be acknowledged that as it is the responsibility of politicians to determine the extent to which public money will be allocated for revenue support, they will also want to be satisfied that it is spent in the most propitious way. It is reasonable to assume therefore that they will expect to do rather more than allow operators to continue in the way they see fit without question and then foot whatever bills might be presented to them. Such an arrangement would be something less than satisfactory for the custodians of the public purse and just as they take professional guidance from their engineers, planners and administrators, so they will wish to have on their staff people versed in the provision of public transport to advise them and implement their public transport policies. Although there have been references in other chapters to swollen administrations as a result of such an arrangement, this was more to bring to notice the danger of overlaps of responsibility with the consequent risk of too many directives and duplication of work. There is certainly no dissent from the declared need of politicians to satisfy themselves that they get value for money and their advisers in this particular field are now an established part of at least the British transport fraternity, albeit with terms of reference somewhat different to those of their colleagues who provide the services. A text book on bus operation should cater for the needs of those involved in public transport from this new angle as well as for those progressing through the operating side and it is for this reason that there is included here a sub-section which discusses public subsidies in a manner slightly different to what might emanate from within the industry itself.

The work of what in Great Britain is a county public transport co-ordinator is largely conditioned by the attitude of his county council towards public transport and revenue support. The more that is paid, the greater will his influence be and it is the social factors and repercussions on highways and land use which county councils take into account. The provision of bus services makes it possible for everybody to move around and thereby enables the daily life of the individual and the nation collectively to continue. There are, however, other social benefits which a bus gives. Although public transport cannot match the convenience afforded by private transport and it is not easy to attract existing motorists away from their cars and on to buses, the existence of a bus system does, nevertheless, reduce to some extent the number of private cars which would otherwise be on the road. This is of considerable importance as the bus is far more economical in terms of road space per passenger carried than is the private car. If there was no such bus network or it was reduced to such proportions that it could no longer cater for all local travel requirements, then those bus passengers who were able to do so would turn to private transport. Even to the existing motorist, the bus has a social value as not only does it hold down traffic congestion to the extent that he is able to use his own car with relative ease, but the bus is also there as a stand-by service when his own vehicle is for any reason not available.

The social benefits of a bus or train service may be summarised as follows:

(a) It helps to reduce traffic congestion and it keeps it at acceptable proportions.
(b) It avoids the need for costly roadworks which would otherwise be necessary to accommodate as far as possible an increase in vehicular traffic.
(c) It helps to reduce fuel consumption which, in view of the energy situation, can only be an issue of increasing national importance.
(d) It reduces air and noise pollution from cars.
(e) It avoids the need for more car parks.
(f) It makes it possible for everybody to move around, including those who have no access to or are unable to use cars and would otherwise be immobilised.

On the question of spending public money, the transport co-ordinator has perforce to take a wider view of things than does transport management. He will need to consider:

(a) The value of the benefits as listed at (a) to (f) above and the situation which would emerge if the bus system either disappeared or was severely truncated.
(b) Fare levels as they would be in the absence of subsidy and the relationship with price and income levels generally and what the traffic can bear.
(c) The desirability or otherwise of subsidising the travelling expenses of any specific categories of people.
(d) Whether cheaper fares attract the right type of traffic to produce overall community benefits.

Furthermore, just as an operator will seek a situation which is most favourable to him, county transport co-ordinators will perforce endeavour to get the most for the least. They will, therefore, try to ascertain what action operators would take if no financial support was forthcoming. For various reasons it would not necessarily mean automatic withdrawal.

If it is decided that a subsidy in some form is justified then consideration must be given to the following possibilities either singly or in combination as a means of helping to determine the extent of that subsidy. It will need to be decided whether there should be:

(a) A percentage ceiling on a subsidy in relation to either farebox revenue or total costs.
(b) A blanket subsidy or selective by routes.
(c) A ceiling on the amount of subsidy per passenger journey (or passenger mile).
(d) A ceiling on the amount of subsidy per head of population, either for the area as a whole or a specific part.
(e) A subsidy set as a percentage of revenue as a method of assessment.

As well as providing for a service, all forms of subsidy are, of course, also to hold down fares at an acceptable level because to charge an economic fare at what would be an unacceptable level is tantamount to not providing a service at all.

The actual amount of subsidy might be decided after consideration of the values of alternative levels of service. If a blanket subsidy is provided, say to keep fares below or service levels above what could be justified on pure economic grounds, there is little influence over operators or incentive for them to conduct their business with maximum efficiency or economy. At the end of the day they just indicate their shortfall. This is not to suggest that managements would tolerate inefficiency but there are nevertheless no built in safeguards for those who are paying other than examination or audit to the extent that they are able. Selective support, service by service, particularly if there is a final upper limit would help to eliminate services which are either very poorly used or inordinately expensive to run and the criteria for service provision as considered in Chapter 5 will have a bearing here. If the policy is to hold down fares, there could be advantage in compensating for each ticket sold. For example, if a 'commercial' fare of 8p is held down at 5p, then pay 3p for each 5p ticket sold and so on throughout the range. In other words pay by results and leave service levels to the operator who would be required to answer for any inadequacies. If there are no passengers then there is no money. If the service fails to operate; again no money. The disadvantage of this system lies in excessive administration and the difficulties in producing the required figures will be seen in Chapter 9. Some co-ordinating authorities may not only be selective in the services which they are prepared to support but willing to meet only the net deficit incurred by that particular group. In other words, they would seek to offset the losses by any profit makers within the routes selected. There is some logic in the argument that if it is good to bear the losses then it is also good to take credit for any profits and the application of this principle is not without precedent. Viewing the matter impartially, however, it is the opinion of the writer that this is not an equitable approach unless the entire network is adopted. Even then, if a business as a whole is profitable and the proprietor is asked to provide a loss making service he is not likely to agree to such an arrangement as the cost would then come out of his profits. There would seem to be an equally strong argument on the part of operators not to include profitable services in any financial agreement.

Free Fares

Although there are very few examples, the concept of a free bus service is not new, even on a commercial basis. There are instances of such facilities being provided for publicity purposes, as a means to induce people to visit certain shops or to encourage recruitment at awkwardly sited factories. Being considered here, however, are the social aspects of a no fare principle applied to a local network and available for everybody to use. Funding entirely through rates or taxes could be accomplished only by a political decision and many readers might have strong personal views regarding the acceptance of such an arrangement. Those reasons are irrelevant in any discussion here, although outside political circles disquiet has been expressed regarding the arguments put forward in support of such a policy. If considerable sums of money are to be spent on revenue support then equally considerable sums must be used for capital expenditure, which might not necessarily be available. If it is not, then to take the extreme case, everyone would have a bus pass but there would be no buses. But more than that. Some money at least would have to come from local rates, and shops and other commercial premises carry heavy liabilities in this respect. This additional burden on the owners could only be passed on to customers and the cost of living would in consequence rise. It is likely that under such circumstances a higher percentage of income would then have to be spent by the lower paid groups than by those who are more affluent with the result that those who would suffer would be the very people whom it was planned should benefit. As a means of reducing traffic congestion by enticing motorists out of their cars and on to public transport, the system is once again of doubtful value. Mention was made in Chapter 5 of the great store that the motoring fraternity puts on the convenience of personalised transport. Even though between the years 1972 and 1977 because of higher prices the average expenditure per household on private motoring doubled, there was still a 10% increase in the number of cars on the road.* This suggests that it will take more than free buses to make much impression on the trend and only car restraints will deal with the congestion issue. There is, however evidence to believe that many pedestrians would become short distance bus riders if they did not have to pay but this would only delay the service and make it less attractive. It would not achieve the desired objective.

For various reasons, therefore, a free fares policy is not likely to find widespread support and it must remain a relatively minor issue in any study of transport operation. Nevertheless, a free fares system is a possibility which some politicians have not overlooked. It is necessary, therefore, to consider, albeit briefly, the effects of such a policy on operating practices.

A free fares system is likely to be preceded by a range of sub-standard fares, being fares held down well below what the traffic could bear, for political reasons. It could be, for example, that existing charges are kept constant with the effect that in a period of inflation, in real terms, prices fall. If this situation remains then, subject to inflation not abating, the time must come when the cost of collecting fares is greater than the revenue that they produce, in which case there is good reason not to charge anything at the time of travel. There are two aspects of a free fares policy which call for consideration. The first involves the economics of the system in terms of bus operation and secondly there are the operating and other complexities which are bound to arise.

It will be quite clear from Chapters 9 and 11 that fare collection involves cost in terms of both capital equipment and labour. Money has to be collected, tickets issued, cash handed in, coins counted and cash in bulk banked together with a need for all of the supporting administration, audit and necessary security arrangements. Conductors could be dispensed with subject to the vehicles being of a suitable type (most of them now are) but conductors are a disappearing breed anyway and as drivers would still be responsible for passengers it is debatable whether they could ever be deprived of their one-man allowance. A free fares policy, however, is not likely to be a part of any national policy.

*Source: *Transport Statistics, Great Britain*; HMSO.

If ever it did come it would more probably be through a local decision and any local free fare zone is unlikely to coincide with a bus undertaking's operating territory. In other words, some bus routes are always likely to be cross-boundary in local authority terms, in which case they would operate only partly within a free fares area. Those services which did go outside such a zone would still be subject to normal charging methods. This being the case, provision for fare collection and all that goes with it would have to be retained although the equipment would be under-utilised. The absence of tickets within a free fares zone would of course eliminate the need for travelling ticket inspectors, but those officials are likely to be required in any case for control work and other supervisory duties. Nevertheless, some savings in administration could be anticipated and furthermore there would be no loss of revenue through tickets not being issued, fares uncollected, passengers overriding etc.

Thus far the exercise is straightforward. The savings are quantifiable but variable according to circumstances although they need not be as great as might at first be imagined. The imponderables come when the repercussions on traffic planning are examined and this is where the criteria for service provision becomes of even greater significance. Remember what was said in Chapter 5. Route statistics are the all-important tool for traffic managers to judge whether their services are correctly planned. Trends can be detected and warning lights can spark off more detailed investigations to see whether any adjustments are necesasry. With a free fares system, all such statistics have, of course, completely gone, but with a purely social service, it does not necessarily follow that a deterioration in demand signals reductions or withdrawals. At this stage buses would come into a similar category to that of other public utilities such as the library service, schools and refuse collection where everybody pays regardless of the extent of use and expects to receive a standard 'product' in return. This could create an entirely new situation and the greater the degree of subsidy, the more remote might the hitherto accepted practices for determining service provision become. Unlike certain other public utilities, the demand for public transport would not be easily predictable as:

(i) The journeys to be made vary considerably.
(ii) The demand for shopping and pleasure travel is not regular and some people do not use buses every day or, indeed, every week.
(iii) Some people do not use buses at all, in which case it would be a waste to make provision for them even though those concerned might not accept the point.

The formula adopted for the other utilities could not, therefore, be applied with the same precision to public transport. But complete rate support could easily provoke demands from some ratepayers for reasonable (undetermined) facilities to be provided for their use regardless of the numbers of people involved.

Free fares would be the final transition from a commercial to a social service and if it ever came, planning and service provision would take on a completely new dimension.

8
Statutory Controls

The Need for Regulation

The provision of a public service of any kind generally implies some sort of control. It might be that a special skill is required which, if undertaken by people not properly proficient, could be damaging or even result in danger to life or property. If it is an essential service, those who provide it might need to be protected from unfair or wasteful competition. If by so doing near monopolies are created, then in turn the public requires protection with its interests taken into account. There would also have to be safeguards to ensure that such essential services are maintained.

Control emanates from the dictates of Parliament. The various edicts which come forth from the legislature either detail in direct terms what will or will not be done, are permissive in that certain provisions may be implemented at the discretion of the appropriate secretary of state or lay down principles and authorise the preparation and issue of regulations, again probably by a secretary of state. Provision must also be made for the requirements of these enactments or regulations to be properly administered and a convenient way of doing this is by the institution of a licensing system, which means the establishment of an issuing authority.

There are two basic types of control, being exercised through *Quality licensing* and *Quantity licensing*.

The terms are self-explanatory. Quality licensing ensures that adequate standards are maintained, that vehicles are kept in a safe and roadworthy condition, that the operators are competent and that the business is properly run. Quantity licensing controls the amount of service and where it may be provided. In Great Britain, bus services are generally subject to quantity control and the operator (being the manager) the operative (being the driver), the vehicle and the service are all subject to quality control. The manager and the driver must be proficient, the vehicle must be properly constructed and maintained and the route and stopping points must be physically suitable.

Railways are equally subject to safety controls but they operate on their own private right of way as was seen in Chapter 3. Under these circumstances direct regulation is applied which is more appropriate than licensing and provides only for quality control.

In view of the diversity of the systems, the statutory control of road and rail public passenger transport will be dealt with separately. All of what follows refers to British law and applies to Great Britain.

Road Passenger Transport

Vehicle Definition

The vehicles which are used for public passenger transport and to which the licensing laws to be described apply are known as public service vehicles (PSVs). A public service vehicle is defined in Section 2 of the Transport Act, 1980 as a motor vehicle (other than a tram) which is used for carrying passengers for hire or reward and carries more than eight passengers or if it is able to carry only 8 passengers or less it is used for hire or reward at separate fares as part of a passenger business (but see under the sub-heading 'car sharing' below). In more familiar terms this generally means buses and coaches.

Traffic Commissioners

The PSV licensing system revolves around traffic commissioners, being semi-judicial bodies appointed by the minister for each of 11 traffic areas which between them cover the entire country. There are three such traffic commissioners for each area, one being a permanent and full time chairman, the other two being nominees from county and district councils respectively. Traffic commissioners are the licensing authorities for the PSV industry and are responsible for the issue of operators' licences, road service licences for stage carriage services and drivers' PSV licences. As a matter of interest, the chairmen of the traffic commissioners are also responsible for the issue of licences for the road haulage industry but in this capacity they are known as licensing authorities.

Traffic commissioners were established by the Road Traffic Act, 1930 when a system of quantity licensing for the PSV industry was first introduced. Following subsequent legislation on this and other matters there was a consolidating act 30 years later, being the Road Traffic Act, 1960 in which the licensing system was brought forward without alteration in principle. Subject to numerous subsequent amendments and additions to the licensing procedure which were aimed at relaxing controls under certain circumstances, the system of licensing both bus and long distance coach services and excursions and tours remained until the Transport Act, 1980 replaced many of the provisions relating to public service vehicles. Today it is the Road Traffic Act, 1960 as amended and re-enacted by the Transport Act, 1980 which is the authority for the PSV licensing arrangements. As it is the traffic commissioners for each traffic area who are responsible for the issue of PSV operators' licences and road service licences, without which operators cannot run their buses, they have considerable control, subject only to appeal. The PSV licensing system and the machinery necessary for implementing it follows.

Quality Control

The Operator

Unlike the other aspects of control, operator licensing is a comparatively recent innovation and is something which came originally through membership of the European Economic Community. The Public Service Vehicle Operators (Qualifications) Regulations, 1977 gave effect to the EEC Council Directive 74/562 on admission to the occupation of road passenger transport operator and the requirement is now contained in Section 19 of the Transport Act, 1980. As has been explained, traffic commissioners are responsible for the issue of public service vehicle operators' licences without which no PSV as such may be run. Before so doing they are required to satisfy themselves that the applicants are suitably qualified. In accordance with Section 21, potential PSV operators must show that:

(a) They are of good repute.
(b) They have appropriate financial standing.
(c) They are professionally competent or they employ a manager who is of good repute and professionally competent.

Apart from certain people who were already in the industry when the regulations became effective, professionally competent means that they are qualified through one of the appropriate professional institutes or they have passed a special examination conducted by the Royal Society of Arts and have thereby gained a certificate of competence.

In respect of such applications, traffic commissioners must also give regard to:

(a) Previous conduct involving operation of vehicles.
(b) Arrangements to ensure that the regulations concerning drivers' hours (to be considered below) are observed.
(c) Facilities for proper maintenance.
(d) Manner in which the vehicle is to be used.

Section 152 of the Road Traffic Act, 1960 as amended also requires holders of public service vehicle operators' licences to observe wages and conditions for their staff which are not less favourable than those which would apply to contracts with government departments resulting from a resolution of the House of Commons.

In accordance with Section 20 of the 1980 Act, PSV operators' licences may be either standard or restricted. A standard licence authorises the holder to use any description of public service vehicle and may be issued either for national only or national and international operations. The restricted licence applies to those operators to which the requirements of the EEC Directive do not apply such as to vehicles with not more than eight passenger seats; a figure which may be increased to 16 if the vehicle is not used as part of a passenger carrying business.

Applications are made to the traffic commissioners in whose area the operating centre is situated. Undertakings could (and often do) have two or more such centres and if they are in different traffic areas then licences must be obtained from all of the traffic commissioners concerned. Once a licence is obtained an operator may run his vehicles, subject to any road service licence requirements (see below), within the area in which the operating centre is located and beyond into any other traffic area.

Traffic commissioners will, vide Section 22 of the 1980 Act, specify the total number of vehicles which may be operated regardless of whether they are stage, express or contract carriages (terms which are explained below). They may also stipulate the maximum number of vehicles within each description and conditions for restricting or regulating the use of such vehicles including stopping places. Their decisions are subject to the right of appeal to the minister and beyond that to the High Court.

The Driver

Drivers of public service vehicles must hold an appropriate licence obtainable from the traffic commissioners vide Section 144 of the Road Traffic Act, 1960 as amended. The issue of such a licence is subject to the applicant showing that he is a fit and proper person and he must also prove himself competent to drive a vehicle of the appropriate type. A PSV driver's licence is not a substitute for a normal driving licence which is still necessary. The issue of a PSV driver licence is accompanied by a badge which must be worn whilst on duty. It is of passing interest that until recently, a conductor also required a PSV licence. It was Section 36 of the Transport Act, 1980 which modified Section 144 of the 1960 Act accordingly.

The Vehicle

The basic requirements for motor vehicles are stipulated in the Motor Vehicle (Construction and Use) Regulations, 1978, the purpose of which is to ensure that motor vehicles and trailers are constructed within statutory dimensions and to acceptable standards. They also set out the requirements for maintenance and use as vehicles must remain roadworthy and not become a source of danger. In the case of public service vehicles which carry more than eight passengers, because of the greater capacity and the even greater need for precautions, Section 17 of the 1980 Act requires that a public service vehicle will not be used as such without either a certificate of initial fitness issued by a certifying officer, or a type approval in accordance with Section 130 of the Road Traffic Act, 1960 as amended although the Road Traffic Act, 1974 makes possible a future repeal by order of this Section 130. To qualify for such certificates, a vehicle must comply with the Public Service Vehicles (Conditions of Fitness, Equipment and Use) Regulations, 1972 (as amended). A decision of the certifying officer is subject to the right of appeal. Subsequent testing of public service vehicles (probably annually by regulation) is necessary in accordance with Section 34 of the 1980 Act which extends the application of Section 44 of the Road Traffic Act 1972 (which requires test certificates for motor vehicles) to PSV's. Furthermore, Section 16 of the 1980 Act empowers certifying officers or public service vehicle examiners to inspect such vehicles at any time.

Further reference to construction and use regulations is contained in Chapter 10.

The Service

The licensing of the service is basically quantity control and as such will be considered in the following sub-section. However, when considering applications for road service licences of stage carriage services (to be explained), traffic commissioners will, vide Section 6 of the Transport Act, 1980 have regard, among other things, to the suitability of the route and stopping places and generally for securing the safety and convenience of the public.

Quantity Control

Quantity control, to the extent that it exists, is administered through a system of service licensing and is perhaps the most interesting part of the PSV licensing laws. The point 'to the extent that it exists' is made as quantity control does not now extend to the entire road passenger transport industry. It applies only to stage carriage services but from the definitions which are about to be given, it will be seen that this embraces really all local urban and rural bus operation, which is what this book is about. Nevertheless, if the licensing system is to be properly understood, it would be impracticable to deal only with the local routes and its application to all services must, therefore, be explained.

The system of road service licensing, like the traffic commissioners themselves as was noted earlier in this chapter was first introduced with the Road Traffic Act, 1930. It was a system of quantity licensing designed to regulate competition, encourage co-ordination and protect existing operators. It was introduced at a time when those undertakings which viewed seriously their responsibilities to the community and thereby endeavoured to give everybody a service by accepting the poor routes along with the good were frustrated in so doing by other less scrupulous operators who muscled in on the more lucrative traffics and 'skimmed off the cream'. Whilst the principal company was adhering to its scheduled timetable the other buses — the 'pirates' — might overtake or even reverse from the opposite direction to get to the point first where most people were standing. Without adequate controls such conduct was possible, the livelihood of the pirate bus was precarious, the regular operator was insecure and whilst some passengers may have had a shorter wait at the time, in the long run it did them no good either as the larger operator was weakened and the others were only interested in good loads, always assuming that they remained in business anyway. This is not to say that there is now no place in the bus industry for small independents. On the contrary, and this was said in Chapter 3, this sector with its lower overheads and more personal service can make a valuable contribution to a bus network if circumstances are right and this applies particularly to rural areas. But proper control was (and still is) very desirable and the system of road service licensing remained in principle virtually unchanged when re-enacted in the Road Traffic Act, 1960. After this time, feelings began to be expressed that the licensing procedure was cumbrous and, as bus operation, particularly in rural areas, became more and more unattractive, unnecessarily inhibitive to people who might otherwise have been prepared to provide a service. The result was a series of relaxations of the licensing rules applicable under certain circumstances. Thus appeared permits, experimental areas, minibuses, car sharing and community buses, all of which, in some small way, enabled the full licensing procedure to be circumvented. Overall, however, even collectively they had little impact on the system apart from making it confusing.

Some of this has now changed. Part I of the Transport Act, 1980 has, among other things, abolished road service licences for express carriages as redefined and made it easier for applicants to obtain road service licences for stage carriages by shifting the onus of proof.

A public service vehicle has already been defined. Section 3 of the 1980 Act perpetuates the earlier classification of PSVs into stage, express and contract carriages but now the definitions are that:

A stage carriage is a PSV used on a local service.
An express carriage is a PSV used on an express service.
A contract carriage is a PSV which does not carry passengers at separate fares.

Both local and express services do carry passengers at separate fares, the distinction being that in the case of an express service, no passenger may be set down at a place which is less than 30 miles from the boarding point measured in a straight line. Section 4 of the 1980 Act precludes the operation of any stage carriage service except under the authority of road service licence. What this means in practice is that most bus services require road service licences. It also means that express and contract carriages do not, the latter being regardless of the length of journey. Unless it is an excursion or tour, however, Section 3 requires operators to keep traffic commissioners informed regarding the routes and timetables of their express services. A contract carriage may carry passengers at separate fares providing, in accordance with Schedule 1, the arrangements are not made by the operator or some other person who would receive remuneration for so doing; all of the passengers travel for most of the journey and without any fare differentiation and there is no previous public advertisement. Even then, there is no objection to local internal publicity through places of work or worship, clubs or other voluntary associations.

Applications for road service licences are made to the appropriate traffic commissioners. If the service has stopping points in more than one traffic area, then licences are required in respect of each of the areas concerned. Whereas at one time it was necessary for the applicant to prove his case, the 1980 Act has created a presumption in favour of the applicant and traffic commissioners will, vide Section 5 of the 1980 Act, grant the licence unless they consider that to do so would be contrary to public interest. In so considering, they will have regard to:

(a) The transport requirements of the area as a whole.
(b) Any transport policies or plans which have been made and drawn to their attention by county councils.
(c) Any other relevant objections or representations.

The last item (item (c)) is singularly significant as it is this which gives rise to the traffic court procedure which is likely to follow an application for a new or an amendment to an existing road service licence. All such applications are contained in a circular entitled 'Notices and Proceedings' which is published by the traffic commissioners for each traffic area once per fortnight. Armed with this information, other passenger transport operators and local councils might see fit to object. Operators are likely to feel so inclined if they think that the application, if successful, would prejudice or abstract their own existing traffic. Sometimes if a new facility is to be provided, more than one operator will apply and it is again a matter for decision by traffic commissioners.

If objections are received to any application, the matter will be considered by the traffic commissioners at a public hearing, hence the traffic courts where proceedings are conducted on lines similar to those at a magistrates court but rather less formal. The onus is on the objectors to prove that an application should be either rejected or modified. At the close of the hearing the traffic commissioners give their decision which will be either to grant, attach conditions, modify or refuse the application. Any such conditions will be as a result of their considerations with particular regard to (a), (b) and (c) above and to general suitability and safety as mentioned under quality licensing. Conditions as to fares are restricted by Section 7 of the 1980 Act. Traffic Commissioners will impose requirements on fares only if they consider that such action is essential in the interests of the public in order to give protection from any unreasonable action on the part of the operator or to regulate competition between different stage carriage services.

Should the traffic commissioners consider that, in connection with any application for a road service licence, there are no other transport facilities available which could meet the needs of the route concerned, then Section 8 requires that such an application will be granted subject always to suitability, safety etc. Under these circumstances, the need to consider outside representations would not arise. Section 9 requires applications for road service licences for excursions and tours to be similarly dealt with providing they would either not directly compete with any other bus or tram service (other than another excursion or tour) or that they would operate only for special events.

Any party who is aggrieved by a traffic commissioner's decision has the right of appeal other than in the case of Sections 8 and 9 and once granted, a road service licence is normally valid for five years.

Such is the procedure for obtaining road service licences for stage carriage services. As express and contract work requires no road service licence, their definitions are of considerable importance.

Relaxations of the PSV Licensing Requirements

Introduction

Passing comment was made earlier that over the years there has been pressure from some quarters for a relaxation of the PSV licensing laws, particularly those which invoked the traffic court procedure for road service licences and the protection which it gave to established operators. Criticism of this kind is not necessarily justified and even with the 1980 Transport Act, Parliament has not seen fit to sweep away all of the quantity licensing control as was done by the 1968 Act in the case of road haulage. Nevertheless, as has already been said, some relaxation of the controls was superimposed on pre-1980 legislation. The 1980 Act itself has produced further easements which have replaced some and perpetuated or amended other parts of the previous arrangements. Whilst in some cases this has facilitated the provision of a service, the system remains somewhat complex and the relaxations have certainly done nothing for the student who is trying to get a grasp of the subject.

Details of the exceptions to the basic PSV licensing system (which must be read in conjunction with what has already been said in the previous sub-sections) follow.

Experimental Areas

The Passenger Vehicles (Experimental Areas) Act, 1977 enables county councils to authorise the use of certain passenger vehicles within defined experimental areas for hire or reward with or without separate fares without the need for such vehicles to be designated public service vehicles. The experimental areas are designated by the minister or as requested by a county council but notice of any proposed authorisations must be publicly advertised and account taken of any representations received and are subject to the approval of the minister. Such authorisations may be applied to private vehicles generally, private vehicles being defined as those which are not otherwise used in the course of a passenger transport business and cannot carry more than a specified number but less than 16 passengers, or they may be issued to specified persons and vehicles. In the case of the special authorisations, however, the vehicles may be private or commercial. The commercial vehicles may be otherwise used as part of a passenger transport business but for this purpose they must be adapted to carry not more than eight passengers. In other words, in this case it is really aiming at taxis and hire cars.

As authorisations within experimental areas avoid the need for the public service vehicle classification it follows that they are not subject to the PSV licensing laws. They do not, therefore, need a road service licence. However, authorisations are subject to the following conditions or requirements:

General authorisations

(a) The journey must not be in conjunction with or an extension of a conventional licensed service if the vehicle is owned by the holder of that licence.
(b) There must be no previous public advertisement.
(c) The vehicles must not ply for hire.
(d) Passengers must have made their travel arrangements in advance.

Special authorisations

(a) Regard must be given to the suitability of the applicants and the vehicles.
(b) There may be specific requirements on any matter including the following:
   The persons by whom specified vehicles may be used.
   The route, timetable and fares.
   Advertising of services.
   Picking up and setting down points.

This system was devised as a way of facilitating the provision of public transport facilities in areas away from the established bus networks. So far, three areas in Devon and four in North Yorkshire have been designated as experimental areas. Vehicles authorised in this way must not cross into neighbouring areas without similar approval from the adjoining authority.

Trial Areas

Section 12 of the Transport Act, 1980 introduced trial areas. These are areas outside Greater London being areas designated for the time being (between two and five years) in which road service licences are not necessary for stage carriage services. The minister may designate areas as such on request by a county council. Within these areas, that part of PSV licensing which applies to road service licences will have no effect although Section 14 requires information regarding such services to be supplied to the relevant county and district councils and also published in the local press.

Minibuses

The Minibus Act 1977 makes provision for use under certain circumstances of minibuses carrying passengers for hire or reward without the need for classification as public service vehicles (and again remember that under such circumstances the normal PSV licensing machinery does not apply). Minibuses are defined (as amended by the 1980 Act) as vehicles which have a capacity of more than eight but not more than 16 passengers. This act enables traffic commissioners and other bodies as may be specified to issue permits to designated organisations (including themselves) which authorise the use of these vehicles for the carriage of certain fare-paying passengers (and this does not mean the public at large) in connection with non-profit making activities. A minibus so used under authority of a permit and subject to compliance with any prescribed conditions is not classified as a PSV.

In accordance with the Minibus (Designated Bodies) Regulations, 1977, the bodies who may issue permits either to themselves or to other allied or subsidiary organisations include non-metropolitan county councils, metropolitan district councils and all kinds of charitable institutions. The types of organisations to which and in whose interests these regulations are aimed are those concerned with education, religion, social welfare or other activities conducted for the benefit of the community. In other words, the acts seeks to facilitate the use of minibuses which are owned, for example, by schools, scout groups and all charitable organisations for such purposes as away sports matches, meetings and other such activities whilst at the same time permitting passengers to contribute to the running costs of the vehicle. If children are to be carried between home and school the consent of the education authority and the traffic commissioners is necessary. Minibuses working under the permit system must not carry members of the public at large and must not be used to make a profit.

The 1980 Act has made certain additions to the 1977 Act which has rather confused the issue and made its title somewhat irrelevant. Section 33 of the 1980 Act refers to small and large passenger-carrying vehicles with the small vehicle carrying more than eight but not more than 16 passengers and the large vehicle carrying more than 16. Whilst the provisions of the 1977 Act remain (as amended) it now authorises the issue of permits to large vehicles as well by the 'other bodies' to which reference has already been made. The same circumstances are necessary for such permits to be issued (ie not for the use of the public at large, not with a view to profit, etc) but in the case of the large vehicles they are not excluded from the PSV category but instead are relieved of the need for PSV operators' licences, road service licences and PSV drivers' licences.

Car Sharing

It was said at the beginning of this chapter that the definition of a public service vehicle (vide Section 2 of the Transport Act, 1980) was that it carried more than eight passengers for hire or reward or, if not so adapted, at separate fares in the course of a passenger carrying business. In other words, this excludes from the PSV licensing system vehicles carrying eight or less in which passengers are conveyed otherwise than as part of a passenger carrying business which, of course, covers private cars. Even so if such a vehicle is part of a passenger carrying business (such as taxis and hire cars) it may still carry passengers at separate fares without classification as a PSV provided that:

(a) Total receipts do not exceed costs.
(b) The arrangements for payment are made before the journey commences.
(c) The arrangements are not initiated by the driver or owner of the vehicle or any other person with a vested interest.
(d) There is no previous advertisement unless such arrangements are as approved by a county council to meet social and welfare needs of a community.
(e) The journey is not a part of or an extension to a licensed service and arranged in conjunction with the holder of that licence for financial benefit.

It was Section 7 of the Transport Act, 1978 which modified the 1960 legislation on the carriage of passengers (at that time up to four) in small vehicles. It is now Section 2 and Schedule 1 of the 1980 Act which has liberalised the conditions of car-sharing schemes and receiving payment for giving lifts without being bound by the PSV licensing machinery. Section 61 of the 1980 Act amends Section 148 of the Road Traffic Act, 1972 and makes insurance in respect of the private use of vehicles to cover use under car-sharing arrangements.

Community Buses

Yet another device for facilitating the use of minibuses is the concept of the community bus as introduced by Section 5 of the Transport Act, 1978 as amended by Schedule 5 of the Transport Act, 1980. In accordance with the provisions of this section, traffic commissioners are empowered to authorise road service licences for stage carriage services using community buses. The following conditions apply:

(a) The vehicle must have a capacity of more than eight but not more than 16 passengers. It does not require a certificate of initial fitness for use as a PSV but must fulfil prescribed conditions in this respect.
(b) The applicant must be concerned with the social welfare needs of the community, but does not need to have a PSV operator's licence.
(c) The service must run without profit.
(d) The driver must be an unpaid volunteer who need not be the holder of a PSV driver's licence but if not, must fulfil any prescribed conditions.

Traffic commissioners may also authorise the use of a community bus for express or contract carriage work (subject to any conditions) should they consider it reasonable in order to provide financial support for the community bus service.

The advantage of the community bus concept is that it means freedom from PSV licensing (other than the road service licence) and hence some of the rigours of quality control which go with it.

School Buses

Arrangements for the transport of special groups such as schoolchildren without the need to conform to all of the PSV licensing regulations are now covered by Section 1 of the Minibus Act, 1977 as amended by Section 33 of the 1980 Act and to which reference has already been made under the sub-heading 'Minibuses' even though the buses concerned could be 'large passenger-carrying vehicles'. Remember that under these special circumstances, the small passenger-carrying vehicle (more than eight but not more than 16 passengers) is not regarded as a PSV whilst the operation of a large passenger-carrying vehicle (more than 16 passengers) does not require a road service licence, an operator's licence or a PSV driver's licence.

Section 32 of the 1980 Act provides that a local education authority may use a bus which is providing free school transport also for the carriage of fare-paying passengers and additionally a school bus which belongs to the education authority may be used by that authority to provide a local bus service when it is not employed on free school transport. Here again there are relaxations from the PSV licensing regulations.

Monopoly Areas

The purpose of the quantity licensing system is, as already explained, to encourage co-ordination, eliminate wasteful competition and protect established operators even though the Transport Act, 1980 has made it easier for applicants to obtain road service licences. Should there be a monopoly situation where only one organisation has authority to operate by force of law, the road service licence and traffic court procedure becomes superfluous. In one instance this has actually happened. The London Passenger Transport Act, 1933 gave to the then newly formed London Passenger Transport Board a statutory monopoly within a defined area around London. This was known as the Special Area and within that area the LPTB had a statutory monopoly and no other bus undertakings were permitted to provide services without its consent. Although the detail is now different, the principle remains. Section 23 of the Transport (London) Act, 1969 prohibits the provision of a London bus service by anyone except the London Transport Executive other than in pursuance of an agreement with that Executive. Section 23A however, as inserted by Section 35 of the Transport Act, 1980, gives a right of appeal to the minister and beyond that, Section 23B provides for an appeal to the High Court by the parties concerned or the traffic commissioners or appropriate local authorities on any point of law.

No road service licence is necessary for a London bus service although there is control over the suitability of the route, etc.

Whilst this is in one sense a relaxation of the licensing laws, it is an easement only for the established operator. Unlike the previous devices which are designed to circumvent in one way or another the normal licensing procedure and thereby encourage in a small way the provision of facilities where otherwise there might be nothing, this is a restriction for everybody except the one nominated undertaking. However, unlike the rural areas, in a massive urban agglomeration such as London there are reasons why a monopoly is desirable and mention here is appropriate as it does constitute an exception to the normal licensing arrangements.

A similar situation could have arisen in the designated passenger transport areas referred to in Chapter 5. Section 19 of the Transport Act, 1968 did, in fact, make such provision but it was permissive for implementation at the discretion of the minister. However, in the event, Section 19 has not been implemented, there is no indication that it ever will be, passenger transport executives still require road service licences the same as any other bus operator and the only exception is London.

Other Statutory Controls

Drivers' Hours

In the interests of safety, limitations are imposed on the hours which drivers of passenger and goods vehicles may work. The principle is not new. Such restrictions were contained in the Road Traffic Act, 1930 with similar requirements brought forward into the Road Traffic Act, 1960. Sections 95 and 96 of the Transport Act, 1968 as amended by the European Communities Act, 1972 and the Road Traffic (Drivers' Ages and Hours of Work) Act, 1976 give the latest situation as far as the British hours law is concerned.

The theory behind the drivers' hours regulations is straightforward. Passengers' lives should not be endangered by a driver who has been dulled by fatigue. The sort of things which the regulations enforce are the number of consecutive hours that a man may drive, overall driving time in the course of a day, minimum periods of rest per day and per week, etc. Unfortunately, the principle is the only straightforward thing about it because the subject has now become extremely complex. Furthermore, the EEC has a different and more rigorous set of standards which are gradually being superimposed on the British laws although as far as urban and rural passenger transport is concerned, the repercussions will not be great.

In British law as contained in Section 95 of the 1968 Act, the limitations on drivers' hours as they concern the passenger side of the road transport industry apply to all public service vehicles and all other motor vehicles which carry more than 12 passengers with either employee drivers or owner drivers who drive in the course of their trade or business (ie not for pleasure). The EEC law as far as passenger vehicles are concerned does not apply to vehicles which do not carry more than eight passengers or to vehicles used on regular bus and coach routes which do not exceed 50km in length. The latter exclusion very much reduces EEC influence in urban and rural passenger transport, which is what this book is about but it certainly does nothing to help the longer distance services or, for that matter, goods transport either.

It would not be appropriate to incorporate the vast amount of detail regarding drivers' hours in a work of this kind. It is sufficient here for the student to be advised that such regulations do exist with an indication as to where full information can be found.

Statutory Undertakings

Reference was made in Chapter 3 to the different forms of ownership within British public passenger transport. Remember that there is a substantial publicly owned sector with the undertakings concerned set up by different acts of Parliament, all of which have their statutory duties and responsibilities. As far as the nationalised bus and coach undertakings are concerned, being the National Bus Company and the Scottish Transport Group, Sections 25 and 26 respectively of the Transport Act, 1968 give them power to carry passengers by road inside and outside their respective countries and to participate in other activities such as vehicle hire, travel agencies and such else as the Minister may agree.

It is the passenger transport executives (including London Transport) which have their powers and responsibilities clearly defined. These undertakings have a two-tier level of control. Policy is determined by locally elected representatives who decide on the principles which are to be followed in accordance with their political doctrines. The executives are the professional managements. Although the structure of London Transport and the provincial PTEs is now similar, their establishment stems from different legislation and they must, therefore, be dealt with separately.

It was the Transport Act, 1968 which first introduced the concept of passenger transport authorities (the political bodies) and passenger transport executives with a view to securing the provision of properly integrated and efficient systems of public passenger transport to meet the needs of the newly designated passenger transport areas. In accordance with Section 9 each executive is a body corporate with perpetual succession and a common seal. In other words, they are independent autonomous undertakings but subject to political directives. As was noted in Chapter 5, they have two basic functions, being operators of the (ex-municipal) undertakings which they inherited and any others which they might subsequently acquire and public transport planning authorities (ie road and rail) for their entire areas. Their powers, which are listed in Section 10, are quite extensive and include not only the carriage of passengers by road but also by any form of land or water transport, all within certain limits. Section 20 imposes a special duty in relation to railway passenger services and although this particular section is permissive, in the event the minister has applied it to all of the existing PTEs. There is now a general requirement, therefore, for PTEs to enter into agreements with British Railways whereby BR will provide whatever services and charge whatever fares on the local lines that the PTEs might require and who in turn will meet the financial deficits incurred. This aspect is referred to in greater detail in Chapter 4. Section 24 calls for the executives and the National Bus Company or Scottish Transport Group, whichever is appropriate also to enter into agreements regarding the services which are to be provided.

With the reorganisation of local government brought about by the Local Government Act, 1972 the county councils became the passenger transport authorities. Of particular interest here is Schedule 24 which adds another section to the 1968 Act (Section 15A). It is Section 15 which details the functions of the authorities and Section 15A states that in addition to the powers which the authorities already have, they may further give any other directions to the executives regarding the exercise and performance of their functions.

The establishment of London Transport in its present form is sanctioned by the Transport (London) Act, 1969. Its status, two-tier control and general functions and responsibilities are similar to those of the PTEs except that as noted earlier it has a statutory bus operating monopoly. Unlike the PTEs, however, it is not required to enter into an agreement with British Railways and financially support local BR lines although it is a substantial local railway operator in its own right.

An underlying principle behind all of this legislation is that there should be controlled planning to produce properly co-ordinated systems of local public passenger transport. The 1968 Act (Section 24) requires the passenger transport executives, the National Bus Company, the Scottish Transport Group and the British Railways Board to co-operate with each other wherever appropriate. The 1969 Act (Section 5) requires similar co-operation between London Transport, National Bus and British Railways and the 1978 Act (Section 1) calls for all public passenger transport operators, non-metropolitan county councils and district councils to co-operate with one another for the purpose of co-ordinating public passenger transport services. However, Section 15 of the 1980 Act relaxes the need for such co-operation in trial areas as referred to above other than to the extent that it would otherwise affect the co-ordinating duties of passenger transport executives or county councils.

Rail Transport

The point was made earlier that as the railway network in Great Britain is provided, in the main, by one operator, control does not need to be exercised in the same way as in the case of road transport. As far as the safety factor is concerned, what is perhaps even more pertinent is the fact that as the railway is the sole user of its own exclusive way, being in contrast to the road, the use of which is shared by a multitude of different users, safety requirements can be imposed more directly. A licensing system is not therefore necessary. The various statutory requirements as they relate to those aspects of railway operation which involve the carriage of passengers in the urban and rural context will now be considered in a similar manner as was done in the case of transport by road.

Routes and Services

As was referred to in Chapter 2, a railway requires its own specialised way. In the case of road transport with its use of a common way, the presence of a road is assumed and no attempt was made in the previous sub-section to explain the legal processes involved in constructing a new road. Neither is it proposed to enter into any such detail in the case of a railway. It is sufficient to note that a railway (like a road) can, for good or for ill, affect the lives of the people resident within the vicinity of the route. It could affect the environment, it could involve compulsory purchase of land and property and people might wish to object. In short, the construction of a railway requires the approval of Parliament and there are in existence many private railway acts which have sanctioned the building of different lines. In return for such powers, Parliament, over the years, has seen fit to impose various obligations on the railway which have been convenient to contain within these authorising acts and which can be repealed only through the normal parliamentary process. Railways can, therefore, have requirements imposed on them in this way. Duties of a more recent, more general and more readily identifiable nature can be traced from the Transport Act, 1962 onwards. It was Section 1 of that Act which established the British Railways Board, Section 3 imposed on it a duty, among other things, to carry passengers by rail within Great Britain and in this connection to provide also such other services and facilities as are expedient with due regard to efficiency, economy and safety of operation. What is important, however, is that there is qualification in the same section that this does not imply an enforceable duty. British Railways is no longer a common carrier and this is explicitly stated in Section 43. It cannot, therefore, be forced to carry any particular traffic. However, as was recorded in Chapter 3, there is a special TUCC procedure which has to be followed should it be proposed to discontinue a service from any station or line.

It follows that apart from any specific local requirement which might still persist, British Railways is free to run the quantum of service it pleases subject more to financial constraints than anything else as is discussed in Chapter 4. In other words, it is commercial viability which, according to the 1962 Act, would play a large part in deciding what would be provided. No special authority has to be obtained for augmenting services and hence no objections have to be countered. However, running local passenger rail services is not a lucrative business and this is where the controls come. If essential services are to be maintained there must be subsidies just as there are on the bus side, the implications of which are again as considered in Chapter 4. For the purpose of this chapter it is appropriate to note that as far as local passenger services are concerned, British Railways is required to operate at least the services as stipulated, subject to the deficits being met. In designated passenger transport areas (ie metropolitan counties) it is the passenger transport executives which determine requirements in accordance with agreements formulated through Section 20 of the 1968 Act as was explained earlier. Elsewhere and in accordance with Section 3 of the Railways Act, 1974 it is the secretary of state who directs British Railways to provide certain levels of services and where. This is known as the public service obligation. However, as was said in Chapter 5, non-metropolitan county councils have a responsibility vide the Transport Act, 1978 to co-ordinate local public passenger transport within their areas and these councils may, should they so wish, also seek the provision of certain railway facilities on payment. There is, of course, also the requirement to co-operate with the other organisations as was mentioned in the road section.

Fares

The history of railway fares and charges is long and interesting but has no particular relevance here. Suffice to say that from the time of their inception right up to the passing of the Transport Act, 1962, railway fares were subject to rigid control. It was Section 43 of the 1962 Act which swept away these controls thereby leaving British Railways free to determine their fares on commercial criteria and this is the situation which now prevails. British Railways will, however, charge fares at scales as may be requested by passenger transport executives on those lines which they financially support. The subject of railway fares, therefore, has little impact on this chapter on statutory controls but has much more relevance in Chapter 7 where pricing arrangements to maximise revenue are discussed.

Safety

Safety controls on the railway grew, rather like the railways themselves, in a somewhat haphazard fashion. Control technology has developed out of all recognition between the time of the first steam trains in 1830 which were slow and ran on sight and the now fast main line trains travelling at speeds of 125mph or more and governed by multi-aspect colour signals controlled by power boxes in charge of over 100 route miles of track. Not that such trains are subject matter for this book but to come back to what was said in Chapter 2, the fast trains and the locals are physically all part of the same system and there must be a common method of control.

As speeds developed beyond the 30mph or so of the earliest steam trains with track layouts becoming more intricate, services becoming more intense and the number of possible conflicting movements of trains thereby magnified, it is not surprising that control beyond what could be exercised by the driver alone quickly became necessary if collisions were to be avoided. Such safeguards were developed in many instances by the railway administrations themselves through their own volition but partly as a result of 'encouragement' by government departments often through public pressure and sometimes in conformity with the will of Parliament. Legislation of this kind often came after a serious accident involving substantial loss of life although the safety record of the railway is, nevertheless, high and such occurrences really only remained highlighted in railway history because of their spectacular nature and the fact that there have been so few of them. Nevertheless, this is the setting in which statutory control over safety measures on the railway has developed over its 150 years of operation.

The Regulation of Railways Act, 1840 was the first of a series of such acts which introduced statutory controls over railway workings in the interests of safety. One of the most important, perhaps, was the Regulation of Railways Act, 1889 which gave the then Board of Trade (now the Department of Transport) power to require implementation on passenger lines of what are now three basic principles of railway operation, being the block system of working (to keep trains apart), the interlocking of points and signals and the fitting of continuous brakes on passenger trains. These various acts originally introduced and gradually extended the powers of government in relation to safety on the railway. To implement the technical function of a government department to exercise such safety controls the 1840 Act established a railway inspectorate, being a branch of the Board of Trade (now Department of Transport). The powers of the railway inspectorate were enlarged by the Regulation of Railways Act, 1871; it has functioned through the years and its principal responsibilities are now to approve new works on railways which involve the carriage of passengers, to investigate accidents and to give technical advice to the minister on general railway matters. The railway inspectorate also has responsibilities of a technical nature in connection with the design, construction and operation of tram and trolleybus systems.

In any examination of safety control on the railway, a little bit of history is unavoidable and parts of some of the 19th century statutes referred to are still valid law. But it is the Road and Rail Traffic Act, 1933 which has brought forward and clarified these statutory requirements. This act is perhaps more often associated with the introduction of quantity licensing into road haulage on similar lines to what has just been described on the passenger side (and which was also subsequently embodied in the 1960 Act but unlike the passenger system was repealed by the 1968 Act). Section 41 of the 1933 Act (which was not repealed) has reinforced the appropriate provisions of the 1871 Act. This section requires the minister (through the railway inspectorate) to satisfy himself that any new works (being new or altered lines) will not be a danger to the public using them before they are opened for passenger use. The basic requirements are summarised in the Department of Transport circular 'Railway Construction and Operation Requirements for Passenger Lines and Recommendations for Goods Lines'. It is nevertheless true to say that the relationship between the railway inspectorate and railway management has always been one of co-operation with a common purpose and a minimum of direction.

Trams and Trolleybuses

Even though Great Britain now has very few trams and no trolleybuses it is necessary that the student should have knowledge of the legal complexities which govern this form of transport, particularly as the predicted oil situation might even stage a partial comeback of one or the other to British transport. It was said at the beginning of this chapter that a tram is not a public service vehicle. For this reason, then, unless there is special legislation to the contrary, it cannot be subjected to the laws which govern PSVs. Trams are, therefore, free from the need for road service licences. Nevertheless, they are by no means above the law. They are, in effect, in precisely the same situation as that which applies to the railway as has just been described and to which mode of transport trams (and trolleybuses) are, in many respects, legally a part. In short, the construction of a tramway (or trolleybus) system or the conversion from one to the other requires the authority of Parliament. The close relationship between the two modes was discussed in Chapter 2 and there is no clear demarcation between a tramway and a railway.

Trams began to proliferate in the second half of the 19th century and to facilitate what was in effect a succession of requests from tramway promoters for authority to construct, some easement to what was a cumbersome and expensive procedure was necessary. The resultant Tramways Act, 1870 was introduced for this purpose and became the basis for subsequent local acts which authorised the construction of individual lines. Briefly, the act states that any persons or bodies are free to apply for provisional orders to construct a tramway and it then details the procedure to be followed. Such orders, if granted, would specify, vide Section 10, the traffic to be carried, the fares and such regulations as are considered necessary by the minister. Here, of course, lies the control; the contents of the order being contained in a local Act. Section 25 requires the route to be inspected and certified as fit for public traffic before it is brought into use. There are limitations on what the promoters may do to the surface of the road and Section 28 requires them to maintain not only the track but also the road extending up to 18in on each side. It is Section 43 which enables local authorities to purchase the system after 21 years as was referred to in Chapter 1. A resemblance of PSV licensing lies in Section 48 which gives local authorities the same licensing powers in regard to the trams themselves (ie the vehicles) and their drivers as they already had with hackney carriages.

There is, therefore, ample framework for statutory

control of trams (and trolleybuses), much of which is (or, more correctly, would be if the occasion arose) the responsibility of the railway inspectorate as already noted and described. Section 9 of the Transport Charges etc (Miscellaneous Provisions) Act, 1954 empowers the Minister to make regulations regarding the numbers of passengers carried on trams (and trolleybuses). A small point on fares, however, is worthy of note. It has just been said that Section 10 of the 1870 Act made provision for, inter alia, the fixing of fares. With the passing of time, these original orders became somewhat remote and not being PSVs, fares on trams and trolleybuses were not subject to the jurisdiction of the traffic commissioners. This anomoly was remedied by Section 2 of the Transport Charges etc (Miscellaneous Provisions) Act, 1954 by putting such fares under the control of the traffic commissioners. However, it has been seen that the Transport Act, 1980 has given freedom of charging (except under certain circumstances) to PSV operators and similarly Section 65 of the 1980 Act has repealed Section 2 of the 1954 Act.

In the case of trolleybuses, the situation is a little more obscure. The trolleybus has been a natural development from the tram and until now, the statutory control of tramways as has just been described has applied equally to trolleybuses. At this particular time the point is academic as there are no trolleybuses in Great Britain. There are a few experimental battery buses which are classified as PSVs and which are, therefore, subject to the PSV licensing laws but the forthcoming energy situation promises a possible return to some form of trolleybus operation. As will be considered in Chapter 12, a new generation of trolleybuses might be of the hybrid type, ie, capable of running both on and off the wires, in which case legal classification with a tram would produce complications.

The relevant parts of the definitions of PSVs in the Road Traffic Acts of 1930 and 1960 and the Transport Act, 1980 are as follows:

1930 Act
A PSV is a motor vehicle used for carrying passengers . . . etc, etc, excluding (inter alia) trams and trolleybuses. A tram was defined as any carriage used on roads by virtue of an order made under the Light Railways Act, 1896. A trolleybus was defined as a mechanically propelled vehicle used on roads without rails but moved by power transmitted from some external source. (Section 121)

1960 Act
This repealed the definition of a tram as contained in the 1930 Act. Section 117, however, defined a PSV as a motor vehicle used for carrying passengers . . . etc, etc, but not including a tram or a trolleybus. Section 257 defined a tram as including any carriage used on any road by virtue of an order made under the Light Railways Act, 1896 and a trolleybus as a mechanically propelled vehicle adapted for use upon roads without rails and moved by power transmitted thereto from some external source. A road is defined as any highway and any other road to which the public has access including bridges over which a road passes (and note that the public does not necessarily have authorised access to the tracks of a segregated light rapid transit system).

1980 Act
This repealed Section 117 of the 1960 Act but Section 2 defined a PSV as a motor vehicle (other than a tram) used for carrying passengers . . . etc, etc. No such reference is now made to trolleybuses.

Added to this, Section 13 of the Transport Charges etc (Miscellaneous Provisions) Act, 1954 introduced 'railways of the nature of a tramway' which were defined as light railways laid wholly or mainly along a public carriageway and used wholly or mainly for the carriage of passengers or railways which, under the statutory provisions relating thereto, are to be treated as forming part of a tramway undertaking. In its definition of a tram, this same section includes also a railway vehicle used on a railway of the nature of a tramway.

Regardless, however, of any confusion about what is or is not a tram it would seem that under the 1980 Act a trolleybus would be regarded as a PSV and hence subject to the PSV licensing system, which would certainly avoid an anomolous situation should the hybrids ever appear. Nevertheless, there is no reason why the erection of overhead equipment for trolleybuses should not remain subject to Parliamentary approval.

Conclusions

The law of business and carriage is a subject in its own right and no attempt has been made in this one short chapter to discuss its many ramifications. Only regulatory and safety matters have been considered which means that the study has been confined to a review of the main features of the more important statutes which affect bus and railway operation in Great Britain. It has not been an exhaustive coverage and it can, therefore, do no more than offer a guide to the student on the sort of controls which exist and where to seek the details.

Enough, however, has been said to show that even this one part of the subject is complex. It is made more so by the fact that new legislation has been superimposed on old and that successive layers of exceptions, permissions and even administrative arrangements have been introduced without always replacing everything that has gone before. The result tends to become a somewhat formidable maze and the process of formulating and introducing bus service changes has, notwithstanding the 1980 Act become complicated, bearing in mind the involvement of not only county councils as a result of the 1968, 1972 and 1978 Acts but also trade unions as was noted in Chapter 3. It all may be a little daunting to the manager on the ground if professional advice is overridden by political whim. Passenger transport executives had their rights and duties clearly defined in the 1968 Act but the 1972 Act required them to follow any other directives they might be given regardless of the fact that the original concept has not been changed. However, unlike London Transport (as it was when it was formed in 1933), the PTEs have required substantial support from public funds almost from the time of their inception and perhaps this is a fair enough reason for political policy control. PTEs have a duty imposed on them to secure the provision of a properly integrated and efficient system of public passenger transport but, again unlike London Transport, they have no statutory monopoly and hence no powers of compulsory purchase. Their 'duty' must, therefore, be achieved through agreement and to this end, all operators are required to co-operate with one another. Non-metropolitan county councils are now the co-ordinating authorities for local public passenger transport within their respective areas and they determine their own policies regarding standards and fares dependent on the price which they are prepared to pay. In designated passenger transport areas the PTEs (through metropolitan county councils) have responsibility for what should be provided and what should be charged on local rail as well as bus services. Even so, the railway has a countrywide network and some if not most of the local lines cross boundaries and the various PTE's may have, and are certainly entitled to have, different policies. Nevertheless, BR must remain, if only for physical reasons, a nationally run enterprise.

To the student this may, at first sight, all seem a little haphazard even though there are reasons for what has been done. Over the years Parliament has attempted to remedy deficiencies in the system which have been brought about largely because of the need to sustain services with money beyond what is contributed by passengers at the time of travel. Many of the difficulties have been overcome but in so doing it might not be too far off the mark to suggest that others have been created. Certainly the administrative machine has become bigger and this alone can only frustrate the process of keeping the business, being the services provided, on an economic footing and abreast with constantly changing demands.

9
Fare Collection

The Need for a Fare Collection System

It is inevitable that in the sale of goods or services, at some stage a money transaction is involved and this is as true in transport as in other trading activity. Even if passenger transport is regarded as a social service and some of its costs are met from public funds, money must be collected from the users and cash must still change hands. The problems are in no way lessened by the fact that not all of the total income has to be collected through fares. It is only when a completely free system, that is free to the users at the time of travel, is introduced that the situation becomes different and this brings with it other problems which are considered in Chapter 7. Apart from the 'free fare' issue, therefore, it must be accepted that, in the case of passenger transport, the customers must pay fares for the journeys which they take. Indeed, regardless of what is the economic function of transport*, the reason why entrepreneurs first went into the transport business was to make a living. Even in a non-commercial situation it is still very much in the interests of managements that everybody who travels pays the correct fare and that is what this topic of fare collection is all about.

Other chapters discuss fare structures and also statistical information, both subjects of which are to some extent linked with fare collection and it is debatable which should be considered first. Methods and types of ticket issue can vary according to the fare structure and ticket issue can also be a source of much statistical data. It could be argued, therefore, that the fare structure and the required statistics should first be determined and the fare collection method made to suit those requirements. This is all good theory but there are practical and financial limitations on the methods and equipment used to collect fares. Although important, statistics cannot be regarded as more than a useful by-product of ticket issue. It is also quite useless to introduce a fare structure for which no satisfactory method of implementation within the set parameters, whatever they may be, can be devised.

The important fundamental issue must not be forgotten. Operators need to ensure that as far as possible they receive all revenue to which they are entitled. To do this, not only must passengers pay the correct fare; those responsible for collecting that fare must surrender the money to their employer and must not divert it to themselves. Cash so collected is handled by various people at different levels within an organisation and cross-checks are, therefore, necessary. Whilst it is right and proper for employers to expect their staff to be honest, in the opinion of the writer it is wrong to submit an employee to temptation unnecessarily. If a person is handling large sums on which he knows there is no check, any lapse is at least deserving of some understanding, if not excuse. There should, therefore, be a system of control. It is when proper audit has been instituted and the misdemeanant has then deliberately set himself out to beat the system that severity can be justified.

*R. W. Faulks; *Principles of Transport*, Chapter 1; Ian Allan Ltd.

Basic Principles

Having established that some sort of cash transaction is necessary in respect of each passenger journey; that many employees at different levels within the organisation are responsible for collecting and handling cash and there is a clear requirement that management needs to receive all the money to which it is entitled, the methods of collection must now be examined.

For long distance travel, be it by aircraft, boat, coach or train, a system of pre-payment is readily accepted by passengers. Such transactions are made in the seclusion of a purpose-built office away from the rough and tumble of actual travel. Tickets will be prepared and cash handled by a booking clerk who is adept at that particular type of work and who will have at his disposal all the necessary aids for ticket preparation and cash security. The actual method of issue may be manual or mechanical and may be linked to a system of seat reservation. Large organisations, notably airlines, are now tending to computerise this work with the result that intending passengers can state their requirements at any one of a chain of booking offices and the clerk is able to confirm promptly the booking (if there is accommodation), ascertain the fare and issue the ticket. But this is getting away from urban transport.

For the shorter journeys on buses and trams, the situation is very different and is far less conducive to efficient fare collection. In the large built-up areas, particularly during the morning and evening peaks, many thousands of people strain the vehicle resources, some travelling for perhaps quite short distances. If they are all to pay at the time of travel, and as far as buses are concerned, at least in Great Britain it has for many years been the custom and practice so to do, then, if speed is to be combined with efficiency, fare collection becomes a science in itself.

Tickets

If a scale of charges is to be properly enforced, which means that every passenger pays his proper fare for the journey taken and at the end of the day that money is credited to the transport undertaking, then a system of ticket issue becomes necessary. A ticket is, in effect, a receipt for the fare paid and an entitlement to travel for that particular journey. Tickets also constitute a record of sales. The conductor or whoever is selling the tickets can, therefore, be held to account for the cash collected. The tickets must be issued on the vehicles unless a separate ticket sales point can be made conveniently available and they should contain at least the following information:

(a) Fare paid
(b) Availability (such as stage boarded)
(c) Identification (such as number of machine)
(d) Serial number

With these details the passenger has proof of payment and entitlement to travel. The ticket is available for inspection and this in turn deters overriding. As far as the ticket issuer is concerned, ticket sales are recorded on a waybill and he is hence accountable for cash so collected.

It was in the early 1880s that the long defunct London Road Car Company first issued to conductors of its horse drawn buses rolls of pre-printed and serially numbered tickets showing fare values. A similar system was introduced by the erstwhile London General Omnibus Company some ten years later and the fact that at the time this contributed to strike action by drivers and conductors suggests that their take-home pay in real terms might perhaps have been lessened as a result. If this was the case, then the need for some form of ticket issue becomes all the more apparent.

The Bell Punch System

At this juncture it is appropriate to consider what was at one time the most popularly accepted system of fare collection on buses and trams. It was in use from the era of the horse until the advent and general acceptance of more sophisticated equipment and it still survives in various parts of the world even today. Its description is synonmous with what was then the title of a well known but not the only manufacturer of tickets and equipment, namely the Bell Punch Company, although as a result of a merger, the trade name 'Bell Punch' has changed.

The original 'bell punch' system involves the issue to conductors of packs of serially numbered and pre-printed tickets, each denomination having a distinctive colour and all being carried in a rack. As the tickets were sold to passengers they were punched so as to indicate availability, eg at the stage boarded, the clipping being retained within the punch. A bell within the punch rang each time a ticket was clipped, which gave audible confirmation of a genuine cancellation. The punch also contained a counter which recorded each time a ticket was so punched and which, incidentally would not function unless one, and only one, ticket was inserted. The opening numbers and quantity of all tickets issued from stock to conductors were recorded on a waybill. At the close of duty the conductor recorded for subsequent check the closing numbers and arithmetically calculated total sales and hence cash taken for paying-in. The punch register needed to agree with the recorded sales and as a further check, the coloured clippings within the punch were available for counting as each denomination was recognisable by its distinctive colour. Ending numbers could be entered on the waybill by the conductor as required throughout the duty, say at the commencement of each journey and intermediately to the extent considered necessary for purpose of supervision by ticket checking inspectors.

So far so good. The system possessed all of the attributes which have been stipulated. The necessary information was contained on the ticket in a clear and understandable way and the conductor had a complete record of sales. Statistics could be derived from the waybill and the system was suitable for any fares structure including return tickets. Very little in life is foolproof, particularly where money is involved and this is as true with fare collection and the bell punch system as with anything else. Over the years many interesting cases have passed through the courts as a result of ingenious devices. But this was not the reason for change. The bell punch system served the industry well for a span of more than 50 years. There were other reasons which made this manual system of ticket issue no longer appropriate for present day conditions. Nevertheless, by becoming as it did so much a part of the business, the system tends to be regarded by busmen today as a standard against which the merits or otherwise of mechanisation are measured.

The disadvantages of a manual system of ticket issue may be summarised as follows:

(a) The fact that conductors are issued with stocks of pre-printed value tickets for which they are held to account means that waybills must be compiled and all of the conductors figures checked. This means a lot of clerical work.
(b) The conductor is involved in a large amount of arithmetic.
(c) Pre-printed tickets of a quality suitable for issue manually must be a part of the expendable equipment.

(d) The act of selecting and removing a ticket from the rack and punching it accurately is a cumbersome process.
(e) The need for the conductor to carry a ticket rack inhibits free movement (although the writer has knowledge of this particular piece of equipment being a useful albeit unauthorised weapon for self-defence!).

The upshot of all this is that the system is expensive in terms of clerical labour and in the production of pre-printed tickets; conductors must be held responsible for the fare value of their tickets which if lost could be misappropriated; waybill compilation could be arduous for conductors who have no particular aptitude for this type of work and operationally, the whole process is relatively slow, both in ticket issue on the vehicle and waybill compilation. It was the combination of these factors together with the ever increasing capacity of new generations of vehicles which put a premium on speed of ticket issue. This led to thoughts of mechanisation and hence the virtual demise of the old bell punch.

Mechanisation of Ticket Issue

In the search for an ideal system of fare collection, different ideas have been developed, not all of which incorporate the collection of individual fares for cash at the time of travel. Fare collection off the vehicle is something which, as far as buses are concerned, has been practised on the mainland of Europe for many years and is now beginning to find acceptance elsewhere. On railways, including urban railways, the reverse is the case. By tradition, railway tickets are bought prior to travel, usually at the station booking office and it is only comparatively recently that British Railways, to quote an example, has arranged as an economy measure for fares to be collected on trains on certain lightly used lines. Mention is, however, relevant as some of the services concerned do penetrate urban areas. In Great Britain trains of this type are known as 'Pay Trains'. Other countries which have adopted a similar system will have different terminology but the principle remains. The guard, who is required in any case, becomes the conductor responsible for fare collection, booking offices and hence booking clerks are no longer needed and stations become unstaffed (which in turn produces a security problem which is considered in Chapter 11). At this stage, fare collection on the railway becomes akin to fare collection on buses, just as any trend towards the purchase of tickets prior to travel on the buses brings with it a similarity to established practices on the railway. Mechanised fare collection is not, therefore, a subject to be examined in terms of mode, but in accordance with these two basic concepts, although the railway does have a built-in advantage over road in the establishment of off-vehicle ticket sales points — being the booking offices and controlled access and egress at stations. First will be considered the mechanisation of fare collection on the vehicle and this will be followed by a review of other methods.

Ticket Machines

Ideally, any system of mechanised ticket issue on the vehicle should possess all of the attributes of the old bell punch but should overcome its deficiencies (a) to (e) as described. Numerous manufacturers, several of whom are very old established (including the Bell Punch Company), have undertaken a lot of development work in this field. Generally, a ticket machine is portable. It is something which a roving conductor must have affixed to his front which means that he must wear it for the greater part of his working day and it must not, therefore, be either too bulky or too heavy. Whilst the ticket machine number and the ticket serial number are pre-set (the serial number automatically increases by one each time a ticket is issued) the fare paid and the stage boarded must be set by the conductor for each transaction. There are various designs for so doing by the use of rotating knobs or dials, but whatever the method, it must be a straightforward, quick and simple job to set the machine, which must be robust and reliable, and then activate it to issue a ticket many times in rapid succession in a crowded and moving vehicle. Operators must be selective in the types of machines which they purchase depending on the length of routes and fare structures. Some machines have a wide range of fare values. Others have a very limited range but easier settings for the values which they possess. Some produce more statistics than others. Speed of issue is crucial for the success of any system. It is usual for machines to have visible registers which record cumulatively the total number and the total cash value of the tickets sold. A very much simplified waybill then becomes possible as there are only two sets of readings. The starting numbers of the ticket register and cash are recorded at the outset of duty and again at the close. By subtracting one from the other, totals in terms of tickets and cash are ascertained and the cash figure is what the conductor is required to pay in. This is the money which he should have in his bag. The tickets themselves are printed on a blank roll of paper which in itself has no value. It is not until a ticket is actually issued and hence is recorded by the machine that the conductor becomes responsible for the cash taken.

If attention is again turned to the alleged disadvantages of the manual system of ticket issue, it will be seen that a portable machine which possesses the features as described in the previous paragraph and functions satisfactorily under arduous conditions could effect a substantial improvement in all of these shortcomings. It will be recalled, however, that the point was made that, apart from the stated deficiencies, the bell punch system met the required specifications for a satisfactory fare collection system. The next question, therefore, is whether mechanisation has, in meeting the bell punch deficiencies, created other shortcomings where the bell punch was satisfactory. The four essentials (a) to (d) as mentioned have certainly been met. However, the texture of a ticket issued from a machine is likely to be inferior to that issued manually from a rack; it will not be of a distinctive colour and hence not immediatley obvious that the correct denomination has been issued and the availability will be indicated only by a stage number which the passenger might well not understand. This latter feature could and did arise with a bell punch ticket, as although it is perfectly feasible in this case to pre-print stage names instead of numbers on tickets, in order to facilitate interchangability between different routes, even some bell punch tickets bore only numbers. At the time, this was often referred to colloquially as the 'deaf and dumb' ticket because it did not tell you anything. As far as short journeys are concerned, there are very few tickets issued today which do tell you anything. What is even worse, with some types of equipment, constant fares revisions make it impossible to retain compatibility between the range of values which the machine can issue and actual fare scales. Under these circumstances there is a practice of replacing the monetary value as shown on the ticket by a code number. Notwithstanding notices on buses, with this system there can be little doubt that few passengers will be able to check that they have been issued with the correct ticket even if they wished to do so and even fewer would be sufficiently sure of themselves to challenge the driver or conductor if they thought it was wrong. Maybe improvement does not always follow progress. One further point concerns statistics. Remember that with separate packs of tickets, not only for each denomination but, if required, for each separate class, for example, ordinary single, return or child, there is a complete record of sales. For the machines as described point entries may be made as necessary, perhaps at the end of each journey, or even intermediately, but for most types this will disclose only total tickets sold without a split by fare values. Setrights, for example, provide a statistical counter to check the number of tickets issued for any one fare. This fare can be pre-set at will and can, therefore, produce a sample statistic in respect of that one denomination. By judicious use of this counter day by day total tickets sold of each denomination over a period can be estimated and this goes some way towards the production of the required figures. The results in this case are not, therefore, as good as the bell punch, but are the figures really required? Or has the industry in the past employed staff to extract information, some of which serves no real purpose and is never acted upon? This is another matter and one which is considered in Chapters 3 and 5.

One-Man Operation

One-man operation is not new. It is of passing interest that the West Metropolitan Tramways Company (a predecessor of London United Tramways which in turn was absorbed by London Transport), when it first introduced horse trams on the western periphery of the metropolis in the 1880s adopted one-man operation on two sections of its lines. There was a flat fare of a penny which passengers placed in a glass box and the driver gave change if required. In the 1920s, the London United adopted one-man operation on one of its electric tram routes which lasted for several years, but by that time many small 20 seater buses were also running without conductors, generally outside the more built-up areas. What is relatively new is the extension of the system to large vehicles. In Great Britain it was not until the late 1960s that double deck one man operation became legally possible, facilitated by the front entrance, rear engined vehicles as described in Chapter 10. This development put a new dimension on fare collection as with a 78-seater vehicle speed is not only desirable, it is crucial if excessive delays at stops are to be avoided.

At this stage it is appropriate to consider one man operation and to see why the system has spread so rapidly in Great Britain over the past decade. Although not strictly within the terms of this chapter, one-man operation (OMO) cannot be divorced from the subject of fare collection as the success of the former is dependent on the efficiency of the latter. The other contributory factor is vehicle design which is dealt with elsewhere. It is the development of double deck OMO which has stimulated extensive research into what has almost become a science in its own right — fare collection without a conductor — and the ideal system has yet to be found.

Bus operators on the continent of Europe and elsewhere have long decried the established British practice of employing a crew of two on a bus, one to drive and the other to collect fares. For many years now, European operators have sought alternative methods of fare collection and where conductors are employed they are usually seated at the point of entry owing to the impracticability of circulating in a large crush loading standee type vehicle. In order to minimise time spent at stops, numerous devices have been introduced, the most important of which involves the advance purchase of tickets with self-cancelling on the vehicle, subject only to occasional spot checks by inspectors. These various methods are to be examined but before so doing, lest it be thought that British busmen are backward compared with what might be regarded as their more enterprising continental colleagues, let it be said that there are good reasons why the Europeans have been able to go where the British have so far feared to tread. These reasons will be discussed as the pre-paid ticket system is explained and, to the extent that the situation is influenced by vehicle design, in Chapter 10 as well.

First, however, it is necessary for thoughts to return to the one-time conventional conductor and consider a direct transfer of the conductors duties to the driver, utilising the same scales of charges and a similar ticket system. It is one thing to do this on a 20-seater single deck bus on an infrequent service in a semi-rural area. It is quite another to do it on a 78-seater double deck bus on a high frequency service in a heavily congested area. Under these circumstances, delays at stops whilst drivers are collecting fares could easily become intolerable, both to passengers and to other traffic and these delays would quickly result in the bunching of vehicles and hence a very ragged service. There must not, therefore, be delays.

There is no reason why a ticket machine cannot be transferred to the driver, although he does not wear it as does the conductor. It is instead fixed to the bus on the near side of the cab. At the same time this brings with it an advantage as it then becomes possible to plug it in to the vehicle's electrical system and issue tickets from the machine so adapted by the press of a button. This is easier and faster than by turning a handle which the conductor is required to do. Generally, therefore, ticket machines similar to those used by conductors can be modified for use by drivers. This method has, in fact, been widely adopted, both in the UK and overseas, particularly in areas where there has been a strong British influence. It has been applied to both single deck and double deck buses with reasonable success except on the very busiest services already referred to, particularly where there is a heavy short distance on/off movement. It is here that the driver really requires some assistance over and above that of an electrically operated ticket machine. It is here also where both operators and manufacturers have undertaken and are still undertaking much research into the need for a fare collection system which is adequate under the circumstances described, complies with the operator's specifications (that is, it can be adapted to the chosen scale of charges) and is acceptable to and understood by passengers.

Fare fixing as distinct from fare collection is considered in Chapter 7. As is said in that chapter, fare scales are set by either economic or political dictates according to circumstances. Ideally, the collection system should fit the fares and not the fares the collection system. In practice, however, some systems are more efficient if used in conjunction with only certain types of fares. This means that there must sometimes be discretion when deciding whether to surrender or modify a chosen method of charging in order to improve the efficiency of collection. By referring again to Chapter 7, it will be seen that in Great Britain by custom and practice, a graduated fare scale is invariably adopted, which means that there are many different fare stages and fares. This materially adds to the complexity of ticket issue. At the other end of the scale maximum simplicity is derived from a flat fare which so far is not characteristic of the UK.

A fare collection system must satisfy all reasonable passenger demands as well as being acceptable to the 'establishment'. In the days when one-man operation was confined to the 20-seater buses and drivers had a bell punch and rack of tickets, they were able to allow all passengers to board quickly at the busier stops and then go round the bus and collect fares either before driving away or even at the next stop if it was in a quieter place. With a larger bus this is no longer practicable and with a fixed ticket machine impossible. Payment on entry must, therefore, be enforced at all times. This not only produces problems when buses are unattended on a stand, which is another matter, it also means that passengers must queue outside the bus to pay, even after it has arrived at a stop, regardless of the weather. It is important, therefore, for more than one reason that passengers can board as expeditiously as possible.

Two-Stream Boarding

Vehicle design has repercussions on time spent at stops and the controversy over a separate centre exit is discussed in Chapter 10. As far as fare collection is concerned, one device to reduce waiting time is to permit two streams of people to board simultaneously. Whilst one stream is required to pay the driver in the conventional manner, the other must utilise self-service equipment. Various manufacturers have produced ideas in this field. One system is for the second stream of passengers to put money into a machine to get a ticket which records the essential details. The only action required by the driver in this instance is to change the stage number by remote control at each fare point unless, of course, management requires the last driver of the day to empty the machine and pay in the money to the cash office. This is a separate issue which is discussed in Chapter 11. A particularly interesting machine of this type is the Videmat which instead of indicating the fare paid, reproduces on the ticket by means of a carbon impression the actual coins (genuine or counterfeit!) which have been placed in the box.

As a broad principle, the two-stream system of boarding has the advantage that in theory it virtually halves the time spent at stops providing passengers split themselves equally between the two different methods of payment. In practice this seldom happens. There is usually a preference to pay the driver for one of the following reasons:

(a) Passengers either imagine they do not know how to use the machine or they are nervous of it with a fear that they might lose their money in full view of spectators, being the people already seated in the lower deck.

(b) They do not know the fare or, therefore, how much money to put in the machine.
(c) They know the fare but do not have the correct money and therefore require change, which only the driver can give.
(d) They are seeking psychological reassurance that they are on the right bus.

A disadvantage of two-stream boarding to the operator is that there is a greater chance of loss of revenue through fare avoidance. At busy stops a driver will be fully occupied with the first stream through issuing tickets and giving change. He will make no attempt to challenge other passengers passing by, ostensibly to help themselves to a ticket. Unfortunately, there are occasions when some passengers misunderstand the operators' intentions, walk past not only the driver but the machine as well and help themselves instead to a free ride. For psychological reasons, this practice is encouraged if the bus has a centre exit and it is not, therefore, necessary to once again pass the driver in order to alight.

The Need to give Change

At this stage it is worth pondering a while on item (c) above and the vexed question of giving change. Much play has been made of the speed at which tickets can be issued. Machines are faster than the bell punch and ticket rack and some machines are faster than others because of the way the stage number and fare have to be selected. Fractions of a second are regarded as all important when choosing the machine most suitable for the job. But it is not the actual issuing of a ticket which takes the time, it is giving change which really delays the fare collection process. Many passengers offer the correct money — a few do not — and some even tender very high money, in the UK perhaps a £1 note or even a £5 note for a minimum fare. There is no legal obligation to give change. It is provided as a courtesy but this service to the few means a dis-service to the many. One person demanding change for a high value coin or note could delay some 70 other people who have boarded without bother or fuss. Operators look to give service but it is important to give it in the right places. Further reference will be made to this aspect of fare collection when the fare box is considered.

Pre-paid Tickets

In the context of both two-stream boarding and change-giving problems, it is opportune to introduce the pre-paid ticket. Such tickets are purchased away from the vehicle and prior to travel. Sales points could be strategically sited dispensing machines or enquiry offices and agents. The all important point is that this part of the transaction is done at lesiure and not amid the hurly-burly of the bus platform. Tickets of this variety may be multi-journey, that is, valid for more than one ride (often ten or even in multiples of any journeys up the value of the ticket) or there could be books of tickets, each valid for one journey corresponding to its face value. If a special cancellator is provided on the vehicle, passengers boarding who have tickets then form the second stream and insert their tickets in this machine. This validates the ticket by printing the necessary details for the journey being taken and in the case of the multi-journey ticket, cancels an appropriate portion. Passengers who take advantage of this system are likely to be regular riders who, therefore, should quickly become accustomed to its use. The inhibitions of using the machines as already described should not, therefore, under these circumstances, apply to the same extent. The classic example of pre-paid tickets is, of course, the season ticket, sometimes referred to as a contract ticket, being a multi-journey facility sold at a specially commuted rate. The regular riders who first used them became known as commuters and the word has now found a place in our present day transport vocabulary. Such tickets may be and are being increasingly extended to buses, which certainly eases fare collection problems on the vehicle. The subject of season tickets, however, falls within the charging process and is therefore dealt with in Chapter 7. The issue of such tickets is still more a part of the railway scene than of road transport.

It should be noted in passing that a season ticket (or any other pass for that matter which is valid for travel) is, in effect, a display ticket and should be capable of being easily shown and its availability promptly recognised. Its size and shape should ideally be such that it can be contained within a standard season ticket wallet. A book type document which has to be opened for inspection fails to meet these basic requirements, passengers are encouraged to show and staff to accept a valueless outside cover and the design is hence quite unsuitable.

Although pre-paid tickets have the operational advantage of eliminating cash transactions on the bus platform (regardless of whether a validating machine is used as they could be checked by the driver), they have their disadvantages which may be summarised as follows:

(a) By using the system passengers must set aside a sum of money for what is, in effect, bulk purchase of travel. Furthermore, if the type of ticket is such that the journeys must be undertaken within a defined period, then they are committed to travel and by that means unless they are to lose their money. In any case, people have to be encouraged to put themselves out sufficiently to go to a sales point, lay out money in advance and then take care not to mislay what they have bought. To do this requires an incentive, which is likely to take the form of a cash discount. In other words, there is a cheaper fare, with the consequent repercussions on revenue.
(b) The setting up of sales points does, in itself, involve additional administration and hence cost. Premises

and staff must be found and sales duly accounted for and audited. The railway does, of course, have booking offices which it may require for its main line services in any case.

(c) If dispensing machines are used, a further capital and maintenance cost is involved and there is also a security problem as is considered in Chapter 11.

(d) If agents are employed, the agents might seek commission on sales, which is a further charge against revenue and cash collecting, accounting and audit is still necessary. Some agents might, however, be persuaded to sell tickets without commission as it does encourage people into their shop.

The ideal is still being sought and at this juncture it is worth taking stock of these British experiences and seeking reasons why, to all outward appearances, various systems seem to be working satisfactorily in Europe but run into difficulties, imaginary or real, when applied in the UK. Vehicle types are dealt with in Chapter 10 and this does have a bearing on the matter. Suffice to say here that in contrast to the areas of British influence there is, in Europe and elsewhere, a strong tendency towards single deck vehicles with plenty of standing accommodation. The result is that there are some very high capacity vehicles, particularly where articulated buses and trams are concerned. At the same time, in some countries, unlike the patient British, the arrival of a bus means for the locals a push and scramble. A further wait to buy a ticket would not always be tolerated for very long. Operators have, therefore, taken stronger measures to enforce the sale of pre-paid tickets and in so doing they have been aided by certain circumstances which do not apply in Great Britain. The point regarding the inability of drivers to check the second stream when boarding has already been made. If boarding is permitted at entrances other than at the front then it clearly becomes quite impossible and passengers must cancel a ticket for which they have paid in advance without any question of direct supervision at the time. Under these circumstances, it is usual for European operators to employ roving inspectors to make spot checks in order to deter faredodgers. So far, nothing has happened which could not be done in Great Britain. The difference lies in the fact that in Europe inspectors may impose an on the spot fine on those caught riding without a ticket. Although UK operators have, over recent years, lobbied for similar authority, at the time of writing, misdemeanants may be charged only the additional fare or excess fare although there are now instances where the amount paid under these circumstances may be higher than the normal fare. Certainly it is contrary to British PSV regulations to travel on buses with intent to avoid payment but to go to court and prove intent is a very different matter to simply accusing a person of not possessing a valid ticket. In the absence of such legislation, it is unlikely that British operators would risk placing all of their passengers on trust in this way. Even so, it is questionable to what extent the on-the-spot fines in Europe do act as a real deterrent. Unless there is a lot of inspectors, and this would be expensive, the chance of being checked might be sufficiently low as to justify the risk of not paying the fare and perhaps operators might prefer not to say how much revenue they are really losing. In one way, it might be a good thing that inspectors in the UK are not so empowered, certainly if their personal safety is of any concern. True, the British are by nature a placid race but unfortunately there is now a minority group which lacks this traditional characteristic, as is noted in Chapter 11. Certain gentlemen who frequent late night buses pay scant regard for persons or property and when they are travelling the least of the troubles might be not paying the correct fare. In the absence of judicial support for the use of strong-arm tactics in the enforcement of proper conduct, the writer for one would have some trepidation in demanding a fine on these occasions. In some countries, the delinquent is allowed more appropriate treatment and control is correspondingly easier.

Another feature often met outside the UK is instead of allowing a discount on the approved scale to those who purchase tickets in advance off the vehicle, to charge a fare much higher than the accepted scale to those who still wish to pay the driver. Again, this is something which is still foreign to British practice, but it does encourage the use of pre-paid tickets. It is also easier to find shops willing to sell tickets at all hours on the continent as tobacconists, for example, tend to remain open much longer there than in Great Britain.

There are reasons, therefore, why certain methods which are followed in some countries are not acceptable in others. Long established customs and practices and the national legislature all play a part. There is, however, one system which has many advantages, which has found general acceptance within the United States and Canada but about which operators elsewhere have been surprisingly reticent. It is the farebox.

The Farebox

The principle of the farebox is popularly regarded as an import from North America. This is not, however, necessarily true as it has already been seen that some of the horse trams of the West Metropolitan Tramways Company in London carried a glass box in which passengers placed their fare. The modern farebox consists of a locked vault within a locked chamber, above which is a glass or perspex dome, within which passengers deposit the correct fare. The farebox is within view of the driver and he can see what money has been placed in the box. Even at this stage, however, the money cannot be retrieved. Once the driver is satisfied that the correct fare has been paid, he presses a button and the money drops through into the locked vault. Providing the passenger knows the fare and has the correct money, it is as simple as that and it is very fast — as fast as with a two-man crew. In North America, however, most people know the fare because it is normally a flat fare or at most a zone fare and no ticket is necessary. These different types of fare scales are considered in Chapter 7 but it does bring out a point already made that although fare collection apparatus should cater for the needs of the desired fares, it sometimes helps if the fare scale is contained within what the machines can deal with. Even in Great Britain, there is no legal requirement to issue a ticket. However, British practices favour graduated fares and if tickets are not issued under these circumstances, there is no subsequent check on where passengers boarded or what they paid and hence no check on overriding. It is fairly safe to assume, therefore, that any operator introducing a ticketless system with a graduated fare scale is destined to lose money. But certain manufacturers have taken care of this by introducing a ticket issuing arrangement in conjunction with the farebox. Instead of having one button to press to release the coins the driver has a bank of buttons. Each does the same job, it releases the coins and simultaneously issues a ticket. The price marked on the ticket, however, corresponds with whichever button is pressed. The great advantage of this system is speed. A mixture of coins (or tokens) of any value and even paper money can be used. It is all just dropped into a receptable, there being no slot to fumble with. Whilst it is accepted that change cannot be given (unless the driver carries a float) doubt has already been expressed on the justification of giving change. Any case of hardship can always be met by giving a passenger a voucher instead of change which could be cashed subsequently at an appointed office but with this inconvenience it is likely that passengers will do this only once. As a matter of interest it is worthy of note that the real reason for introducing the farebox in the USA was not to speed the service but for security. Armed robbery in that country is now such that for their own safety drivers can no longer have money in their possession — hence the locked vault. Speed, however, has proved to be a useful by-product and many passengers feel that this is a small price to pay for the much improved quality of service. Nevertheless, security was the real reason for the farebox and what happens in North America has a habit of spreading across the Atlantic in due course. But that is a matter for Chapter 12. A further point, however, before leaving North America is one which calls for a slight refinement to the statement that a ticketless system requires a flat fare. With a two zone system and no tickets, passengers travelling in the first zone can pay as they enter whilst those boarding in the second zone pay as they alight. By this means those travelling through both zones (ie the longer riders) pay twice and still no tickets are necessary.

It was noted in Chapter 7 that if a flat fare is in operation there could be a need to offer transfer facilities. Again the best examples are in North America and in many instances transfer facilities are available even with the farebox without ticket type of fare collection and no other sophisticated equipment. The driver has pads of dated paper transfer tickets pre-printed with lines at each quarter hour. The pad is held in place on the vehicle with a bulldog type clip, the position of which is moved every 15 minutes to accord with the time of day. When passengers alight the driver tears off a transfer ticket on request and hands it to the passenger which is evidence that a fare has been paid and at what quarter hour the change of vehicle is being made. This piece of paper is accepted in lieu of money by the driver of the next bus who is able to check by the time that it is reasonable to regard this second trip as part of the same journey.

Having extolled the virtues of the farebox in terms of both speed and security on the bus, it does produce one complication which lies in the process of emptying. This, however, is another matter for Chapter 11.

A development of the farebox system which has found its way into the UK is the turnstile. The equipment is installed inside the bus just behind the entrance at the expense of a fair amount of seating capacity. Whilst, however, the correct money must be dropped into a farebox, the turnstile requires not only the correct money but the right coinage as well which must be inserted in the appropriate slot to cause it to open and allow the passenger to pass through. The use of pre-paid tickets presents a problem although there could be provision for the use of tokens. This does, however, seem to be an expensive, complicated and cumbersome alternative to the farebox without any obvious advantages.

Applications to the Railway

Most of what has been said so far refers to road passenger transport with fares being paid on the vehicles and pre-paid tickets being checked on the vehicles, be they buses, trolleybuses or trams. The point has been made, however, that for reasons of economy, it is sometimes advantageous also to collect fares on trains, in which case the same thinking applies as with conductors on buses. It does prompt the thought, however, that if traffic is so low as to make the conductor/guard system practicable there might not be any real justification to run the trains at all. The railway is an expensive animal. It is also a bulk carrier and this is where it reaps its economies — but this is repeating what was said in Chapter 2. To get back to what British Railways call 'Pay Trains', they are, of course, two-man operated, not OMO in the bus sense. It would be a lot to expect train drivers to collect fares. Nevertheless, operationally, not only are one-man trains practicable, with full automation there is no technical reason why trains should not be entirely un-manned. In this case, however, the ticket issuing equipment would be on the stations and not on the trains and this is where any developments in the field of fare collection on the railway are likely to be.

Coming back to the older established methods of ticket issue, the origins of this particular facet of railway operation are not dissimilar to that of buses and trams except that traditionally, railway tickets have been bought prior to travel (usually immediately prior to travel) at a station booking office. The tickets themselves were pre-printed on card, serially numbered and with a face-value, similar to the bell punch system except that station booking clerks would possess an infinitely greater selection than would a bus conductor. Tickets were not just printed by face values, there were separate prints for each specific journey. There was, therefore, no need for punch holes when tickets were issued, although ticket collectors did and still do clip tickets in order to make fraudulent travel more difficult. What was done at the time of issue was to date the tickets. The system was introduced by a Thomas Edmondson in the 1830s and the one-time familiar 'clop' (or 'clop clop' if it was a return ticket and had to be dated at each end) of the Edmondson dating press can be heard even today at some country stations where ticket issue has not been mechanised. Like the bell punch of the bus conductor, Edmondson's system involved a lot of clerical work. A bus conductor's waybill becomes a sizeable ledger in a railway booking office in which must be recorded on a daily basis the ticket stocks, the opening and closing numbers of each set of tickets followed by a calculation of the cash taken.

Mechanisation has had to come, therefore, to the railway just as much as to the road and particularly to those stations which have local urban services about which this book is concerned. Heavy short distance traffic can quickly produce queues at a booking office window. In the confines of an office with all its facilities, change giving is not the problem that it is on a bus but speed of ticket issue is crucial. Many different types of ticket dispensing machines are available; some of which record the price on an otherwise pre-printed ticket, whilst others might print the ticket on a blank roll. At very busy stations such as those of London Transport, the popular destinations can be dealt with by a series of buttons. According to which button is pressed the appropriate ticket comes immediately to the counter and a change giving machine promptly supplies the necessary change. Even so, queues still form and booking offices are supplemented by a series of self-service ticket machines clearly marked with their price and the range of destinations for which they are valid. Such machines are also able to give change for certain values of coin.

Remember, of course, that where pre-paid tickets are involved (and on buses it is the exception, rather than the rule but on the railway it is the rule with some exceptions, hence these remarks are associated with the railway) the fare collection system does not end with the person who sells the ticket. Selling a ticket is a very important part but steps must be taken to ensure that as far as possible the ticket is used correctly. If it is not, then some of the revenue to which the operator is entitled will have been lost. On the buses, it has been seen that drivers, roving inspectors and special cancelling machines all play their part but on urban railways (and on main line railways as well for that matter) as has already been noted, it is possible to do more than that. Being a segregated system with relatively infrequent boarding points and with those boarding points (the stations) being, in effect, private property, access to the platforms and hence trains can be controlled. Exits can also be governed in the same way. It is common practice, therefore, to have ticket collectors posted, in the case of some organisations only at the exit barriers but more often at both the inwards and outwards control points. One step further and the process is automated. Electronically coded tickets open the barriers at the stations of origin and destination (providing they are valid) and this is the beginning of automatic revenue collection.

10
Vehicles and Rolling Stock

Introduction

There is no particular magic in the title of this chapter which presupposes some distinction between vehicles and rolling stock. As far as the movement of people is concerned, a vehicle is essentially a land carriage and buses and coaches are the obvious candidates for this classification. By definition, it does not exclude coaches which run on the railway. However, the term 'rolling stock' with its interpretation as locomotives, carriages, etc, of a railway is equally correct and has more popular acceptance. Whilst, therefore, the two terms are synonymous, both are spelt out as an indication that the subject covers road and rail. The detail is sufficiently different, however, to warrant treatment in two separate sections.

A feature common to each mode is the conflict between comfort and capacity. In any given space the greater the provision which is made for one the less room will there be available for the other. Hence the different configurations for different types of service.

The propelling power may either be incorporated within the carrying unit itself or contained in a separate tractive unit. As far as buses and coaches are concerned, there are very few examples of separate tractive units, although on the road haulage side, articulated vehicles which are of this type are very numerous. On the railway the situation is different. Locomotives are used to haul trains of non-powered coaches. But generally this applies to the main line services. Local trains in particular usually have their motors incorporated within the passenger coaches whereby powered and non-powered coaches are semi-permanently linked to form a two, three or four-car multiple unit (electric or diesel) set. Such an arrangement permits trains to be driven from either end. This permits easy reversing (an essential requirement for the type of terminal station as illustrated at the end of Chapter 6) and there is a constant power/weight ratio. If two four car units, for example, are coupled to form an eight-car train, the additional power comes automatically with the additional coaches. This would not be the case if four more coaches were attached to a locomotive hauled train. The characteristics of the multiple unit are, therefore, particularly appropriate for busy local services.

In terms of motive power, there is a similarity between the two modes as both are heavily dependent upon diesel fuel. The railway, however, being a fixed track system, is able to exploit the advantages of electric traction wherever it is economic so to do. In view of the energy situation, both are likely to face the common problem which leads into thoughts on trams and trolleybuses as will be considered in Chapter 12. A more immediate possibility is the conversion of buses to run on alternative fuels such as propane gas. Whilst, however, such an arrangement could be economic quite apart from the availability aspect, the price of fuel is always somewhat artificial and subject to rapid fluctuation in view of the high element of tax. What was cheaper could suddenly become expensive should governments so decree and it is unwise to base forward planning only on the current price of fuel and its alternatives. Availability is another matter.

Buses and Coaches

Definition

The legal distinction in Great Britain between stage, express and contract carriages was explained in Chapter 8. In this context it is more appropriate to note that a vehicle built for express coach work is not necessarily suitable for use on a town bus service which brings out the fundamental difference between a bus and a coach. There is no rigid distinction as such except by common practice and use and although both terms are used but applied to different types of vehicles, it is really only playing with words. A coach is a large road or railway carriage, the road version in its original form being known as a char-a-banc. The prefix 'omni' meaning 'all' when attached to the stem 'bus', thereby producing 'omnibus', means a vehicle for all. In popular parlance it is usually the bus which caters for the shorter distance riders whilst the coach is a more luxurious vehicle unsuitable for short stage work with its heavy pick-ups and set-downs because of narrow entrances, gangways, etc. but is used for longer journeys. Operators sometimes have a few vehicles in their fleet of a general purpose design with seats rather more comfortable than those of a bus but with entrance/exit and general layout nevertheless suitable for bus work, which can be used for all types of operation.

Basic Features

The evolution of the bus was dealt with in Chapter 1. The features of that review which must be brought forward for discussion here are capacity and the position of the power unit. Both have had a profound influence on the design of the body.

In most countries and certainly in the United Kingdom the dimensions of buses and coaches are strictly controlled by regulation. The Public Service Vehicles (Conditions of Fitness, Equipment and Use) Regulations, 1972 as amended stipulate in a depth of detail statutory requirements regarding the construction and use of buses and coaches in Great Britain. To give the student a broad idea of their magnitude, the following summary shows the features covered in the order in which they are presented in the regulations:

Fitness

Stability: Both double deck and single deck, when loaded to be able to tilt to specified degrees without overturning.
Suspension: No excessive body sway.
Turning Circle: Vehicles to turn within a swept circle of maximum defined radii according to length (a swept circle is that which is traced by any part of the body of the vehicle and not just the track of the wheels).
Guard Rails: Minimum requirements between front and rear wheels.
Side Overhang: Limitation on the protrusion of the body beyond the wall of the outer rear tyre.
Brakes, Steering Gear and Hubs: Technical requirements.
Fuel Tank and Exhaust Pipe: Requirements regarding positioning, filling and fuel to the engine.
Locking of Nuts: Need for lock nuts or split pins.
Lighting: Minimum requirements and methods of fitment.
Body: General construction requirements with dimensions stipulated for body sides, steps, platforms, stairs, entrances and exits, doors, emergency exits and their access, gangways, seats and driver's cab.
Windows including Windscreens: Demisting device and provision against breakage.

Equipment
Fire extinguishers and first aid equipment.

Use
Various requirements about passengers not obstructing exits or the driver, adequate interior lighting, the carriage of dangerous substances and if a stage carriage with more than a certain number of seats, the need to carry a conductor unless authorised to the contrary by the traffic commissioners.

Separate regulations apply to minibuses.

The re-positioning of the engine from front to rear has made it possible to replace the one time traditional half-cab with a full fronted and front entrance (that is in front of the front wheels) vehicle. This feature together with a relaxation in maximum vehicle lengths has permitted the production of a double deck 78-seater bus (and there are still larger models overseas) which is in contrast to the standard front engine, half-cab, rear entrance 56 seater bus of the 1940s. At the same time, the design enables passengers to pass the driver as they board which makes it physically possible for him to collect fares. In the 1940s the maximum sized vehicle which was permitted to operate in the United Kingdom on a stage carriage service in this way was the small 20-seater single deck with special dispensation being possible for up to 26 seats. Even when the longer full fronted single decks (with underfloor engine) came at the beginning of the 1950s a conductor was still needed. From here to single manning on the 78-seaters is productivity indeed and small wonder at the need for mechanical aids to fare collection as was considered in Chapter 9. But as was seen in that chapter, fare collection methods have also progressed from the original rack of tickets and it is the opinion of the writer that the one-man operated double deck bus should be the standard for now and into the future. It is true that further relaxations in maximum permitted lengths have enabled the capacities of new single deck buses to approximate those of the smaller type double deck vehicles. If this capacity, which could be in the 50+ region, is adequate for traffic purposes there is a strong feeling amongst operators that it would be better to standardise on this type of single deck bus. The writer disagrees with the principle for reasons of economy in road and garage space and manoeuvrability. The difference in capital costs and running costs is not necessarily great; both can be one man operated and the opinion is here expressed that where the headroom is available (and in Great Britain the standard clearance on British roads permits double decks) this advantage should be exploited. There is so often the odd occasion when the extra capacity is valuable indeed. Even so, the performance of the rear-engined buses has, over the years, left something to be desired, partly because the driver cannot hear any warning sounds and his first intimation of trouble is complete failure, by which time damage has been done. The body layout, however, has made such a deep impression on operating practices that there can be really no thought of a return to the design of the stalwarts of the 1930s and 1940s. Some manufacturers have produced vehicles outwardly similar to those with the rear engine but instead with the engine forward beside the driver whilst at the same time preserving the front entrance. A disadvantage of this arrangement is that the driver cannot easily enter his cab from the interior of the bus and must have instead a door on the offside. To get into the bus from the cab, therefore, should he have need to do so entails getting out and walking round, leaving his cash and ticket machine temporarily unattended. Securitywise this is not an ideal arrangement for one-man operation although vehicles of this type are used in this way.

Entrances and Exits

Fitment of Doors

Front entrance buses are fitted with doors which are under the control of the driver. It has been the trend over many years to fit doors on buses, partly (with the assistance of heaters and forced ventilation) to give better control in winter over the interior temperature but more importantly to prevent boarding and alighting accidents. Even before one-manning, doors were being fitted to both rear and forward entrance buses (a forward entrance is an entrance at the front but behind the front wheels). At first these doors were worked manually by conductors and their use was impracticable on busy town services. Although subsequent development permitted them to be opened and shut by the driver or conductor at the push of a button, they have always had a mixed reception on local routes. Whilst passengers are glad of the extra internal comfort which a door provides in inclement weather they often resent the obstruction which doors make to boarding and alighting at places other than approved stops. 'Hop on a bus' was a well known catch phrase launched to encourage local riders and one of the characteristics of this mode of transport is its convenience for local trips for which the ability to hop on, take a short ride and then hop off was appropriate. The advantage of this practice is particularly apparent when buses are stationary in heavy traffic. People are able to board vehicles which they would otherwise have missed and tempers quickly become frayed when they have to stand on the platform, but are unable to alight whilst the bus is held in congestion and cannot get to the stop. London is still a classic example where large numbers of rear entrance vehicles without doors are still in service and where passengers frequently board and alight in this way. Once doors are provided, passengers have no alternative but to use the authorised stops. On some busy town services the additional time taken to complete a journey for this reason when buses with doors have been allocated has been noticeable. Of course, without doors there are boarding and alighting accidents which the industry cannot condone. In any case, the use of rear entrance buses without doors for one-man operation would be out of the question. For more than one reason, therefore, doors are here and here to stay. Their provision is in the interests of safety and comfort but not of speed and convenience.

Centre Exits

The full front design with front entrance and driver's cab contained within the vehicle as with the later family of double decks just described was already in vogue for single decks (which had underfloor engines) when the rear engined double decks were introduced. This put up the height of the floor and hence the need for steps at the entrance but, be that as it may, vehiclewise, the way was thus paved for single manning. When, therefore, British regulations were relaxed in the mid 1950s and buses larger than the 20- or 26-seaters became eligible for this type of operation, (single decks at first), thoughts turned to how boarding times could be minimised. At first it was those existing vehicles with front entrances which were converted, but the next generation was to be designed with one-man operation specifically in mind. Outside the United Kingdom and particularly beyond the areas of British influence, circumstances were a little different. Overseas local bus passengers, by custom or use, are not generally as comfort conscious. Some get a seat but many others stand with the maximum load governed by the number which can physically squash on, boarding either at the front, paying the driver and circulating through towards the back or boarding at the rear, paying a seated conductor and circulating through towards the front. In conditions such as this a separate centre exit is a physical necessity. When the door opens, passengers alight (voluntary or otherwise) and more can then board at a separate entrance. For the same reason, standee type buses, even in the UK, do require a separate centre exit, although whether the principle of maximum standing space should be extended is another matter. The point here is that the separate exit, hitherto adopted only in isolated instances, developed into a recognised option and became a regular specification in Great Britain for one-man buses. When double deck OMO appeared on the scene, so also did double deck buses with their separate exits but with one staircase, the position varying between front end and amidships. The theory of the separate exit was that alighting and boarding could be undertaken simultaneously, thereby reducing the time spent at stops. Whilst, however, the need for a separate exit on standee buses is accepted, on a double deck bus where everybody has a seat and the crush situation does not arise it is not and there has been much controversy over this particular issue. With only one set of stairs, passengers cannot board and alight at the same time except to the extent that the first few people can board and block back at the foot of the centre staircase whilst other passengers are descending and alighting. At the same time there are disadvantages in both the construction and use of double decks with centre exits which may be summarised as follows:

Construction

Lower capacity (usually four seats less which, on a frequent service, could mean the allocation of an additional bus).

Unpopular seating arrangements in the forward portion of the lower deck.

Higher initial capital cost.

Use

Passenger safety hazard.

Inability of drivers to check on the number of passengers

alighting with consequent difficulty in knowing how many may be permitted to board without overcrowding.

Difficulties with shelter and queueing arrangements at stops.

Pollution of the atmosphere of the lower deck by smokers whilst passing through to the upper deck.

What, in the opinion of the writer, is of overriding importance, and this applies to all types of centre-exit buses, is the safety hazard which results from the driver no longer being able to observe directly the alighting point. It has already been noted that the unguarded exit of the erstwhile standard rear entrance bus was a potential source of danger, even with a conductor and there were alighting accidents. The introduction of the first front entrance bus with a door under the control of the driver was rightfully acclaimed as a significant move towards greater safety. With a centre-exit that advantage has been annulled unless the vehicle is so equipped that its wheels cannot turn whilst the doors are open.

Much research has been undertaken by various bodies including the Transport and Road Research Laboratory of the Department of Transport into boarding times with different types of one-man operated buses. There is evidence to show* that a separate centre exit on a double deck bus does not achieve a faster alighting/boarding rate. Furthermore, with any type of bus it is only at those stops where there are passengers both boarding and alighting where there could be any possible saving in time and according to TRRL data this represents no more than about a third of the total number of stops. The alleged safety hazard is, however, a very real one. There are numerous cases of fatalities and serious personal injuries resulting from passengers being trapped in the centre doors. A one time popular arrangement was to operate the doors through a sixth gear position, but even then there are circumstances where the bus can still move whilst they are open. To overcome this danger it is necessary to fit a transmission interlock which directly links the operation of the doors with the movement of the wheels. This, however, has been shown to increase, sometimes quite substantially, the time spent at stops and more than cancels out any advantage in speed which there might otherwise have been. For various reasons, therefore, most operators are now veering away from separate centre exits.

The writer is strongly of the opinion that passengers should both board and alight at a point adjacent to and in full view of the driver. Only in this way can the interests of safety be properly served. If a separate centre exit needs to be provided, ie for standee buses, then it must be accompanied by a transmission interlock regardless of the delay factor.

**Bus Boarding and Alighting Times,* (LR 521-1973); TRRL.

Steps

Closely allied to entrances and exits are steps and their height. Quite clearly, the fewer the steps the better as some passengers find them physically difficult and sometimes impossible to negotiate. More is now being done, with statutory backing, to help disabled people to get around. Nevertheless, the fact must remain that the most important role of the bus is to move the masses in the peaks. The needs of the many should not be subordinated to the requirements of a few, deserving as their case may be, but if designs can be adapted to help the disabled without excessive cost or inconvenience to other passengers then this should be done. The principles to follow are the step up from the kerb on to the front platform to be as low as possible and steps from the front platform through into the lower deck as few as possible. Of course it is difficult to win whatever the design. It is interesting to recall that the old rear entrance type had a step up from the platform into the lower deck. Then Bristol/Eastern Coachworks brought out the Lodekka in the 1950s with a rearranged transmission and rear axle which permitted a lower floor level on the bottom deck with a consequently lower overhall height. This eliminated the step from the platform into the lower saloon which was ideal for the purpose under discussion except that some passengers continued to step up the step which was no longer there and fell just the same.

Ways and means of helping people who find it hard to get around seems to be exercising everybody's minds. Whilst on the subject of the disabled, but slightly off the point of steps, it might be noted that one idea which is done at virtually no cost is to indicate on a few easily accessible seats that they are reserved for the lame and handicapped should they require them. On a front entrance coach, the obvious pair of seats to be so earmarked are the ones in the front; the very ones which are the favourites of tourists who want to see the view and enjoy the ride. It is irritating indeed if they have to give them up, particularly after they have queued to get them. If passengers are streaming on to both decks of a double deck bus and on the same principle, if by the time the benevolent act has been accomplished the vehicle has become filled to capacity and the conductor will not take passengers standing, the result is even more irritating, but this is digressing. Nevertheless, it is a valid point that steps have a bearing on the disabled and it must be noted that there are problems.

Miscellaneous Arrangements and Fitments

Although there is not a large number of different vehicle manufacturers and they each produce their own fairly standard types of body shell, unlike the private motorist, operators are still a long way from buying their buses 'off the peg'. Certainly, in Great Britain there has been a greater degree of standardisation in requirements over recent years but this is more because of amalgamations amongst the operating companies. Different managements order basic types in accordance with their preferences and availability but they are careful to prepare their individual internal specifications. Alternatives to be considered are the layout, design and covering of the seats depending on the required ratio of seated to standing passengers, the degree of comfort that is wanted and resistance to vandalism. Greater comfort will of course be achieved by a lesser number of larger and more luxurious type seats which will be at the expense of capacity. Fibre glass gives the maximum protection against malicious damage but at the expense of comfort, although it is more hygienic than moquette.

The position of the staircase and the controversial separate exit (if one is to be provided) have a major impact on the internal layout. Of the few operators which still specify separate exits, some prefer them off centre and nearer to the front entrance served by a staircase at the front. But regardless of whether there is one door or two, it is for decision which way the staircase should ascend, being with or against the direction of travel. The writer suggests that the internal layout should be so arranged as to permit the former, that is, in the same style as the rear entrance bus or, in other words, the passenger faces the driver as he ascends. If there is an emergency stop whilst the passenger is on the stairs and he is thrown forward, the results are not likely to be as serious if he is propelled into rather than away from the body structure.

It is for consideration what provision will be made for passengers' luggage and other chattels and for unaccompanied parcels. It is convenient for double deck buses on town routes to have a small area near the front where passengers can deposit bulky articles. It is likely that seats will be placed as close together as possible and although this provides maximum capacity it does little to help the passenger lumbered with an awkward parcel or, for that matter, the person sitting next to him. It is on the rural routes where such space is also likely to be useful for unaccompanied parcels. For longer journeys, overhead luggage racks are desirable. The availability of space for parcels at the front is to some extent conditioned by the fare collection equipment in use. A ticket machine beside the driver takes up no room and a farebox not much more; it is positioned on the floor but right at the front. It is when two-stream boarding is adopted with secondary help-yourself equipment or ticket cancellator that more space is needed. Right at the extreme in terms of space requirement comes the turnstile and when this sophisticated apparatus is in position there is precious little room left for parcels or passengers either.

With the single manning of double decks it is never easy for the driver to know how many vacant seats he has available on the upper deck. With centre exits it is sometimes quite impossible for him to know as has already been noted. A periscope will be fitted which gives him a view upstairs, except possibly for the front seats, but even then his task is a difficult one. Equipment has been produced which gives a numerical indication visible to the driver in his cab and to the passenger at the foot of the stairs how many seats are vacant. If accurate, this is a most useful accessory but in arduous service conditions, perfection is not always the rule and wrong information is worse than no information at all.

One further point in vehicle design which arises from the fact that passengers now have direct access to drivers is the need for his protection. Assaults on bus crews both in Great Britain and overseas are becoming prevalent and in certain areas of some countries a protective screen is provided between the driver and the outside world. In some places this is necessary and in the UK there are isolated examples where it is being tried. At present it is not a particularly popular innovation but the author's view is that unfortunately the time will come when it will be inadvisable to drive a bus which is not so fitted.

Another matter of detail on which operators have their different views is the display of destination blinds. Most undertakings adopt a route numbering system and this, together with the ultimate destination, must be exhibited, at least in the front. What else should be shown besides the final destination is a matter of opinion and there can be no undisputed answer. Whilst in one sense there can never be too much information if the stranger is to be catered for, a wealth of detail becomes confusing; expensive in terms of blind display; longer blinds become necessary which can only cover a lesser number of routes and therefore make vehicle allocation more inflexible and there is a greater likelihood of incorrect blind display (and again incorrect information is less helpful than no information). The writer feels that route number and destination only is reasonable providing there is adequate supporting publicity in the form of maps or timetable leaflets supplemented by information exhibited at stops, although it is appreciated that wilful destruction is giving the latter provision a serious problem. Side blinds are helpful, particularly when buses are standing nose to tail and there are divided views on the provision of information at the rear. Some managements would like rear blinds but have difficulty in persuading one-man drivers to change them and settle for a compromise of a route number only without the need to alter the destination at the end of each journey. Others maintain that a rear display is essential and that people living in towns where buses are not so embellished 'don't know what the're missing'. One final point on blinds is the display of the route number. An old established practice but one which has become more widespread in recent years is separate blinds for each digit with up to four aspects (to make provision for three figure numbers plus a suffix letter). This arrangement is often not as neat as the individual figures are sometimes not displayed in perfect alignment and, according to the permutation, cannot always be in the centre of the box. However, the system makes for economy in blinds and gives maximum flexibility. In an emergency, a correct route number with everything else blank is much better than nothing.

Articulated Buses

In road haulage terms an articulated vehicle is one where a separate tractive unit hauls a non-powered semi-trailer. Apart from isolated examples such as airport buses, the design is not used for passenger vehicles in the UK although there are limited examples overseas. A more common adaption of the articulated principle for passenger work is the linking of two passenger carrying units. This principle is widely adopted in Europe where the standard headroom generally precludes the use of double decks. In Great Britain this is not the case and the same need does not arise. In fact it was not until very recently that domestic legislation allowed this type of bus; it was the Transport Act 1980 which made it legally possible.

The articulated bus is a long one, about 56 feet in fact but for its length, surprisingly manoeuvrable. It also has a very high capacity; up to 150 if only 40 seats are provided with the remainder standing, and all with only one driver. For this sort of number three sets of doors need to be provided and if OMO the fare collection system must be geared to a pre-paid or help-yourself basis. If this is not acceptable and it is felt that provision must be made for passengers who wish to purchase a ticket in the conventional manner, then one possibility is for those passengers to board at the back and file past a seated conductor. To do this, however, would achieve little in terms of manpower compared with conventional double deck OMO. The use of vehicles of this type really comes back to the double deck/single deck issue already discussed and the articulated concept is most useful where there is a height restriction. Its development in the UK, therefore, where a lack of headroom is the exception rather than the rule, is bound to be controversial.

Whilst acknowledging certain benefits, the articulated bus has a number of disadvantages compared with double decks which may be summarised as follows:

(a) Unless it is fully loaded, it takes up more road space per passenger carried and road space is a scarce commodity in urban areas.
(b) It takes up more garage space per vehicle; it is not as easily manoeuvrable for shunting inside garages and it cannot use the normal pits for inspection and repair purposes.
(c) It does not mix easily with conventional buses at stops as it requires different queuing and shelter arrangements, it makes the design of bus stations more difficult and reduces the number of stands.
(d) It does not exploit the air space which (at least in the UK) is usually freely available.
(e) Following on what was said in respect of centre exits, if proper safety precautions are to be observed, a transmission interlock must be fitted to prevent the wheels from turning whilst the doors are open. This together with additional time taken to join traffic streams is likely to annul any time saving achieved by the greater number of doors.
(f) If the potential capacity is fully utilised, passengers must travel in considerable discomfort.
(g) One man operation is practicable only if accompanied by a supplementary pre-paid or help-yourself ticket system.
(h) The lower cost per passenger carried is valid only when it is heavily loaded. It has more technical complications and if the capacity is not fully used it is cheaper and more satisfactory to build on an upper deck rather than employ what is a very expensive articulated vehicle.

In short, the big advantage of the articulated bus is capacity and, incidentally, it does not have to be single deck, although there are very few examples to the contrary. The type under consideration here is the single deck standee variety as is used extensively on the European mainland and which is beginning to spread elsewhere. Its capacity is approximately twice that of a double decker and three times that of a single decker but only at the expense of items (a) to (h) above. All of these factors are important but, in the opinion of the writer, of particular significance is item (f). If the bus industry is really anxious to attract traffic and, in the national interest, encourage people to come out of their cars and on to public transport, then it must do something better than herd them into standing positions on crush loading vehicles. In thinking about this, students should not allow themselves to be swayed by the protagonists who point to the greater popularity of the lower deck. Do not forget that more and more people are finding smoking distasteful and some refrain from travelling on the upper deck where smoking is generally permitted not because they object to the stairs but because they cannot tolerate the polluted atmosphere. If smoking was banned on both decks instead of on just the lower, then the upper deck would become more popular.

The writer sees a potential for the single deck standee articulated bus only on routes which:

(a) are for physical reasons restricted to single deck
(b) the average length of the journey is short
(c) there is heavy traffic necessitating a frequent service.

To elaborate on (c), if traffic is such as to justify a 10-minute headway of conventional single deck buses, and the articulated bus can carry three times as many people, then a 30-minute service of artics would suffice. Any greater frequency would result in under utilisation and would be uneconomic but only two buses per hour would not be sufficiently attractive for an urban route, hence the need for a heavy demand. A two-minute headway converting to a five or six-minute frequency, for example, would be more readily acceptable.

Standardisation

Standardisation has already been touched upon on the manufacturing side. For consideration here is the wisdom of fleet standardisation within an undertaking. It is a policy long since practised by the erstwhile Tilling Group, now a part of the National Bus Company and by London Transport. There are advantages. Apart from a few routes where for physical reasons a different type of bus is essential, if there is standardisation then there is flexibility in allocation, drivers and maintenance staff become more familiar with the vehicles, fewer spares need to be kept, there is interchangability of parts and perhaps some savings in bulk purchases. Standardisation can, therefore, produce economies and if such a policy is to be followed, it is for decision what the standard vehicle will be. Of particular importance is capacity. An average size might result in a little over-provision of seats on some services whilst on others more buses have to be run than would be necessary if larger vehicles were available but if there are compensating advantages in standardisation, this is not necessarily a bad thing. Perhaps the biggest drawback with a large number of identical vehicles is when, with new innovations, different designs permit more efficient operating practices. In these circumstances there is a danger that the entire fleet could become obsolete whilst still having a period of useful life remaining. If part of the fleet was replaced with latest designs year by year advantage could be taken at an earlier stage but it would militate against the realisation of the economic advantages of standardisation.

Trams

Although the design of a tram is equally as important as the design of a bus, for various reasons this section need not be a long one. With engineering tchnicalities not being a part of this study, this leaves the design of the body as the main topic for consideration as far as vehicles are concerned and the principles and preferences already expressed in respect of the bus apply also to trams although not necessarily with the same force. The traditional British tram which is now a museum piece was a double deck. The current official concept of trams, presumably drawn from European practices, seems to be a single deck and possibly of the articulated variety with plenty of room for standing. Once again, the writer questions why passengers should be subjected to enforced discomfort on a lower deck when they could be provided with comfortable seats on an upper deck, although the argument is not as strong as it is in the case of a bus. The quality of the ride of steel wheel on steel rail, assuming always that the track is in good repair, is superior to that of a bus using the public highway. Furthermore, if the road is straight then the tram track will be straight whereas the bus will continue to weave around other traffic. Standing in a tram, therefore, is not as tedious or exhausting as standing in a bus but in the opinion of the author it is still not good enough if alternative arrangements (such as seats on an upper deck) are a possibility. The length of an articulated vehicle is of less concern if the tram track forms a segregated private way. Even then there seems to be no good reason why double deck trams cannot be used, loading gauge permitting, joined if necessary in the peaks to form trains of trams with one driver. Special arrangements for fare collection would be necessary in any case, but with a train of trams (single or double deck) single manning becomes impracticable. Unlike the articulated units, there is no physical communication between the two vehicles and each separate trailer, therefore, requires an attendant. On the other hand, trailers can be detached when not required for traffic purposes, which economises in power.

A feature of the tram compared with the bus is that it can be driven from either end. Operationally, this permits a change of direction in the way that can be emulated by no other road vehicle. Subject to there being a crossover in the tracks (or the tram is on a single track) a reversing movement can be accomplished even in the centre of a road without any of the special arrangements as are needed for a bus or trolleybus. This applies equally to an articulated tram but it could not be done if there are non-powered trailers. For reversing purposes it is necessary that a driving cab be provided at each end, which has repercussions on costs and space and there are considerable consequential effects on body design. Entrances and exits must be provided on both sides of the vehicle (which again takes space) and seats must either be so arranged that half face one way and half the other or they are reversible. A seat where just the backrest can be moved across the base might not be as comfortable as a rigid design but otherwise some passengers are likely to have their back to the driver which tends to be unpopular. There are, therefore, advantages in body design of single-ended trams but the route must always have a return loop at each end. This, of course, precludes any short workings to intermediate points where there is no such facility or for turning in an emergency in the event of a line blockage. For emergency use and shunting in depots it is advisable, however, even for single-ended trams to have driving facilities also at the 'back'.

In the UK the railway inspectorate as referrred to in

Chapter 8 is the responsible authority for approving the design of trams.

Railway Rolling Stock

The design of passenger rolling stock on the railway is conditioned by its intended use. A national railway system caters for various types of traffic and it will, therefore, have different classes of coaching stock. Features which have a bearing on design are summarised as follows:

(a) Length of journey

Longer journeys call for a greater standard of comfort than short ones. Furthermore, on long distance trains there will be less intermediate turnover of passengers and doors can be confined to the end vestibules. Conversely, with short distance traffic there is likely to be a considerable turnover combined with a high density timetable. Time available for stopping at stations will, therefore, be strictly limited. Under these circumstances generous provision must be made for boarding and alighting. The standard of comfort provided on local trains is not as important but for the same reasons as were said in the case of buses and trams, it must not fall below an acceptable level. Also dictated by the length of journey will be the need for restaurant and toilet facilities and sleeping accommodation.

(b) Loading gauge

The loading gauge more than the track gauge determines the overall dimensions of rolling stock. The more liberal the loading gauge, then the larger can be the stock which in turn gives scope for more spacious accommodation. For local work in particular the space can be used for additional seating. Extra width enables more seats to be provided crosswise whilst greater height makes double-deck coaches practicable.

(c) Speed

Whilst speed has a strong bearing on suspension and other features necessary to maintain proper stability, the main direct effect noticeable to the passenger is what he sees through the window. A deep window on a fast train can produce visual discomfort to some people. On the other hand, maximum depth is desirable on local trains where traffic is heavy and this includes depth both at the top and bottom. It helps to reduce an overpowering effect if seated passengers are surrounded by others who are standing whilst those who are standing need to be able to see outside, if only to read the names of the stations.

(d) User Classification

For various reasons there may be a demand for a superior class of accommodation which is able to attract a premium fare. In the developed part of the world business executives travelling on expense accounts are likely customers for first class travel. On high density commuter services sufficient capacity might not be available for this purpose and if under crowded conditions some compartments remain under-utilised for this reason, criticism can be expected. In certain territories overseas, particularly where large numbers of people of mixed races are travelling, the provision of different classes of accommodation might not necessarily be economic but is for ethnic reasons essential. Also in this user classification must be considered the extent to which accompanied or unaccompanied parcels, mail, perambulators, invalid carriages, bicycles, livestock and other sundry effects are likely to be catered for.

(e) Climate

Climate may call for heating, air conditioning or both, generous ventilation, sun blinds and tinted glass. If temperatures are extreme there could be some influence on door provision and the manner in which they are used.

(f) Track and Equipment

The placing of lineside equipment, positioning of platforms, the height of bridges and the width of tunnels are the kind of things which determine the loading gauge which has already been referred to. But there are also other effects on vehicle design. If the line is predominantly in tunnel and particularly if there are stations in tunnel, hinged doors are something less than ideal. Whilst in areas of British influence station platforms approach floor height, this is not necessarily the case elsewhere and if not then coaches must be designed with accessibility from ground level. If the line is in a tube, provision for an emergency exit is necessary through the centre and out through each end of the train.

(g) Public misconduct

It has been noted elsewhere that robbery, violence and rape are becoming popular pastimes amongst certain sections of the community. Such acts are more prevalent in some areas than others but the habit is spreading. It is already necessary for armed police to patrol trains of the rapid transit system in New York and what happens in America today comes to Great Britain tomorrow. In difficult areas, therefore, it is advisable that coaches should be so constructed that police and railway officials can patrol trains from end to end whilst they are in motion.

(h) Statutory requirements

Apart from an interesting little piece of railway history, the British government does not exercise control over the design of railway rolling stock except for certain requirements on tube lines (which is important in this context). But first the exception which concerned main line railways. In the 1830's, which was before the advent of continuous brakes and the ride was sometimes a little jerky with a derailment every now and then, 3rd class carriages were little better than open trucks. Passengers had virtually no protection either from the weather or anything else with the result that occasionally they fell out. After one particularly spectacular tragedy the railway inspecting officer of the day expressed certain misgivings. The outcome was that the Railway Regulation Act, 1844 obliged railway companies to run at least one train per day in each direction over each of its lines at a reasonable charge (set at not more than 1d per mile) and in carriages the design of which would be approved by what was then the Board of Trade. This meant that on those particular trains (which became known as 'parliamentary trains') the carriages which were provided for the lower class travellers would have proper protection. So there has been an example of statutory control over rolling stock. There are also other cases where modifications have been suggested as a result of accidents. The requirements* in respect of tube stock, briefly summarised, are:

(i) Material for construction must be metal wherever possible.
(ii) Main electric cables must not be carried through the train.
(iii) Emergency lighting from an alternative supply to be provided
(iv) Must be possible to alight in an emergency from both ends of the train.
(v) Passenger doors to be power operated.

Of all these different parameters which help to determine the make-up of railway passenger coaches, the most fundamental is the length of the journey. The needs of the long distance and short distance riders are very different and provision must be made accordingly. A national railway is likely to carry all types of traffic except possibly the very shortest local riders and from what has already been said (eg door provision in item (a) and depth of windows in item (c)) this means something more than just different internal fittings. Any national railway administration which uses a common body shell based on its long distance stock modified as far as is practicable for suburban work suggests either that it sees the local services subservient to its main business of trunk haul or that it is not properly geared for short distance mass transit. These are two very different types of traffic and if, in any main line railway administration, the former predominates, as it is likely to do, it is but another argument for complete segregation with a self-contained locally operated system catering for short distance traffic. This, of course, is provided always that traffic is of sufficient volume to justify such an organisation.

To get back to the point of this chapter, the design of passenger coaches for intercity and even inter-continental journeys is one thing and for local urban rapid transit, be it tube, sub-surface, surface or elevated is another. These are the two extremes. There are other classes of traffic in between. These include the longer distance commuter services out from the main centres of the large agglomerations to the surrounding dormitory areas and also the rural branch lines and cross-country routes. In short, there is quite a variety and although standardisation between the extremes has just been castigated, if every service had purpose built stock there would be diseconomy and loss of flexibility. Just as in the case of buses, therefore, a measure of standardisation is to be expected. The long distance intercity movement does not fall within the scope of this work and although it is a very important part, if not the most important part, of railway operation, it is not for consideration here. What is for consideration is the railway which moves the masses in the built-up areas, the stage beyond the tram through light rapid transit into heavy rapid transit. This does lead in to the commuter services to the outer suburbs which are physically a part of the main line system and which more understandably take their cue from the intercity business.

For railway rolling stock on local lines once again the controversy arises over the ratio of seats to standing accommodation. The writer came down rather heavily against standee buses. This was largely because an alternative was possible in the form of a second deck. The aversion was to some extent modified in the case of the tram on account of the superior quality of the ride. Whilst under no circumstances can crush loading be accepted as an ideal standard, there are yet further reasons for limited condonation when it comes to mass transit. With the track contained in a segregated right of way, the journey time is likely to be shorter; if it is largely tunnel there is little to see out of the window other than the station names (and this is one of the reasons why there should be some windows of adequate depth) and by custom and practice passengers do not seem to object and sometimes even prefer to stand when travelling short distances on trains of this type. But more than that. When it comes to the volume of traffic which is necessary to justify a rapid transit system anyway, the numbers travelling in the peak are likely to be such that it would either be physically impossible or costwise prohibitive to give everybody a seat. It becomes a case of moving people not always in complete comfort but as expeditiously as possible and this could well mean some standing with even a degree of crush loading at times. This being the case, stock must be designed accordingly.

At this point the loading gauge comes back into consideration. A railway in a tube is something which is very expensive to construct and the wider the diameter of the tunnel the more costly it will be. But a small diameter tunnel, even though it can have standard gauge track, requires specially constructed stock to pass through it. It means that the floor level of the coaches must be lower

**Railway Construction and Operation Requirements for Passenger Lines and Recommendations for Goods Lines of the Minister of Transport 1950;* HMSO.

than standard with shallower platforms. This in turn means that like a double deck bus, wheel arches must appear within the interior and at these points there is nothing for it but to have longitudinal type seating facing inwards. This, however, straight away lends itself to maximum standing accommodation. Plenty of door space must be provided, being at each end and at discretion once or twice intermediately in double or single configuration. On tube trains they will be sliding doors with a requirement that they be power operated. What space free of wheel arches is left may then be used for transverse seating. If the line has sharp bends there could also be a restriction on the length of each coach and this again could influence the internal layout.

Progressing beyond the tube train, track in shallow tunnel (cut and cover) and that on the surface and on elevated structures is more likely to be capable of accepting stock of standard dimensions although there could still be a restriction on car lengths. Trains might be catering for traffic identical to that of the tube. If that is the case, the same seating layout which gives maximum room for standing could be installed although as the floor might be at standard height, wheel arches are not necessarily an inhibition. Under these circumstances there might be justification for a standard body shell for short and medium distance commuter lines with seats in the latter all in the transverse style. Like the tram, it is for consideration whether the seats should be reversible but in the case of the train there is little chance that there will be a reversing loop. Most likely the train will change its direction of travel when departing from the terminal station via a scissors crossover. The generally accepted railway practice is for permanent seats to be provided placed facing each other and back to back in pairs. An alternative arrangement would be for seats to face opposite directions on either side of the gangway or even within alternate coaches.

The pedigree of rolling stock on the outer suburban lines tends to be conditioned according to whether it is a part of the local rapid transit or national railway system. This is understandable and either way satisfactory designs can be produced. On those trains where passengers have a longer ride more attention must be paid to comfort although even here some standing might be inevitable and it is a matter for discretion whether first class accommodation should be provided.

A study of the evolution of the British and European railway carriage really goes back to road transport, for that is where it has its roots. The first compartment coaches in Great Britain were horse carriages on trucks and development from there was not without its parallel on the road. In order to maximise seating the early motor coaches (or charabancs) had rows of transverse seats with side doors at the end of each row and no centre gangway, or, in other words, the 'toastrack' arrangement. The same concept was adopted on the railway but with the rows of transverse seats in pairs back to back with side doors for each pair. Again there was no centre gangway but transverse partitions were provided where one pair of seats backed on to another and so the compartment coach was born. It was very suitable for suburban work as the arrangement provided for maximum seating with ample doors for rapid boarding and alighting. As there was no centre gangway there was no communication between compartments but the concept was successful to the extent that it stood the test of time and although the design is now regarded as obsolete, there are still examples in daily service. In North America, things began rather differently. The compartment carriage was not adopted on the other side of the Atlantic. There, the open type of coach was preferred from the beginning and it is only now that this principle is also becoming standard in Great Britain.

Satisfactory as the compartment coach is it has disadvantages:

(a) Although maximum seating is provided the accommodation is not good for those who have to stand.
(b) Hinged doors must be opened and (hopefully) shut by passengers. If they are not shut there is delay whilst station staff do so.
(c) As passengers cannot circulate through the train they will be selective in the compartment they choose which can lengthen station stops.
(d) With doors under the control of passengers they are tempted to board and alight whilst the train is in motion, which is not in the interests of safety. Furthermore, the outward opening hinged doors are liable to strike other passengers standing on the platform.
(e) With the increase in public misconduct a small self-contained compartment gives the miscreants greater scope. There is no possibility of patrol by railway staff and there is a growing security risk, particularly for female travellers.

A breakaway from the conventional compartment stock on suburban services came with the abolition of the internal partitions and the provision of a centre gangway. Certainly this reduced the number of seats but it gave more satisfactory standing space and thereby helped to overcome the disadvantages listed above except (b) and (d). On the branch lines and on other services where traffic is not as heavy it has been possible to dispense with some of the doors but by and large the basic design features of this second generation of stock have kept fairly standard. In recent years, however, main line suburban stock has undergone yet another change with features much closer to those of the rapid transit systems already described. The biggest impact on design is the provision of power operated sliding doors which must influence the internal arrangements. This latest class, however, does overcome all of the disadvantages (a) to (d) (at the expense of some seats) and the problem at (e) has been mollified as much as carriage design alone can do.

Much was said about the virtues of double deck buses but little reference has so far been made to double deck trains although the principle is equally valid. The difficulty lies in the loading gauge to which reference was made at the outset. In Great Britain the loading gauge is restrictive in comparison with most other national railway systems. An experimental double deck suburban train has been tried but the cramped conditions made passenger circulation difficult when traffic was heavy which tended to delay boarding and alighting with consequent extended station stops. Overseas, this is not necessarily the case. It is ironic that whilst the UK with its greater highway clearances and double deck buses, cannot accommodate double deck trains, whilst in Europe, North America and elsewhere, where double deck buses are the exception rather than the rule, double deck suburban railway coaches are coming into more extensive use.

11
Operational Control

Introduction

All that has been said so far relates to the infrastructure, equipment, functions and professions which collectively form the ingredients of a passenger transport system. Without such hardware and expertise there could be no foundation and no direction or guidance. But the engineers, accountants, planners and staff and commercial managers, important as they may be, cannot alone actually make the thing tick. They may lay down the framework, give guidance and provide the wherewithal. There is, however, another band of people at ground floor level, being the controllers and supervisors under an operating manager, who are in direct day to day control and in whose success or otherwise the efficiency of the undertaking will be judged. They work at or are attached to garages, depots or similar establishments, are responsible for implementing the procedures and directives imposed upon them by their headquarters organisation and they must transmit those orders to the platform staff. If things go wrong (and they do sometimes) it is for them to take the immediate remedial measures. If the results of their endeavours are not satisfactory then the situation catches the public eye. Passengers complain if the service is disrupted; staff complain if they are asked to do something a little more onerous than they expected and it is the supervisors on the road and in the garages who are on the spot to collect these reactions which in any case can only result from circumstances over which they have had little or no control. Surely, then, this is the 'heart' of the business.

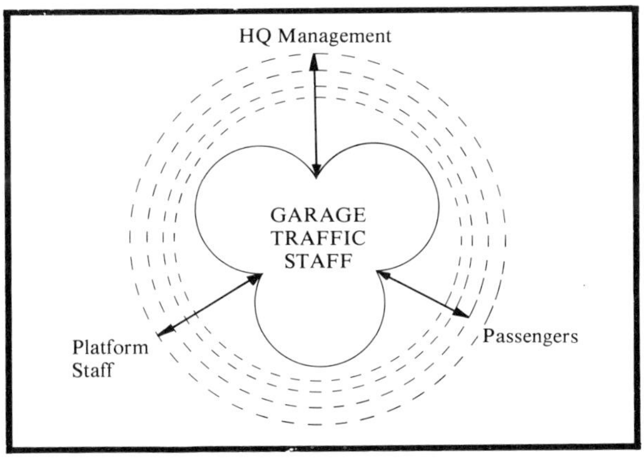

The supervisors and other garage staff are the links between management/administration, platform staff and customers and the control rooms and garage offices are the places where the pulse beats and is kept even.

This is the level where theory and the written directives become practical reality. Services have to be maintained, emergencies have to be dealt with, shop stewards have to be consulted, platform staff have to be solicited (agreements regarding duty changes might preclude the right to give a direct order) and quick decisions have to be made. There are occasions when many things happen at once. The conflicting demands of the passengers and the staff have to be reconciled with the rules of the job and resources are often limited. If, therefore, there is a level where experience counts, then this is it and no busman can really regard himself as having graduated until he has served for a year or two in these various traffic supervisory roles. This chapter deals with this day to day work.

Bus Control and Supervision

Speed Schedules

The time allowances contained in the scheduled vehicle runnings (and this means both the average speed of the service and the amount of layover time at the terminal) have a marked effect on the standard of timekeeping and the ability to rectify late running. Unfortunately, what is advantageous during periods of heavy vehicular traffic has the opposite effect when the roads are clear as not enough running time in the peaks is just as detrimental to good timekeeping as is too much running time in the slack. The only difference is that in one instance buses run late and in the other they run early and the latter is something which should never, ever be condoned. This leads into the subject of determination of average speeds which is a prerequisite for time schedule compilation as was seen in Chapter 6.

It was acknowledged in Chapter 6 that trade unions like to play a significant role in schedule preparation and speed schedules, service by service, do not escape their interest. In the schedules exercise an average speed of 12mph was set but in practice it will vary according to circumstances and for some routes, 12mph might prove to be a little fast. However, the relevance in this context is that it is at local superintendent level that time tests will be conducted and agreed with representatives of the platform staff. To ameliorate late running in the peaks a popular device is to introduce differential running times, that is, varying average speeds according to the time of day and day of week. Certainly this helps but to express a personal opinion, the writer is against such a practice for the following reasons:

(a) The degree of congestion is not necessarily consistent day by day and it is not always the same journeys which are affected. Additional running time cannot therefore be applied with any precision.
(b) When congestion is really bad the few minutes extra per trip which might be given will still not be realistic and to allocate more would produce an unnecessarily unattractive timetable bearing in mind that some of the time lost will hopefully be made up en route anyway.
(c) It was said in Chapter 6 that regular repetitive timings are the ideal as they can be more easily remembered by passengers. With differential running times this is not possible and irregular headways must result.

The view of the author is that any allowances for late running should be built not into running time but into additional layover or recovery time at terminals. By this means buses do at least have a better chance of making the return journey according to schedule without the disadvantages outlined at (a), (b) and (c). However, the industry is not unanimous on this point.

What there can be no argument about, and this should be clear from Chapter 6, is that if additional running time has to be provided, even if it is only an extra minute, it could have a profound effect on schedules and hence costs. If existing schedules are efficient then there is likely to be no slack in which to accommodate anything extra. If more running time is to be provided then it can only mean more vehicles and more staff with poor utilisation. It is part of the job of the local chief inspector, superintendent or whoever to agree running times with the platform staff and a lot depends on the success of his endeavours.

The Bus Control Office

The control inspector is responsible for the maintenance of scheduled services. If everything is running and running on time then his work is not particularly difficult but with a large and complex network this is seldom the case. It depends on physical factors whether, in fact, there is a separate control organisation at all. In the smaller provincial towns, for example, with a rural hinterland the degree of congestion and late running and the number of untoward incidents might not be very great and certainly nothing that could not be dealt with by the output staff at the garage and the general duty inspectors on the road. On the other hand, the job of keeping the service going is, in some areas, of sufficient magnitude in its own right to justify a separate organisation for the purpose.

The most sophisticated method of control is that which was touched upon in Chapter 2 in connection with urban traffic control. Remember the references which were made to closed circuit television and the possible linkage with bus managements. This, of course, is quite practicable. Bus controllers are able to have their own set of television screens and be provided with the same traffic information as is available to the highway authority or police responsible for general vehicle movement. Coupled with this a two-way radio system enables controllers to make contact with drivers on the road and possibly with mobile inspectors as well. Other equipment is available (although not widely used) which gives a visual indication of the times which buses pass certain points and this type of control office also invariably has direct lines to the emergency services, being police, ambulance and fire. This, then, is the ultimate in control equipment. It is costly to install but if its potential is properly exploited it is invaluable in maintaining the best possible services where traffic conditions are difficult. The two-way element in the use of radio is important and if the system is to be successful, drivers must co-operate and keep control properly informed of the changing road conditions. Any resistance on the part of trade unions as was witnessed with tachographs on the road haulage side could, therefore, render the whole concept ineffective. This, however, would be a particularly ill-conceived and short-sighted approach as a better standard of service is in the interests of everybody, including the staff, and the availability of radio with which the driver is able to summon the police quickly in the event of an emergency gives him added security.

Radio has particular significance in the case of the dial-a-bus service as referred to in Chapters 5 and 7. Indeed, this method of operation could not function without it as the whole concept of dial-a-bus is to pick-up passengers where they are and take them to where they want to go; that is, subject to physical practicalities and within a defined area. To summon a bus, passengers telephone the control office from where the driver on the road is contacted.

Control work really comes into its own when buses are either missing or running late due to heavy traffic, breakdown, accident, sickness, non-availability of staff or any of the many other causes which might prevent the bus from getting through. Corrective measures include on the spot intructions to staff to turn short in order to regain lost time, working through but covering their second spell of duty, working through to a different destination on another service, arranging for substitute vehicles, transferring passengers to other services and any other emergency arrangements which might have to be made. Liaison is necessary with the staff or duties clerk and the engineering staff at the garage if there are revised but important changes in staff or vehicle requirements. Bigger problems arise, of course, when these additional resources are not available and very often they are not.

It is because of the control aspect that there tends to be a divergence of views on the merits of cross-town services in urban areas. What were seen as advantages in this type of route in Chapter 5 are likely to be viewed in a different way by the local operators whose job it is to maintain service. If buses come into town and layover prior to return to the place from whence they came then there is a chance to minimise the effects of traffic delays but if they are on a through cross-town service there is no such possibility and any dislocation experienced on one side of the town is likely to be projected through to the other. To give a recovery allowance in the centre on a through service would be irritating to passengers and would defeat the object of providing such a facility as well as having to find more stands in what is likely to be a very congested area.

Inspectors' Duties

Bus operation is centred around the schedules as described in Chapter 6. Examples of bus runnings identified by running numbers were appended as also was a specimen duty schedule. The crew will be in possession of a copy of the actual duty being worked and a copy of the bus running will remain on the vehicle for the entire day, being collected from the garage office by the first driver and handed in by the last driver. The scheduled working of the bus is, therefore, known by the crew and any inspector who may care to board and inspect its running plate. Inspectors will be in possession of timetables but if a road inspector is stationed at a roadside control point which is passed by a large number of buses, perhaps on different services, a 'straightdown' is desirable. This is, in effect, a list of departures in chronological order showing route number, running number and destination. Many inspectors compile this information for themselves from the main schedule but it is a laborious task and with the advent of computers it should be possible to obtain this information quite easily by this means. What is also of material assistance to road inspectors is the display of the running number outside the vehicle. In this way each bus can be readily identified without the need to board but surprisingly few undertakings adopt this practice.

Then there is the unscheduled bus and coach work, always of course within the limits of available resources and any provisions of the road service licence. This is work which is arranged locally, usually on inspector's instructions, according to demand, probably in the form of duplication and covered by either spare staff, overtime or rest day working. Once on the road, however, these vehicles are subject to the same control as are the regular scheduled services. In fact they must have more attention as to avoid waste they need to be curtailed or withdrawn as soon as they are no longer required.

The uniformed road inspector is a general supervisor with many different responsibilities. He is the eyes and the ears of the undertaking and he performs a key public relations role. His observations are important and it is through his reports that management might first hear of changing demands, surplus accommodation, inadequacies and any new circumstances which might affect future traffic patterns. There may be different grades of inspector undertaking different types of work, the two basic groups being those who are basically static at a roadside control point and the roving inspector on ticket checking duties and dealing with anything else which presents itself at the time. Duties might be arranged to do part and part, perhaps a little bit of control work at the busier times but what is important is that ticket checking contains an element of surprise. For this reason there should be no pre-determined schedule of buses to be checked. It should be left to the inspector's discretion and his daily checking sheet will contain a record of the work done. It is customary for checking sheets to show in respect of all vehicles checked the route, running and vehicle numbers, place and time boarded and alighted, number of passengers on the bus and any irregularities found for subsequent processing by a chief inspector or some other appropriately senior official through the disciplinary procedure. If the offence is a serious one, the driver or conductor concerned might wish to be accompanied at a hearing by a union official and it is likely that the inspector would need to be available to give evidence if required. Under these circumstances, a decision, which might range from a warning to suspension or discharge is likely to be subject to the right of appeal to more senior management. The arrangements might be that the official conducting the first interview has limited powers and if he considers that the gravity of the charge warrants more than he is empowered to award, he would himself refer the matter to higher authority.

Road inspectors are often equipped with a portable two-way radio in a similar way to police constables. This is a valuable aid for road control purposes and some undertakings adopt this practice as a cheaper alternative to equipping all of the vehicles in this way. Although in urban areas most inspectors are on foot, it is impossible to cover a wide rural area in this way, particularly if the services are infrequent. For coverage of territory of this type there is advantage in making inspectors more mobile by the allocation of a small van or car. Unless, however, they travel in pairs, an inspector must find his own way back to his vehicle which he left to board and check a bus. The system of employing a squad of travelling inspectors to check buses over a wide area is not unknown. It has the added advantage that these inspectors are more likely to be strangers to bus crews. Some local officials are inclined to mix with platform staff on rather familiar terms and this arrangement, rather like the village policeman, does not create the best atmosphere in which to enforce discipline.

One other grade of supervisor employed by some undertakings to considerable advantage is the plain clothes inspector. The system is only practicable in a large organisation as, if they are to be effective, they must remain completely unknown to the staff. They can be afforded no privileges. They must take their turn in the queue to board and they must pay their fare. But this, of course, is an essential part of the exercise as they are then in a good position to check the re-issue of dead tickets, tickets issued under value and all other operating irregularities. Plain clothes inspectors cannot undertake road control work but they are sometimes useful in checking on any suspected licensing infringements of other (probably independent) undertakings such as by getting a ride on a bus over a section where the operator is prohibited from carrying local traffic.

Accident Procedure

An accident to a bus in service generally takes the form of a collision with another vehicle or pedestrian or a fall within the bus itself. It does not necessarily involve serious personal injury or, indeed, any injury at all but there is usually a delay factor and often a subsequent claim for damages. It is important, therefore, that management is in possession of the full facts and that is why every incident has to be reported in considerable detail. It is, of course, the bus crew that is immediately on the spot and the first steps following an accident must be taken by them. It is only by coincidence if an official happens to be present although if the vehicle is fitted with radio one can be quickly summoned, as can the emergency services. Should a lengthy delay be expected, the onus is on the driver or conductor to transfer passengers to another bus, assuming that one is available and to contact the bus controller for further instructions.

In view of the subsequent importance of the availability of complete and accurate information, staff should not only be properly versed in the procedure to be followed but also provided with a printed form, the completion of which will ensure that no detail has been omitted. This form will contain provision for at least a description of what happened with a diagram if appropriate, particulars of injuries and/or damage to property, insurance details of other vehicles involved, names and addresses of people concerned and witnesses as well as date, time, place, etc. Whilst the police and the fire and ambulance services will look after their own particular responsibilities, it is incumbent upon the operator not only to restore normal service as quickly as possible but also, if necessary, to remove any of its vehicles if they are disabled. Many of the larger undertakings have their own vehicle recovery service, but it is legal for the vehicle concerned to be towed away by another PSV.

Staff Coverage

This is about the allocation of drivers and conductors to buses. It is a task which has to be done at the local operating garages and may be undertaken by depot inspectors or by a special duties clerk. Once again it is necessary to refer back to Chapter 6 which dealt with schedule compilation and which produced a specimen duty schedule and duty roster. If the system which was suggested is followed then the duties clerk at the garage will have played no part in the preparation of the schedules. He will have received the duties and the roster as a finished job and all he has to do is to fit names to it. So far so good and if he has got sufficient names to set against the roster and having so allocated the staff they do not go sick or absent, then the job is done. But that is not always the case.

The specimen roster contained in Chapter 6 had 27 lines. Therefore, at least 27 drivers (or drivers plus conductors) are required. It is a question of fitting names to the lines and then to drop them down one line each week in order that they rotate through all of the early and late shifts with their different rest days. It was noted at the time that this is something with which the staff show a particular interest. They expect to be consulted when the schedules are prepared and they look for similar treatment with day to day allocation at garage level. This means, however, that there are many different systems in operation. An interesting point is that in some countries, the United States being one and Israel another, it is common practice for staff not to rotate through the schedule but to select in order of seniority their line on the roster and keep to it for the life of the schedule. This means that they work precisely the same journeys each week, be they early or late and take the same rest days. Operationally, there is merit in this as the driver becomes thoroughly accustomed to his particular duty and probably also to his passengers and the service becomes more personal. To the staff, the more senior they are, the wider is their choice. They might, for example, prefer a line which has fairly light duties. On the other hand, they might like long spreadovers which have low work content but high penalty payments. The more common British practice, however, if for staff to drop down one line each week. If this system is adopted, a duty list must be prepared week by week which fits names to lines on the roster and changes accordingly. It might, however, involve more than 27 drivers (to quote the example). Even if there is no lateness and absence without leave, there is always holidays and sickness to be covered, which necessitates spare staff. It might be reasonable, therefore, to add, say another three drivers to make 30 in all, the bottom three lines being to instructions, that is, to work as allocated locally by the garage duty clerk.

The real problem with staff coverage arises when not only is there insufficient staff to carry spares but insufficient to cover even the basic scheduled requirements, or, in other words, there are blanks on the duty list. This means that scheduled duties have to be covered by overtime and rest day working as well as taking care of any unscheduled requirements. It is here, of course, that the drivers' hours regulations really aggravate the issue and their sheer complexity does nothing to assist the duties clerk in his arduous task of covering all of the bits and pieces of duties which remain unstaffed. If they cannot be covered, then the buses must come out of service. Some journeys are missed more easily than are others. One bus might have a driver but no conductor, another has a conductor but no driver. Rapid adjustments have to be made, assuming always that the staff are willing and prepared to cooperate. This is the responsibility of the official in charge of output who will also issue ticket machines, running plates and any other necessary items of equipment. At the end of the day a complete record must be made of what everybody has worked if the right money is subsequently to appear in their respective pay packets.

Under the system described, if the payrolls officer had a copy of the duty roster and weekly duty list, he would know what every man was entitled to be paid assuming that he worked his schedule job. It might be convenient, therefore, and this practice is adopted by some undertakings, for the garage officials to advise the payrolls department only of any variations to rostered duties and positive advice would have to be given only in respect of spare staff who are not rostered for any specific work. The alternative is for garage officials to supply information is respect of the entire workforce for pay purposes. In a small undertaking they might even prepare the payroll themselves but the work is more suitable for a specialised department. It is possible, however, that the garage staff might be required to make up the packets and pay out.

One further point on staff coverage is the economics of maintaining a full complement of staff even if it is possible to do so. The cost of a driver (or conductor) is rather more than his weekly pay as the following items must be borne in respect of each employee to the extent applicable:

Employer's contribution to national insurance.
Employer's contribution to superannuation.
Allowance for paid holidays.
Allowance for paid sickness.
Allowance for any staff amenities.
Uniform
Cost of staff administration.

It is a question of balancing this cost against the premium payments for a limited amount of overtime and rest day working to cover vacancies. It could be that a small shortage could be financially beneficial and could also be preferred by the staff as it gives them the chance of extra work and hence extra pay which would not otherwise be available. A policy, however, which relies to a small extent on voluntary overtime does make the system more vulnerable in the event of industrial action.

Receipt and Safe Custody of Cash

Security

Remember from Chapter 9 that the use of buses and trains involves payment, usually at the time of travel. Many hundreds of thousands of separate financial transactions, therefore, take place daily. Each one involves the collection of a small amount of cash for which a receipt (in the form of a ticket) is normally given. Straight away, therefore, there is a big security question. In this context, however, security is not interpreted as drivers and conductors receiving and accounting for the proper fares. That aspect was dealt with in Chapter 9 and in the earlier part of this chapter which covered the duties of inspectors. At this stage it is assumed that the correct fares have been paid, proper tickets have been issued and the money is in the possession of the platform staff. Adequate facilities must, therefore, be available for one-man drivers, conductors and conductor/guards of pay trains on the railway to dispose of that cash with safeguards for both the undertaking and themselves. Having got thus far, those responsible for collecting the money on behalf of management must also have facilities and safeguards and bulk cash must in turn be disposed of into the banking system. That is what security is all about.

Paying-in

Cash offices need to be placed at strategic points where it is convenient for platform staff to finish duty. These paying-in points are often but not necessarily a part of the garage traffic office. In order to avoid the need for staff to carry unnecessarily large amounts of money around with them, some undertakings might consider it reasonable to allow them to pay in money part way through their duty as well as at the end if they happen to be in the vicinity of a paying-in point. In any case, there must be a pay-in at the end of the duty and it follows that the process could take place at almost any time of the day or night. What is quite clear is that much of the paying-in will take place outside normal office hours, which is traditionally a middle shift. The question arises, therefore, whether depot inspectors, garage cash clerks or whatever they might be designated be on duty throughout the traffic day or should their numbers be fewer and confined to normal office working or should, indeed, they accept cash direct from drivers and conductors at all. If the latter alternatives are adopted it is certainly cheaper in terms of salaries of garage officials but some method is necessary for staff to pay-in without an official in attendance. This can be overcome by putting the cash and completed waybill into a special bag and depositing it into a drop safe or night safe as it is sometimes called. The contents of these bags are then counted the following day. Whilst, however, this overcomes the shift problems of the cash clerks, the disadvantage of this system is that the driver or conductor is not present when the money is checked and he is not therefore available for challenge should there be a shortage. This can lead to disputes which can only partially be resolved by the bags being opened and the contents counted in the presence of a second official as a witness or, what might be preferable to staff, one of their own representatives. The system is not ideal and machine manufacturers are developing systems which enable staff to deposit their money and have it counted with the amount being indicated to them. If they are satisfied they can then release it for deposit in a secure place and at the same time receive an appropriate receipt. Suitable records are also made for the garage staff to check susbsequently the amount paid in by each person against the respective waybills.

Fareboxes

All that has been said so far relates to cash collected in exchange for the issue of serially numbered tickets for which there is a record. There is a cross-check and each stage is subject to audit. This is not the case, however, with the farebox type of fare collection system as was described in Chapter 9. Here it will be recalled money is deposited by passengers into a box which can only be released (by the driver) into a locked vault. Where flat fares or zone fares are applied as in the United States, no ticket is necessary. For graduated fares, a ticket must be issued if there is to be any check on overriding and the system marketed by Control Systems Limited, for example, does combine the issue of a ticket with a farebox. However, there is no adequate direct cross-check as such and in any case the cash contents at the end of the day will have been received by several different drivers. In short, buses arrive at the garage on run-in with full boxes but with no record (or certainly no adequate record for which staff could be held to account) of how much has been put in. This presents no problem as far as the driver is concerned. The most he will do is take the locked vault to the cash office. He might not even do that, but the fact remains that by some means the locked vaults must be conveyed from the bus to the cash counting centre. Once inside they will be opened and the contents counted, probably by emptying into the receptacle of a coin-counting and sorting machine. The weakness lies in the fact that in the absence of records, the staff of the cash office are not subject to check and temptation is put in their way.

Some of the larger undertakings in the United States go to great lengths to reduce this risk and consequent theft and thereby protect their interests. Examples are a bank of machines at a centralised counting house attended by several cash counting officials who are required to change from their outdoor clothes on the premises into special pocketless overalls and pass through a metal detector with the window of the chief cashier's office (fitted with one-way glass) overlooking the counting area and all under the watchful eyes of armed guards. Still, of course, there is no positive check, only every possible discouragement. Perhaps the most ambitious method adopted in the United States is the emptying of farebox vaults by vacuum whilst in situ on the bus. With this system a large pipe links the base of the farebox with the receiving end of a coin counting and sorting machine and the contents are counted with the minimum of human contact. Nevertheless, there is still a point where unscrupulous hands might find their way into the hopper of the counting machine. The ideal, of course, is for this to be impossible until the coins have passed through the apparatus and are registered, after which it does not matter if they are accessible as there is a cross-check and the cash counting staff can be held responsible for the money recorded. The difficulty is that access is necessary at the point of entry into and also within the counting mechanism as should the machinery jam, the blockage must be attended to by hand. The cause is likely to be the presence of bent coins and other extraneous material placed in the fareboxes which must be removed but if the rubbish can be extracted then so also can the genuine articles.

To this extent, therefore, there is a degree of weakness in the system which brings in locked boxes of money without any record of what the contents should be. On the other hand, this method of fare collection has been developed largely for security reasons, but on the road and not in the garage. In many parts of the United States and particularly in certain neighbourhoods of the larger towns on the eastern side, it is quite unsafe for staff (or passengers) to carry money. They cannot now even have provision for a float for the purpose of giving change as drivers have been killed through armed robbery. The solution is a locked vault which is accessible (by orthodox means) only by authorised garage staff. The security aspect of the farebox method of fare collection is, therefore, very real. It also has considerable advantages in service in terms of speed and this is something which was considered in Chapter 9. If the farebox method is to be introduced, and there is much to commend it, particularly as it can be linked to a system of ticket issue, it is likely to be advantageous to count all of the cash in a centralised counting house. An exception would be if the vacuum method of emptying was used as this is done in the garage. Otherwise, it might be economic to convey the vaults in vans between the garages and a single counting house. Whilst transport involves cost, there then needs to be only one set of sophisticated counting equipment and security arrangements.

Retention and Disposal of Cash

Once an undertaking has accepted the cash from its platform staff it must be safely stored until such time as it can be banked, either on the following day or as soon as possible thereafter. This calls for the provision of an adequate safe or strong room in garage offices or wherever the money is paid in and proper defined procedures which determine responsibilities of the staff concerned. Disposal of cash to the bank is often entrusted to an outside contractor who specialises in this type of work. It could, of course, be undertaken internally, possibly by the use of a spare bus and driver subject to the availability of suitable escorts. What tends to be to some extent unique is that money collected for bus rides usually contains a high percentage of small value coins. With the farebox system this is even more so as passengers will be tendering the exact fare. Even quite a small undertaking can produce several tons of copper and silver coinage each day and this is not necessarily popular with banks. Suitable arrangements must, therefore, be negotiated and the question of bank charges will arise. An alternative method which could to some extent ease the banking problem imposed by bulk coinage is to sell prepaid tickets and tokens.

Prepaid Tickets and Tokens

The issue of prepaid tickets (which includes season and 'anywhere' type tickets) is primarily a commercial consideration and as such has been mentioned in Chapter 7. But the subject does also impinge on security. If a passenger is in possession of a prepaid ticket, be it valid for one ride or a multi-journey type, the driver may cancel part of it, the passenger could insert it in a machine to do the same thing or, if it is an unrestricted pass, the driver would merely inspect it. The important point in this context is that no money changes hands and the amount of cash for which the driver or conductor is responsible is reduced accordingly. If tokens are used, then the platform staff receive them in lieu of the national currency but their intrinsic value is not quite the same. They are paid-in in the same way as other coins, they can be used in fareboxes and (assuming that they are made of metal) be sorted and counted through the normal machines. They do not, however, have to be banked but merely returned to the selling points for reissue. To this extent, therefore, the use of prepaid tickets or tokens considerably lessens the security risks. In reducing one problem, however, it creates another. Sales points become necessary, the economics of which have been considered in Chapter 7. But they must be conveniently sited for easy purchase and if a sales counter is not practicable an alternative is to install a vending machine. But herein lies a security risk. At best the machine has to be replenished and emptied of cash and to do this in a public place is not ideal but at worst, is liable to be a target for vandalism and at the extreme the contents ransacked. This naturally leads into another aspect of security; protection from vandalism.

Vandalism

So commonplace has the habit of wilful and wanton destruction of other peoples' property become, that the Vandals, those people who in the 4th and 5th centuries ravaged the area around the western Mediterranean, have become immortalised with their name now accepted by general consent as a household term used to describe the malicious practices undertaken by some members of the community today. Public property in public places is a common target for their activities. Public transport is no exception and the majority suffers at the hands of a minority. What has been rampant in the United States for a number of years is now spreading eastwards across the Atlantic and is already making its mark on the British public transport system. Buses and trains and the crews who man them are targets for attack, particularly in the late evening. Payment of fares is refused, behaviour is obscene, vehicles are damaged, often delayed and sometimes even destroyed. Staff are injured and instances of industrial action in the form of refusal to operate last journeys are growing. It is not the job of bus or railway managements to cure this social malaise, they can only live with it; but in so doing it does to some extent influence the way in which they run their services and probably it will do more so as time passes. The subject is for further discussion in Chapter 12. As it is, vehicles, and particularly the seats, have to be designed with this in mind, publicity often cannot be maintained at bus stops, costly aids to deter and detect are being introduced, particularly radio but also even television cameras with recording video tape. Railway stations unmanned as a result of the pay train system are becoming derelict shells. Even signals are being tampered with. Those in charge of public transport have always had to plan for the travel requirements of their passengers; they now also have to plan how to minimise the effects of wilful destruction inflicted by a few of those passengers. It is now a part of the operating scene.

Lost Property

The necessity to handle lost property is one of the minor irritants of all passenger transport undertakings. Whilst operators would wish to give every consideration to their customers, the careless act of leaving belongings on a bus or train does have a strong nuisance value and not only to the person who suffers the loss. Lost property has to be taken into custody by conductors, guards, cleaners or whoever might have the job of searching the vehicles. It has to be conveyed to a supervisor, duly registered and forwarded to a lost property centre. If it is not claimed it has to be disposed of. Enquiries have to be dealt with. All of this involves administration and this means expense. It puts additional work on to staff who must adhere to a strict procedure. Valuable items involve greater responsibility and temptation. If staff fail to observe the lost property regulations there is trouble and although there can be no excuse, it does seem a little unfortunate when a breach of this kind which involves disciplinary action would never have happened in the first place but for somebody else's negligence. As far as buses and coaches (public service vehicles) in Great Britain are concerned, the procedure to be followed is covered by law.

12
The Future

A Projection from the Past

This book began with a brief review of the past. That was a straightforward exercise because the facts were known. The salient features were discussed in the hope that the reader might thereby get a clearer reason why things are done in the way that they are today. The thought was expressed in the very first paragraph that by studying this process of evolution a trend might be established which could help to predict what might happen in the future. If this chapter was being written in 1960 then, with the benefit of hindsight, it could have been predicted that buses would get larger, their engines would move from the front to the back whilst the entrances would move from the back to the front. A lot more one-man operation would appear, including double decks. There would, therefore, be greater productivity but also more staff militancy could be expected. Whilst a large number of officially recognised national stoppages were not to come, transport, like all other industries, was to suffer from localised industrial action. Some branches of transport were to be affected more in this way than the buses. The railway would be dislocated occasionally and thousands of people were destined to be delayed or stranded at airports from time to time as a result of labour troubles at home and abroad. In the air, aircraft were to get larger and a few were to travel at more than twice the speed of sound. Bus route patterns would not be changing much (the origins of some services can still be traced back to the horse tram era). Many timetables would be reduced in frequency and numerous services, particularly in rural areas, were to disappear altogether. But there were to be substantial reorganisations, changes of direction and changes of control. A reorganisation of local government was to be accompanied by a certain devolution of power with much tighter financial and hence policy control of local road and rail transport in the hands of county councils. This responsibility was to include authority to subsidise and different patterns of service were to appear, county by county, according to the attitude of each towards public transport and the amount of money that they would be prepared to spend which would affect indirectly the resultant level of fares and hence passengers carried. Certain inter-city trains were to get into the 125mph category but local services were to do little more than partly fade away except in certain conurbations where, with financial aid, some lines were to be resuscitated. Also two new tube lines would appear in London and a new rapid transit system in Newcastle would come into operation. In Great Britain steam traction was to totally disappear with a changeover to diesel amid certain misgivings about reliance on imported fuel although Britain was destined to develop its own oil resources. Even so, in due course a few diesel trains would temporarily cease to run due to an oil crisis as a result of political instability in the Middle East. At the same time there was to be a sizeable electrification programme.

If these few brief notes had been written in 1960 they would have given some idea of at least a few of the things which were to happen in the ensuing 20 years. A lot has been accomplished and there have been many changes. On the other hand, to the man in the street it could be said that there might not be very much noticeable effect except for the cost of living which includes rising fares and, indeed spiralling wages. These circumstances have made their mark on bus and train travel which in some cases has become prohibitively expensive and the counter attractions of motoring and television have tended to reduce the interest in public transport except for essential journeys. This factor is very important: public habits and preferences have changed and with it travel patterns and the use of public transport. Many people are now able to seek the convenience of their own private cars with the result that the use made of public transport for local journeys, particularly for pleasure purposes, has fallen dramatically whilst the congestion and parking problems being created by private cars is becoming intolerable.

If the trends of the past are projected forward like lines on a graph the result becomes illogical. Apart from the possibility of more use of articulated vehicles, it is difficult to see how buses can get bigger, particularly with one-man operation. Trains will no doubt get a little faster and a few more local services might reappear. Road passenger transport would no longer be required as if the trend is followed, the last customer will have completed his journey. They will instead all be in their cars which will not be able to move anyway, at least in urban areas, because there will be too many of them in the available road space. There would, therefore, be no need for wage claims to price the buses out of business or for militancy to lower the quality of the service as the demand would have disappeared. But more than that — the immediate past has covered an era in which oil has been readily available at a reasonable price. The new energy situation could alter things completely. Something more than a simple progression is therefore necessary if there is to be an intelligent assessment of what is to come. Technology and politics — things which cannot be included on a straight projection of trends — have a commanding influence on the future.

Future Demand

The demand for public transport is not necessarily falling. Airline traffic is buoyant as is that of the short sea ferries. Inter-city railway trains have good loadings and long distance scheduled coach services as well as excursions and tours are not without their clientele. It is the medium and shorter distance bus and train services, particularly in rural areas, which have suffered. For these journeys most people prefer to use their own private cars, which suggests that patronage of public transport is at risk in cases where private transport is a feasible alternative. But for some people, private transport will never be an option, being precluded by age or physical condition. Regardless of the popularity of the private car, therefore, it is inevitable that a hardcore will remain in need of the public services and who will suffer hardship if they are not provided. This, of course, assumes that there will still be the same demand to move around. Optional travel must surely remain. People will still wish to visit their relatives and friends and to change their environment in their hours of leisure but the private car is a strong competitor for journeys of that kind. Whether there will always be the same need for journeys to work and for shopping is not quite as predictable. Depending on developments in other spheres of activity, the pattern of life could change dramatically just as television has emaciated the cinema queues of 30 years ago. It is conceivable, therefore, that there might not be the same need or even desire for mobility as there is today.

Environmental and Social Issues

Environmental and social aspects have already been examined in previous chapters. The impact of the private car with its insatiable demand for more roads, wider roads and faster roads along with its noise and pollution of the air is a particularly sensitive issue. There is no shortage of opinion and advice on this matter from the environmentalists but, nevertheless, they, like other people, enjoy the convenience which the car provides. What this can only mean is that private transport is a bad thing for everybody except them. Be that as it may, it is abundantly clear that people will continue to want cars and as was said in Chapter 2, no government is going to suffer the unpopularity which restraints would undoubtedly bring without some compelling reason, able to be seen and generally understood. It is likely, therefore, that local buses and trains and particularly the lesser used branch lines will continue to run into the red if indeed they run at all. Nevertheless, as at least a limited demand is likely to remain then, other things being equal (but they might not be), urban and rural transport could become still more of a social service. It seems inevitable, therefore, that such provision will remain a political issue and, in the UK, a controversial one at that. Financial support means public expenditure for which there are competing demands. Surely there must be a limit to the amount of money which can be made available through rates and taxes, particularly for non-essential purposes such as concessional travel for the elderly, although if the mid-1970s is anything to go by there could be excuse for doubting even that. The allocation of public money raises the question of priorities which is not something that transport managements will have to decide or a subject which is appropriate for further discussion here. But government decisions, whatever they might be, will have a profound effect on managements who must continue to keep the sectional interests of their own particular industry to the fore when such matters are considered. The UK is already behind the rest of Europe in giving public support to public transport. In some other European countries the degree of subsidy for local transport tends to be much greater and is more of an accepted way of life unaccompanied by reactions from the press and elsewhere which would result in this country. Where subsidies are provided better facilities result. At the same time, co-ordination might be a little more forthright without what to some people is the strange British practice of allowing separate publicly owned undertakings to weaken themselves by competing for the same traffic. With EEC influence growing stronger, there could be a pointer here as to the way things might go. But custom and practice dies hard. With the present day hierarchy the members of which were reared in true commercial style at a time when buses were run on a shoestring but nevertheless giving a good service at no cost to the community other than reasonable fares, it is not easy to change in such a fundamental way. The next generation of management will need no such adaption. The social concept will not be strange to them and this could be yet one further reason why what is at present a still relatively new phenomenon will in the future become even in Great Britain more naturally an established and generally accepted fact of everyday life.

Still on the social plane is the malaise referred to in Chapters 5 and 11 — violence and the destruction of property, which is now rampant. There is a grave danger that this will escalate in the future and this increase will have its effect on the pattern of demand for public transport in the years to come. In some areas people will be in fear of walking the streets; they certainly will not use segregated pedestrian ways except at times when there is safety in numbers, nor will they stand at lonely bus stops or on platforms of unattended railway stations. Potential riders, could, therefore, be confined to those who the bus and train crews will not be prepared to carry. Seats in buses will have to be the uncomfortable fibreglass variety, drivers will not be able to have possession of money, which means only fareboxes or pre-paid tickets and they will need protection from passengers at least in the form of a screen and acceptance by passengers of an unattended upper deck will be unlikely.

It is inevitable that those who man the trains and the buses are in the front line against attack from the rougher members of the community. Train drivers are exposed in their cab to missiles hurled from overbridges and the effects of unauthorised lineside obstacles. Pay train guards and bus conductors suffer abuse and violence when they seek their rightful dues. Their situation is not an enviable one and they are incensed when they do not get the support of other passengers when they are attacked. Industrial action results and late night journeys fail to operate.

Maybe passengers do not always go to the assistance of bus crews because they in turn are displeased with the service (or lack of it) which has on occasions been meted out to them. Bus crews have been known to run early and leave people stranded, fail to stop when hailed, refuse passengers when seats are available, show misleading information on destination blinds, sit and smoke at the terminus and thereby pollute the atmosphere in the bus, depart late and when spoken to leave civility wanting. They will complain, rightly or wrongly that their standard of remuneration leaves something to be desired and when compared with their colleagues in other countries, they may have a point. It is accepted that driving a one-man bus, for example, is a responsible job but have they maintained the reliability, prestige and self-esteem generated by their grandfathers 50 years ago? If appearances and, in the case of some, standards are anything to go by, they have not, which again is sometimes in contrast with their colleagues overseas. However, it is not fair to censure only bus crews for changes in values in society. This is only leading on from what was said in Chapter 3, but outside Great Britain there is a much greater appreciation and acceptance of the fact that if employees are to prosper then their employing organisations must also prosper. No more real money can be got out of a machine than is put into it and the way ahead depends very much on whether organised labour ever accepts this fact of life. If it does not, then the service will suffer. Job satisfaction will continue to deteriorate and retention of staff will become yet more difficult. Falling standards will further discourage traffic and networks will contract. If these sort of circumstances persist there could be a trend towards automation, costly as it may be but justified if the alternative is disproportionately expensive and this would mean more fixed track systems. Of course, none of this may happen, one cannot tell the future with any degree of certainty. Of the students who read these lines, some will be bus crews. They will be seeking betterment. Some will reach supervisory and control status and others will become the managers of tomorrow. They will no doubt understand the points being made and are not likely to be contributing to this industrial disease. Not everybody is. But it is hoped that they will play their part in the difficult task of restoring pride in the service. This is surely one of the things which will have a profound effect on the years which lie ahead and whether those who provide urban and rural transport indeed have any future at all.

From the gloom and despondency which has been dispensed so far, students might be excused should they begin to doubt the wisdom of their choice of calling. But not to despair. It is to be hoped that the years to come prove the previous paragraph to be a timely warning rather than a justified prediction. It has already been said that some people will always need buses and trains but in meeting that need there is one other factor which is very topical to this chapter and which could change everybody's way of life. It is the energy situation.

The Energy Situation

There is now much talk of the forthcoming energy situation and there is really no doubt that the world's supply of oil will one day be exhausted — the only uncertainty is when. At present there is still plenty left and any shortages are politically inspired rather than caused by a lowering of natural stocks, and oil products remain freely available. The full benefits of Britain's own oil production is only now being realised and new sources may yet be discovered both at home and abroad. Commercial production has been geared to accessibility and fields regarded as uneconomic have not yet been exploited. Scarcity increases value which brings justification for working areas hitherto regarded as unviable. Under these circumstances, supplies could continue but at inflated prices. Without going into technical details, what might be a fair assumption for long term planning purposes is that oil will cease to be available for energy needs perhaps sometime in the first half of the next century. Clearly that date will be conditioned by the development of new technology to enable extraction from hitherto inaccessible places and the rate at which available stocks are used. This in turn depends upon the development of alternatives.

Much has already been written and doubtless much more remains to be said on substitutes for oil as a source of power. It is not appropriate here to include a technical treatise of the problems and prospects but once again the fundamentals might give an indication of things to come.

The obvious alternative to the diesel engine is of course electricity. This is a basic and easy assumption but one which raises a host of questions. The simple course for electric power lies in fixed track systems, the concept of which is far from new. In fact, as was said in Chapter 1, many such networks have now been abandoned and replaced by diesel buses. But the most important of such systems — the world's national main line railway undertakings — at present rely heavily on diesel powered locomotives. Even without new technology, therefore, change there must be. Likewise, some power stations burn oil to generate electricity but although coal can be and is similarly used and stocks are available, alternatives are being considered. What is important in this context, however, is not how electricity is produced in power stations but how it will be used for public and private transport.

Still with regard to the fundamentals, derv and petrol are commodities which can be carried around conveniently on the vehicle and the fuel tanks can be easily replenished. Not so with electricity which has to be fed from power stations via suitable conductors through to the motor on the vehicle; unless, of course it could be stored on the vehicle to permit free running independent of any power cables leading in from the outside supply source. But herein lies the problem. Again, battery vehicles are not new but their application is limited. They have been in use for local milk delivery purposes for a number of years and for this role their peformance is satisfactory. But heavy duty bus work is much more demanding. Good acceleration, a fast sustained speed and a range of about 150 miles at least before re-charge are parts of the specification, all with a high capacity vehicle. The volume and weight of a bank of conventional batteries necessary for this performance would leave very little accommodation for passengers and new technology is, therefore, indicated. Development of new techniques in the battery field is another story but to put it briefly, all that can be said at present is that progress is being made.

This, of course, has far reaching repercussions on private as well as public transport. Given that oil will be available for a few more years yet, the production of an acceptable battery car complete with rapid re-charging facilities remains a possibility. Depending on circumstances, however, the developing process might be overtaken by a restriction on oil supplies coupled with substantial increases in cost. For an optional use, the demand for the private car has remained remarkably inelastic. So far there seems to be no financial limit beyond which the private motorist will not go to keep his car on the road. But there surely must be a time when at least some of the motoring population will no longer be prepared to bear the continuous imposition of heavy surcharges. If this situation comes, therefore, at least a limited swing from private to public transport could be anticipated. For the same reasons, public transport undertakings would consider a move away from oil and at the present stage of development, fixed track systems readily lend themselves to this type of traction. Remember from Chapter 1 that the street tramway was abandoned partly because it was confined to its tracks and was considered to be unsatisfactory in heavy traffic. Rather than foresake electric traction the trolleybus came, even though it was far less flexible than the conventional bus and one reason why the mode was finally abandoned was that costs became high in comparison with diesel. Even though electrically powered systems are capital intensive, this trend might now be reversed with history once again repeating itself. If and when oil becomes a scarce commodity it is not inconceivable that parliament might step in with measures to conserve such stocks as are available. This could, for example, take the form of infrastructure grants or tax incentives for those undertakings prepared to develop electrically powered systems. If all this came to pass there would be a very real possibility that trams or trolleybuses might once again become a part of the British transport scene.

New Technology

For consideration now is what sort of systems are most likely to be developed. Conventional trams and trolleybuses would certainly meet the energy crisis as would monorails and light and heavy rapid transit. Monorails would no doubt find support from the armchair planners, some of whom seem to see a mystical built-in formula which makes this particular mode the obvious answer to all urban transport problems. Unfortunately, monorails are not blessed with this virtue as witness the number of systems now in commercial service. The classic example is at Wuppertal in West Germany where the physical layout happens to suit this type of transport. In this instance there is an elongated area of commercial, industrial and residential development astride a river valley with the course of the river forming a natural path for a monorail line. In terms of both capital cost and capacity it comes somewhere between a tramway and a rapid transit system and the characteristics of the monorail happen to be suitable, both physically and operationally for the Wupper Valley. But a situation such as this is not encountered frequently and as can be seen from the illustrations it is akin to the elevated railway in that it produces a visual intrusion.

The trolleybus has much to commend it as although technically a fixed track vehicle powered by electricity, it does not require steel rail. It is free running on a normal road surface which means that the system is less capital intensive than the trams and the vehicles are more manoeuvrable. Even past generations of trolleybuses carried a supplementary power unit in the form of batteries which enabled them to move short distances, albeit very slowly, free of any outside power supply. It is reasonable and logical thinking then that the next stage might be a vehicle which can travel under the wires along heavily used common sections of routes and then able to move on its own stored power into the suburbs and back, where it would again re-charge under the wires. That might take care of the more lightly trafficked outer ends. If towards the centre, the volume of traffic was such that there was more of a case for segregated light rapid transit systems, it is not beyond imagination that the trolleybus might be adapted even for this purpose. The specially constructed way, instead of consisting of steel track would instead be so designed to give linear constraint to a rubber tyred vehicle. If a system of this kind was developed to a state of acceptable operating performance it could combine the best of three worlds, being light rapid transit with its segregated right of way and hence high speed and capacity, the trolleybus with its need for electric power rather than oil and the conventional bus with its flexibility and minimal infrastructure requirements. Then, of course, there are the battery buses which might possess all of the attributes of diesel traction but they are still the subject of research.

At this stage of development, the following represents a summarised review of the possible options insofar as road (ie non-rail) vehicles are concerned:

Trolleybus
A proven system but inflexible with operational problems due to the need for overhead wires. Capital intensive and, at present levels, prices compare unfavourably with diesel buses although as far as the fuel element is concerned, this could change.

Hybrid Battery/Trolleybus
The hybrid would operate from overhead wires along part of the route whilst at the same time charging on board batteries which would become the source of power for the remainder of the journey. The vehicle would therefore need to accept twice the amount of current compared with the conventional trolleybus to allow for both running and charging batteries and the resultant rapid charging would shorten battery life. Costs are therefore likely to be high.

Other Types of Hybrid
Other combinations include a diesel/trolley and a diesel/battery electric. The diesel/trolley is a vehicle with duplicated motive power; in other words a trolleybus which also has a diesel engine and can therefore run 'under the wires' or as a normal diesel bus. Such an arrangement would certainly reduce oil consumption but the vehicle is likely to be expensive. The diesel/battery electric would carry a small diesel engine which would run at a constant speed to drive a generator. This again would be costly and would appear to have little to commend it.

Lead Acid Battery Bus
Satisfactory for specialised work such as milk delivery but at present the range is insufficient for bus operation. The range could be extended with interchangeable batteries but this would be expensive in terms of batteries, infrastructure and staff.

Advanced Battery Bus
There is ongoing research into batteries capable of giving an extended range of say 160 miles or more. This would be attractive but is not yet a reality; at present the sodium sulphur battery seems to be the most promising. If it is ever perfected its characteristics would be superior to the previous alternatives mentioned and in performance and use, comparable to that of a diesel bus as well as offering an alternative to oil.

From the foregoing it seems likely that the advanced battery has the greatest promise if only it was a reality; but for the present it is not. If a breakthrough came then the concept might well be superior to the trolleybus or even the hybrid. The unknown is whether the sodium sulphur battery or an equivalent will come before oil disappears. If it does then capital expenditure for trolleybus equipment would seem to be unnecessary. If it does not, then a reappearance of the conventional trolleybus (or tram) or the development of some form of hybrid becomes rather more than a remote possibility.

Looking into the future involves a deal of speculation although it is fairly clear that those who are now embarking on a career in transport will see many changes during the course of their 40 years of superannuable service (or will even that change and become 30 years?). They will see a change of behaviours and the way of life and in the types of vehicle which will be available to them to carry the traffic as it will then present itself. The managements of tomorrow will no doubt have with them many of the problems which are with us today but they might have some others as well and in this the author wishes them well.

Index

(Note: If consecutive pages have relevance, only the first page number is shown)